AF327061

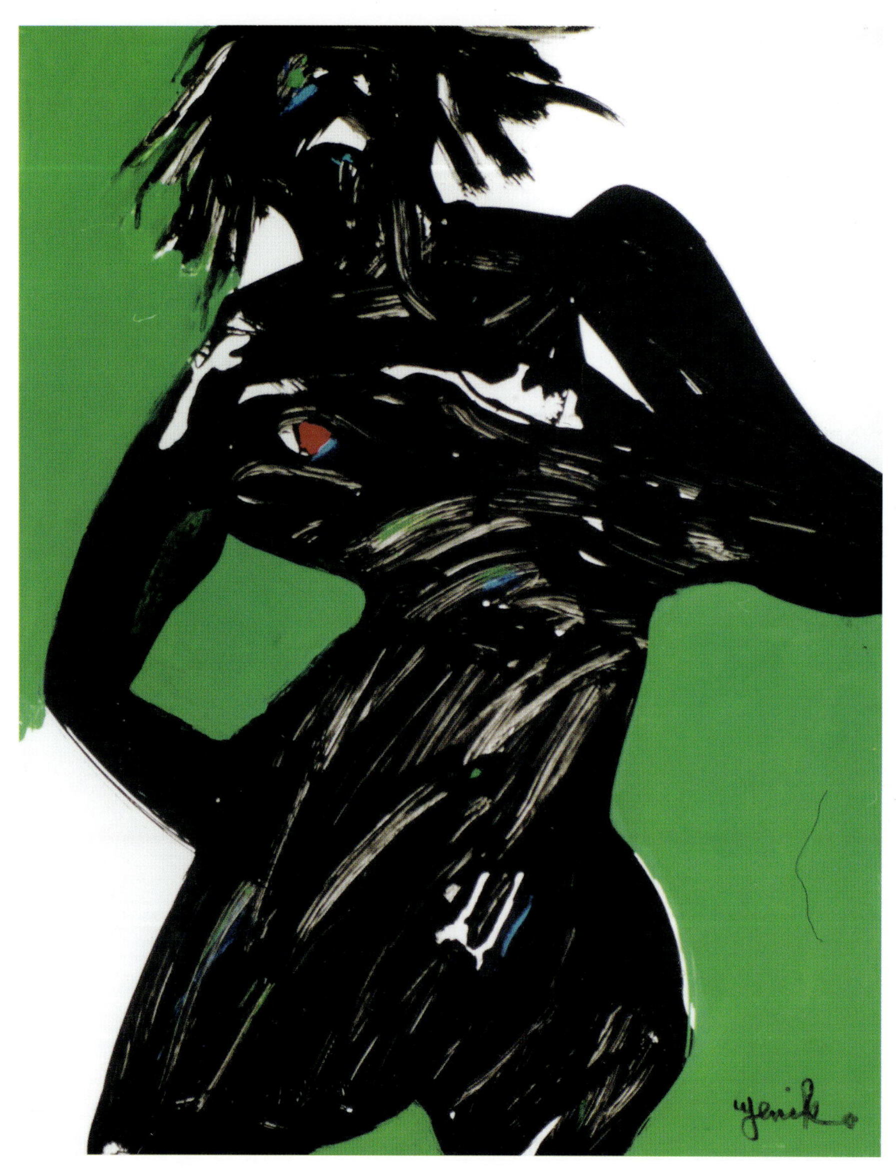

Preface

THE ARTIST HERSELF

When the influential German and, later, American painter and teacher Hans Hoffmann told art critic Katharine Kuh in the early 1960's that his paintings "are always images of my whole psychic make-up," he was responding to a question about his reflections of his own "immediate moods and emotions" within his work.

"You cannot deny yourself," Hoffmann elaborated. "You ask, am I painting myself? I'd be a swindler if I did otherwise. I'd be denying my existence as an artist."

In the same way, the arts of Jenik Cook, for whatever else their subject matter may suggest, can just as reliably be recognized as portraits of the artist at work. Their most immediate quality, their essential identity, is instantly gordianed into the persona of their creator and identifiable by the character of gestures which compose them.

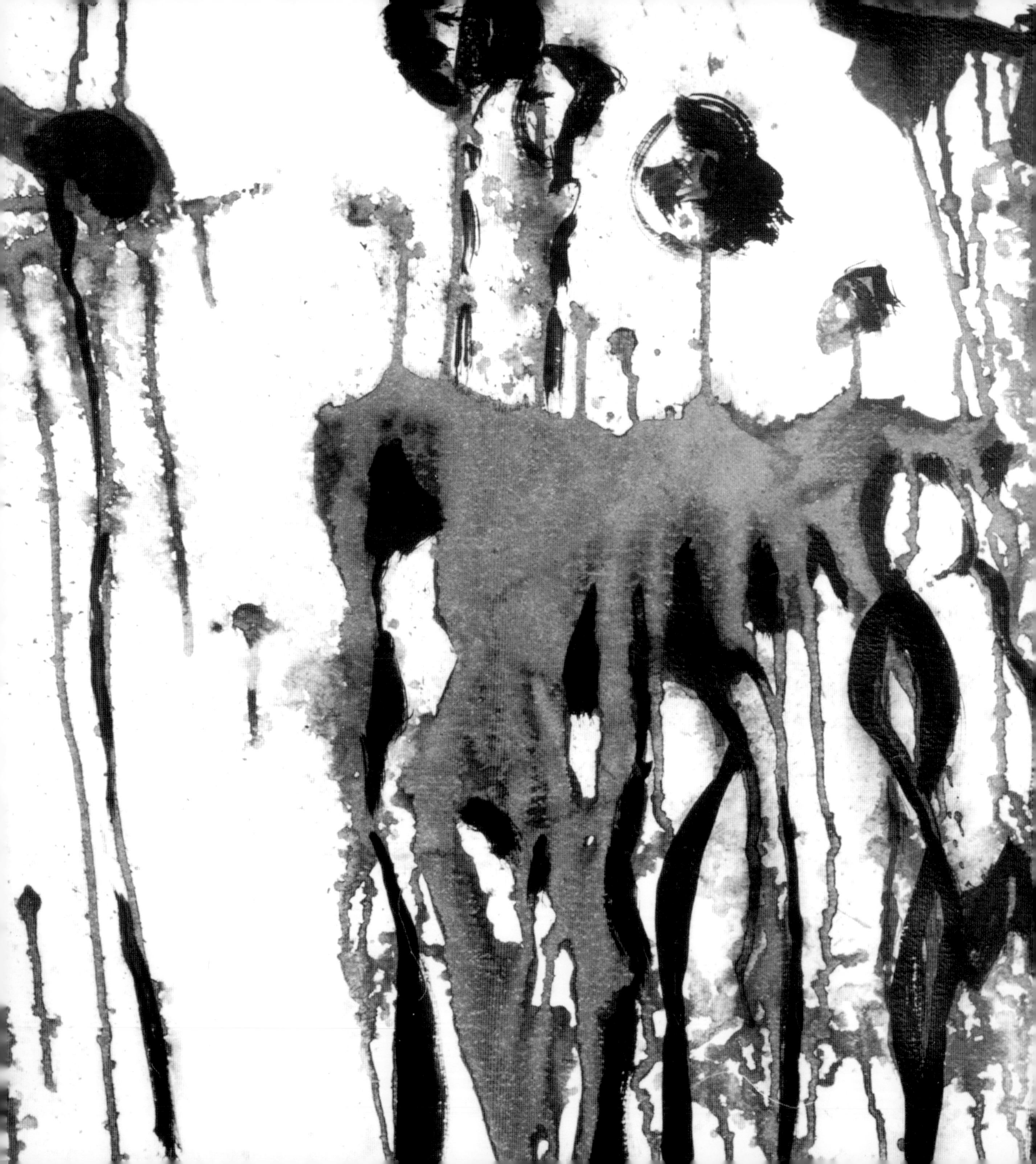

JENIK

G. Alexander Irving

Cover:
Inseparable

Frontispiece:
Artistic

Editor: Jeremy Sedley
Production: Natalie Gains
Graphics: Nicole Digilio
Copy Editor: Eugenia Buerklin
Publisher: J. S. Kaufmann

Published in the United States of America
in 2004 by Book Art Press

ISBN 0-9713859-8-X   0-9713859-9-8 (pbk.)

Acknowledgment

A Retrospective
The Schacknow Museum of Fine Arts
Plantation, Florida

Photography: Paul Moshay
Los Angeles, CA

Contents

THE ENERGIES OF JENIK COOK

Emotions are real; they are as tangible as the physical experiences of pleasure or pain to anyone who has experienced them.

When emotions are the subject of a painting, one might expect them to be visible. Yet, in the early debate over the properties of subjectivity and objectivity, passions must be observed as non-visible entries. We may see the *effect*s of emotion, though not the feeling, itself. Only depictions of emotional effect may be rendered to eye as an objective reality existing outside of the mind. You cannot photograph an emotion. The question of whether or not you can *paint* one is a matter of conjecture hinging upon individual interpretation. That you can *evoke* an emotion through proficient manipulation of hues and forms is a generally accepted premise. But how does one *describe* such a sensation with similar techniques?

It is only in the arts that we find direct experience of emotion communicated with an adequate enough clarity to be meaningful to those parts of human awareness configured to comprehend the message. It happens instantly and with a minimum of intellectual engagement.

William R. Everdell, who considers abstract art "a gift to skeptics" in his treatment of Kandinsky in *The First Moderns*, skirts the point by wondering "whether it is possible in any philosophically precise sense to paint a picture without a subject" and asking "Did not every expressionist at least paint states of mind? Did not even Kandinsky, who snorted at the idea that he might be painting music, claim to strike notes in the soul and there compose something, however ideal? Kandinsky painted colors, as did every other painter; and are not colors in some sense a subject?" Well, it depends, Mr. Everdell, on how you look at them...

In his critical writings, Ernst Cassirer isolated the vision of the artist by declaring: "...I see the landscape with an artist's eye. I begin to form a picture of it. I have now entered a new realm- the realm not of living things but of 'living forms.' No longer in the immediate reality of things, I live now in the rhythm of spatial forms, in the harmony and

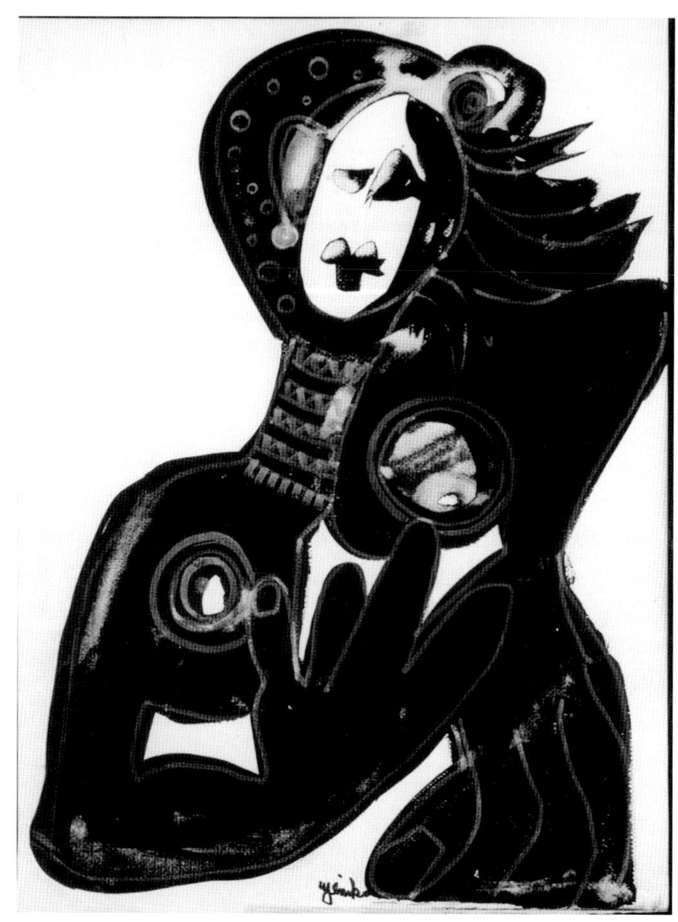

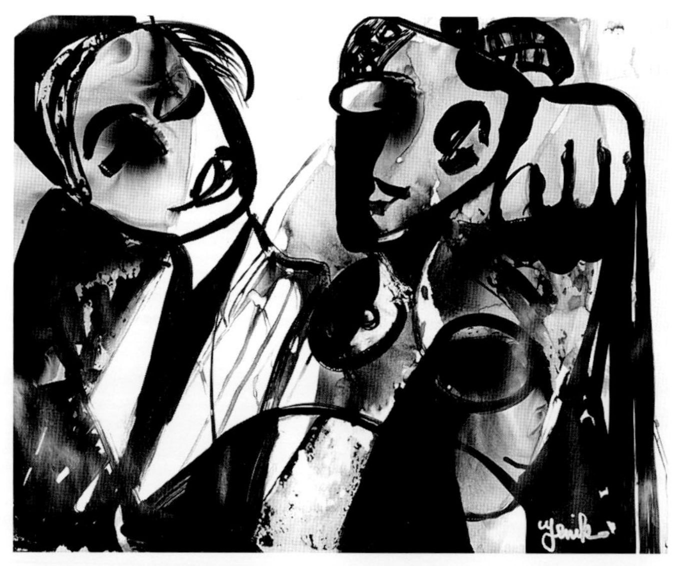

contrast of colors, in the balance of light and shadow…"

Having distinguished a kind of consciousness apart from that which we consider "normal" consciousness, William Butler Yeats found *feelings* attendant to an artistic state of mind—feelings which find reference in his system of symbolism almost as an *ingredient* of consciousness.

"All sounds, all colors, all forms," Yeats observed, "either because of their preordained energies or because of long association, evoke indefinable and yet precise emotions, or, as I prefer to think, call down among us certain disembodied powers, whose footsteps over our hearts we call emotions…"

In the art of Jenik Simonian Cook, we find frequent recourse to a deliberate and devoted focus upon the heart. Not in any terms of contrived sentiment in subject or the superficiality of mood but in pure emotional content. There is an immediacy in the artist's method and vision which translates directly to us her *experiences* of the painting.

When asked about the symbolism of his paintings, Franz Kline once remarked that there was imagery in the paintings but that he did not consider himself a symbolist.

"In other words, these are painting experiences," Kline said. "I don't decide in advance that I'm going to paint a definite experience but, in the act of painting, it becomes a genuine experience for me."

While we may credit emotions with far more shades than visibly possessed by a full spectrum of colors, a correspondence of color, gesture, form and emotion can be profitably traced in the human psyche. However, in Jenik's work, it is our *experience* of emotion which is brought to the fore. Mitigations of the pure surge of joy in color sensation and the effects of visual rhythms creating motion on the painting surface undercut the urgency of static pictorial category. As we gaze at a given canvas we see that it may not be a painting of *joy* itself but in it, not paradoxically, we can see joy. In that realization, we find that joy, or any given emotion, may be attached to any object or activity regardless of its intellectual content but that it is perceivably manifest in the *experience* of the painting just as Yeats' footsteps over the heart shift our vantage points.

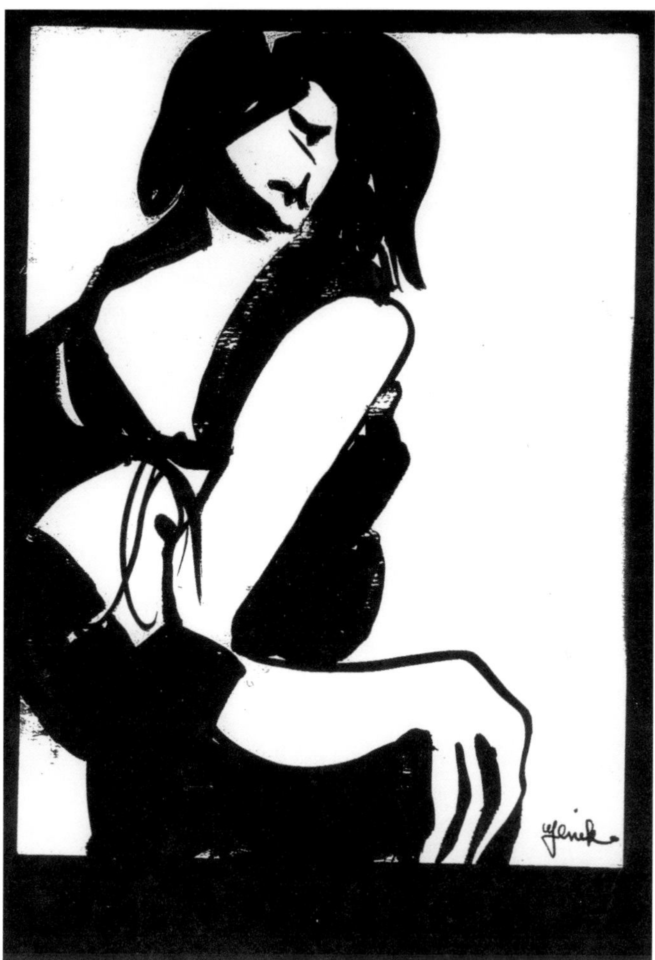

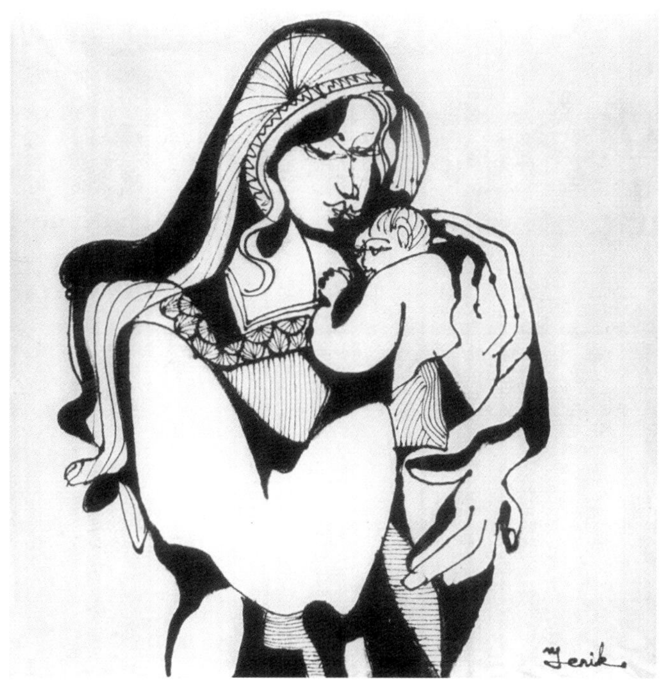

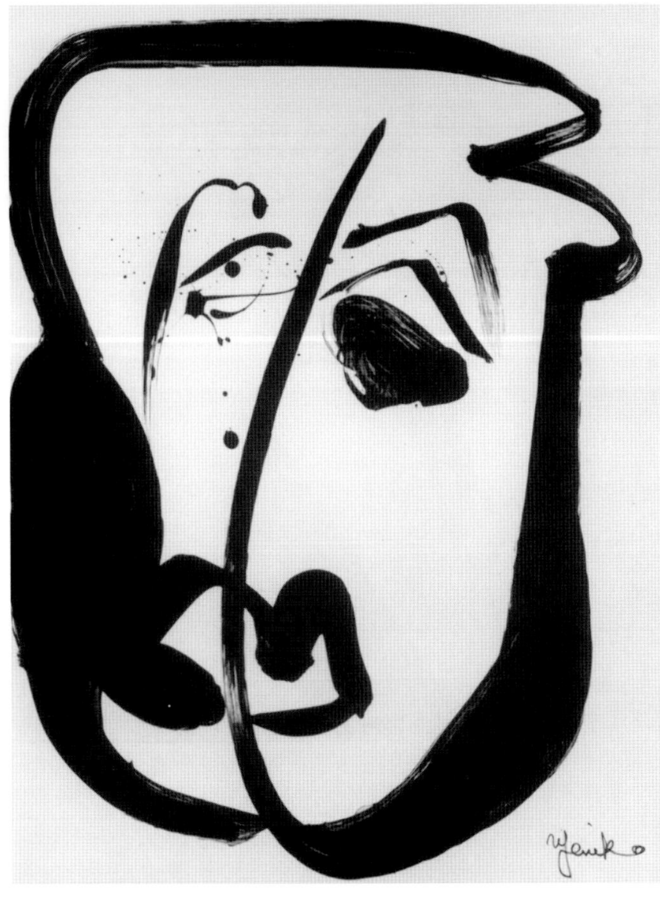

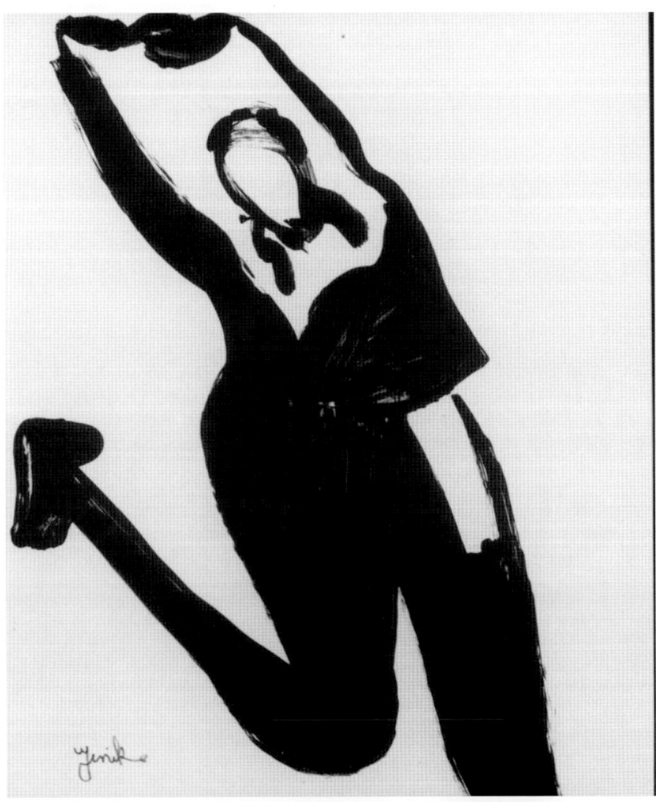

In terms of style, a consideration somewhat secondary to the exuberance of her approach, we find Jenik passing reference to formulas and movements which could not presume to *contain* her impulses but, without a working knowledge of, would lead a less informed artist to disaster. The bold self-assurance of her images derives as much from a comprehension of the disciplines and techniques of the most honored revolutionaries of art as from her own confident reasons for overriding their borders.

While Jenik ventures occasionally into the realm of those inner reflections of reality which emerge under particular impacts from forces of modernism as pure abstraction or harmonic figuration, her vision manifests largely in an Orphic region of influence which incorporates not only objects and beings but our reactions to them. In this, she achieves a "motion" beyond emotion- a stirring of vital essence which Ernst Cassirer described in the 1940's.

Pointing out that Rousseau and Goethe, through their recognition of what they termed "characteristic art," provided foundation for aesthetic theory in later revisions of artistic ideals, Cassirer announced that characteristic art had "gained a definitive victory over imitative art. (But) it is not enough to lay stress upon the emotional side of the work of art. It is true that all characteristic or expressive art is 'the spontaneous overflow of powerful feelings'."

Cassirer ups the ante by surmising that "if we were to accept this Wordsworthian definition without reserve, we should only be led to a change of sign, not to a decisive change of meaning. In this case art would remain reproductive; but, instead of being a reproduction of things, of physical objects, it would become a reproduction of our inner life, of our affections and emotions." He points out that conception is not art without the *experience* of its creation and that it "cannot be expressive without being formative."

Quoting R.G. Collingwood's *Principles of Art* to stress that "[w]hat the artist is trying to do is express a given emotion," Cassirer declares that "an artist who is not endowed with powerful feelings will never produce anything except shallow and frivolous art..." This harsh judgment is based firmly upon that which Cassirer believes art is meant to *do*.

"If what art tries to express is no special state [or emotional feature] but the very dynamic process of our inner life," Cassirer reasons, then, taking him just slightly out of context, any effort which does not record that experience of creation "could hardly be more than perfunctory and superficial. Art must always give us motion rather than mere emotion." He notes that "for a great painter, a great musician, or a great poet, the colors, the lines, rhythms, and words are not merely a part of his technical apparatus; they are necessary moments of the productive process itself."

The distinction drawn by Cassirer relates directly, we should note, to the essence of Jenik's most outstanding achievements upon canvas. Her ability to activate the "artistic eye" with the motions of her brush and bring the *experience* of the painting forcefully to our attention. As Cassirer elaborates: "In his essay 'Of the Standard of Taste' Hume declares: 'Beauty is no quality in things themselves; it exists merely in the mind which contemplates them.' But this statement is ambiguous. If we understand *mind* in Hume's own sense, and think of self as nothing but a bundle of impressions, it would be very difficult to find in such a bundle that predicate which we call beauty. Beauty cannot be defined by its mere *percipi*, as 'being perceived'; it must be defined in terms of an activity of the mind, of the function of perceiving and by a characteristic direction of this function... The artistic eye is not a passive eye that receives and registers the impression of things. It is a constructive eye, and it is only by constructive acts that we can discover the beauty of natural things. The sense of beauty is the susceptibility to the dynamic life of forms, and this life cannot be apprehended except by a corresponding dynamic process in ourselves."

This ability of the artist is the result of an evolution through a progression of influential factors which funneled the realization of this dynamic process. Although active presently in her studio in Los Angeles, the components of Jenik's American artistry must first be sought in the far-off land of her birth.

Armenian Origins

Situated on a high plateau corridor of land between Southern Russia and the Middle East and between the Black and Caspian Seas, Armenia possesses an extraordinary history of

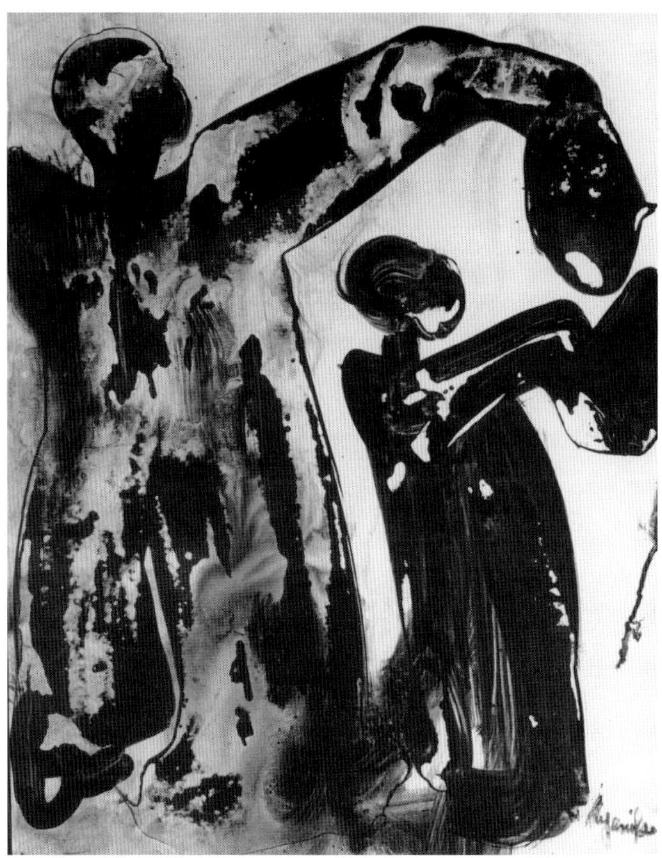

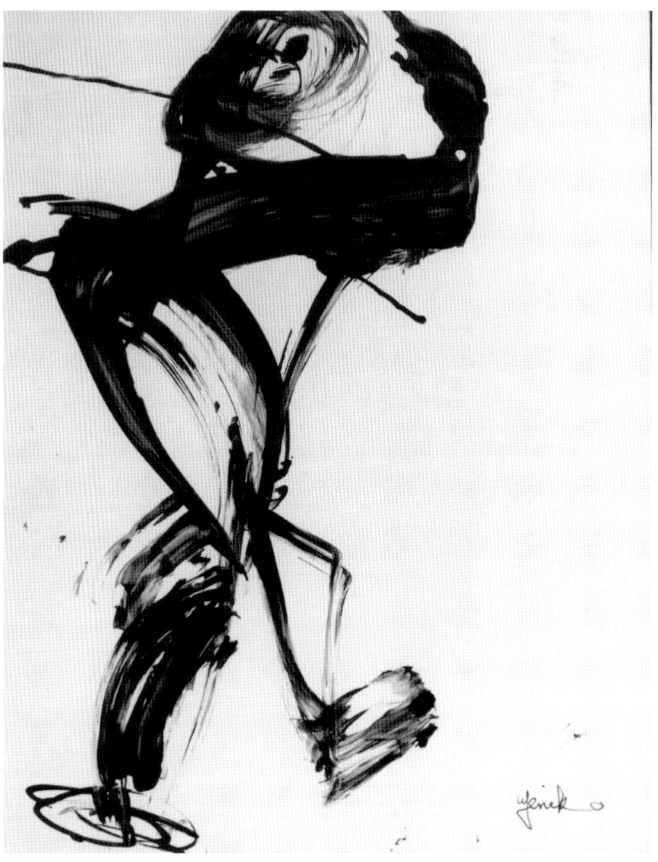

turbulent cultural impacts upon an intrinsic core population descended from contemporaries of the ancient Egyptians and Accadians. With an archaeological record reaching back some 8,000 years, human presence in the region left its traces at places like Karahoonj, which translates roughly to "stones of sound" and is thought to be the world's oldest observatory with a history of 7,500 years and associations with the younger Stonehenge site of Great Britain. The history of metal-working in the region goes back at least three thousand years.

Early temples, historic records and myths were largely obliterated by a succession of occupying forces and, particularly by the clergy of the fourth century after Armenia had become the world's first nation to adopt Christianity, several centuries earlier, as a state religion. This was one of several significant factors in setting Armenian culture apart from that of its neighbors. Armenian painting is generally observed to have originated with the protected post-Christian illuminated manuscripts which show a peculiar blend of enriched Byzantine and other Western influences with Oriental themes and formulas from the East.

The modern tradition of Armenian painting began to blossom in the nineteenth century under the effect of a Russian tsarist empire that had wrenched control of the Transcaucasia area from the Persians and the Ottoman Turks. Many of the artists who emerged in Armenia toward the turn of the century and into the 1920's had studied in Moscow or in one of the Western European cultural centers which beckoned to aspiring artists from afar. Yervand Kochar (1899-1979), for example, lived in Paris from 1921 to 1936 following his education in Moscow while Hakob Kojoian (1883-1959) received his training at an art school in Munich. But when Armenia is mentioned in the world of modern art, it is a remarkable painter with an adopted Russian name who springs first to mind.

Jenik and Gorky

As the subject, in recent years, of two major biographies[1] and ever widening recognition in the world of arts, Arshile Gorky is finally beginning to receive an overdue appreciation for his role as one of the principal bridges between the European and American art scenes in an historic era of development.

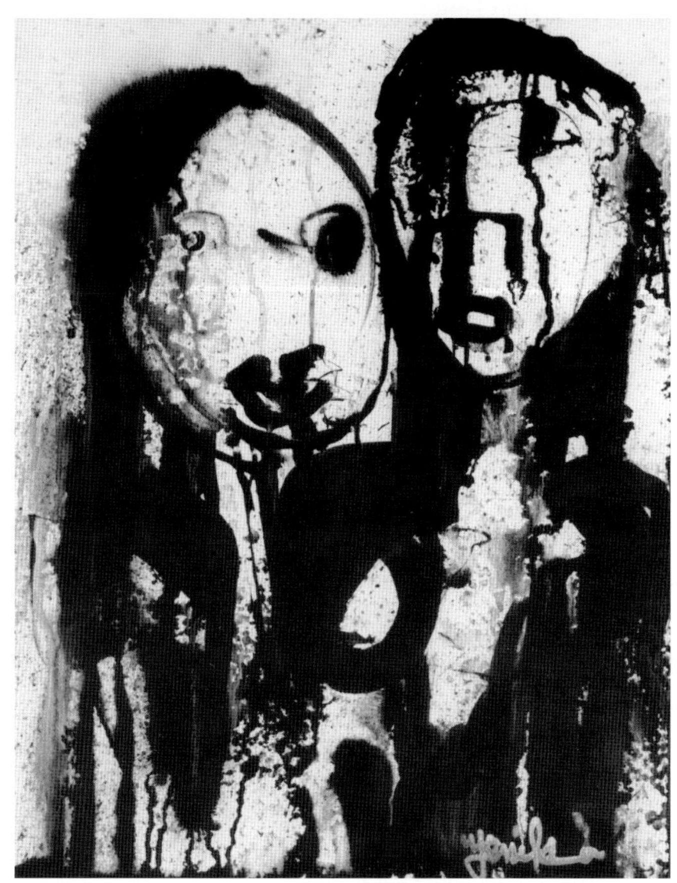

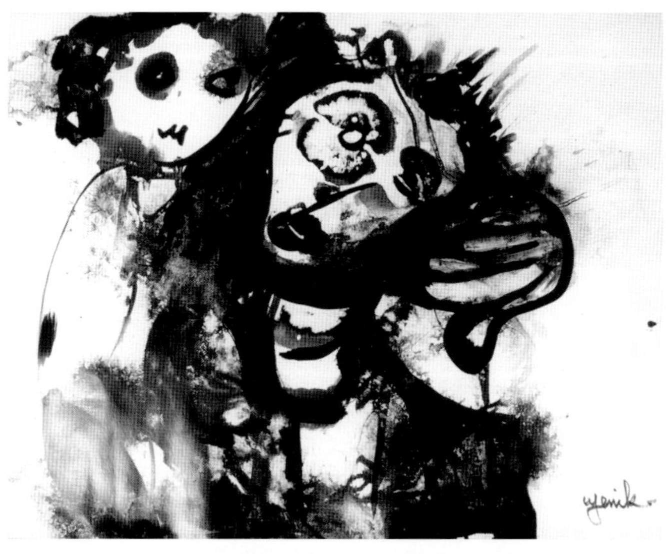

Footnote 1- Matthew Spender's *From a High Place* (Knopf, 1999) and Nouritza Matossian's *Black Angel: A Life of Arshile Gorky* (Overlook Press, 2000). The latter book also supplied primary inspiration for Atom Egoyan's motion picture *Ararat.*

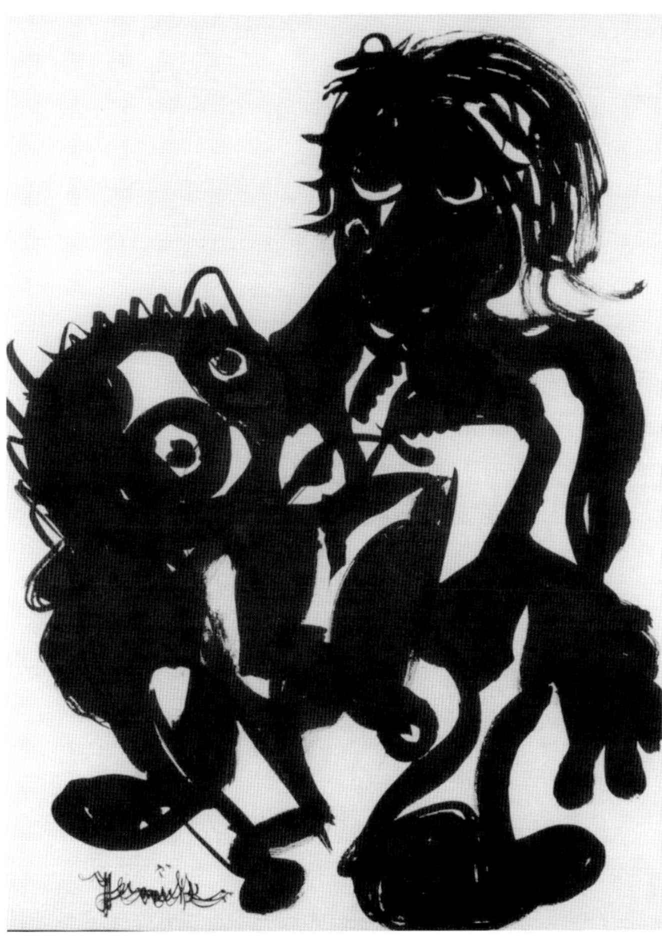

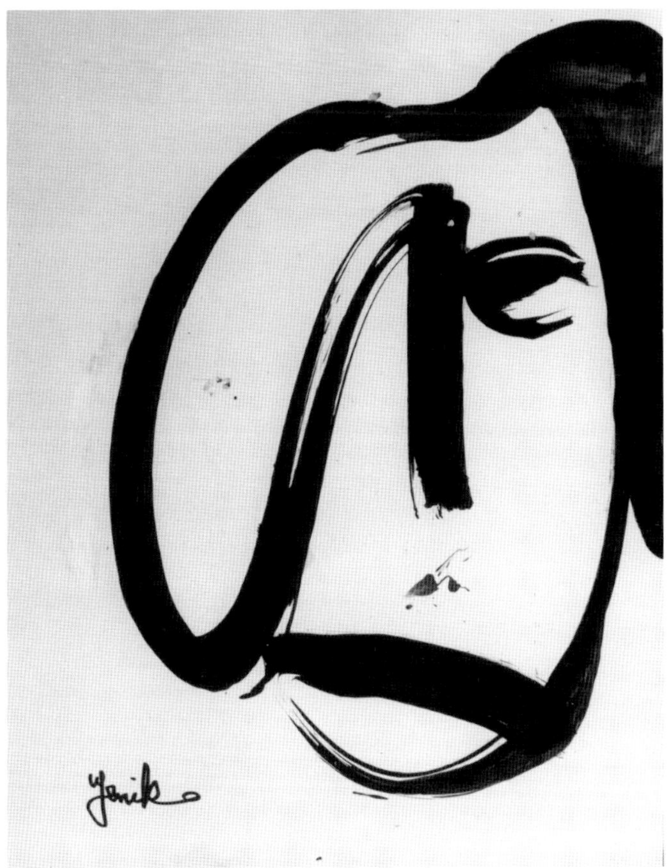

Gorky's life began on April 15, 1904 in the shadow of the tragedies and horrors of his homeland, including the Turkish massacres of 1896 (during which both his father and mother lost their original spouses) and was ended by his own hand in New England when he was overcome by a series of personal tragedies- a factor which undoubtedly muted his immediate legacy in the arts. Even so, his pioneering presence in the world of Western Art left deep and lasting impressions in his native country which would have been obvious to the young Jenik.

Born Vosdanik Adoian, Gorky, as part of a rural farming family, was well-acquainted with the tints of the countryside as his mother, Shushan, provided his earliest introductions to artistic sensibilities. Likewise, Jenik recalls being identified as "an artist" in the school years of her childhood without quite being able to grasp the significance of the distinction. "We had land and there were all the colors, she told Art writer Josef Woodard in 1998, "There were the vernal shades of green. There were many different colors of grapes. The peach trees and vegetables like eggplants and tomatoes were glistening in the sun. Apricots were glowing in rich yellow orange. To me, this is where my art is coming from, from nature."

Gorky's father, Setrag Adoian, sought work in America, when the boy was six, to avoid conscription and, hopefully, support the family from afar. But Gorky never quite forgave his father's absence during the genocidal atrocities imposed upon Armenians in the following years. The family was force-marched 150 miles north to a relocation camp at Yerevan in 1915, where his mother died of starvation in his arms four years later. Fleeing with his sister, Vartoosh, Gorky arrived in Massachusetts in 1920, at age 15.

Frequenting the Boston Museum of Fine Art as he worked a factory job and studied painting, at first privately, and then at Boston's School of Fine Art and Design and New York City's National Academy of Design, Gorky adjusted optimistically to his new environment. In this era, to rid himself of a troubling past in a ravaged Armenia, he invented his "Russian" identity as Arshile Gorky (which translates to "Achilles, the bitter one").

14

In New York, Gorky became enthralled by the theories and styles of Cèzanne, Picasso, Miró, Matisse and other European pioneers of visual experience. He began teaching at the New School of Design in New York, where Mark Rothko was among his students, and joined the explorations pushing beyond surrealism toward the realization of an abstract expressionist realm. Ultimately, his efforts- along with the advances won by his friends deKooning, Pollack and others in the so-called New York School he helped to shape- would contribute to the liberation of Jenik's brush.

To understand the full dynamics of Jenik's informed liberation, it is helpful to briefly recall the impetus, determination and implication of the movements in art during the first half of the twentieth century. It was, of course, scientific discovery which made artistic re-evaluation and exploration necessary. While looking at the timeline, primed as it is by the remarkable breakthroughs in the final decades of the nineteenth century, it is easily possible to conjecture a cause and effect relationship between Planck's Quantum theory of 1900 and the first stirrings of Fauvism a few years later or Einstein's publication of theory in 1905 with the rise of Cubism in 1907. The discovery of subconscious terrains and logics uncovered by advances in the field of human psychology would also have profound effect upon aesthetic theory and insist that investigations into the "new reality" be humanized. Artists were now challenged to consider our response to natural forms and situations and the prospect of making visible not only our world but our relationship to it.

Rapidly, a world shaken from the security of a reality based in the witness of sensory perception found itself having to cope with an infinitely more subtle and complex universe. Philosophy shuddered and took on the task as scientists delved deeper and ripple effects spread directly from philosophy into the visual arts.

As changing concepts of reality opened new area for modes of thought, it was recognized that Man's critical relationship to visual reality required adjustment. We clearly needed new systems of reference. In reaction to the

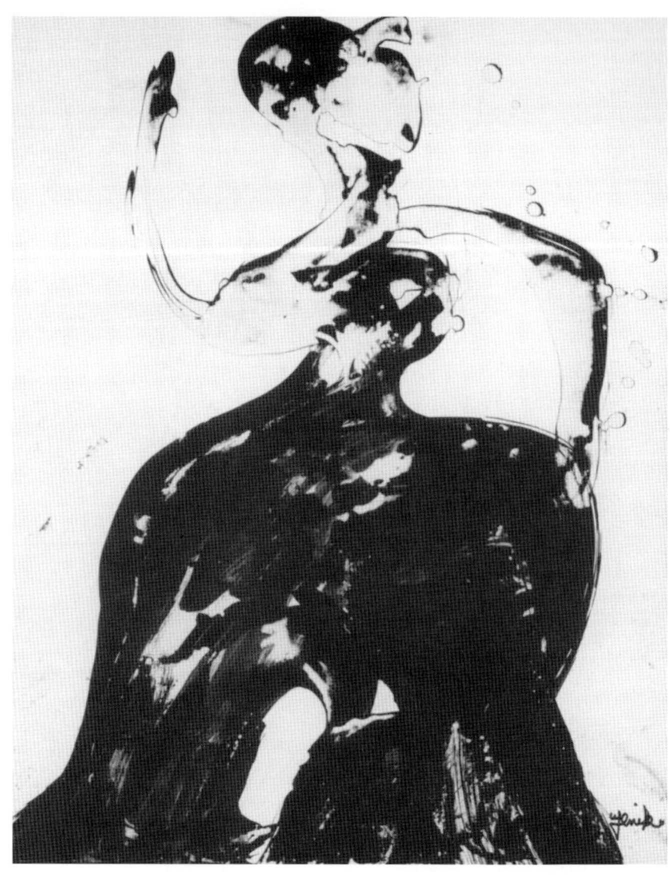

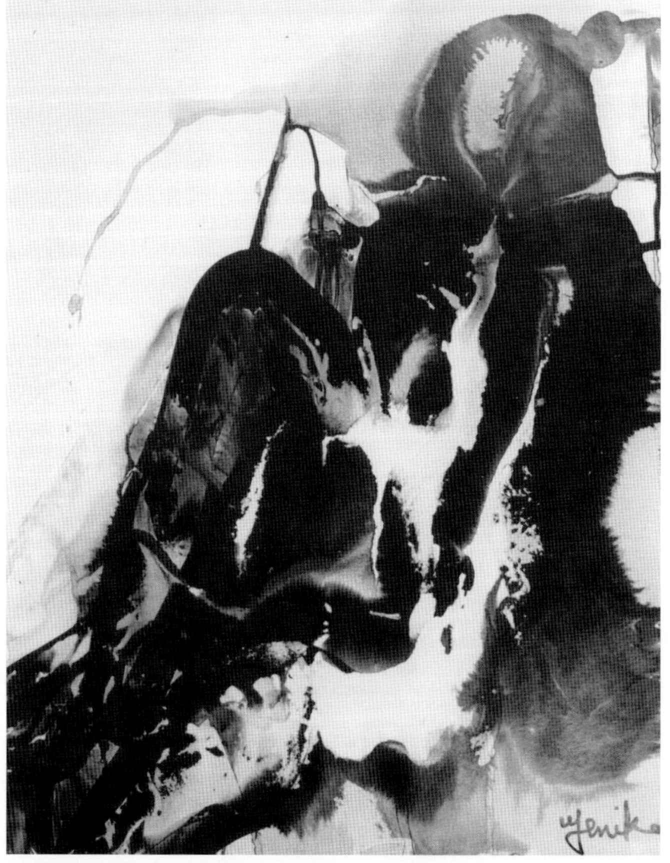

burgeoning expansion of knowledge about the natural world, instinctive questions arose as to what we were really seeing when we looked at a figurative scene. Conveying an illusion of depth upon a flat surface in imitation of what the eye beholds suddenly seemed but one layer of existence among many hidden beyond the narrow bands of perception within which our sensory organs guided us. Painters were compelled to consider expression of objects and energies upon a wider plane of existence and elements of the nature of a subject more fully developed in the space-time continuum... "A rose is a rose" turned to a rose is a bud, a seed, a burst, a bloom, a velvety touch, dried petals, a tube of thorny points, vibrant wave clusters interrupting waves of light to cast a bulbous shadow, and so on... In other words, a rose is more than the rose we thought it was and *how* can we reveal the rest?

The disclosure of Minkowski's space-time mathematical theorem in 1908 was followed within two years by the emergence of abstract art and theory. Questionings and explorations of visual reality strove to blossom beyond their two and three dimensional boundaries and the new reality was expressed in the "transcendent realism" of Max Beckmann; the "magic reality" of Carlo Carrà and the Futurists; the facetted space of cubism; and other strategies designed to present equivalents or parallels of deeper experience and make visible the inner content of things.

This, in brief, was a primary motive for the various modernist dialogues which evolved in the past century. Gorky's role in the development of these insights was turned back at the height of his creative powers when his studio and many of his works burned in a barn-studio fire in early 1946. Within a month he was diagnosed with colon cancer and his health ravaged despite a surgery which checked the spread of the disease. The same week that a marital betrayal separated him from his beloved children, he suffered devastating back and neck injuries as a passenger in a car crash, losing the use of his painting arm and requiring the use of a large leather brace to keep his head upright. The reasons for his suicide hold few mysteries.

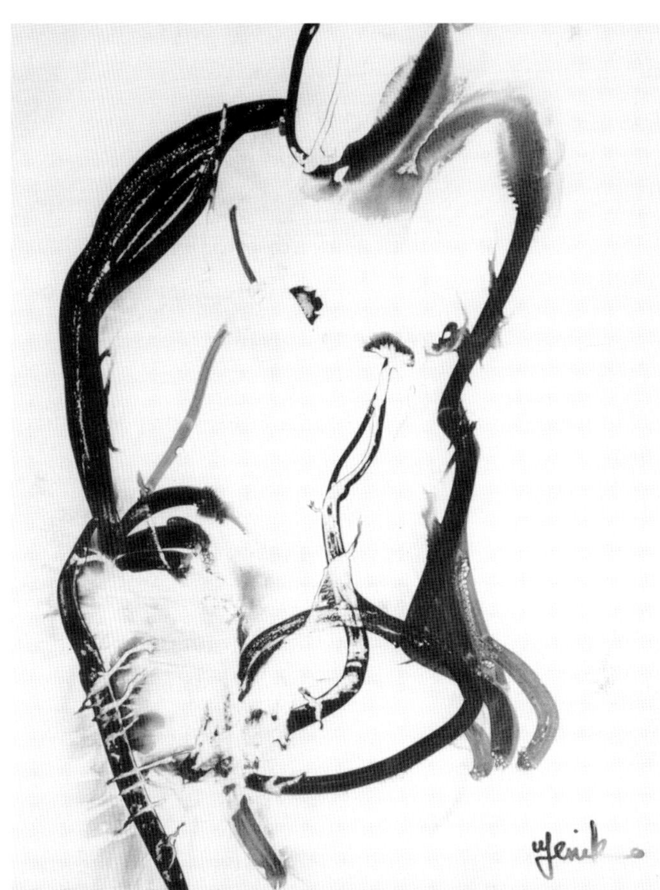

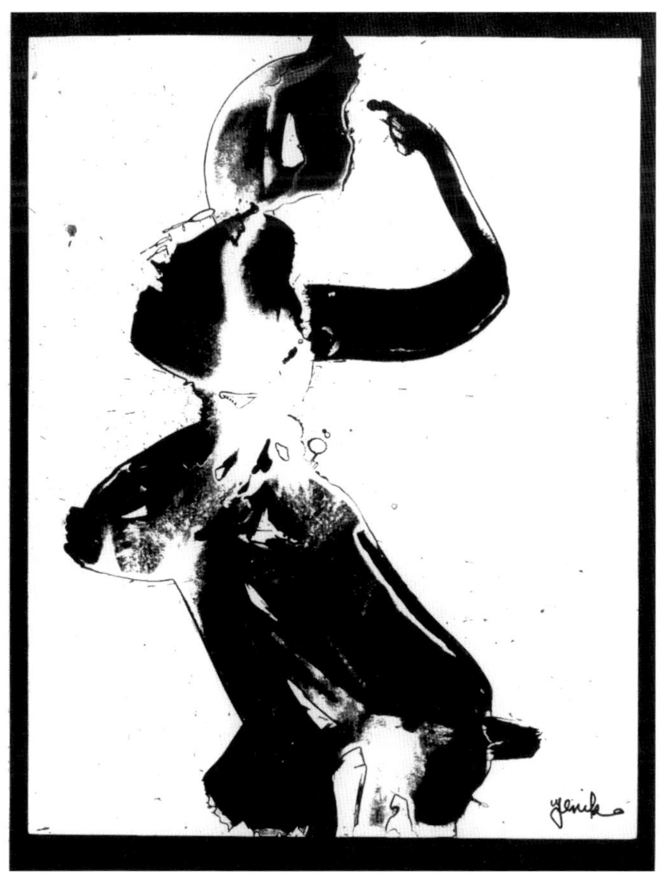

Before his demise, Gorky had painted himself forever into the abstract expressionist landscape and prowled new paths where non-objective figuration stands toe-to-toe with surrealism. You will find gestural and biomorphic elements in Jenik's paintings which reflect back to her countryman's contributions but you will find also some of the emotive qualities with which Munch informed us and, often, signals from the spatial envelopments and suspensions of the cubists.

The end point of these observations is that Jenik has absorbed and assimilated these lessons from modernist masters, eventually assigning them to a supporting role as factors in her work much as light might be considered, or palette... Where you may have the sense that sometimes Gorky's motions of image were trapped within the formula of whichever theory he was investigating, Jenik's thrust of core purpose in the creation of an image escapes the pull the theorem's gravity. Her pictorial impulses are informed by such knowledge but not instructed by it. Foremost is the freedom of the image's own internal rationale of color and form and the motion it compels to achieve itself. Always, there is a sense of narrative, however oblique, commanding the performance of the brush.

This resolve of intention and self-assurance combine to instill the most essential features of Jenik's images—their phenomenal energies. It is as if there are no errors to be made in a stroke, that the brush is in command and knows full well that momentary misbalance is correctable- even desirable; as is the slight body lean on a bicycle in motion which begins an agreeable turn of direction- and that unforeseen imprints may merely indicate a portion of the image's anatomy which was not previously obvious. And, as much as art embraces spontaneity and innovation, this is as it should be; as it *must* be in achieving a masterly touch.

Lesser, but still important, elements of style include the Armenian and Mid-Eastern heritage alluded to by Marlene Donohue in a 1996 essay on Jenik's work as a tradition one "feels more than sees" in the final motif. "It is detectable in [Jenik]Cook's love for flat, animated pattern and simple schematic shapes reduced to their essence to tell great generic or ritual tales," observes Donohue discerningly.

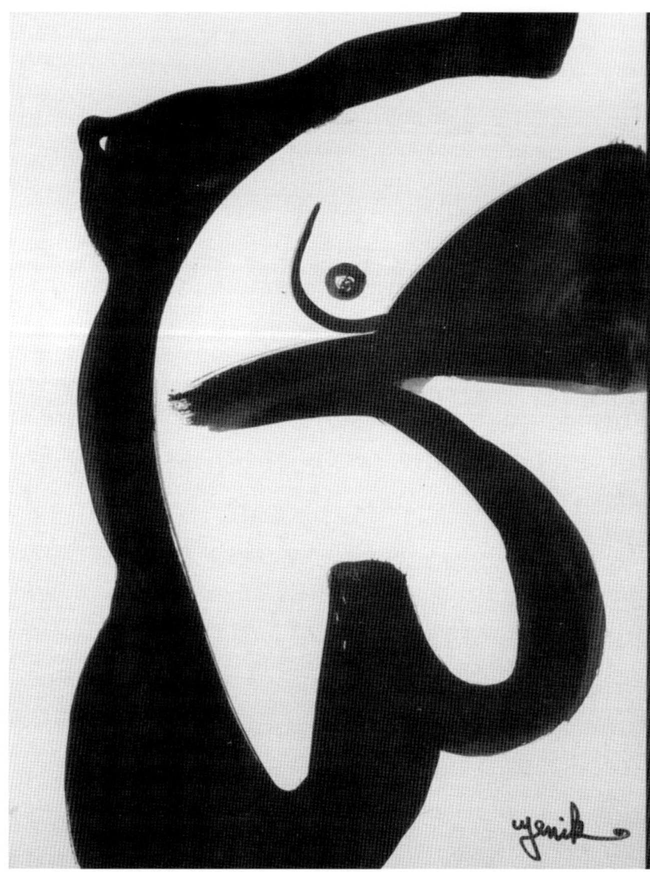

Jenik studied art in Iran before moving to England at age seventeen in 1970, studying in Scotland with a private instructor while there. But even intonations of Persian culture are modified by Western influence in contemporary Iran even though, as this is written, the Iranian government is busy divesting the Tehran Museum of Modern Art of works by Renoir, Van Gogh, Pollock, Ensor, Toulouse-Lautrec, Bacon and others. Jenik also lived for a time in Holland, France and Norway, benefiting from their abounding museum collections before moving to California in 1978 and resuming a more formal approach to artistic study.

In some of her work, you will find broad, lingering traces of a calligraphic instinct drawn early from oriental influence and an ancient prohibition against the making of pictorial images. There are also bold and flavorful injections of an even more ancient primitivism wherein intellectual cautions are suppressed in favor of more direct impressions. This, too, was a fundamental aim of Picasso and other architects of modern painting and Jenik articulated it succinctly to Donohue:

"I feel as if I spent the last twenty years or so of my life turning an innate talent into sound foundation, mastering the fundamentals, knowing composition, color and line, learning how to draw exactly what I saw as it appeared in the world. I have spent the last six years having the courage to forget all of that; to use that information indirectly so as to paint from within myself, not with my brain but with my heart. When an artist realizes that he or she isn't tied to copying the exact appearance of the world, that the goal of art-making is pure expression of an inner vision, this is a great revelation. There is much more risk in this leap of faith, in this act of learning to trust one's self. It involves the release of immense energy when you find that you catch the fish from within; that the wellspring is inside."

The energies captured by the hand of Jenik Cook are those which define the experience of the moment with all of its attendant visual and emotional cues. Her art is less about what is painted or states of "having painted" or "about to paint"- it is all in the act of *doing* it and doing it with all of the faultless poise of *being*. As Walter Pater observed in *Studies in the History of the Renaissance*: "Not the fruit of experience, but experience itself is the end." The object is not a thing to see but to *feel* by looking. It is not situated in memory but in the forces that renew us moment to moment and, so, in Jenik's work, frequently visited motifs always hold variant and fresh connotations.

Pater reflects that "if we begin with the inward world of thought and feeling, the whirlpool is still more rapid, the flame more eager and devouring. There it is no longer the gradual darkening of the eye and fading of color from the wall- the movement of the shore side, where the water flows down indeed, though in apparent rest- but the race of the midstream, a drift of momentary acts of sight and passion and thought."

Jenik's brush is carried by the emotional force of the experience of painting and the knowledge that, momentarily, an emotion becomes the memory of emotion. Experience is sidetracked by contemplation, as Pater notes, and reduced to "a swam of impressions."

"...reflection begins to act upon those objects (and) they are dissipated under its influence; the cohesive force is suspended like a trick of magic; each object is loosed into a group of impressions- color, odor, texture- in the mind of the observer," Pater observed. "Analysis...tells us that those impressions of the individual to which, for each one of us, experience dwindles down, are in perpetual flight; that each of them is limited by time, and that as time is infinitely divisible, each of them is infinitely divisible also; all that is actual in it being a single moment, gone while we try to apprehend it, of which it may ever be more truly said that it has ceased to be than that it is. To such a tremulous wisp constantly reforming itself on the stream, to a single sharp impression, with a sense in it, a relic more or less fleeting, of such moments gone by, what is real in our life fines itself down. It is with the movement, the passage and dissolution of impressions, images, sensations, that analysis leaves off- that continual vanishing away, that strange perpetual weaving and unweaving of ourselves."

To enter the moment and record one's impressions of it requires a dynamic stability in motion which is granted to or earned by few artists among the multitude. It is small wonder that Jenik declares herself filled with joy as she paints. She is in that moment. Her paintings show us that and, in doing so, become vital reminders of its presence.

We may all visit there. It is ever within reach. We can even condition ourselves to extend our stays. But to work there with confidence and competence requires an adequately informed intuition and a drive to create. Jenik possesses both.

Pater sums it up eloquently; "To burn always with this hard gemlike flame, to maintain this ecstasy, is success in life. Failure is to form habits; for habit is relative to a stereotyped world; meantime it is only the roughness of the eye that makes any two persons, things, situations, seem alike. While all melts under our feet, we may well catch any exquisite passion, or any contribution to knowledge that seems, by a lifted horizon, to set the spirit free for a moment, or any stirring of the senses, strange dyes, strange flowers, and curious odors, or work of the artist's hands, or the face of one's friend. Not to discriminate every moment some passionate attitude in those about us, and in the brilliance of their gifts some tragic dividing of forces on their ways is, on this short day of frost and sun, to sleep before evening..."

—*G. Alexander Irving*

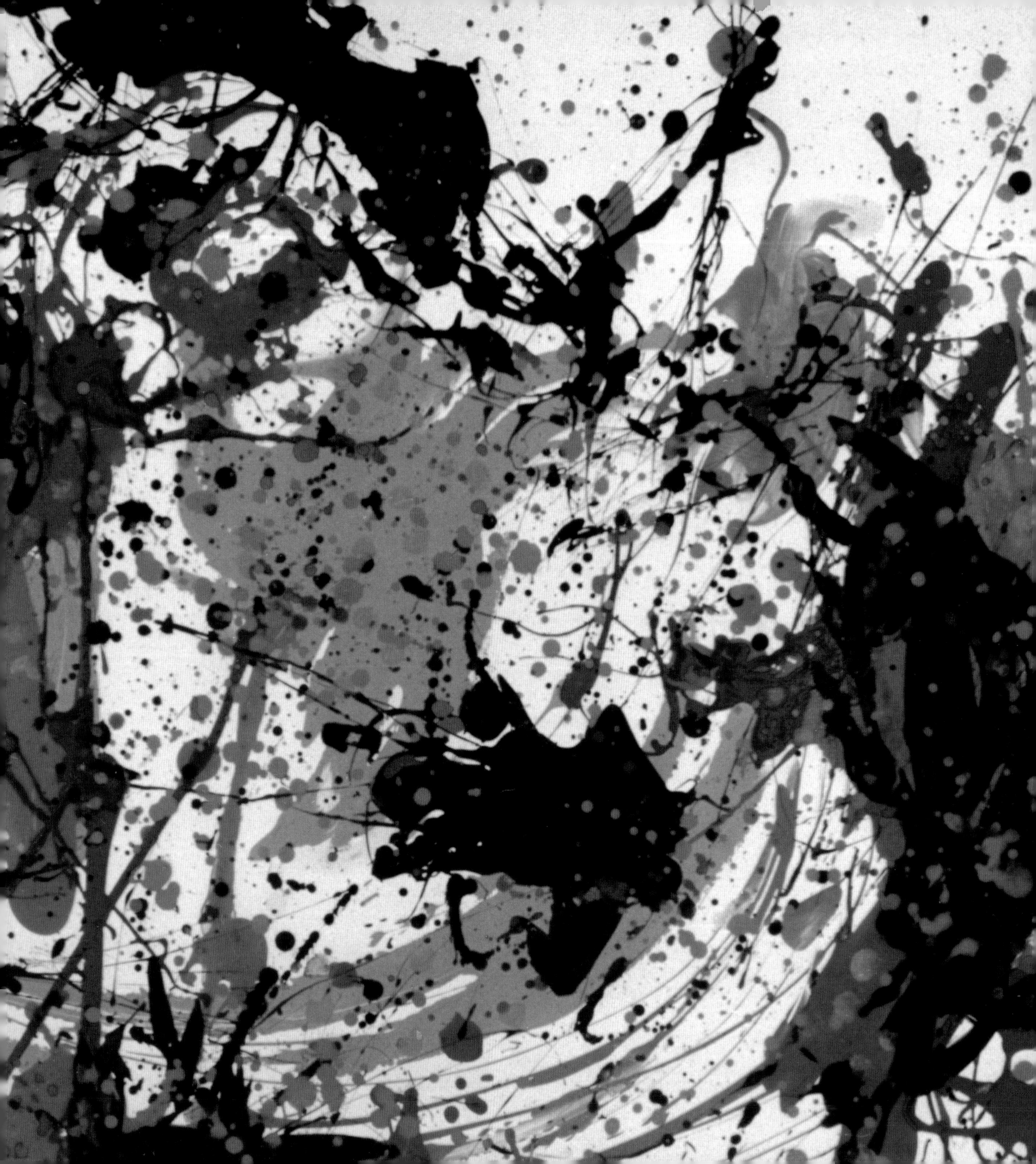

Aesthetic ingenuity and invigoratingly spirited application distinguish the nonrepresentational excursions of the artist. Her robust and audacious extemporizing of decorative and amorphic design gently lift one's instinctual disposition.

ABSTRACT

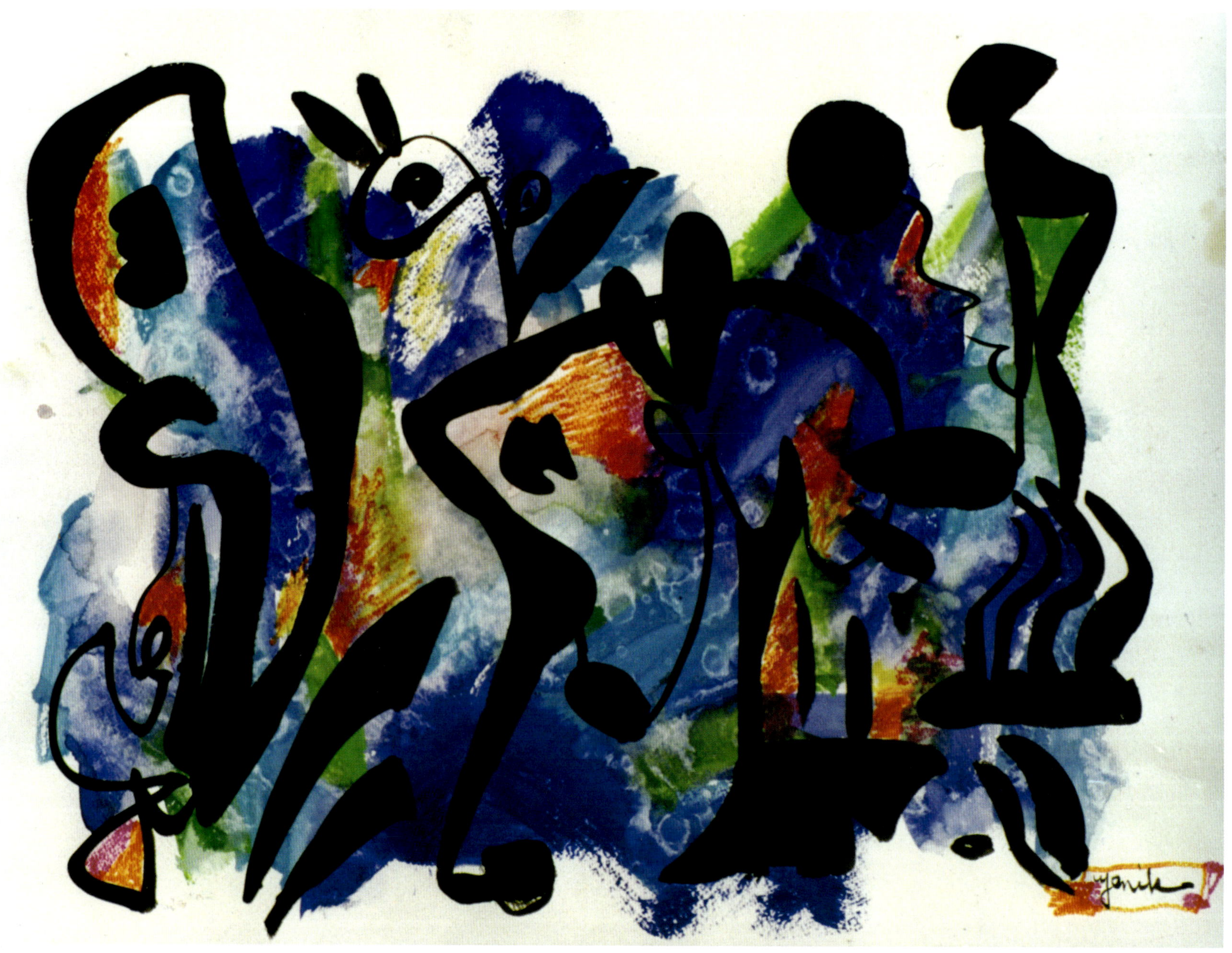

ABS No. 74, Watercolor, 18" x 24"

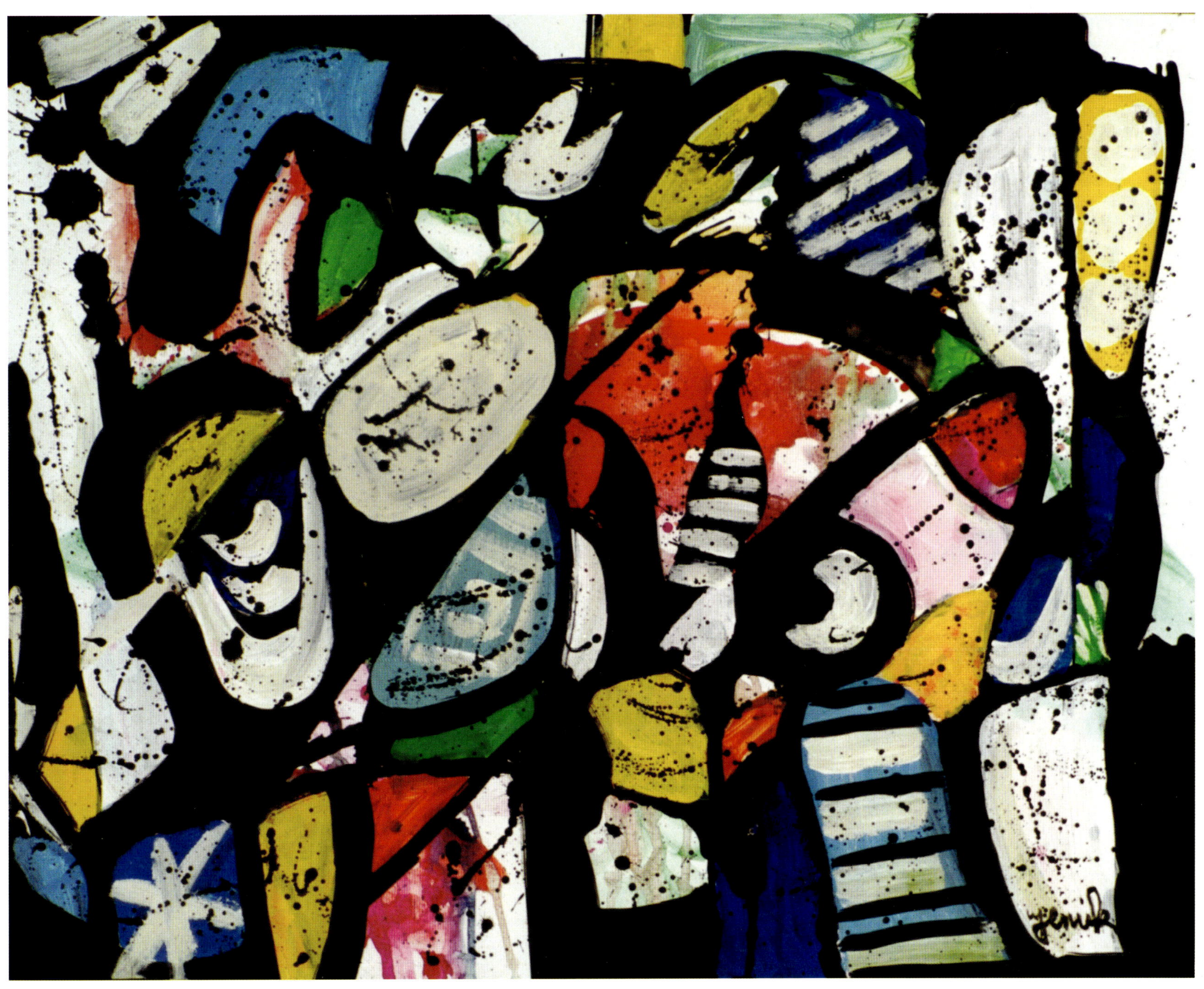

ABS No. 42, Acrylic, 22" x 28"

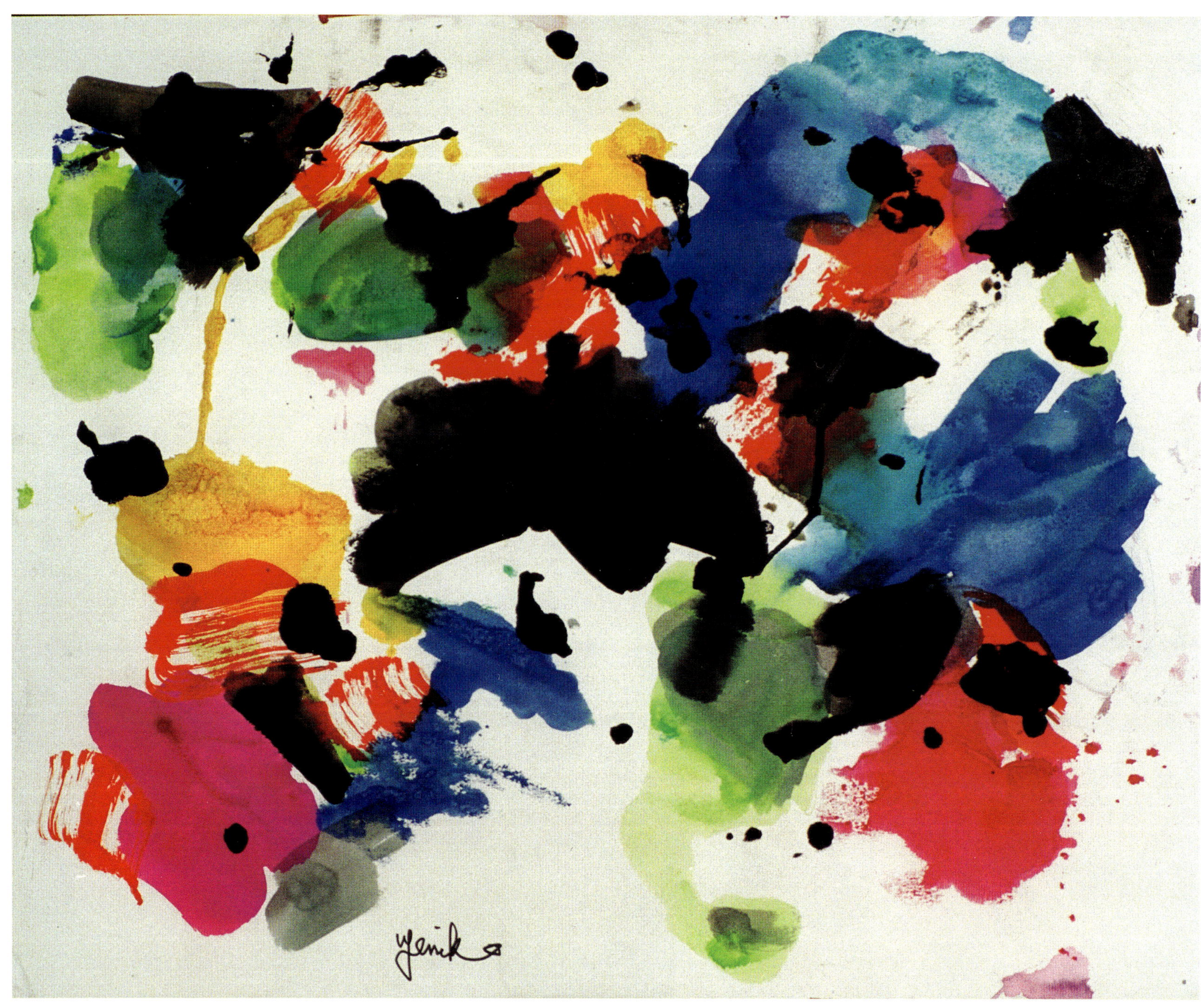

Abs. No 50   Watercolor   18" x 24"

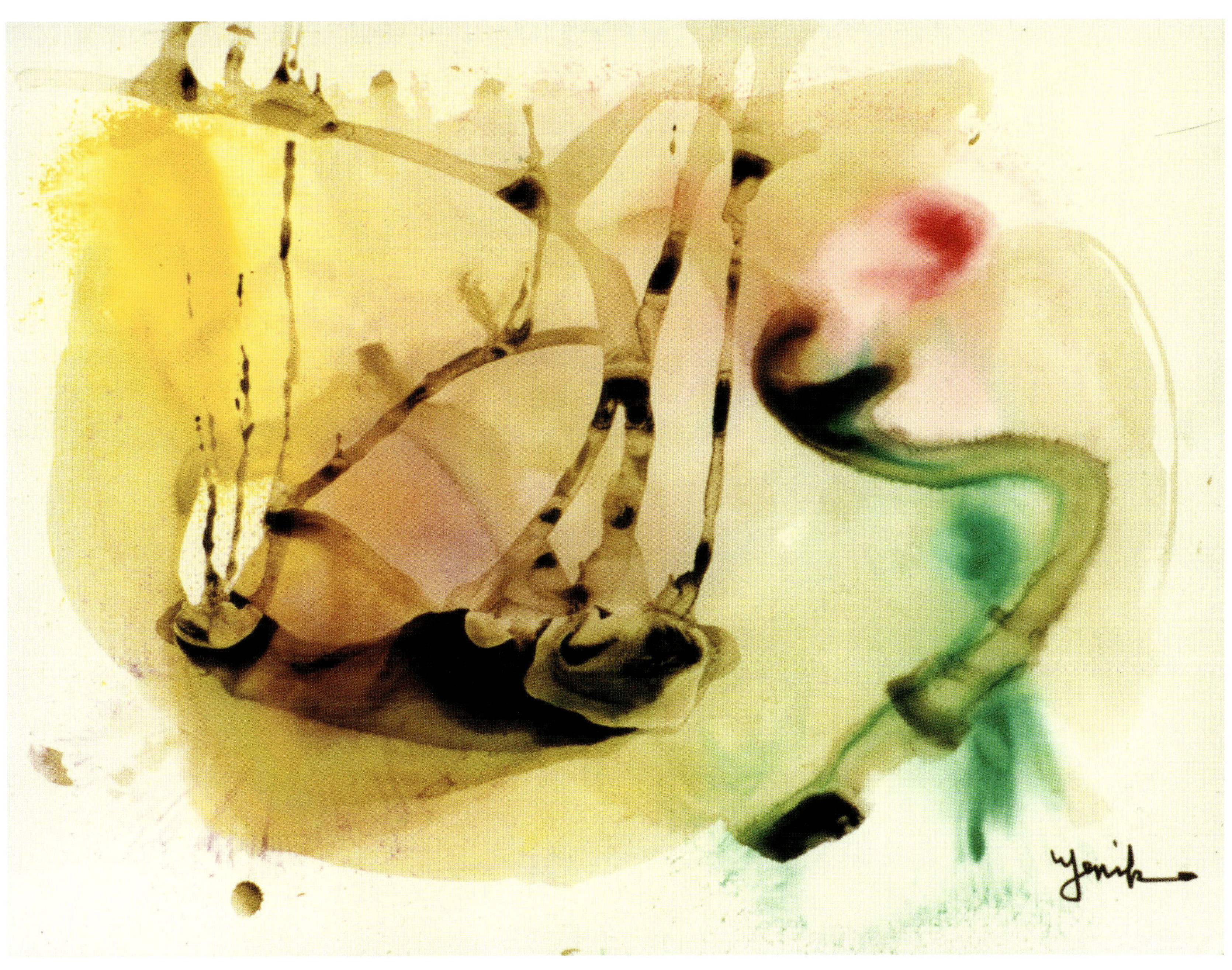

ABS No. 72, Watercolor, 18" x 24"

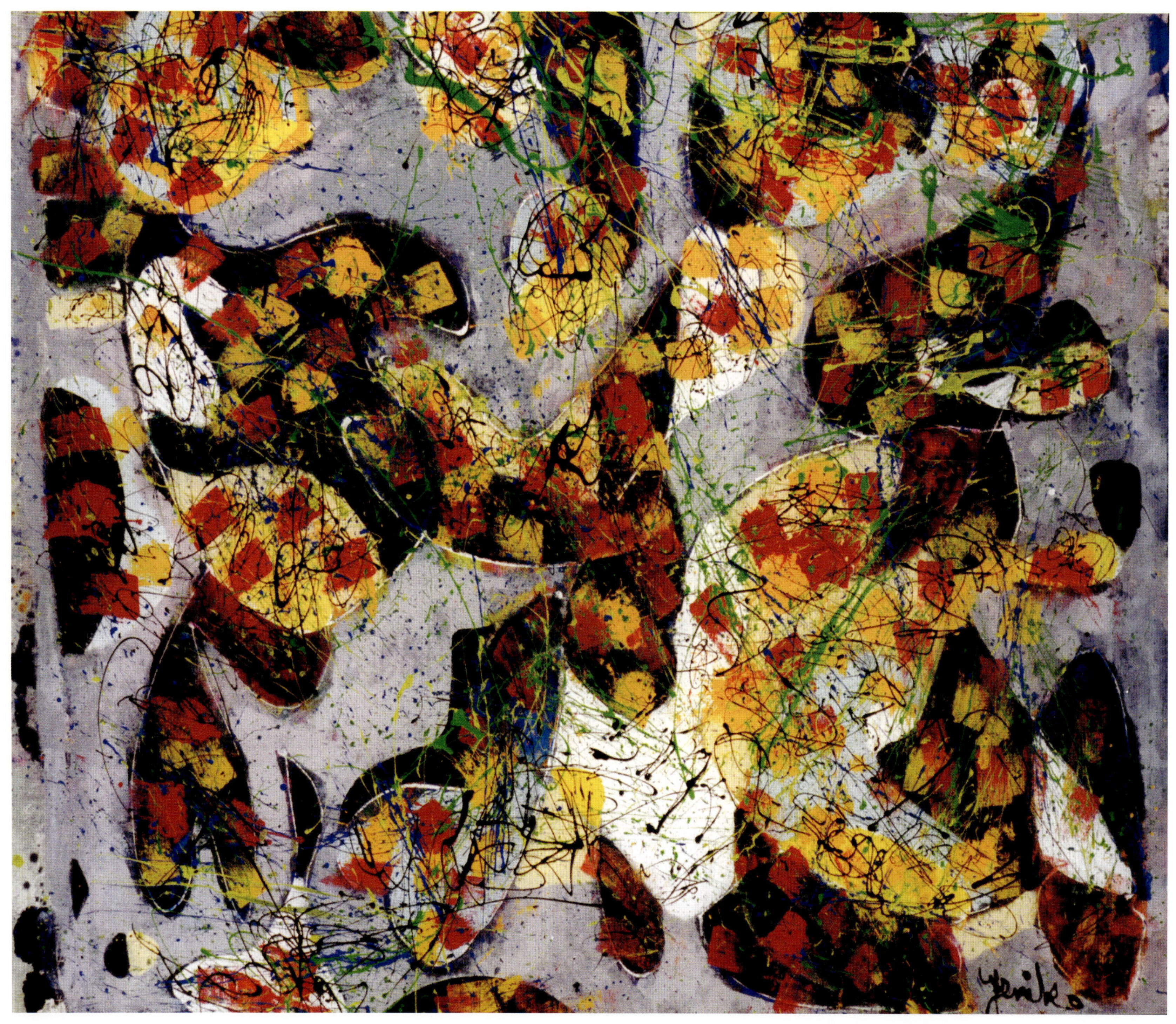

ABS No. 20, Oil, 54" x 64"

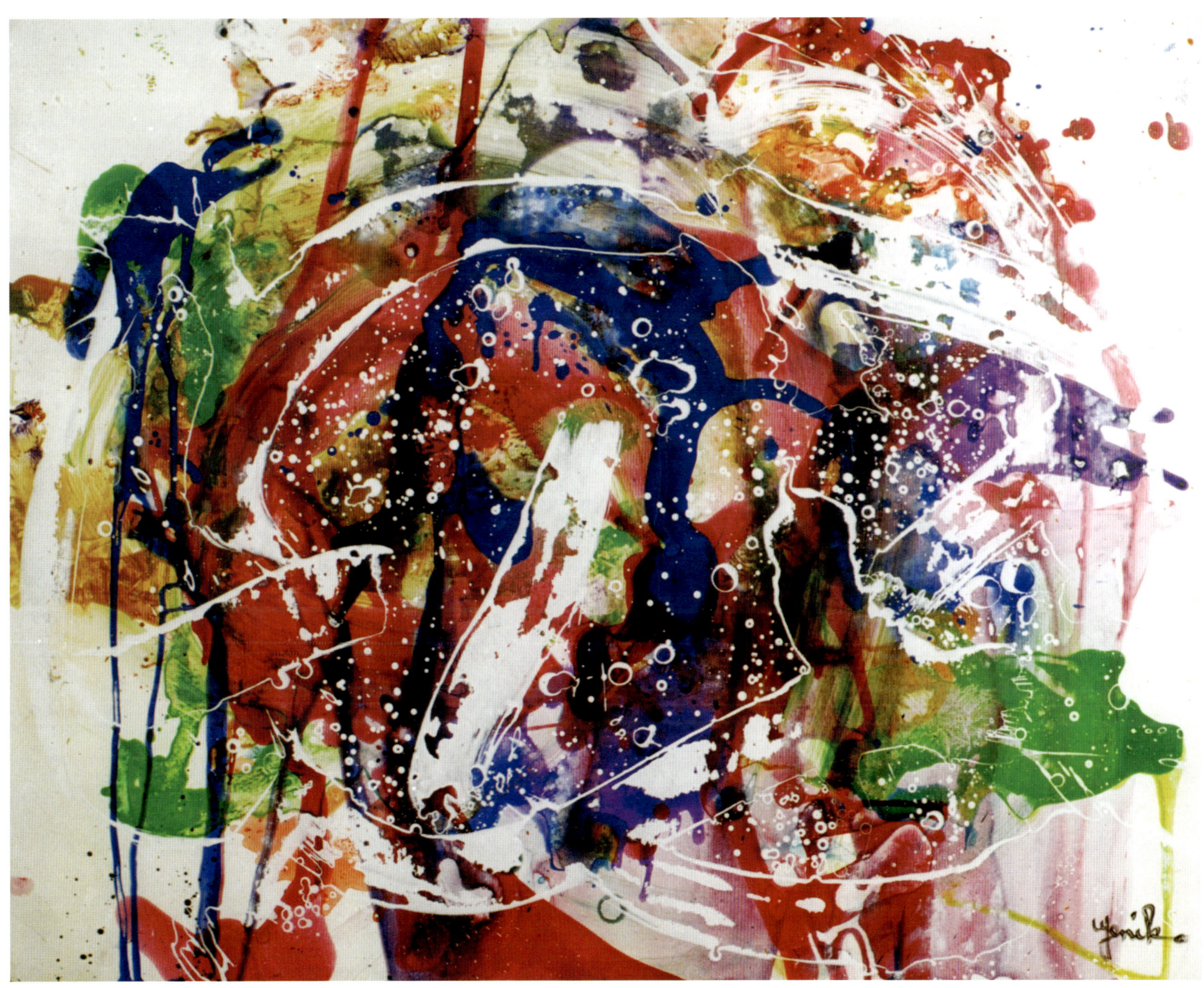

ABS No. 36, Mixed Media, 24" x 30"

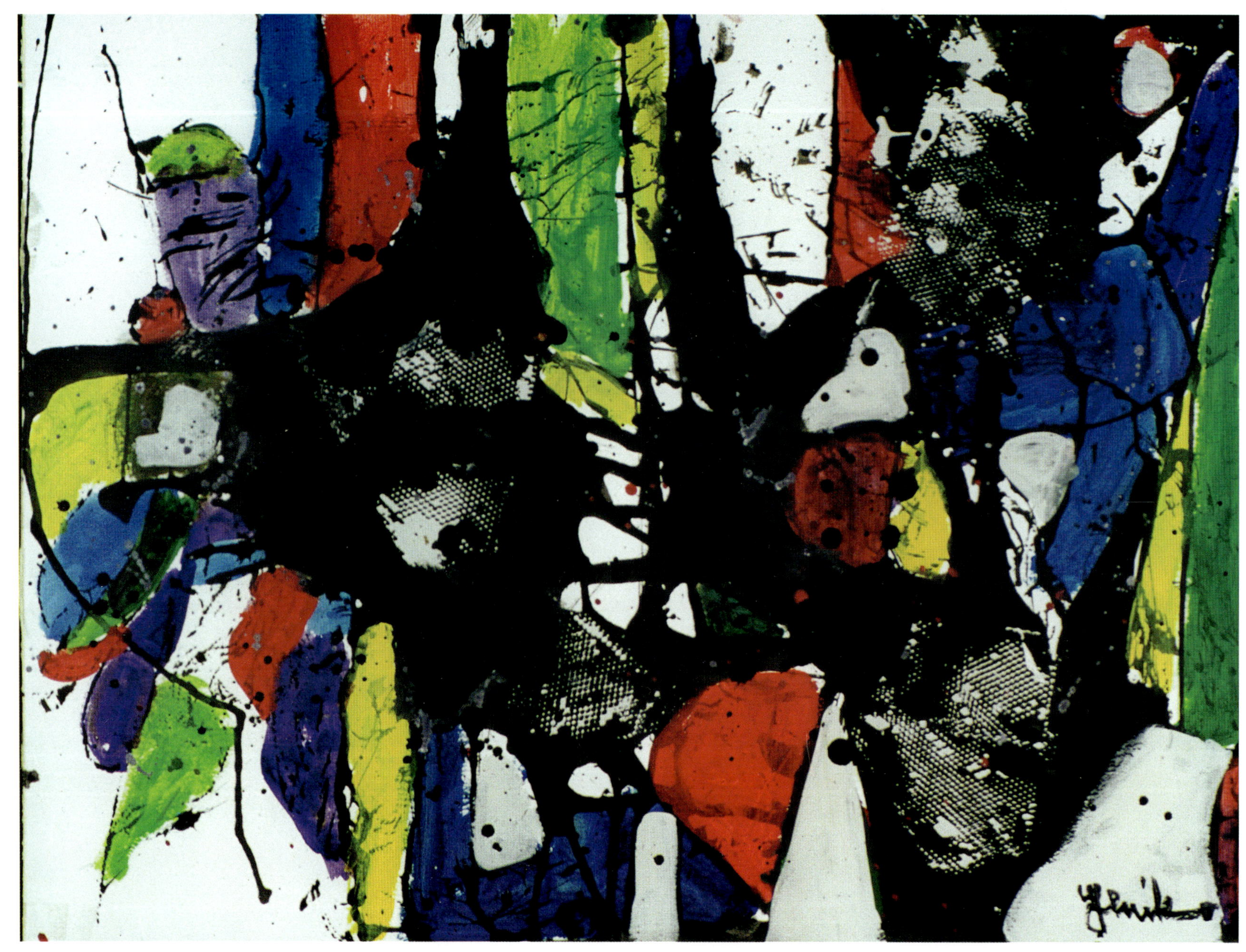

ABS No. 75, Watercolor, 18" x 24"

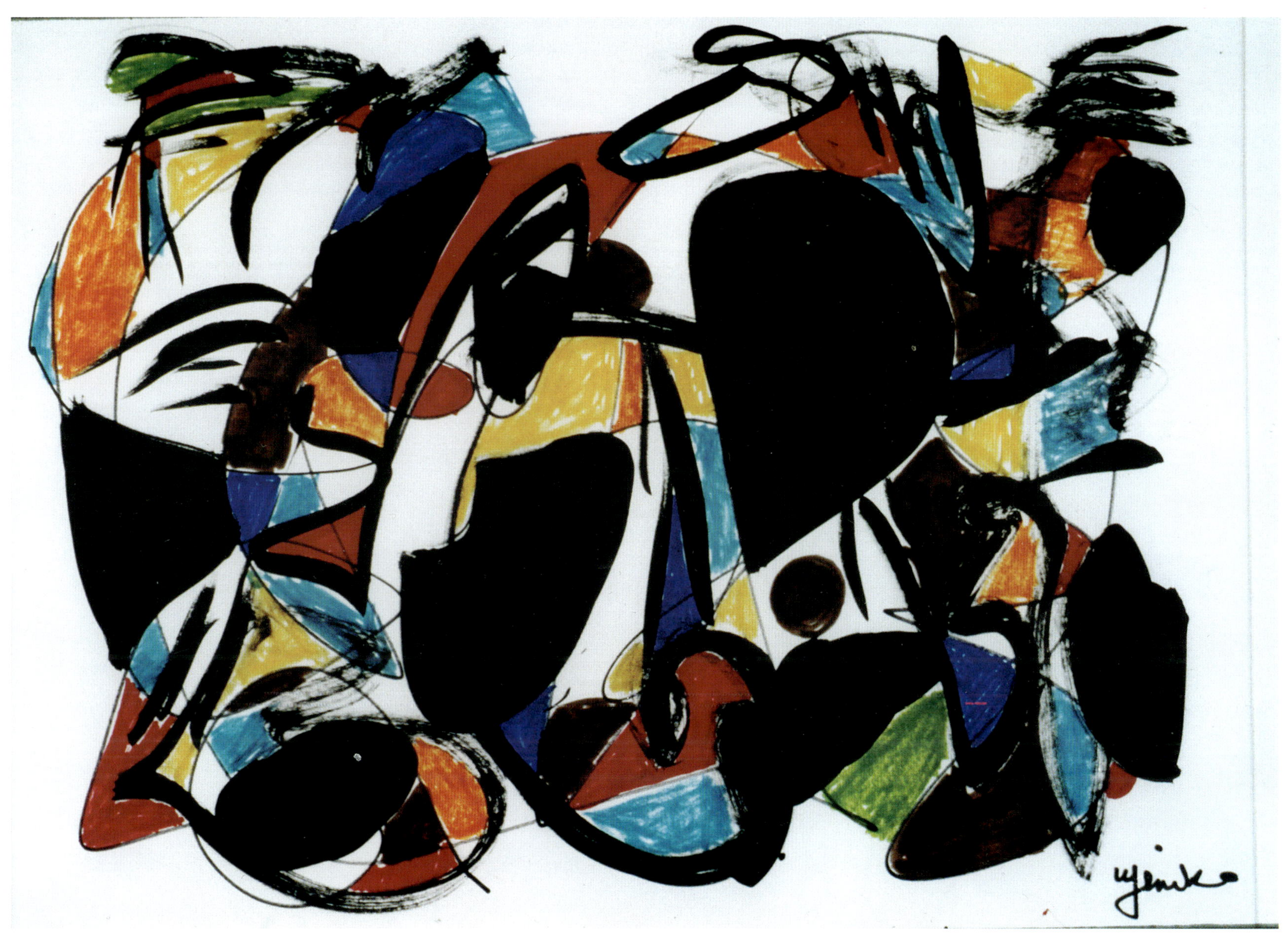

ABS No. 69, Watercolor, 18" x 24"

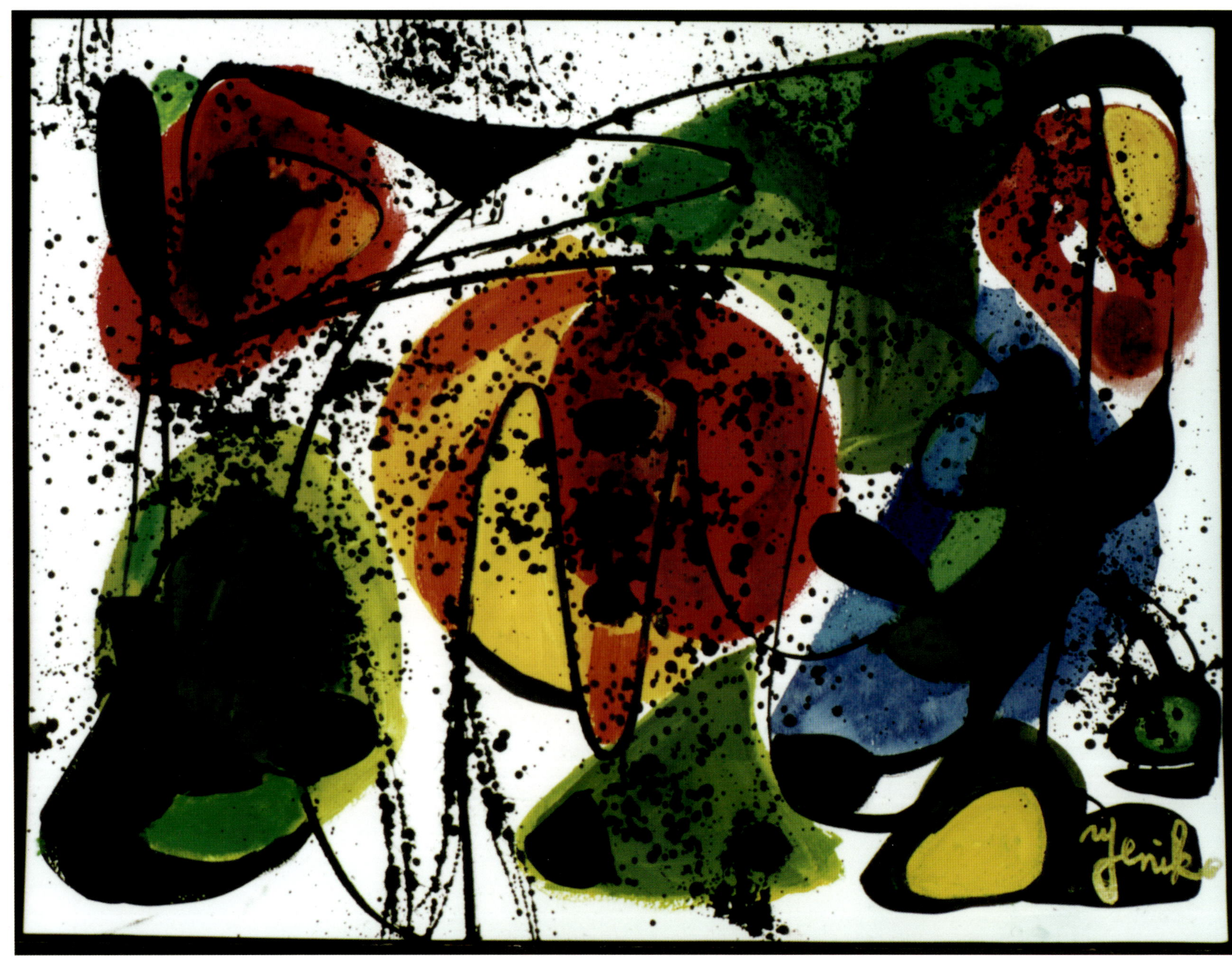

ABS No. 68, Watercolor, 18" x 24"

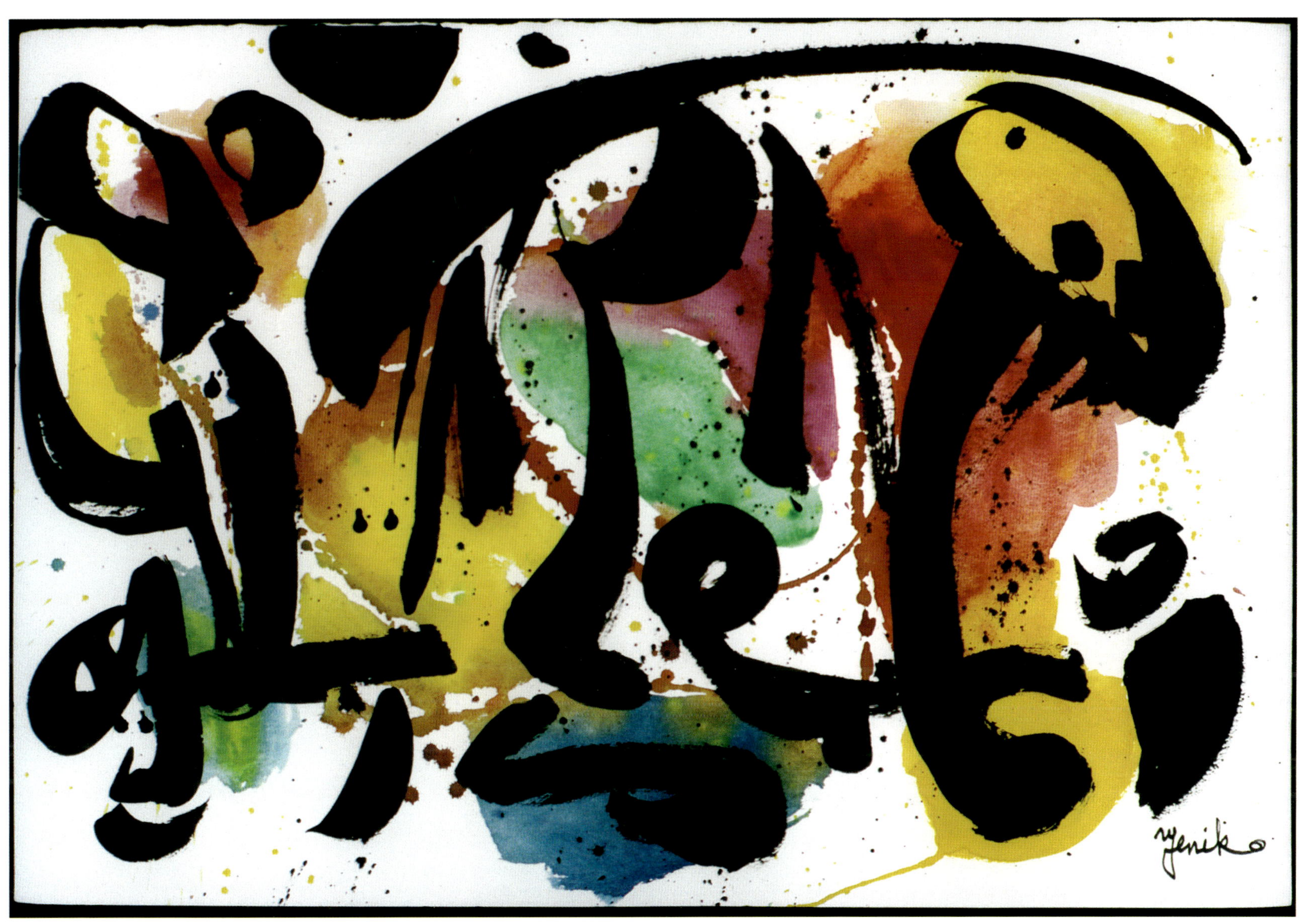

ABS No.35, Water Color, 24" x 34"

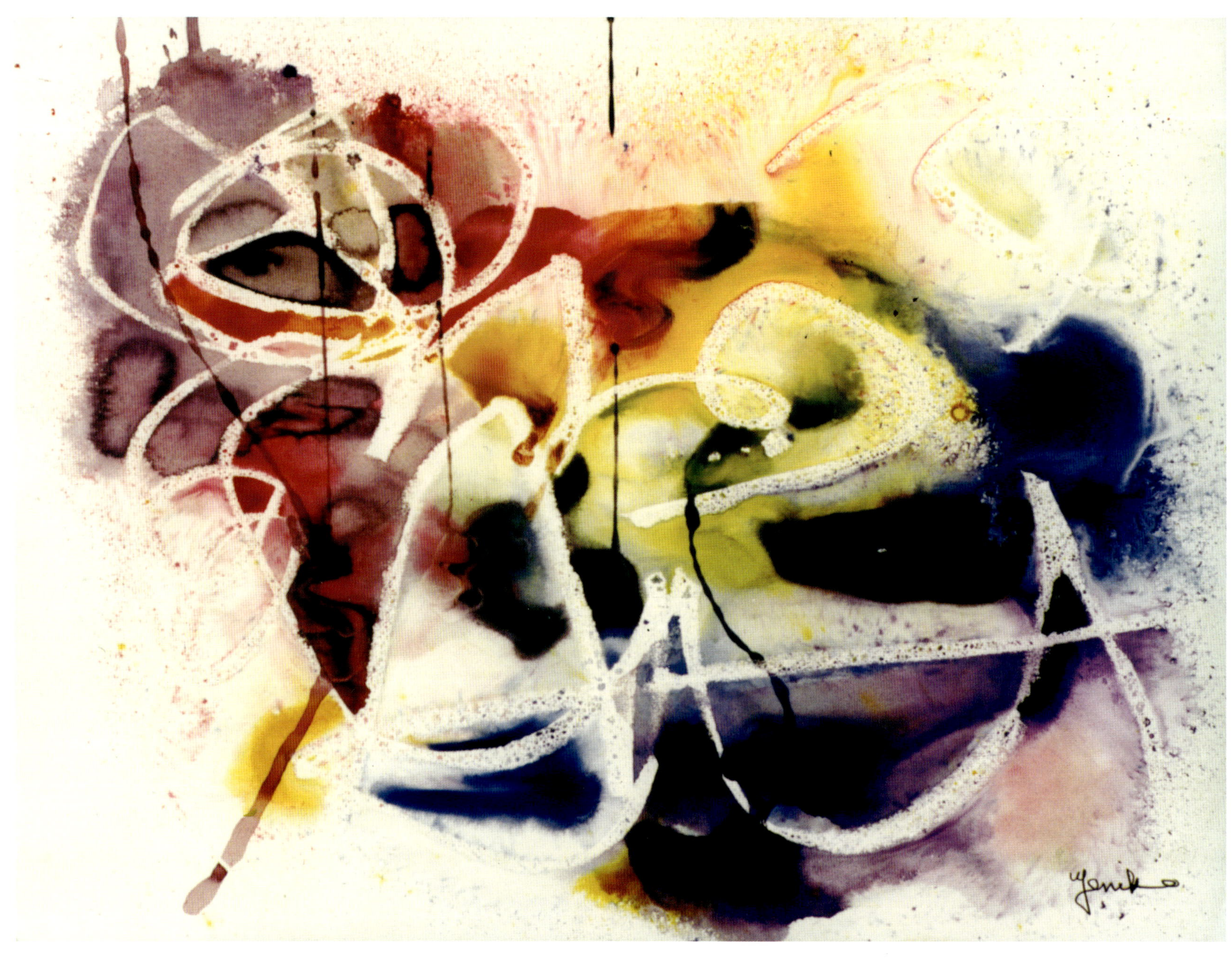

ABS No. 82, Watercolor, 18" x 24"

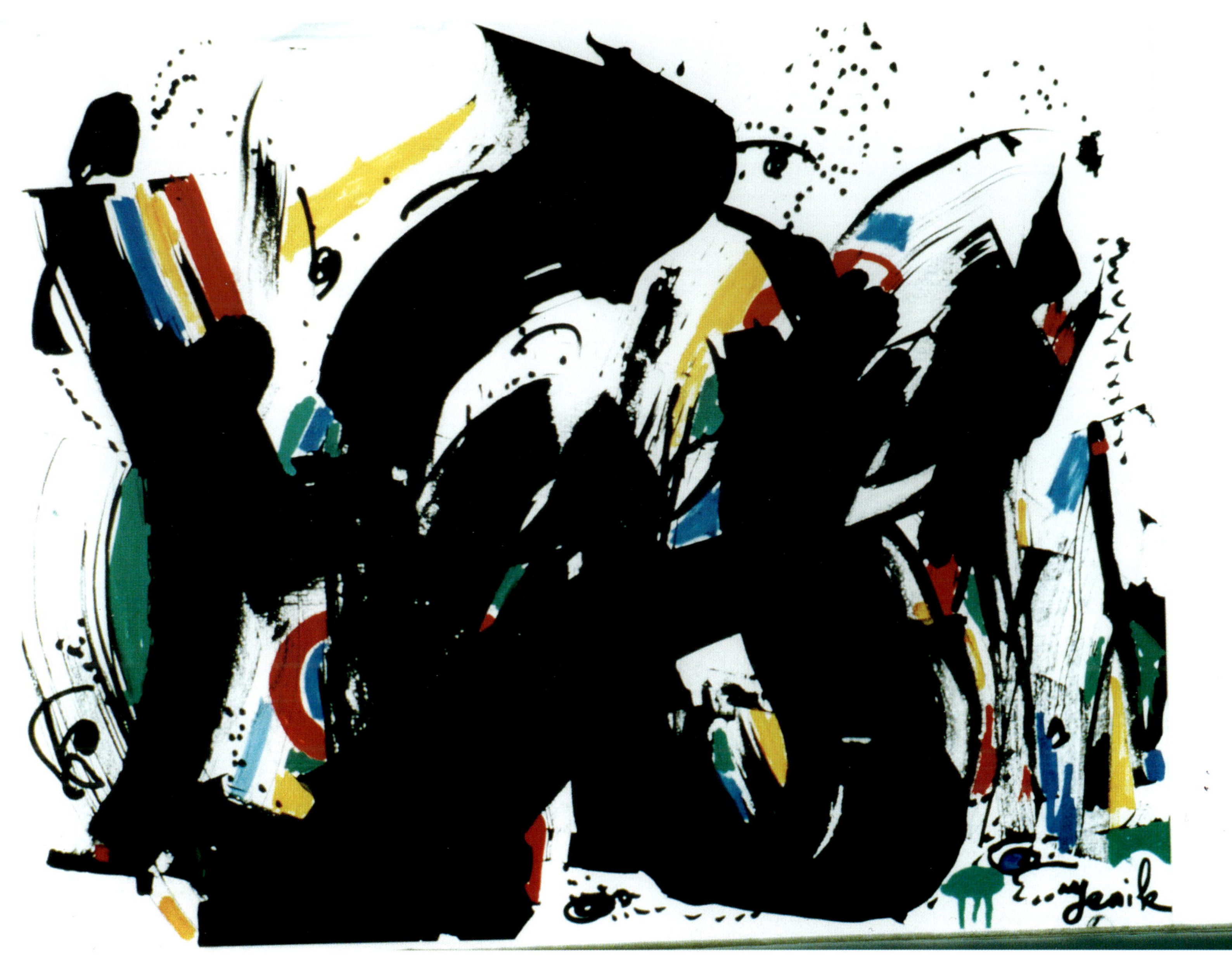

ABS No. 52, Watercolor and Acrlic, 18" x 24"

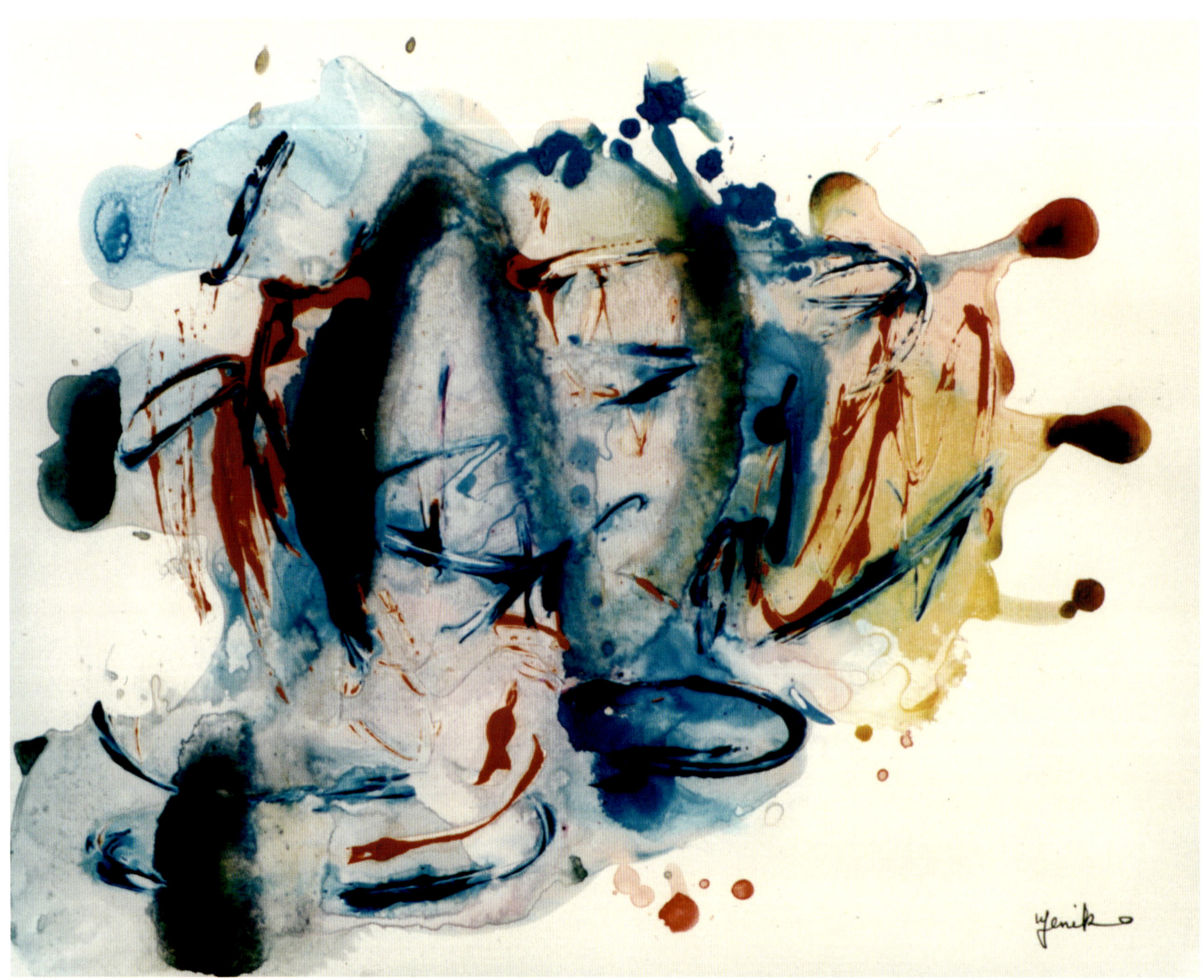

ABS No. 79, Watercolor, 18" x 24"

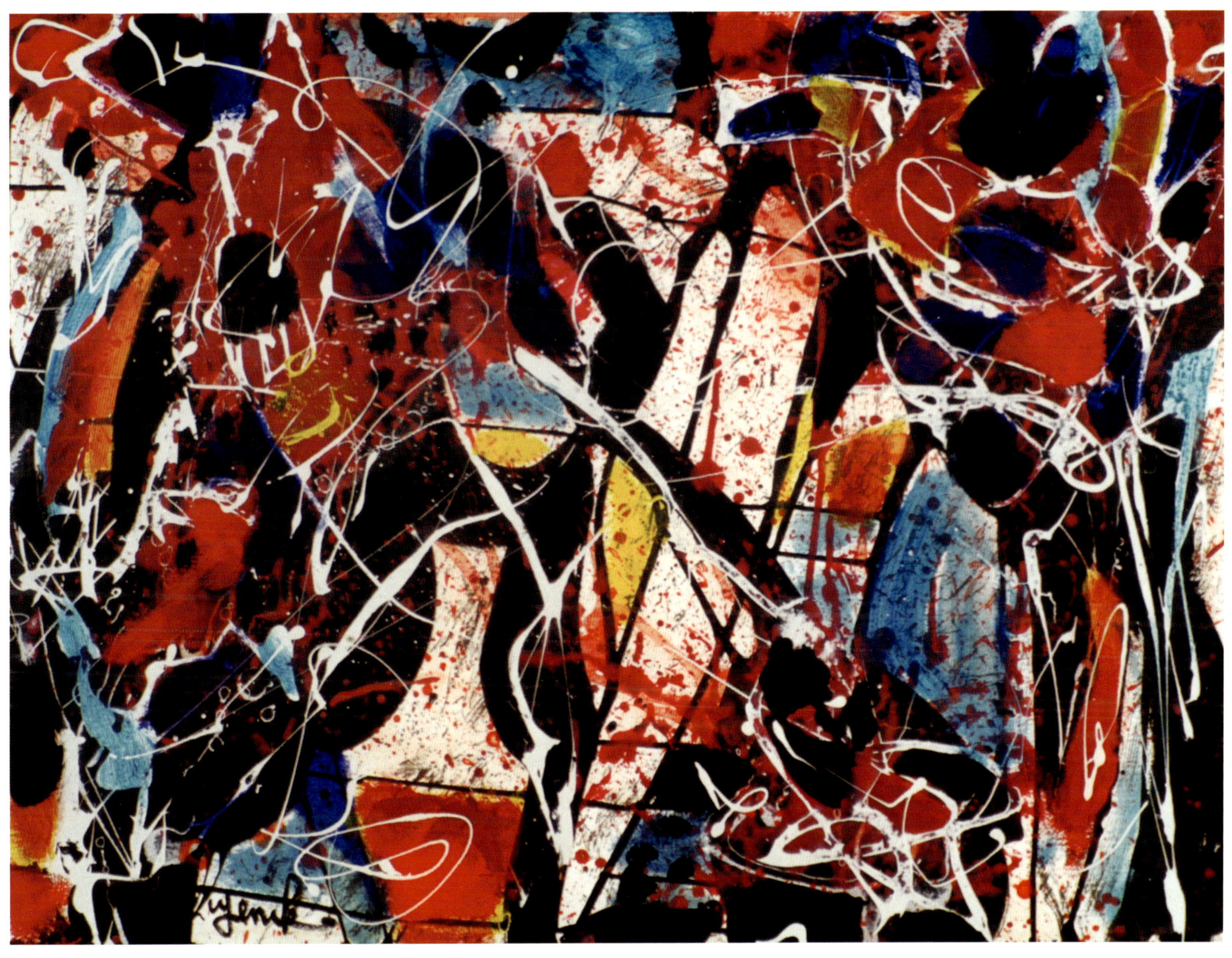

ABS No. 48, Mixed Media, 18" x 24"

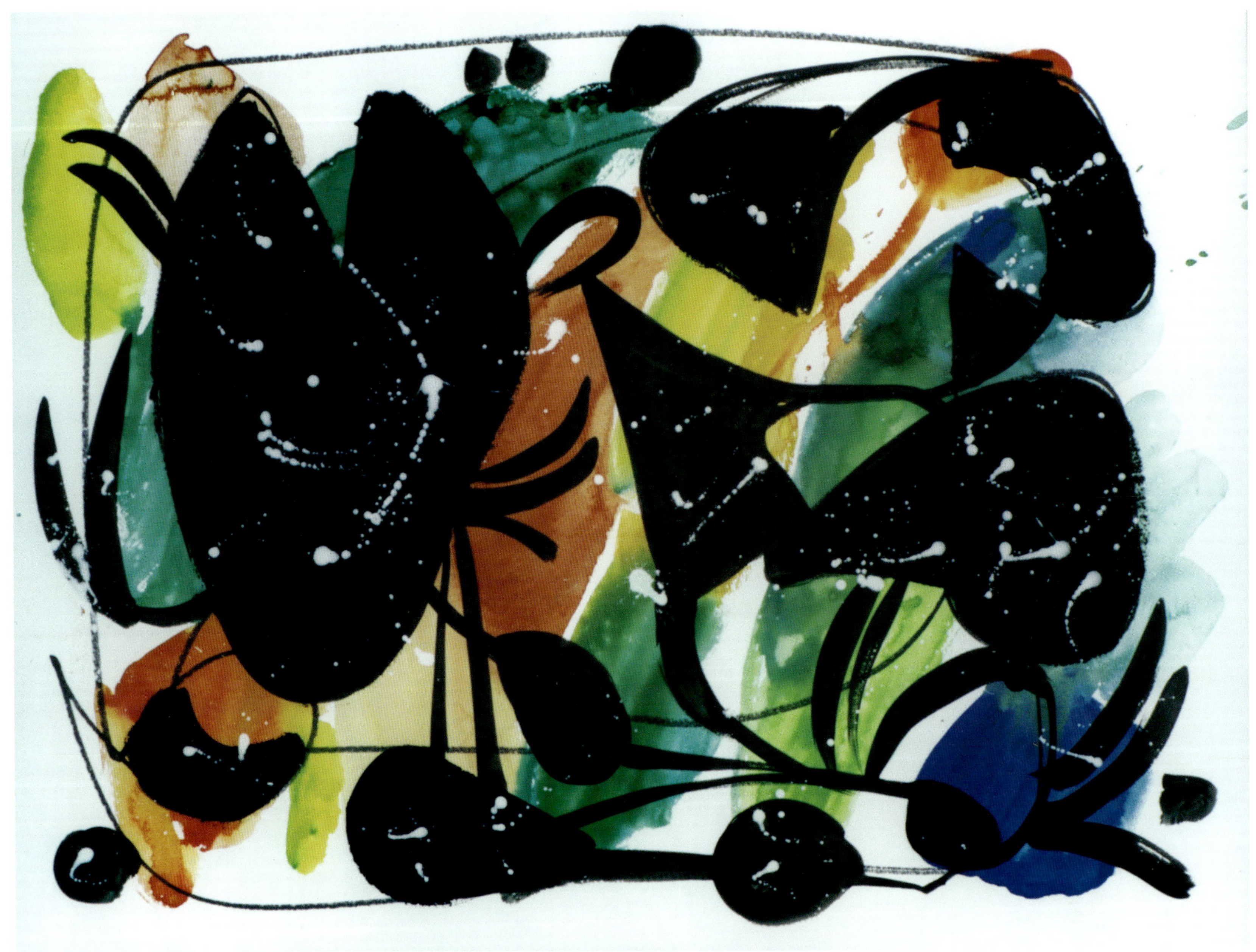

ABS No. 56, Watercolor, 18" x 24"

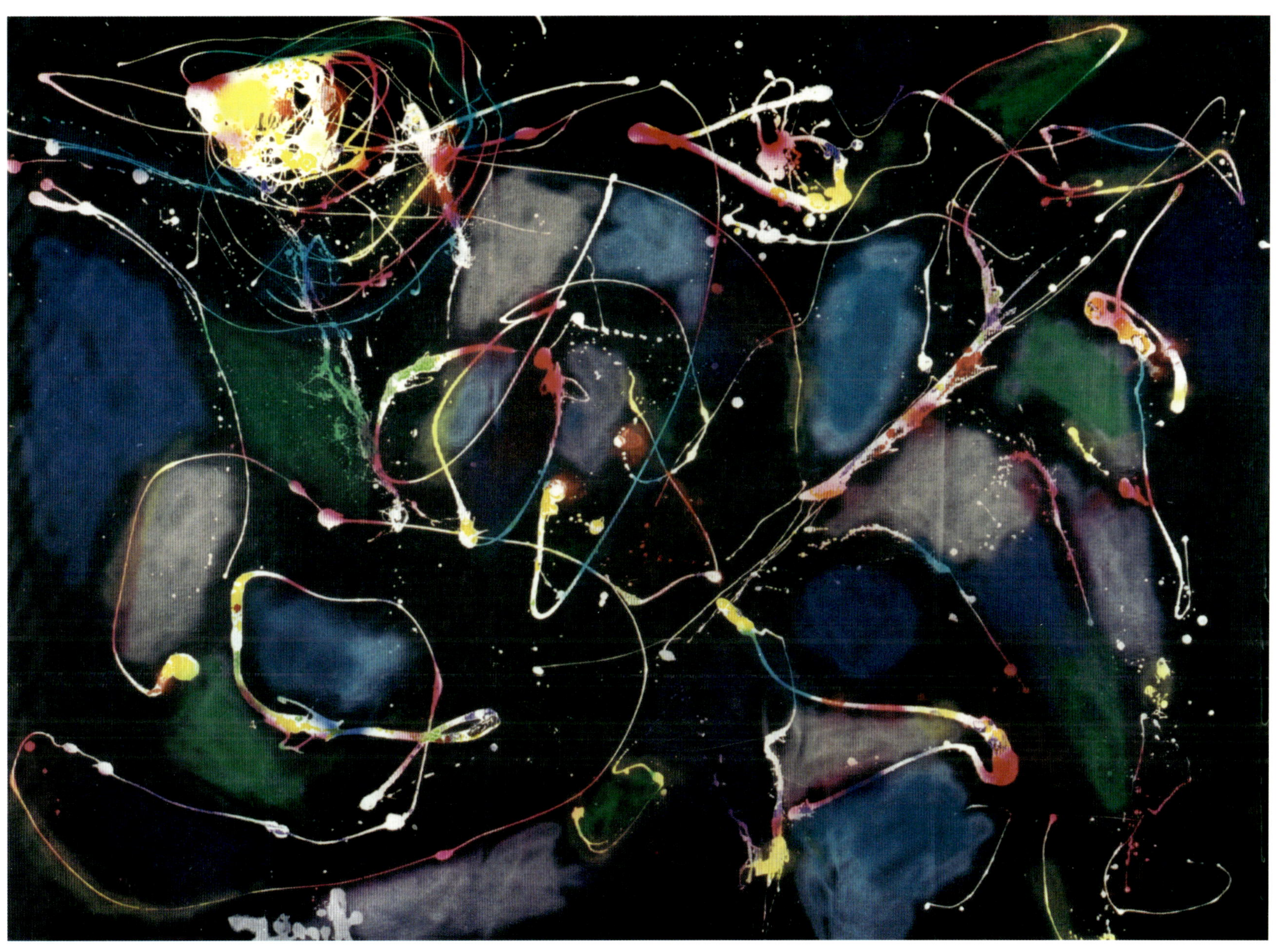

ABS No. 28, Acrylic, 56" x 68"

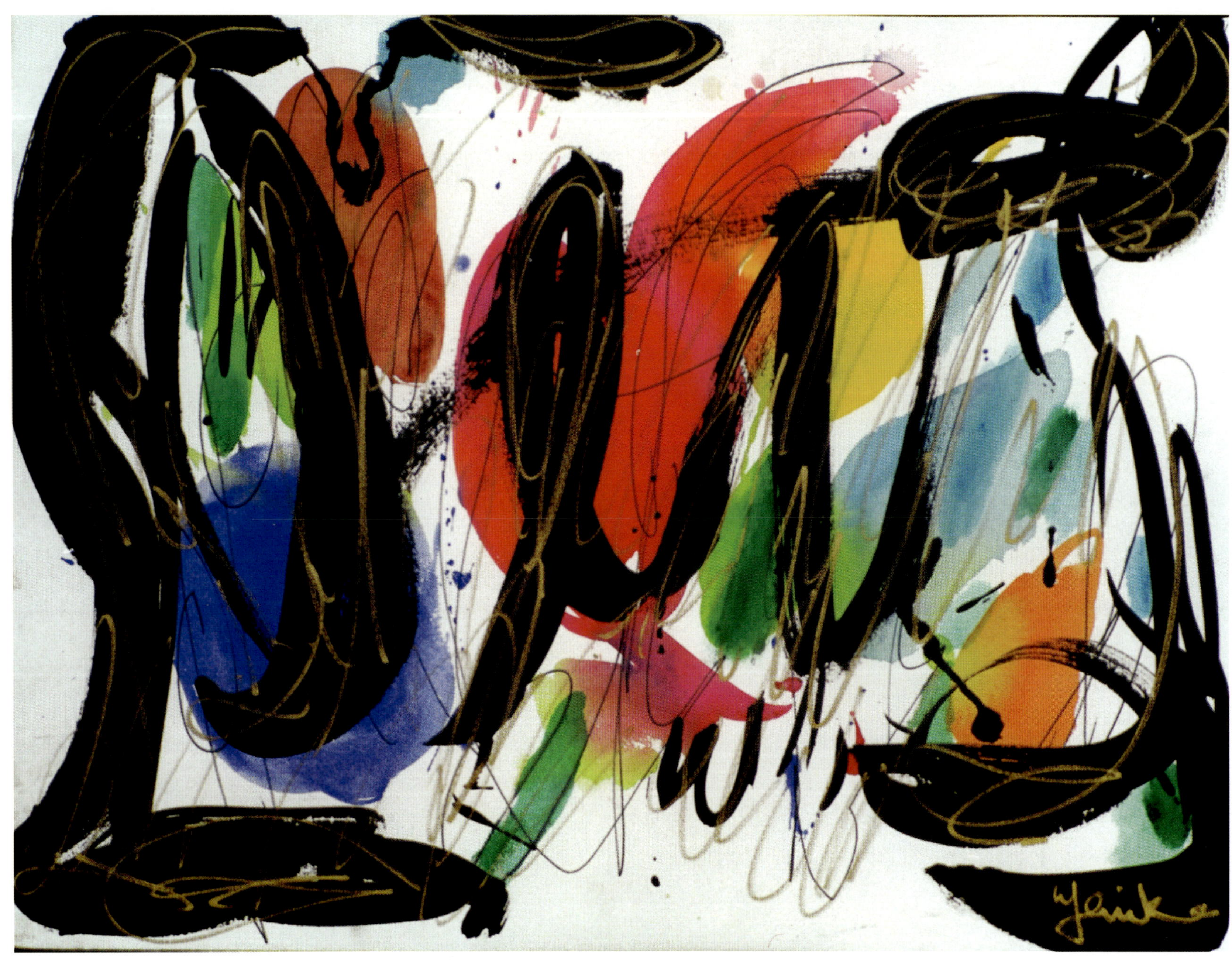

ABS No. 67, Watercolor, 18" x 24"

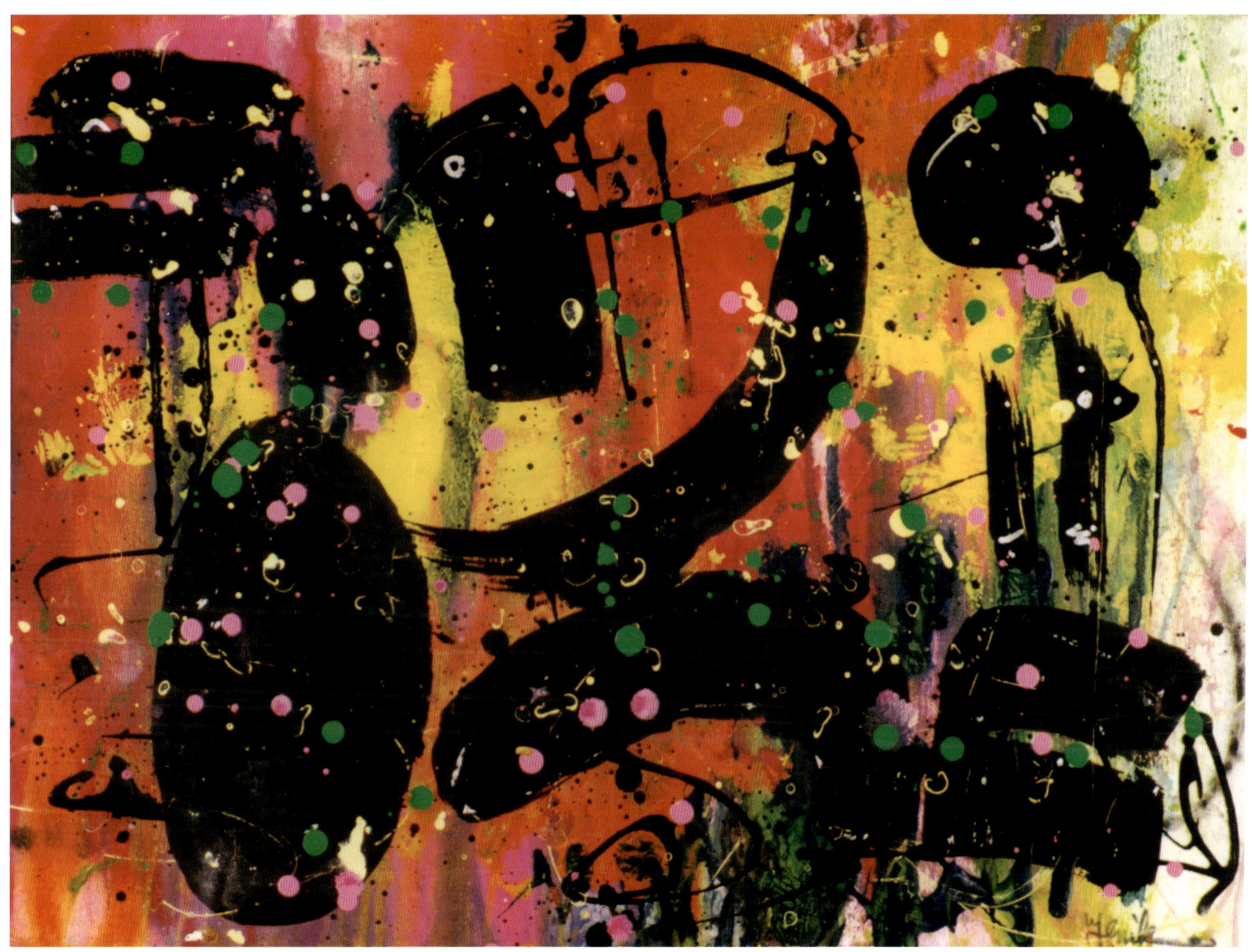

Dreaming, Watercolor, 18" x 24"

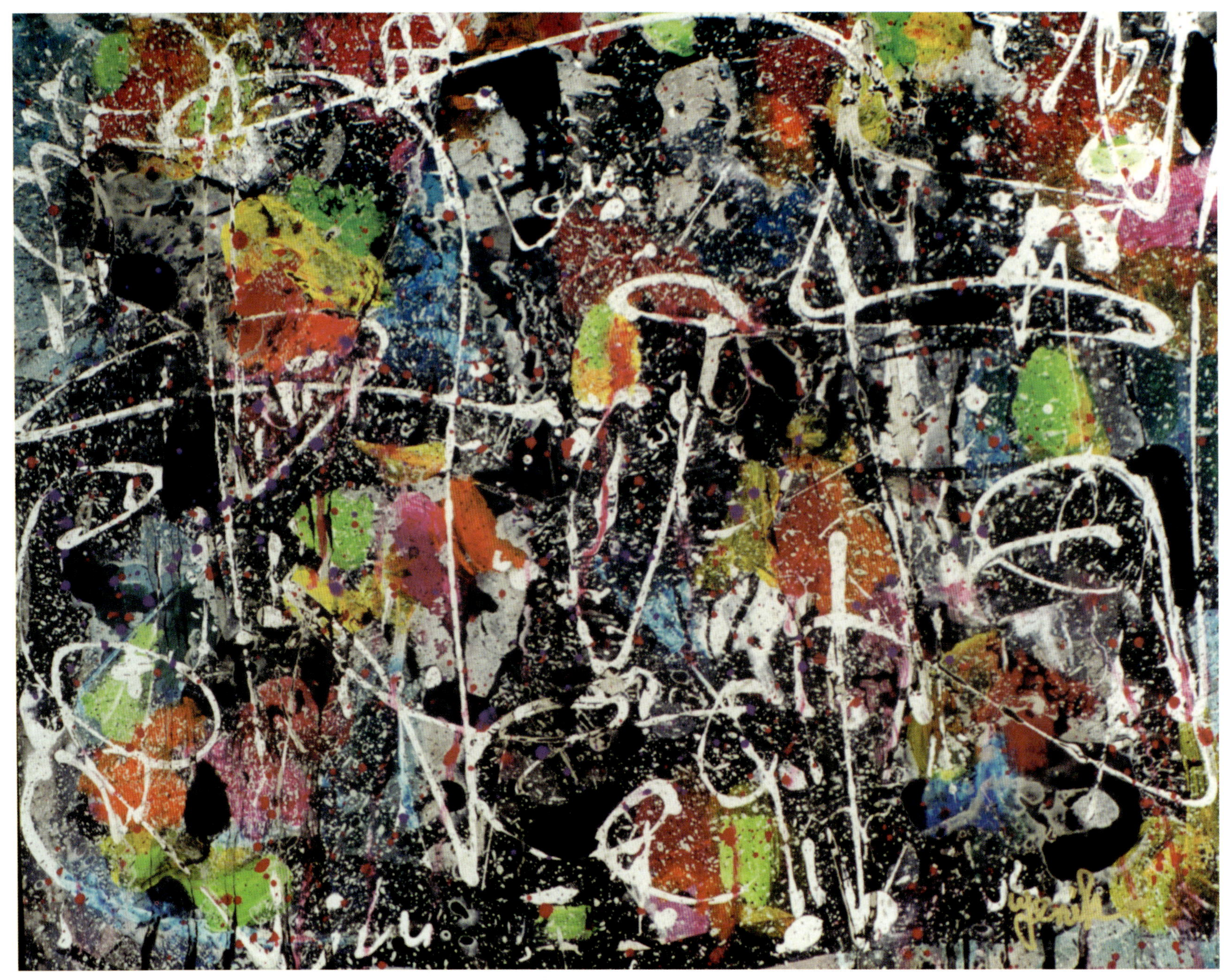

ABS No. 49, Watercolor, 18" x 24"

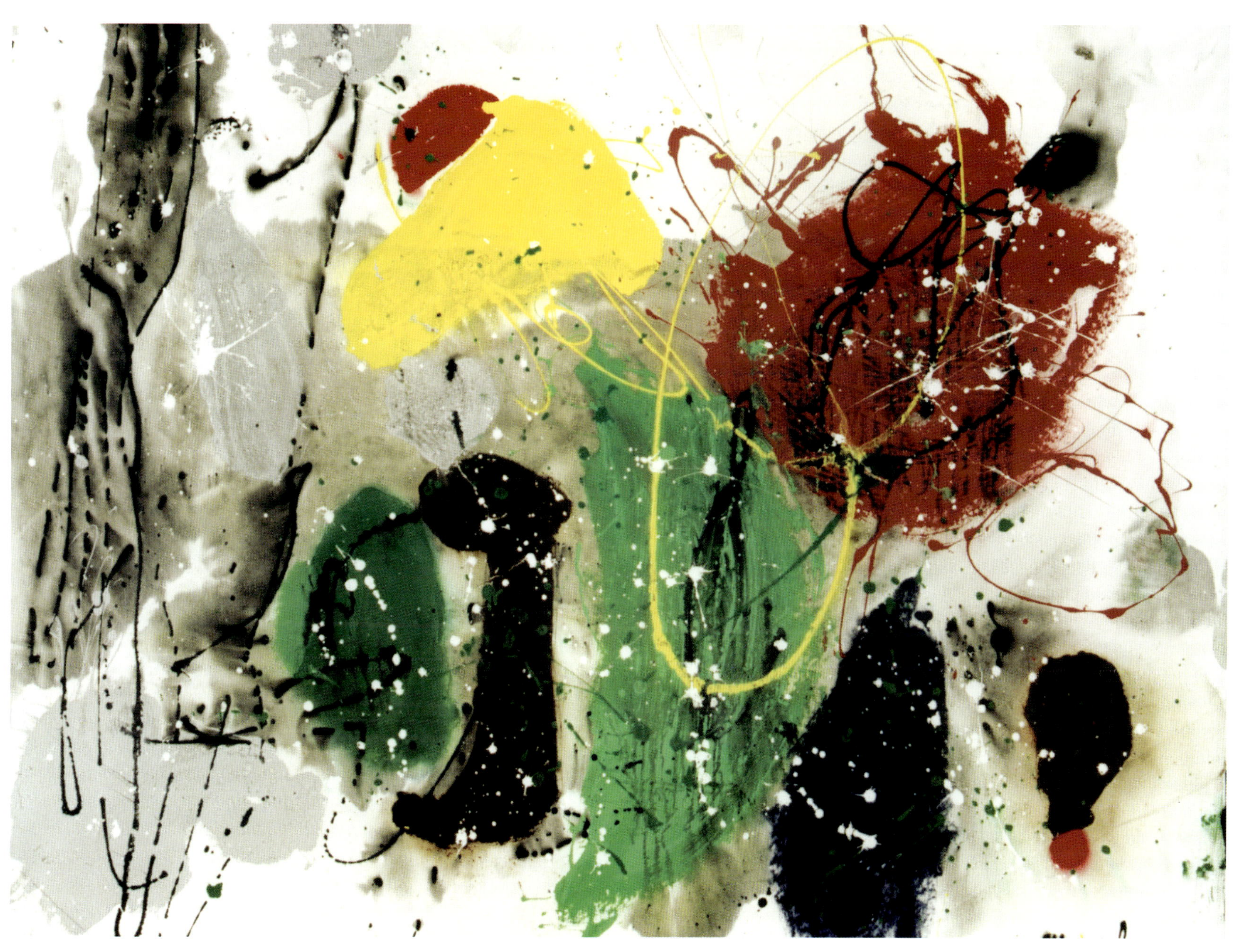

ABS No. 24, Acrylic, 46" x 66"

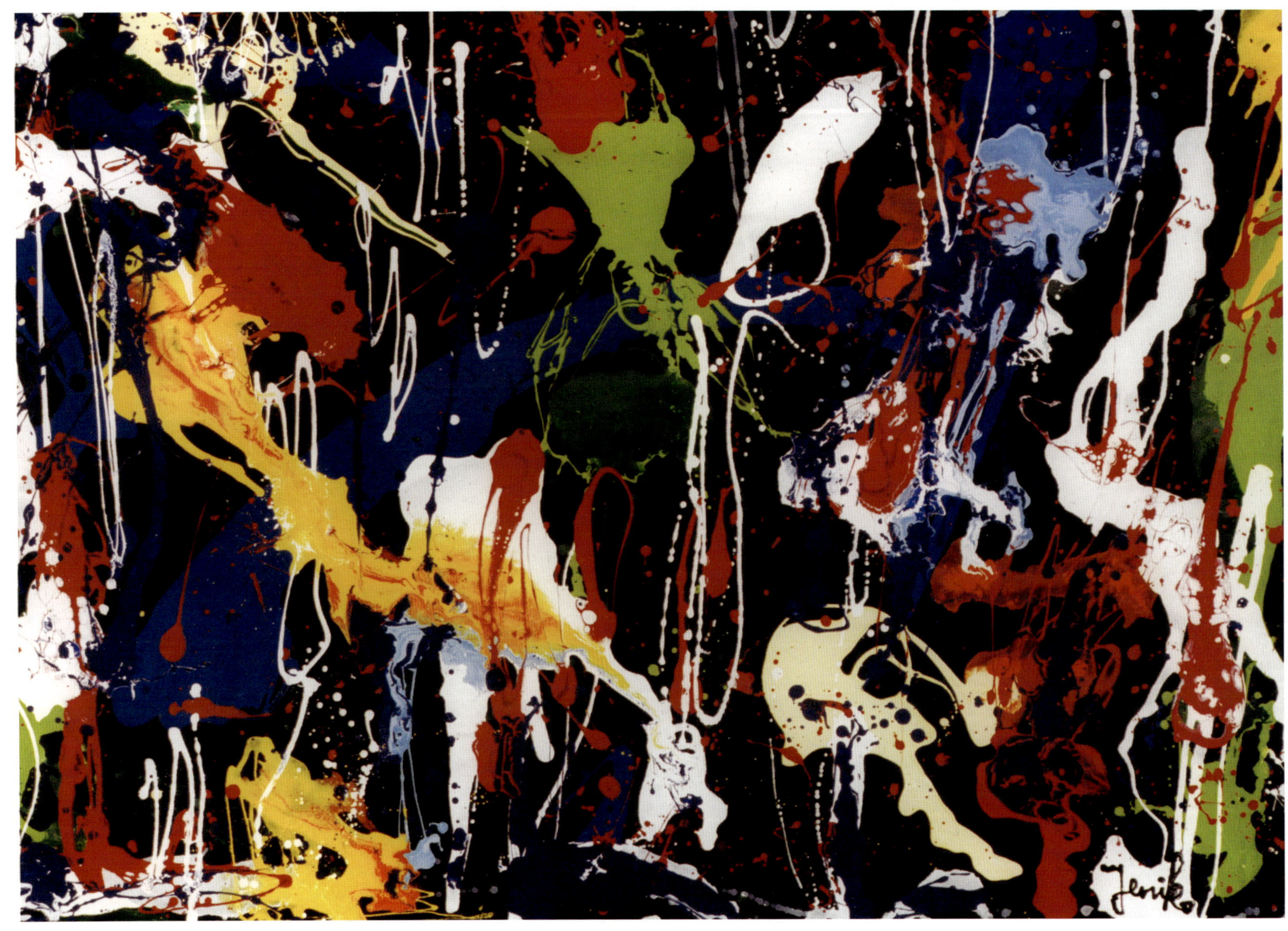

ABS No. 9, Acrylic, 46" x 60"

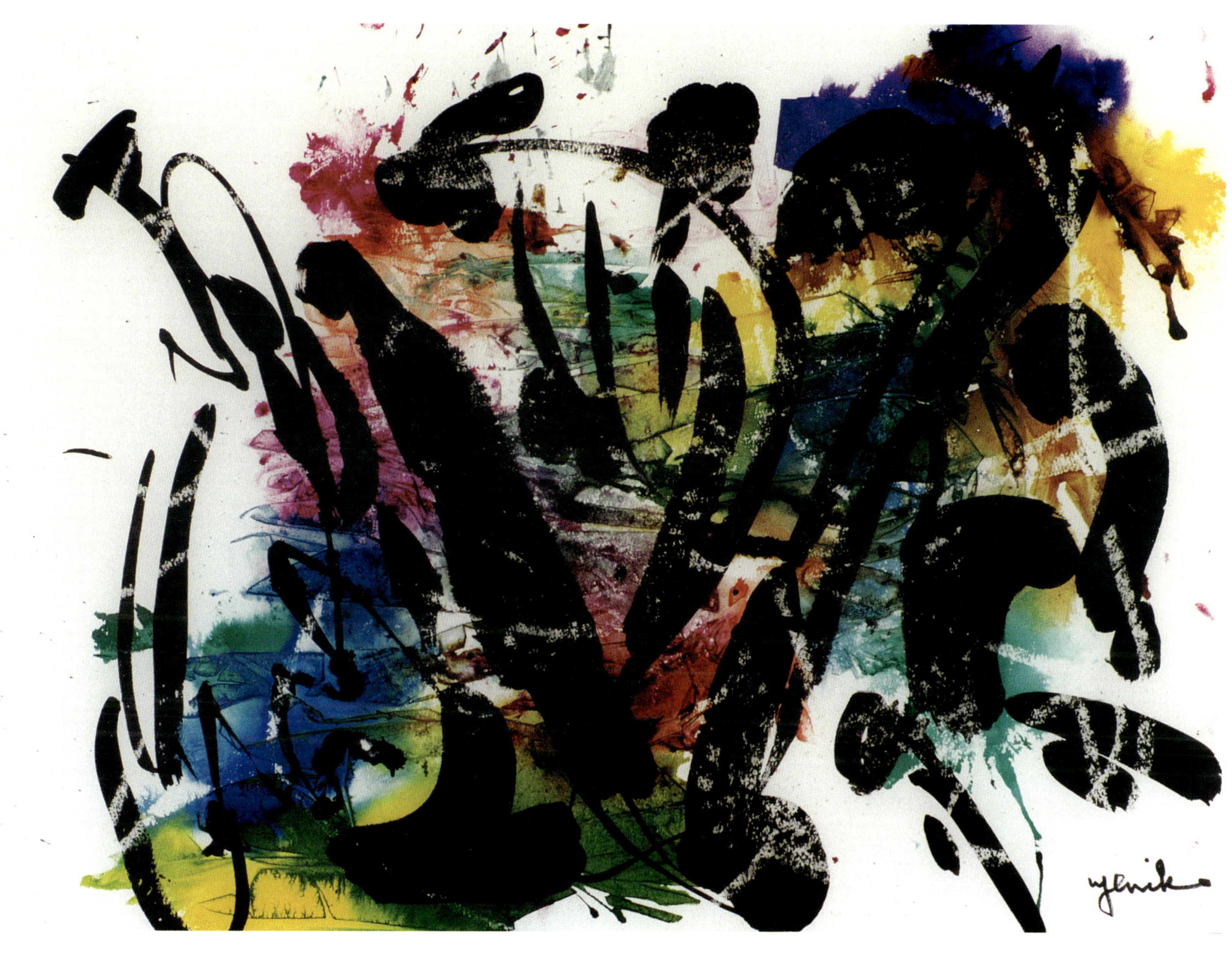

ABS No. 54, Water Color, 18" x 24"

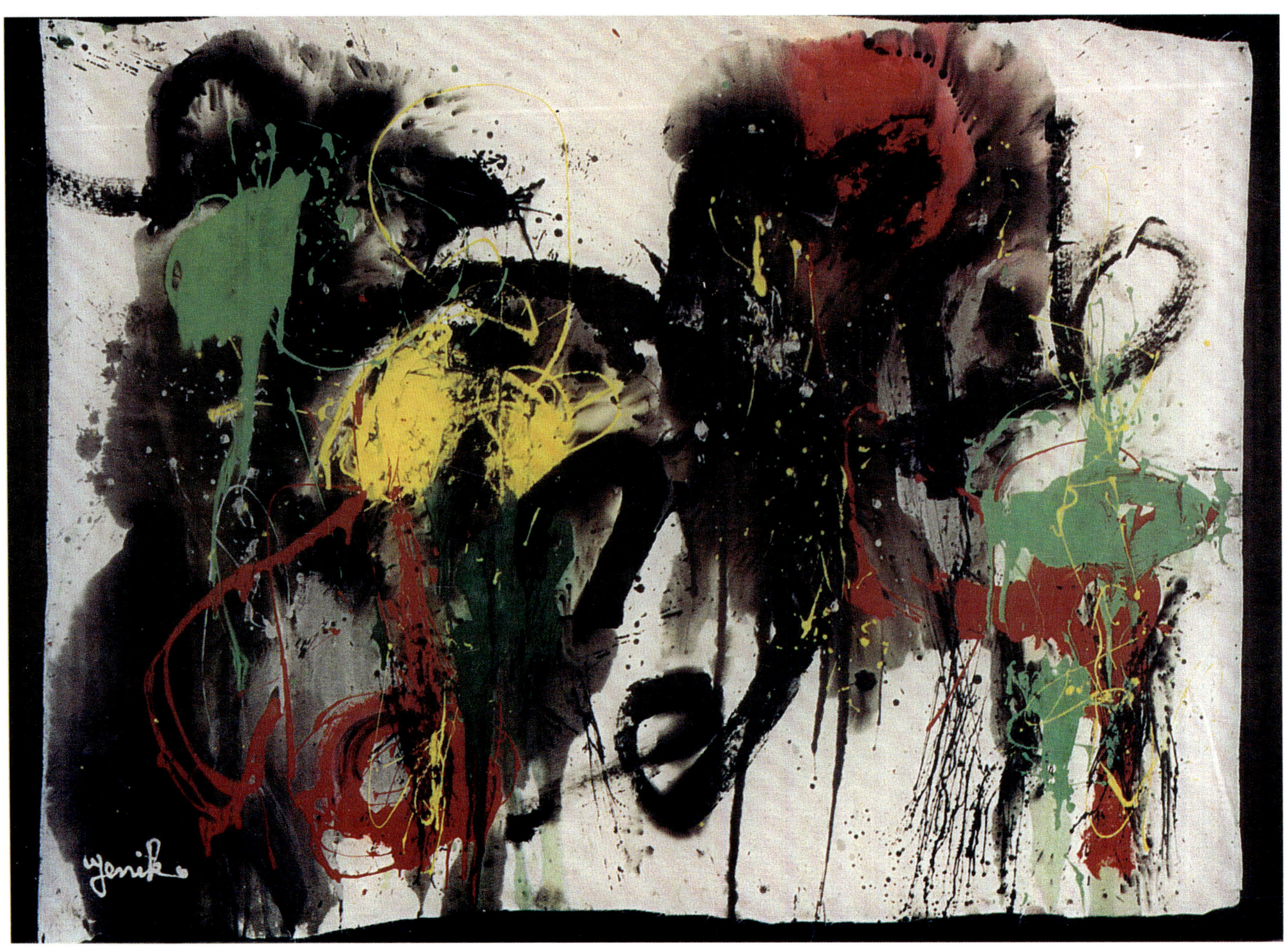

ABS No 14   Acrylic   46" x 66"

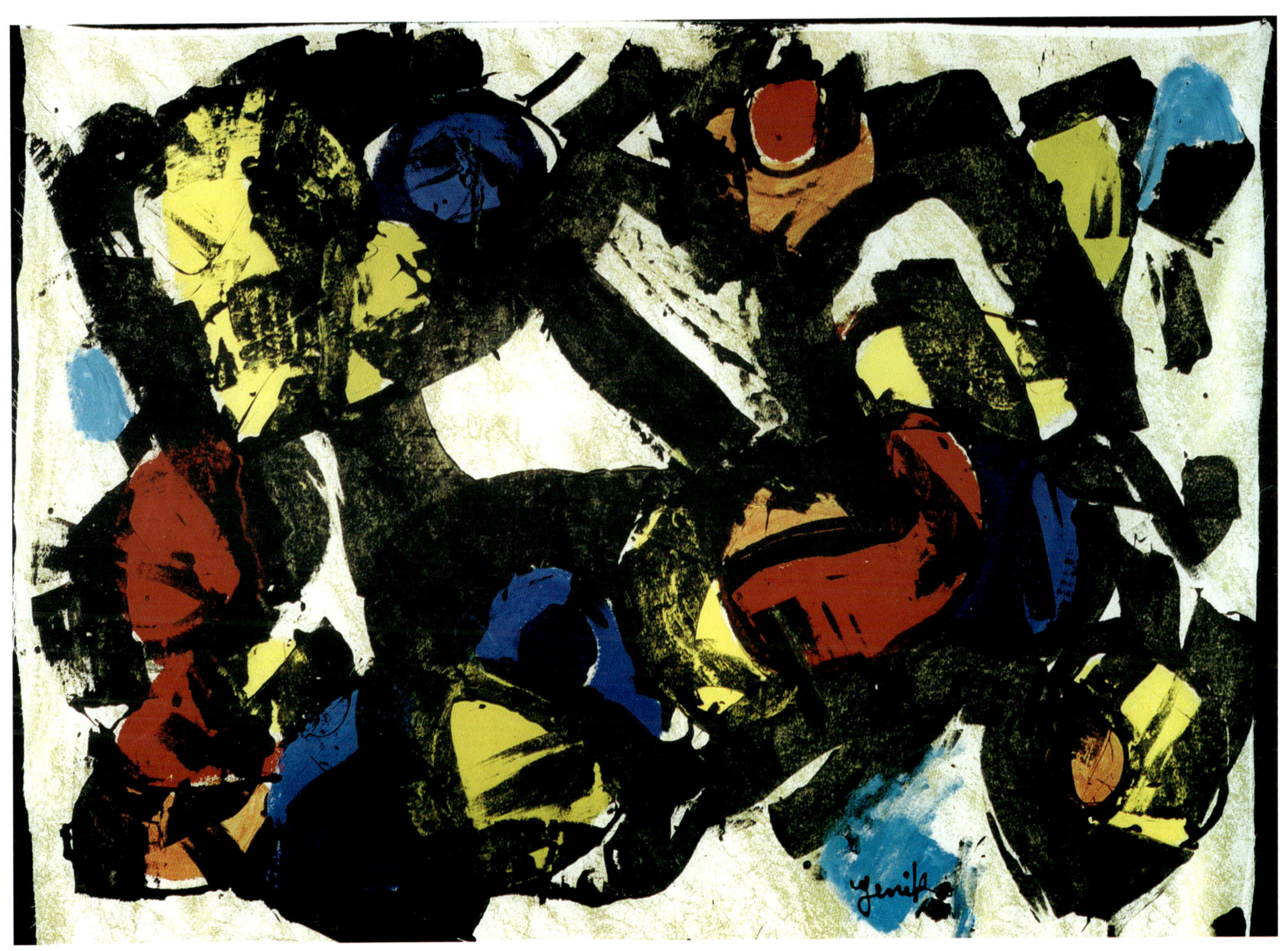

ABS No 10   Medium Oil   54" x 74"

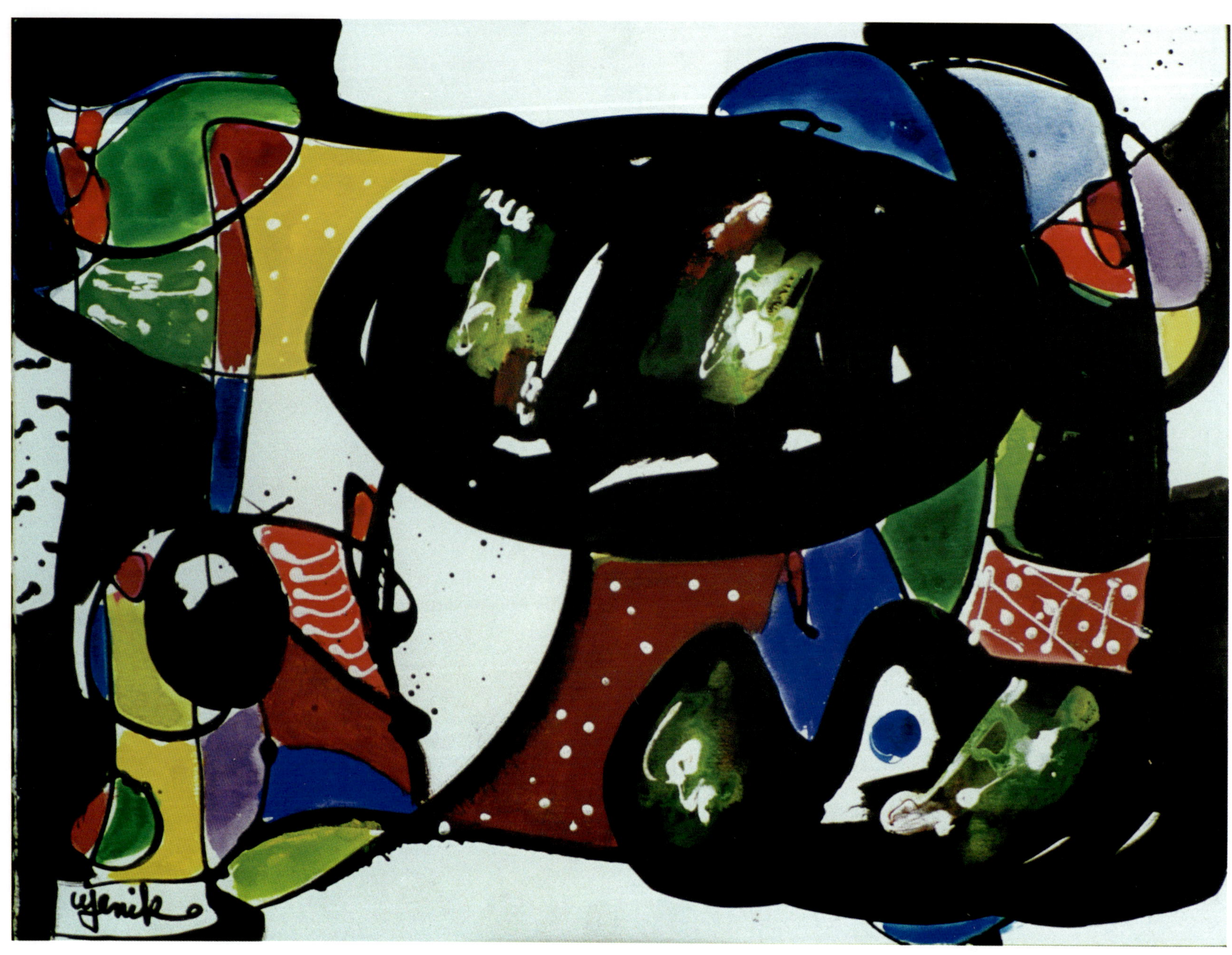

ABS No 66   Watercolor   18" x 24"

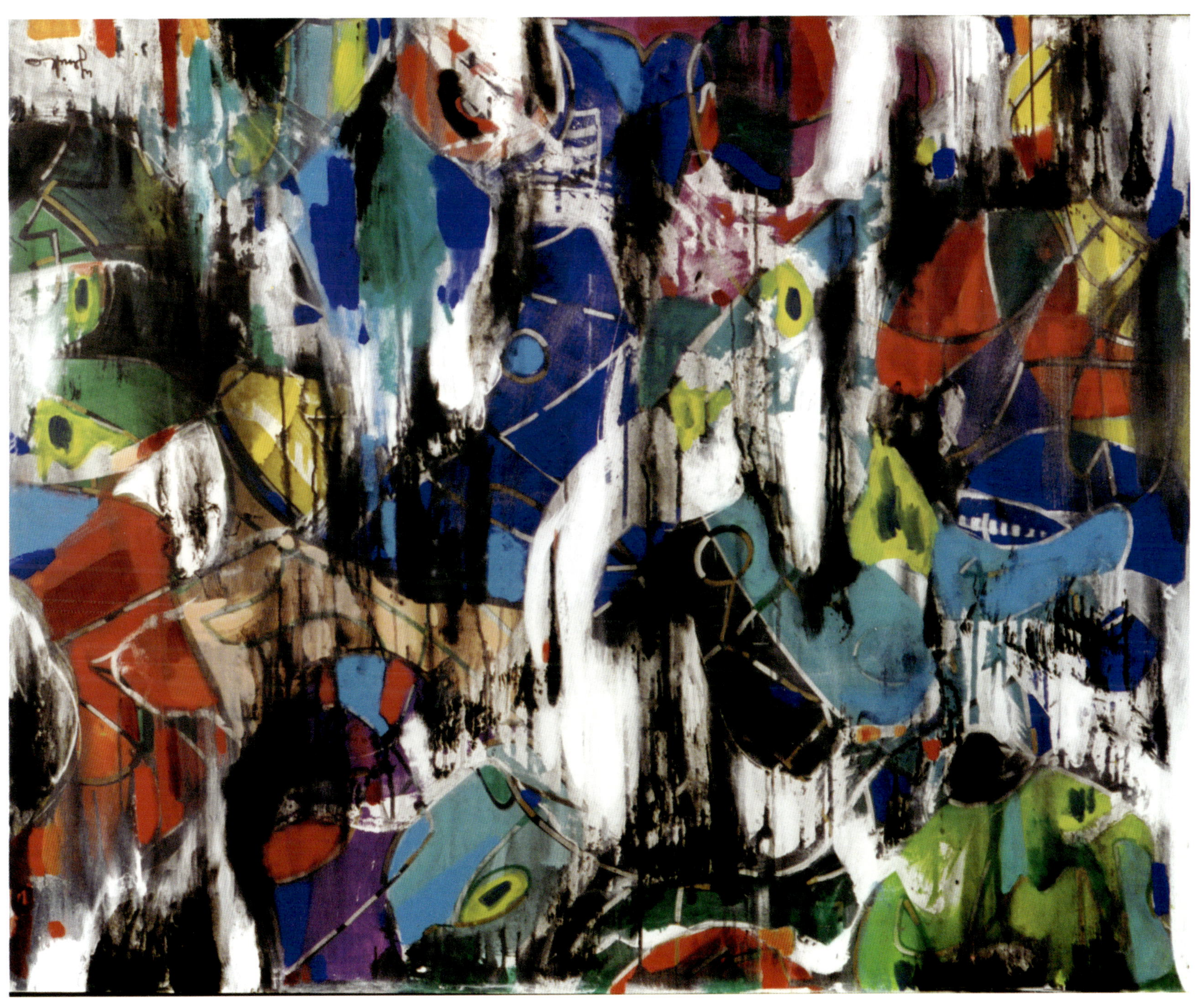

ABS No. 8   Oil   44" x 60"

RS

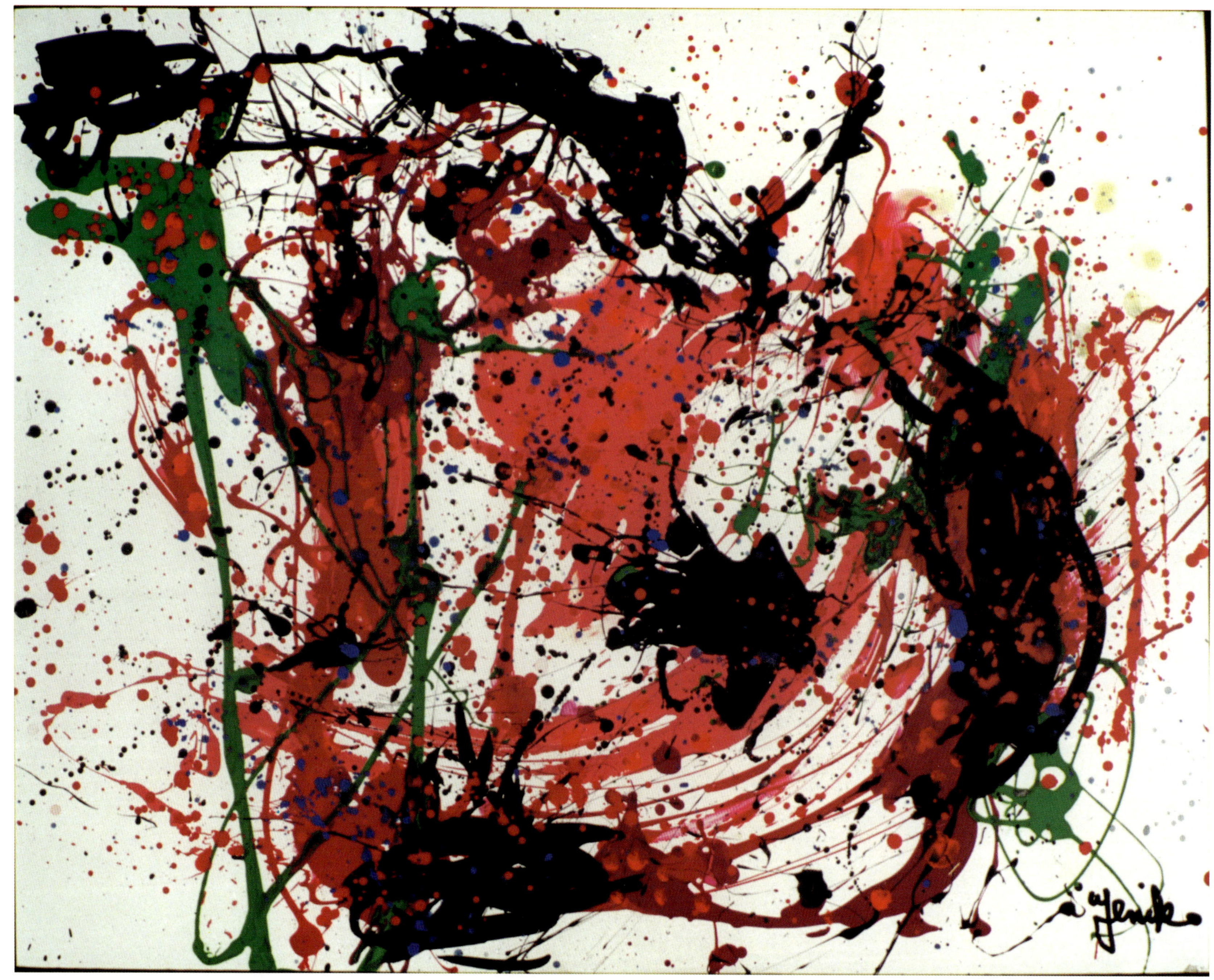

ABS No. 36   Mixed media   24" x 30"

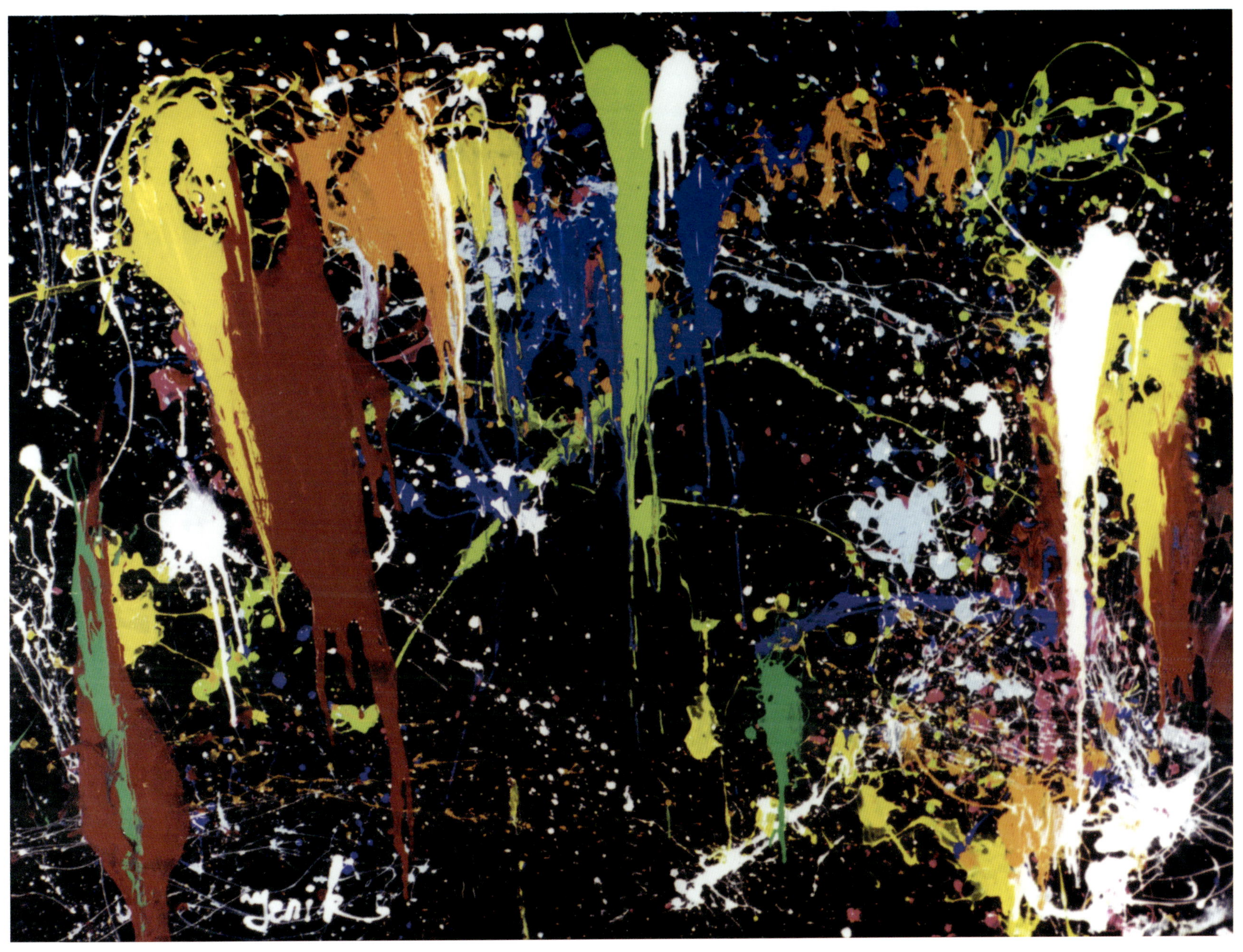

ABS No. 22, Oil, 54" x 74"

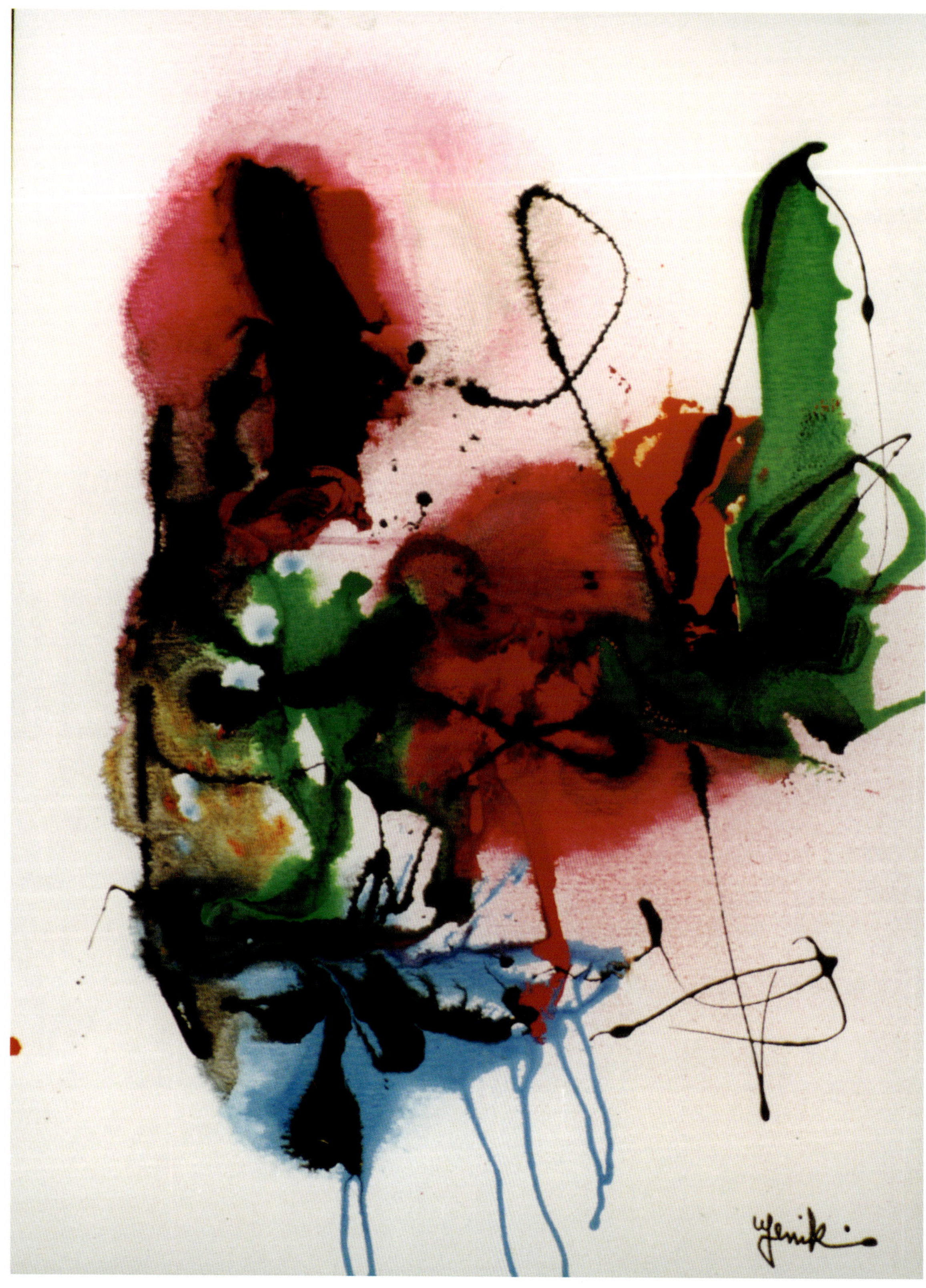

Connection   Watercolor   24" x 18"

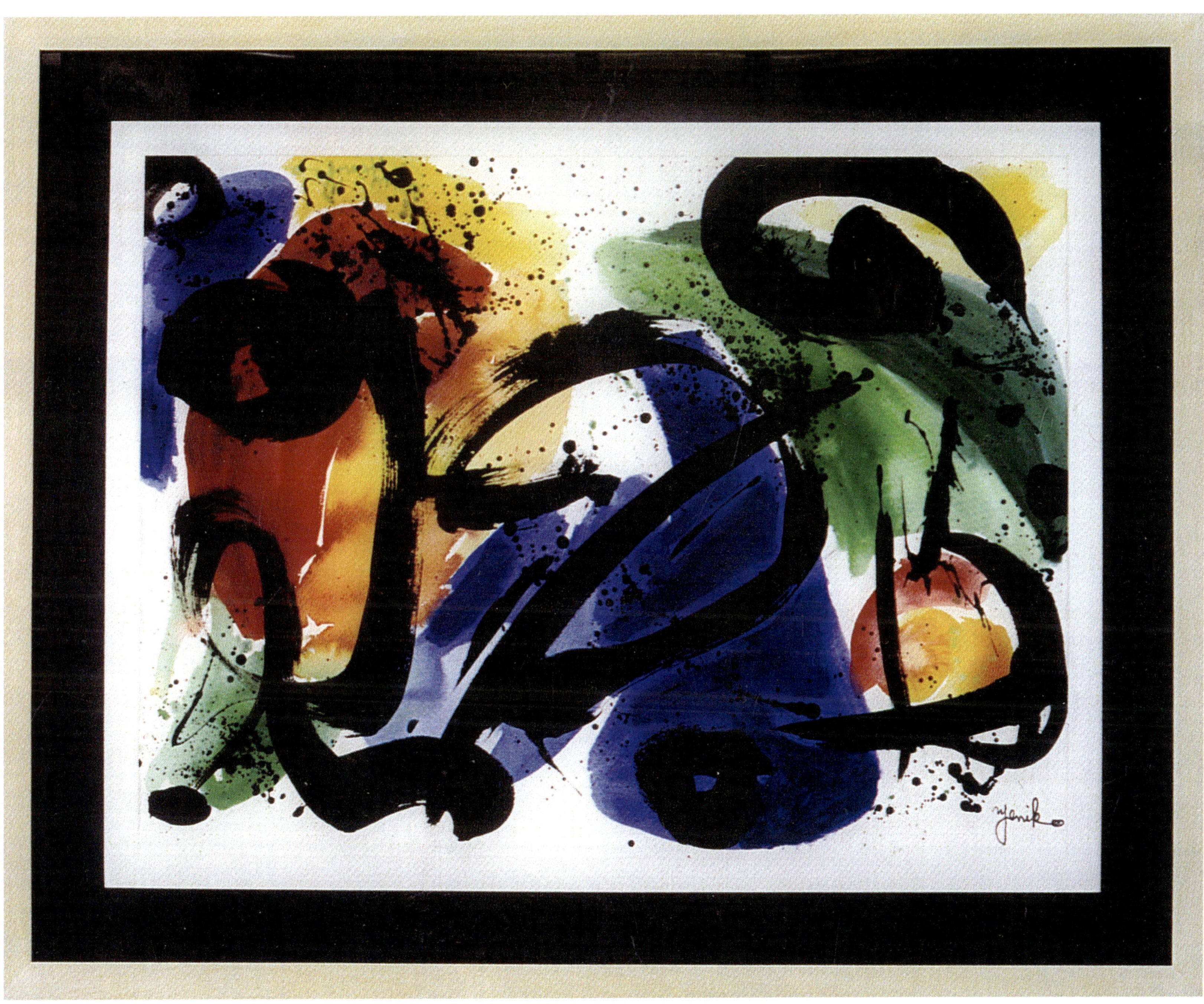

Zazy   24" x 30"

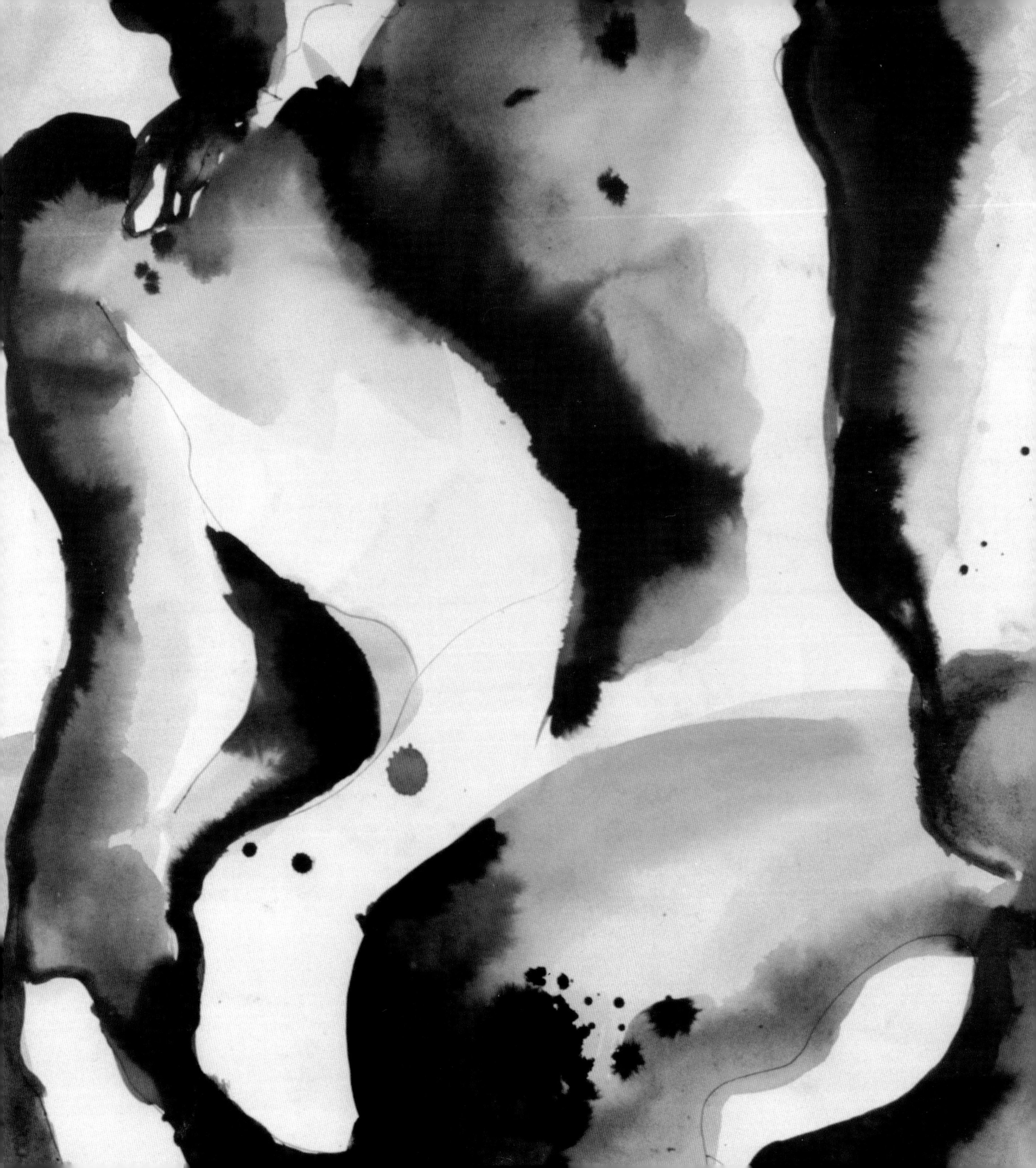

Jenik's similitudes embrace a variety of human
involvements and activities, melding substance
and force into harmonious considerations of
space and design.

FIGURATIVE

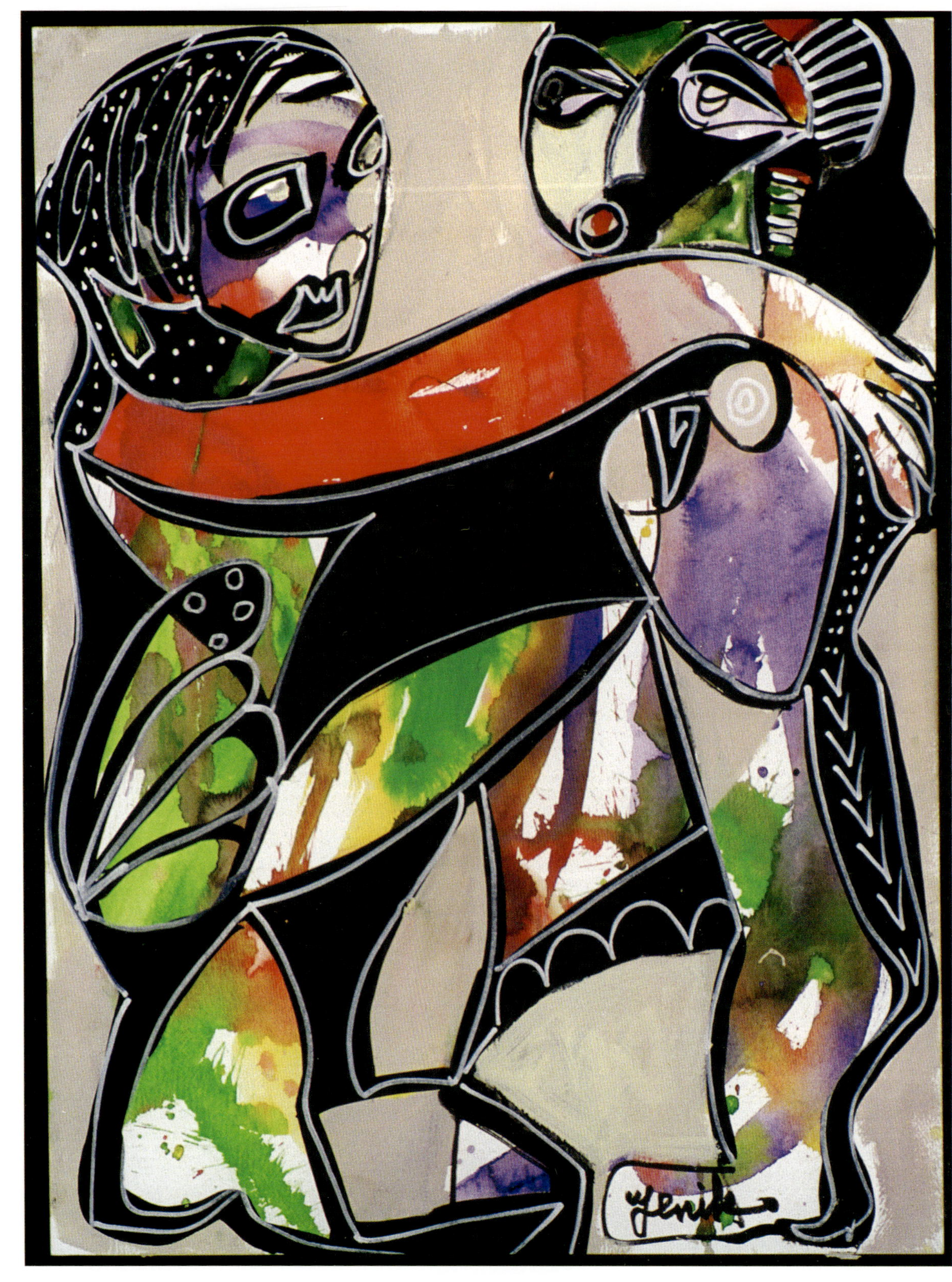

Greetings Watercolor 24" x 18"

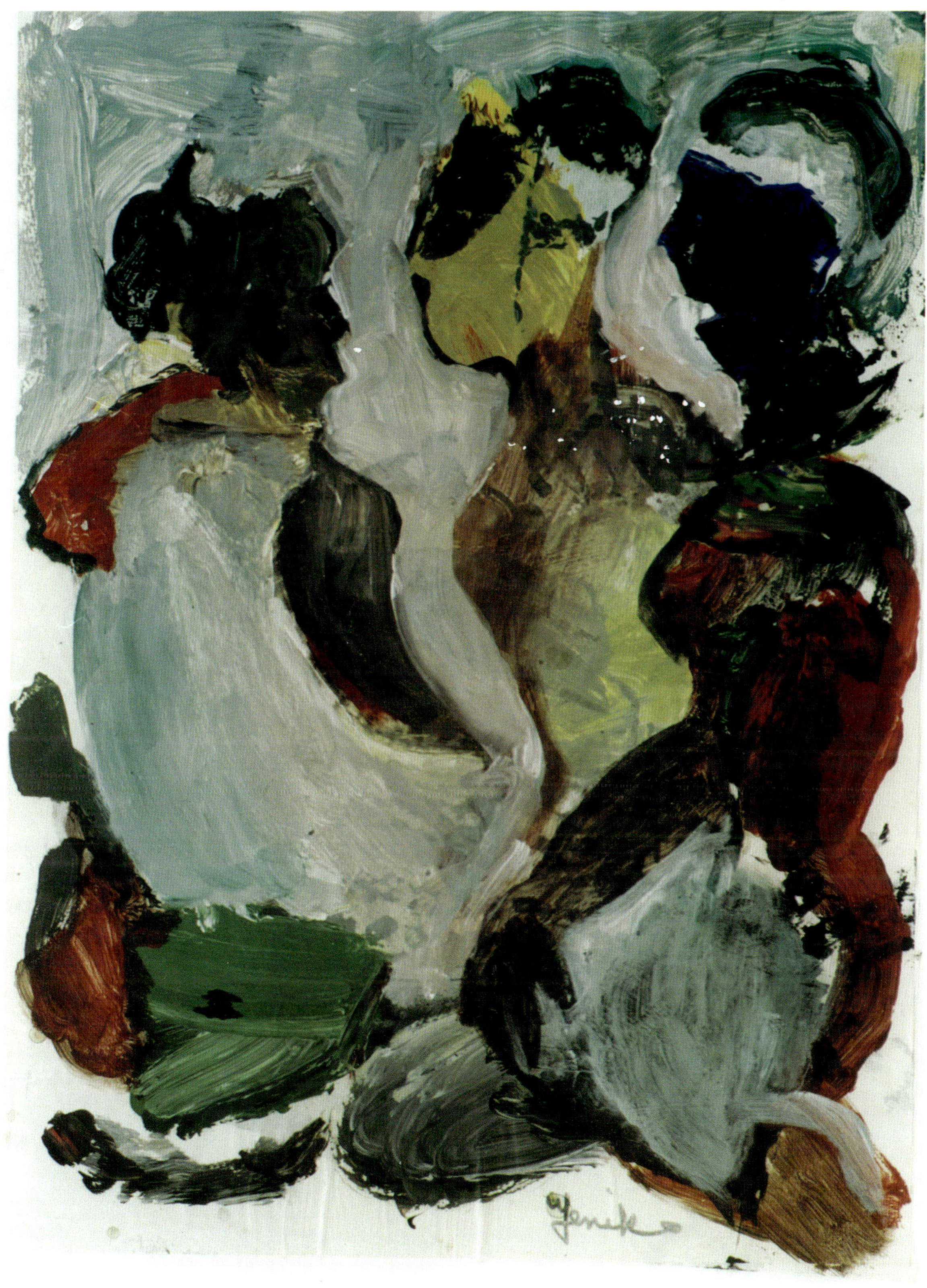

Company Oil 18" x 14"

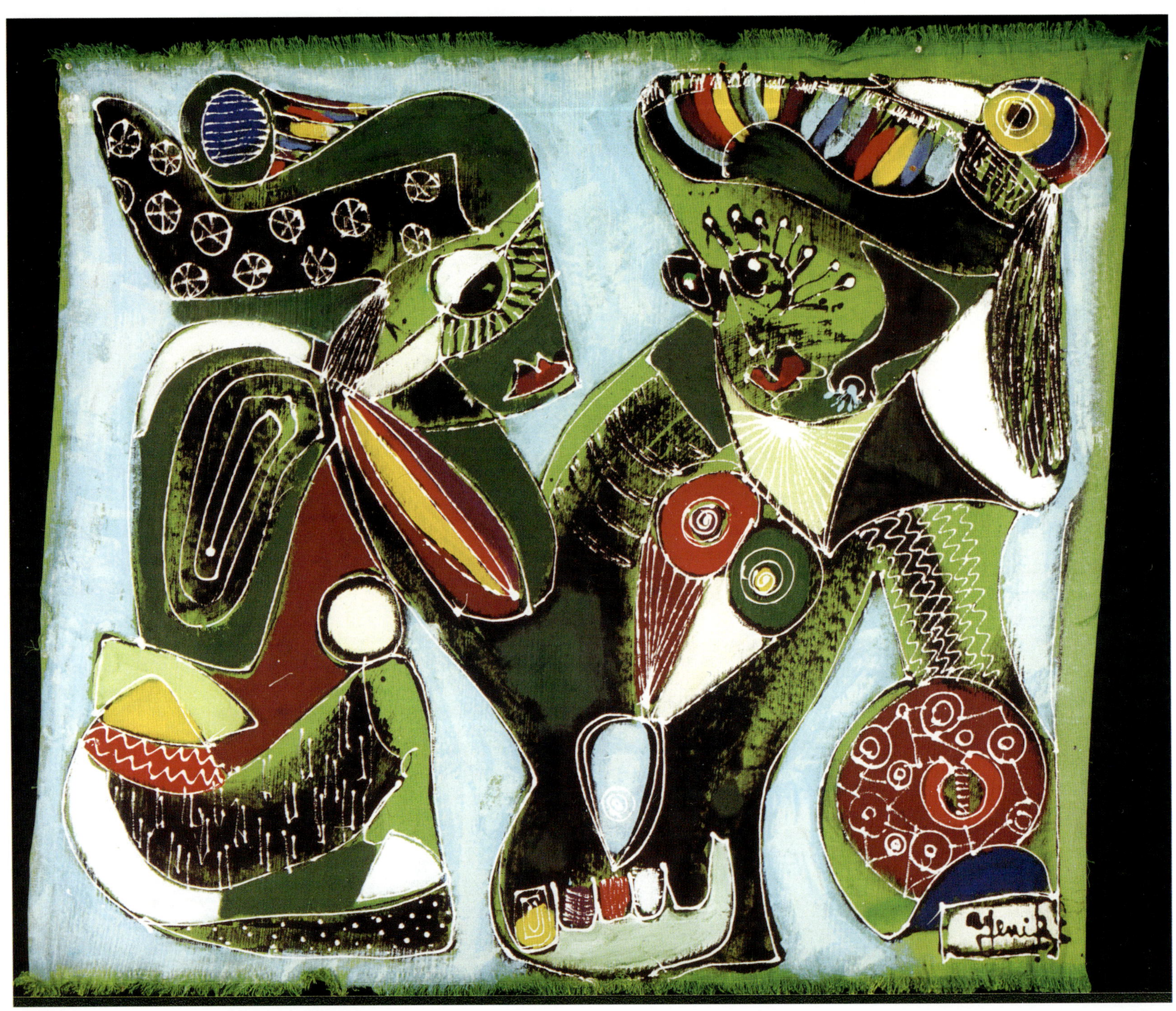

Conversing   Acrylic   52" x 64"

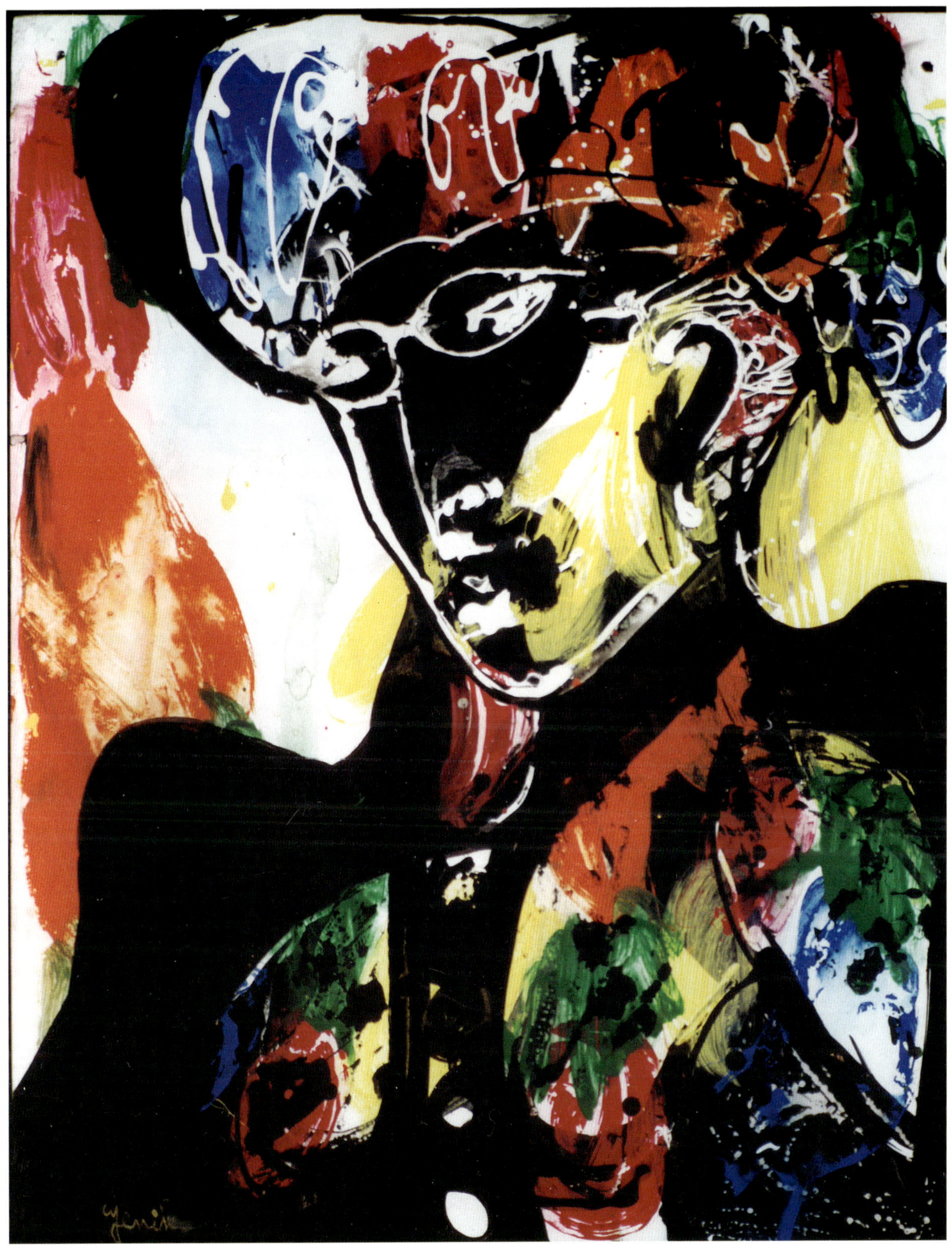

Metador   Watercolor, Acrylic   28" x 22"

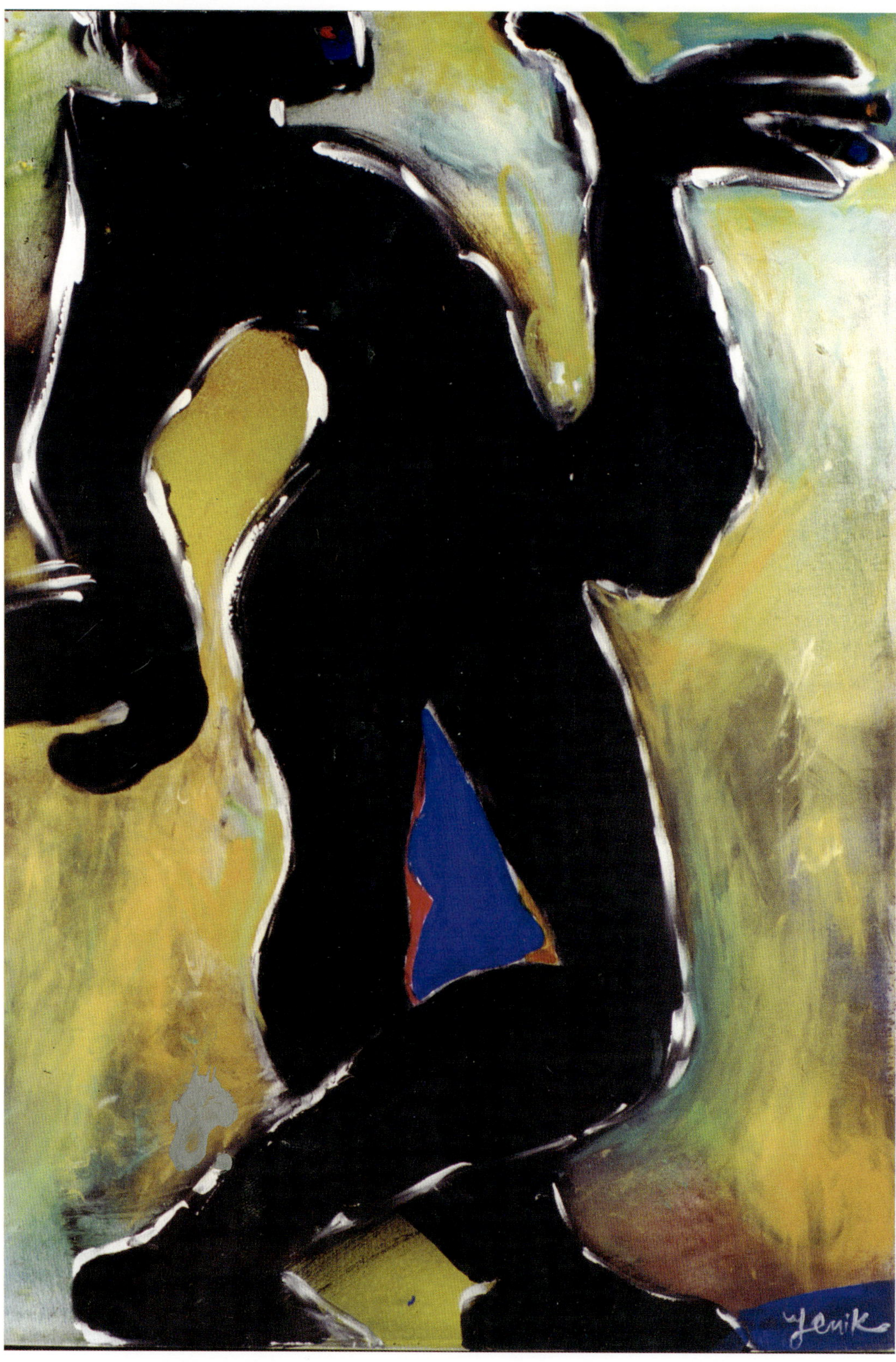

Walk the Talk   Mixed Media   42" x 38"

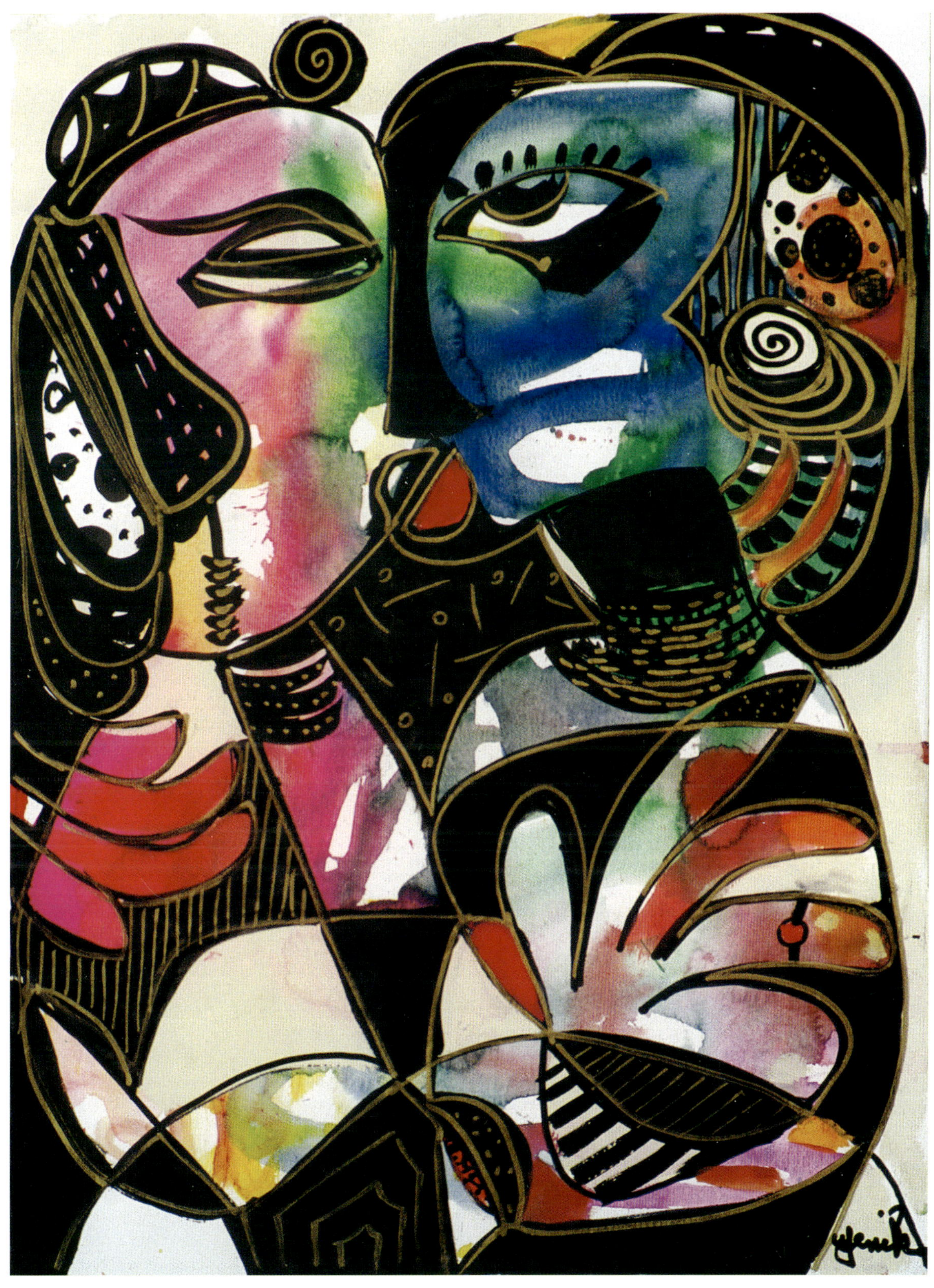

Cool & Warm, Watercolor, 24" x 18"

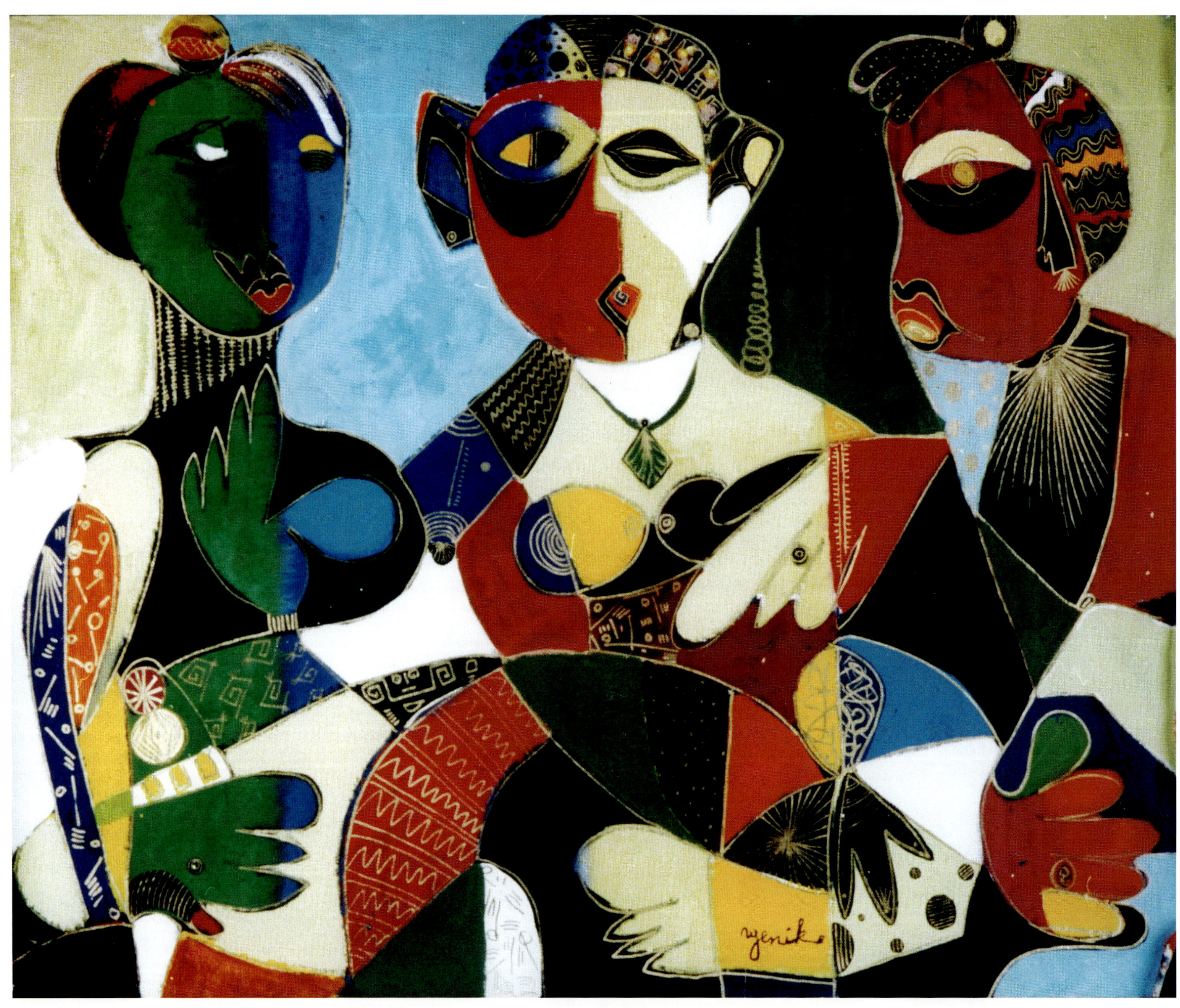

Ancient Beauties   Acrylic   64" x 78"

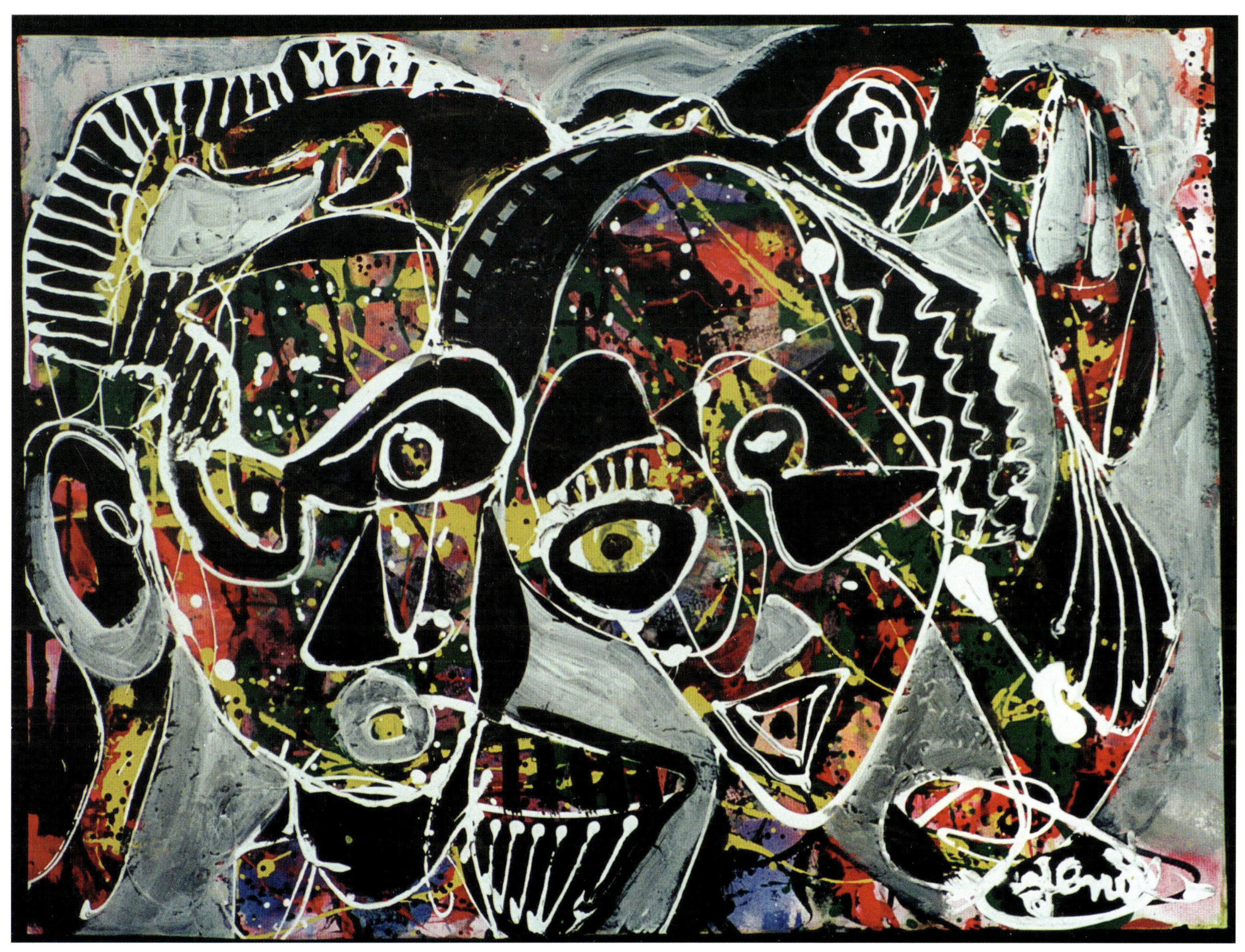

Remember, Mixed Media, 22" x 28"

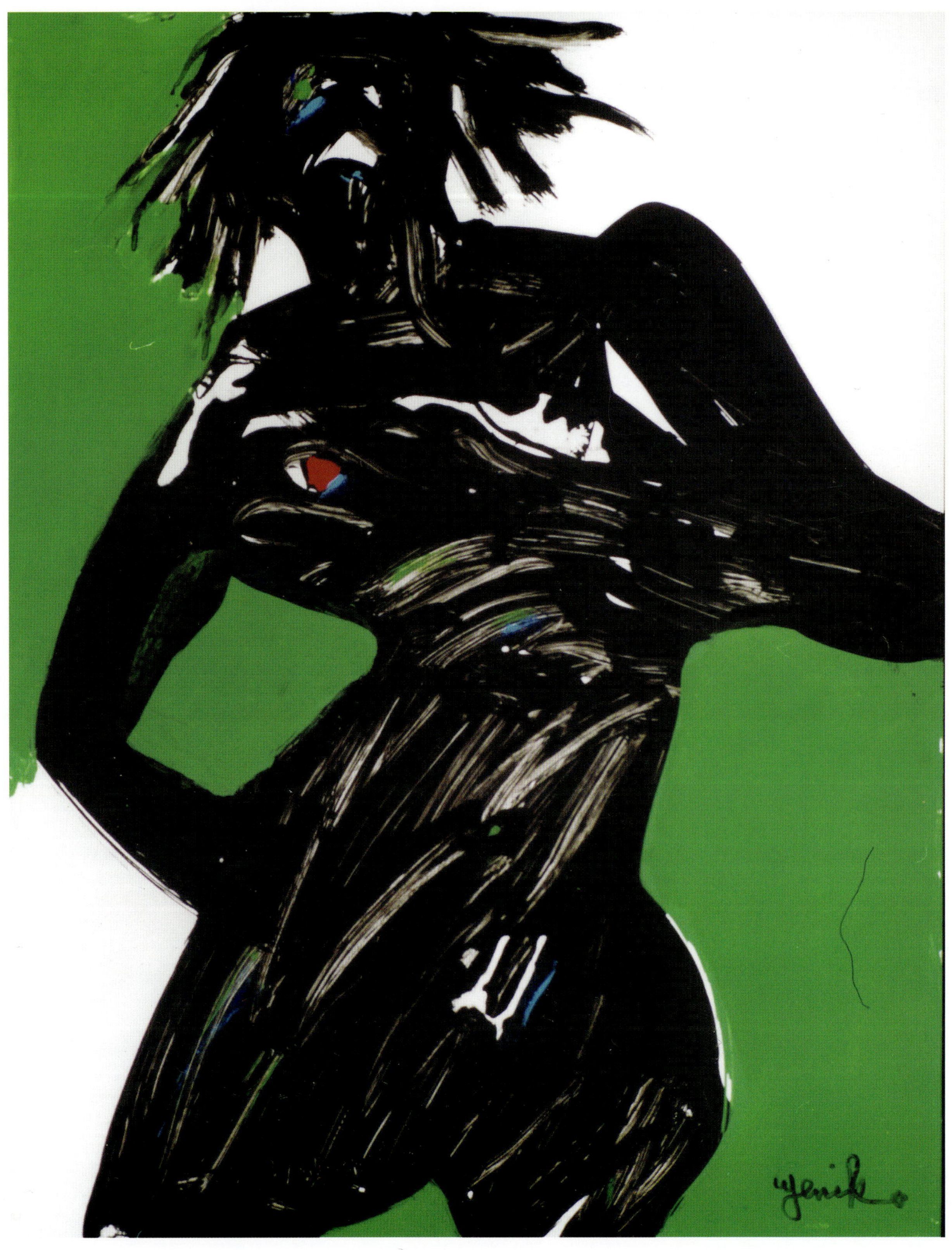

Artistic   Acrylic   28" x 22"

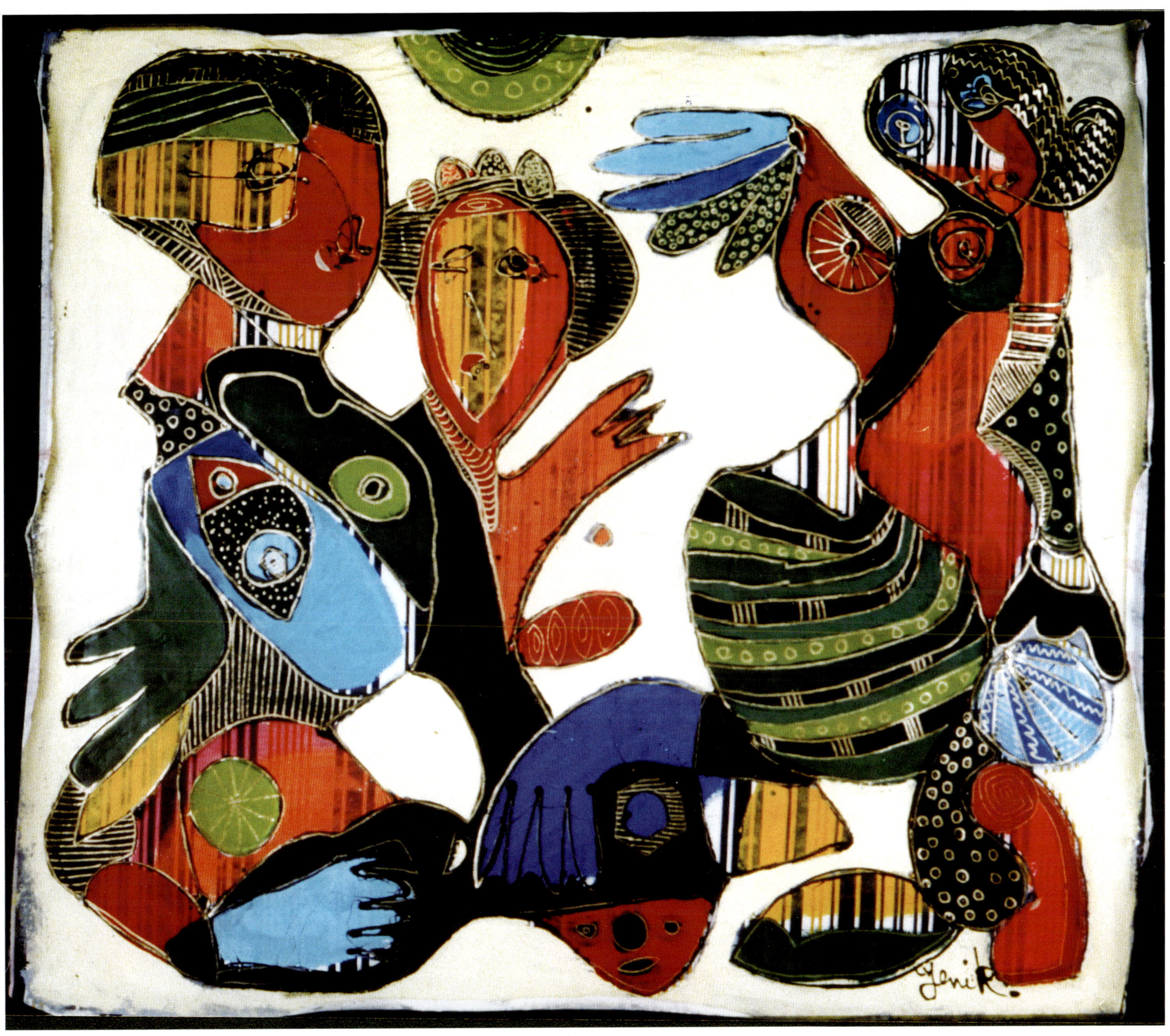

Blessings, Acrylic, 60" x 66"

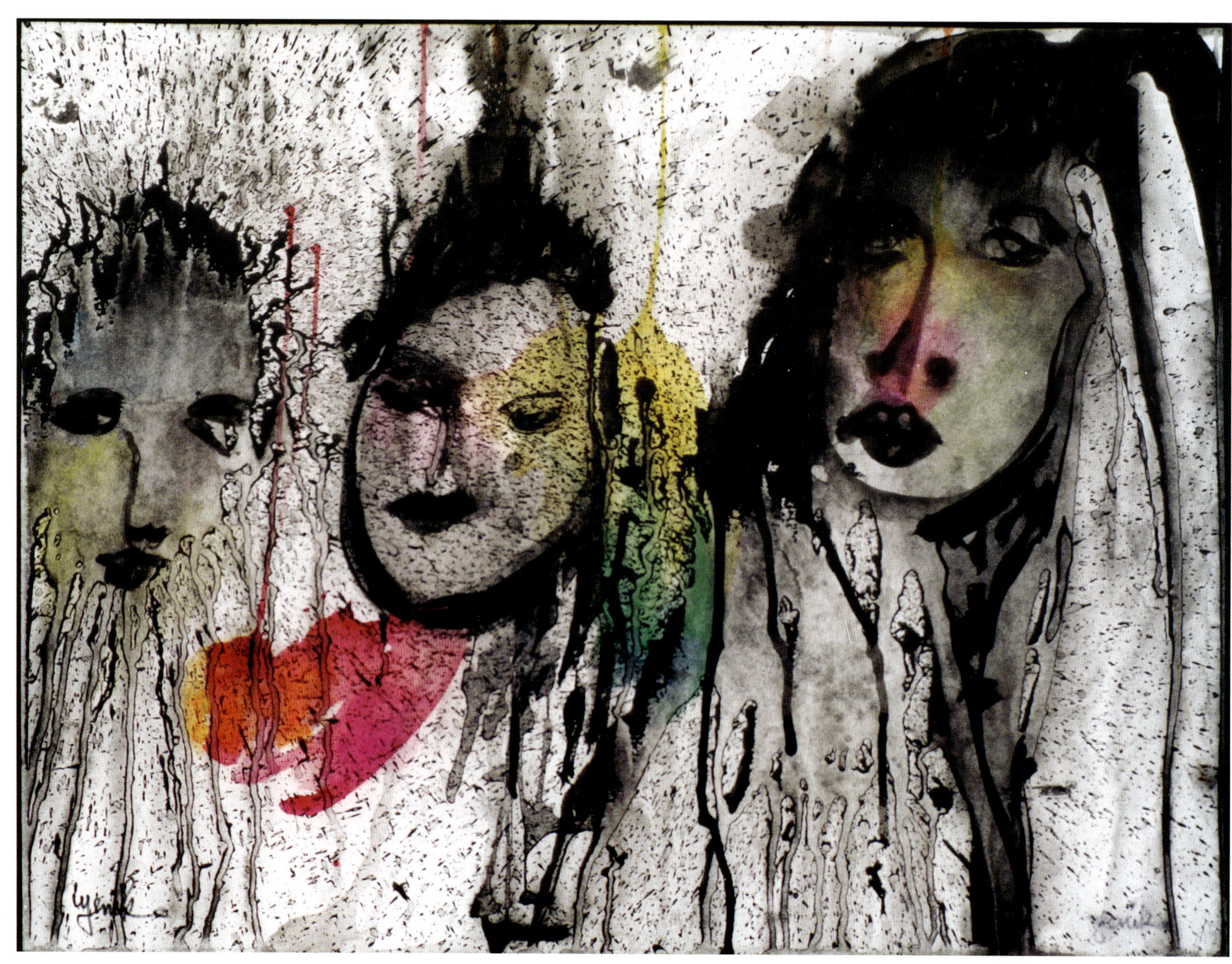

Three Graces   Waterocolor   18" x 24"

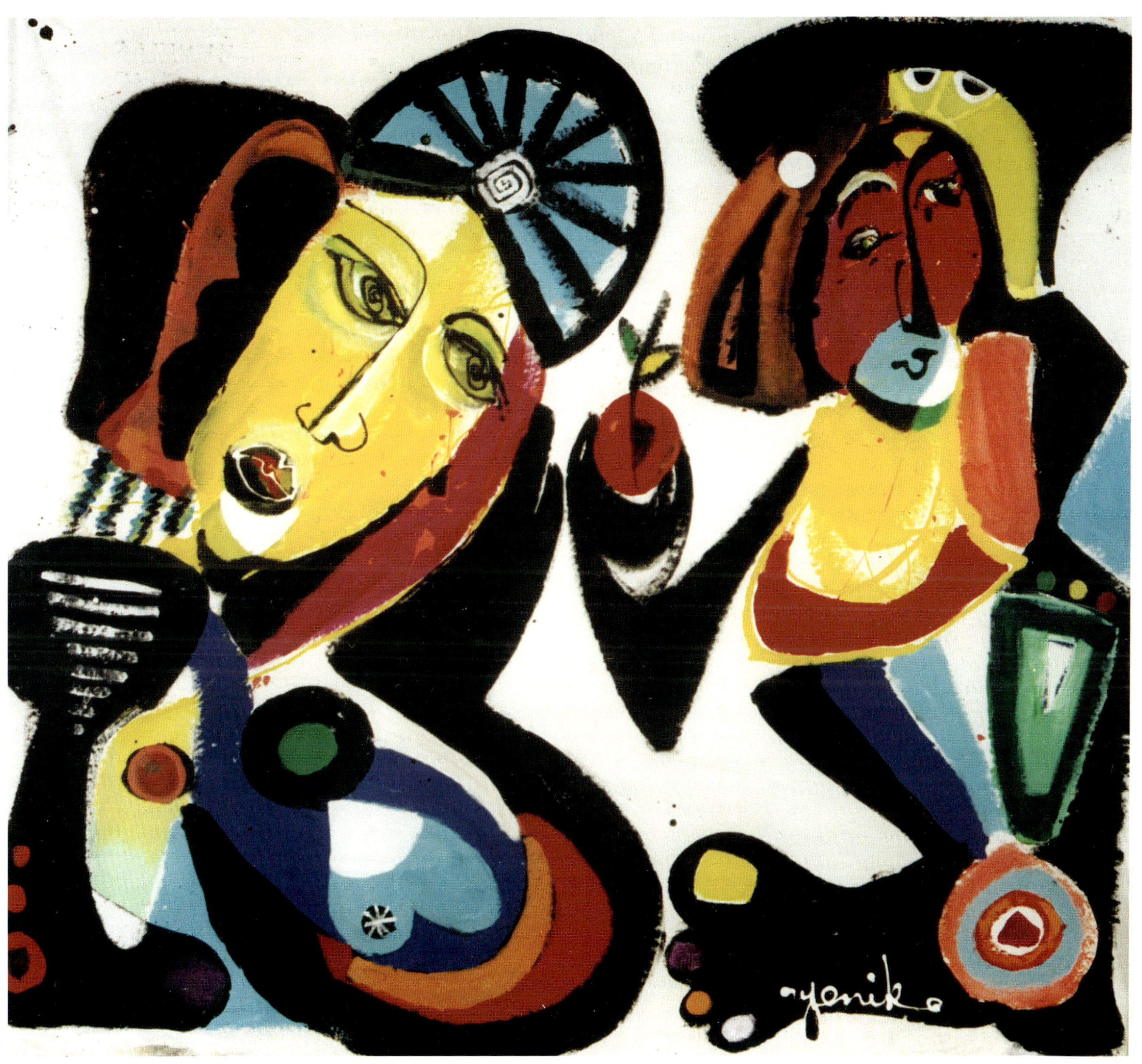

Tempter Acrylic 54" x 64"

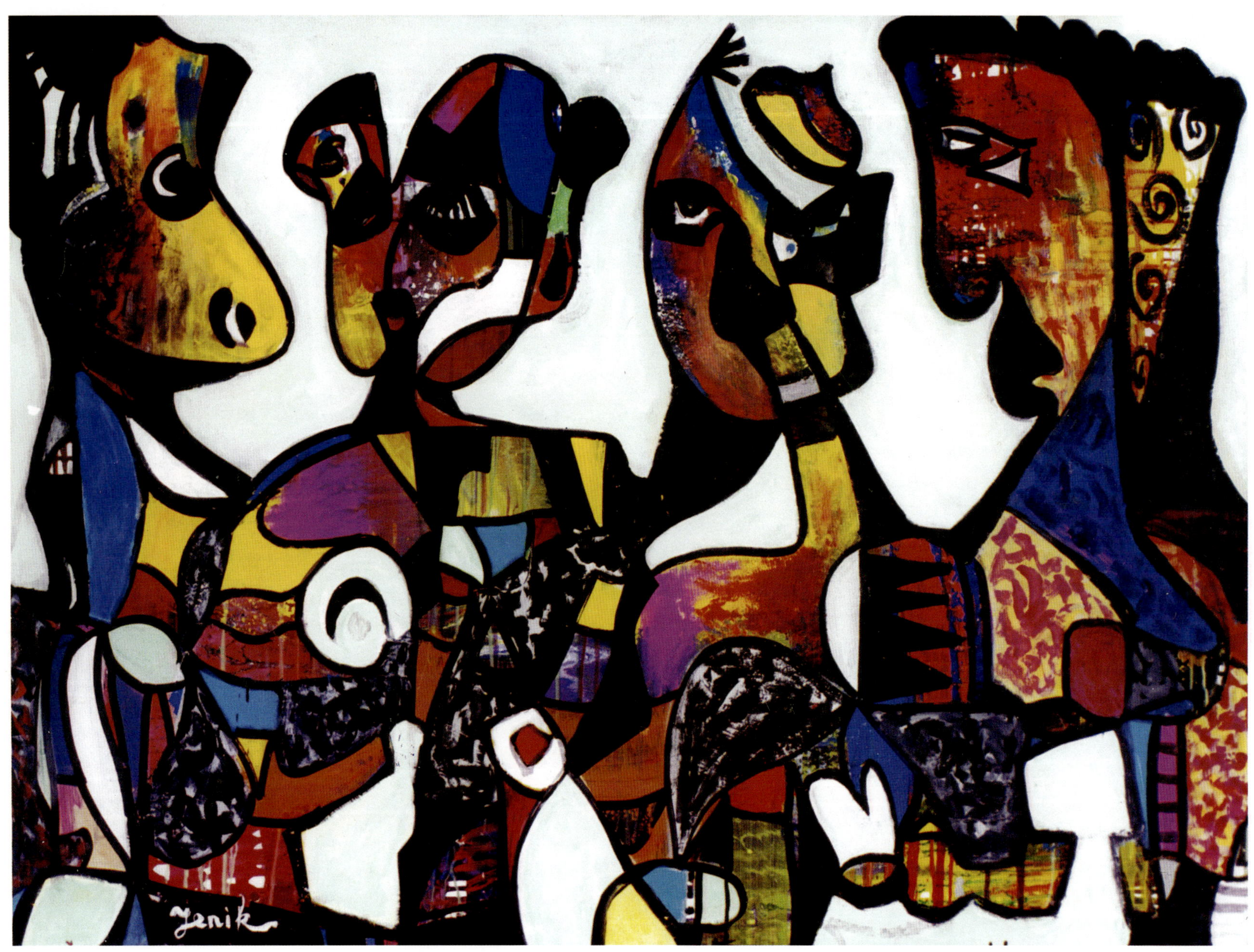

Dimentional Release   Oil   60" x 40"

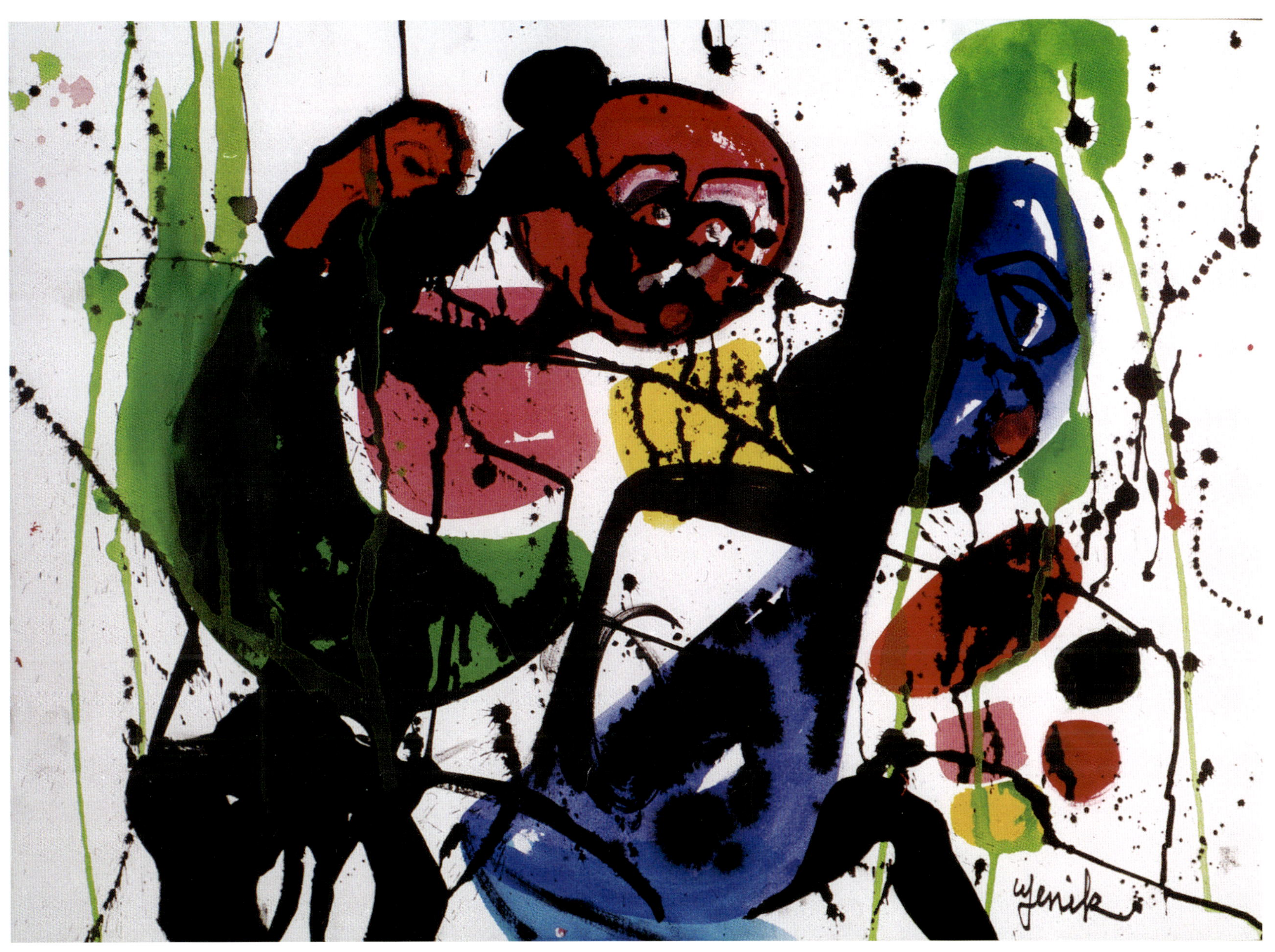

Return, Watercolor, 18" x 24"

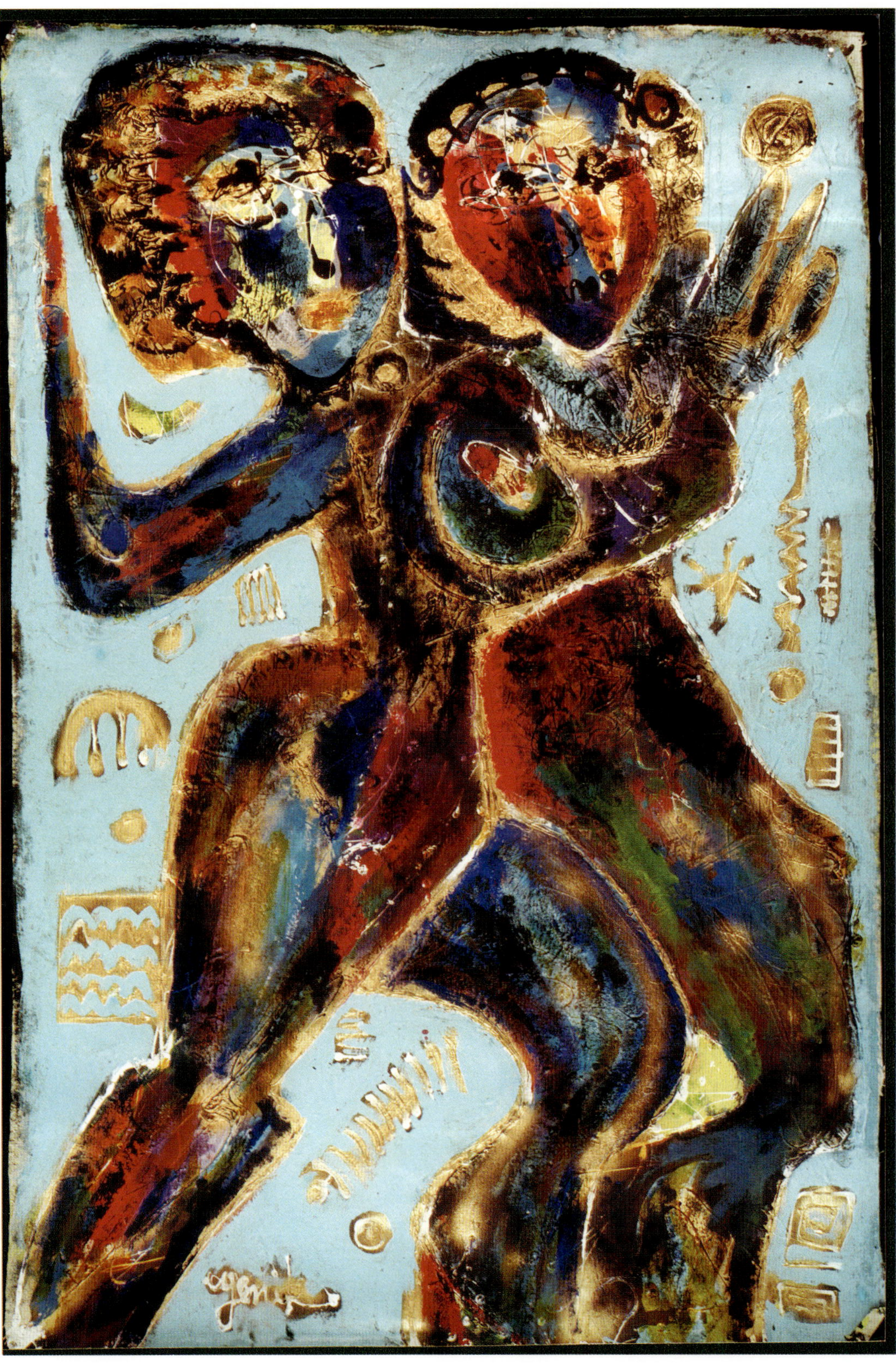

Unified Acrylic 64" x 42"

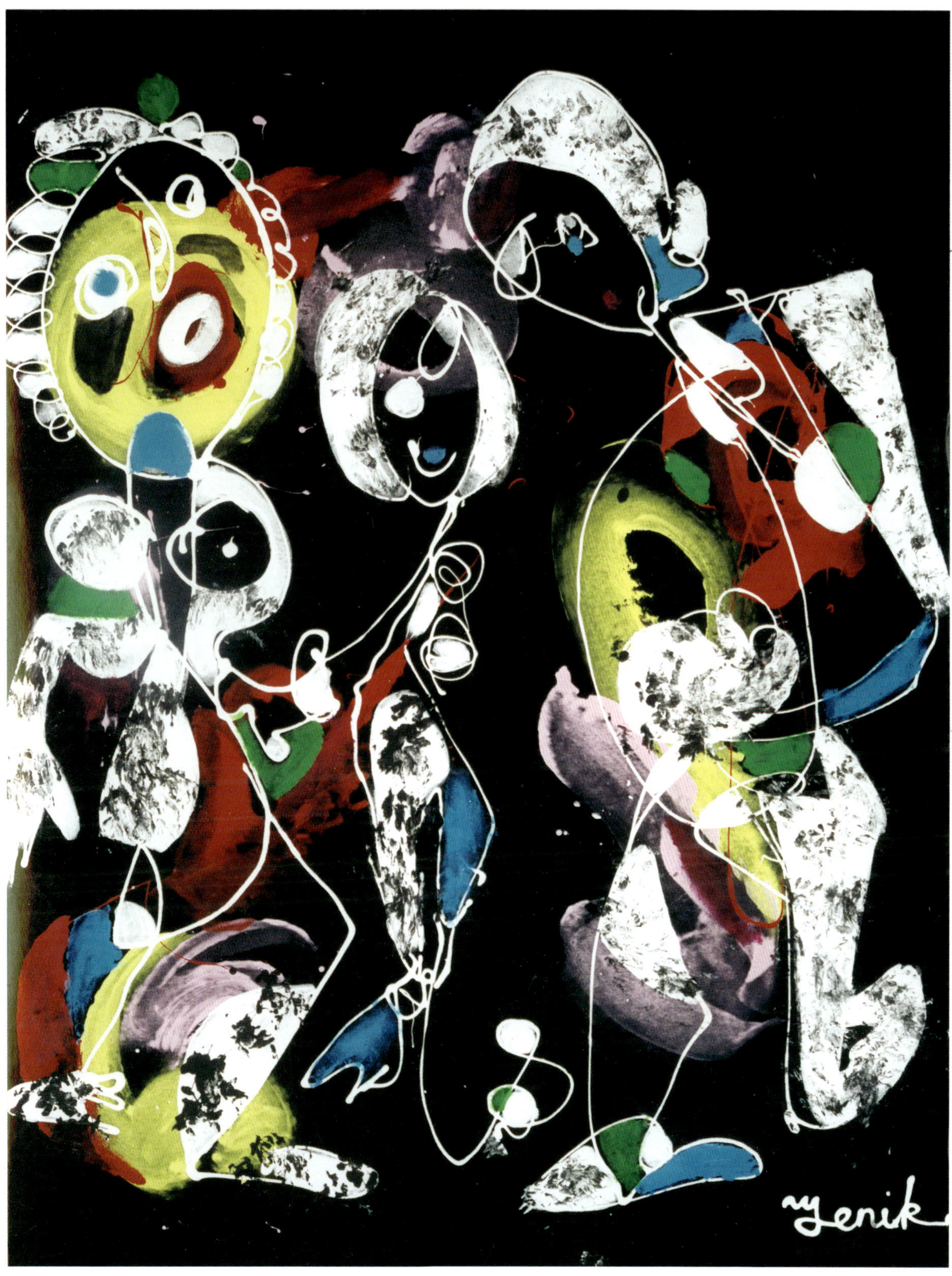

Caring, Acrylic, 60" x 50"

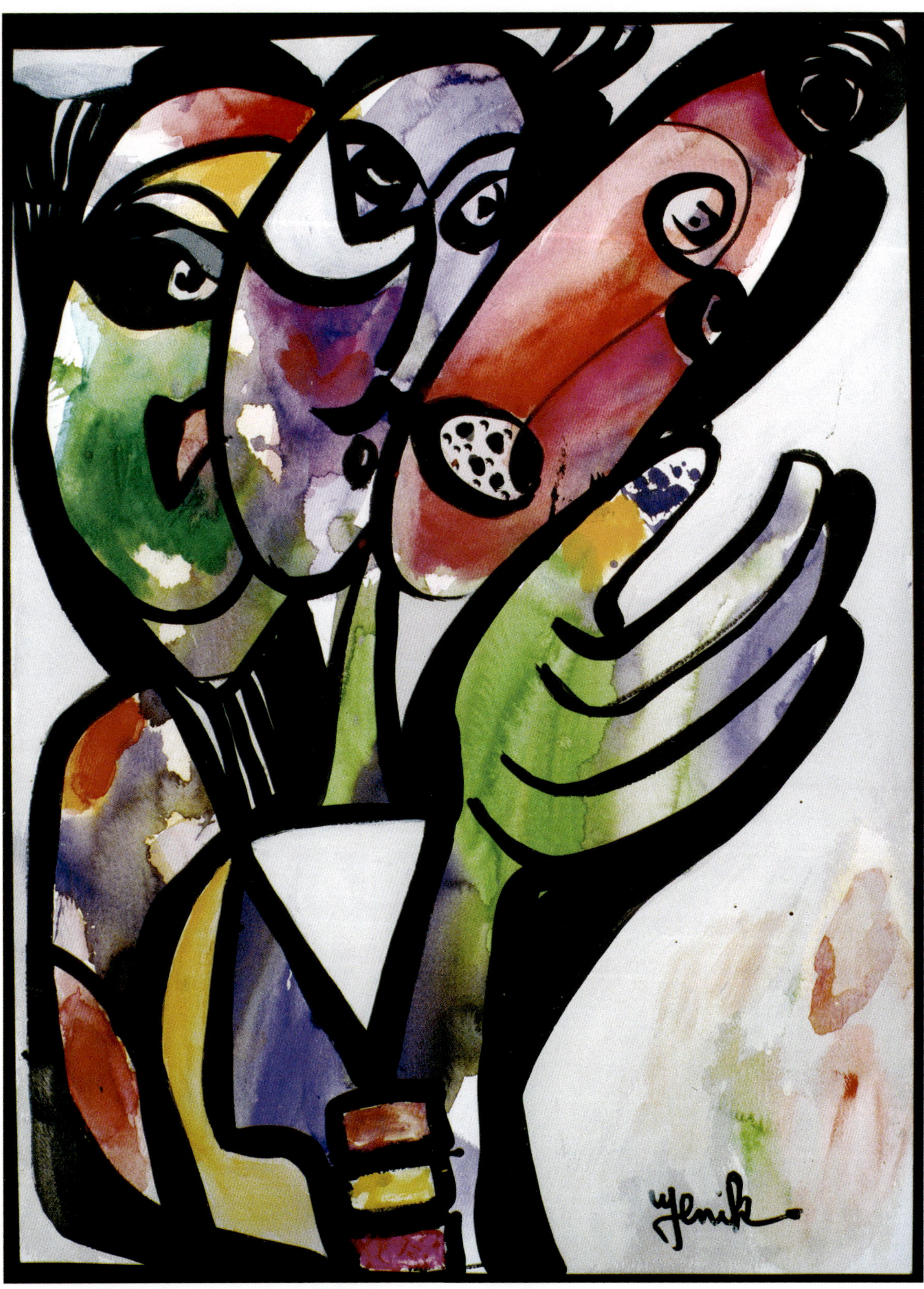

Sisterhood   Watercolor   24" x 18"

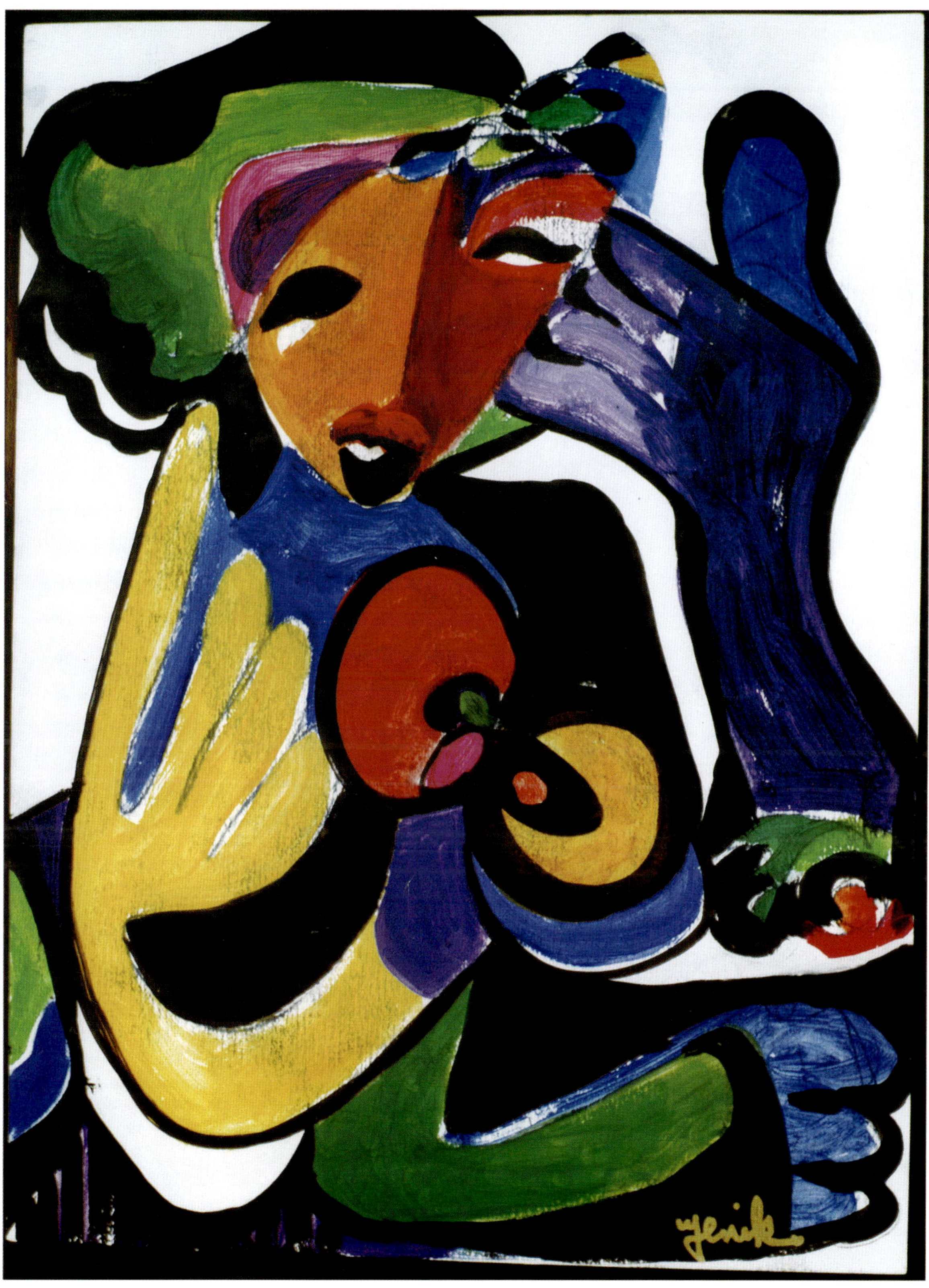

Shania   Watercolor   24" x 18"

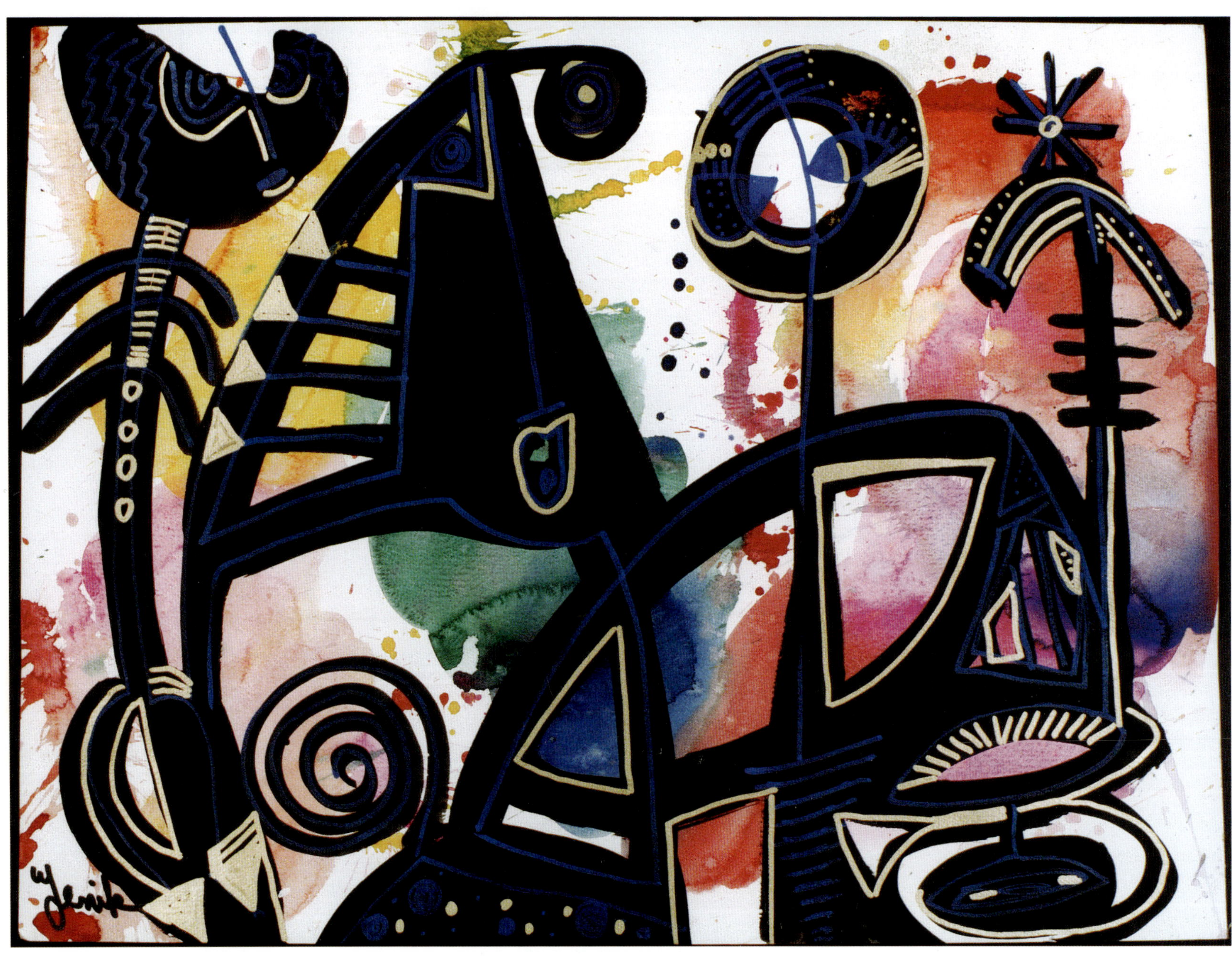

Observing   Watercolor   18" x 24"

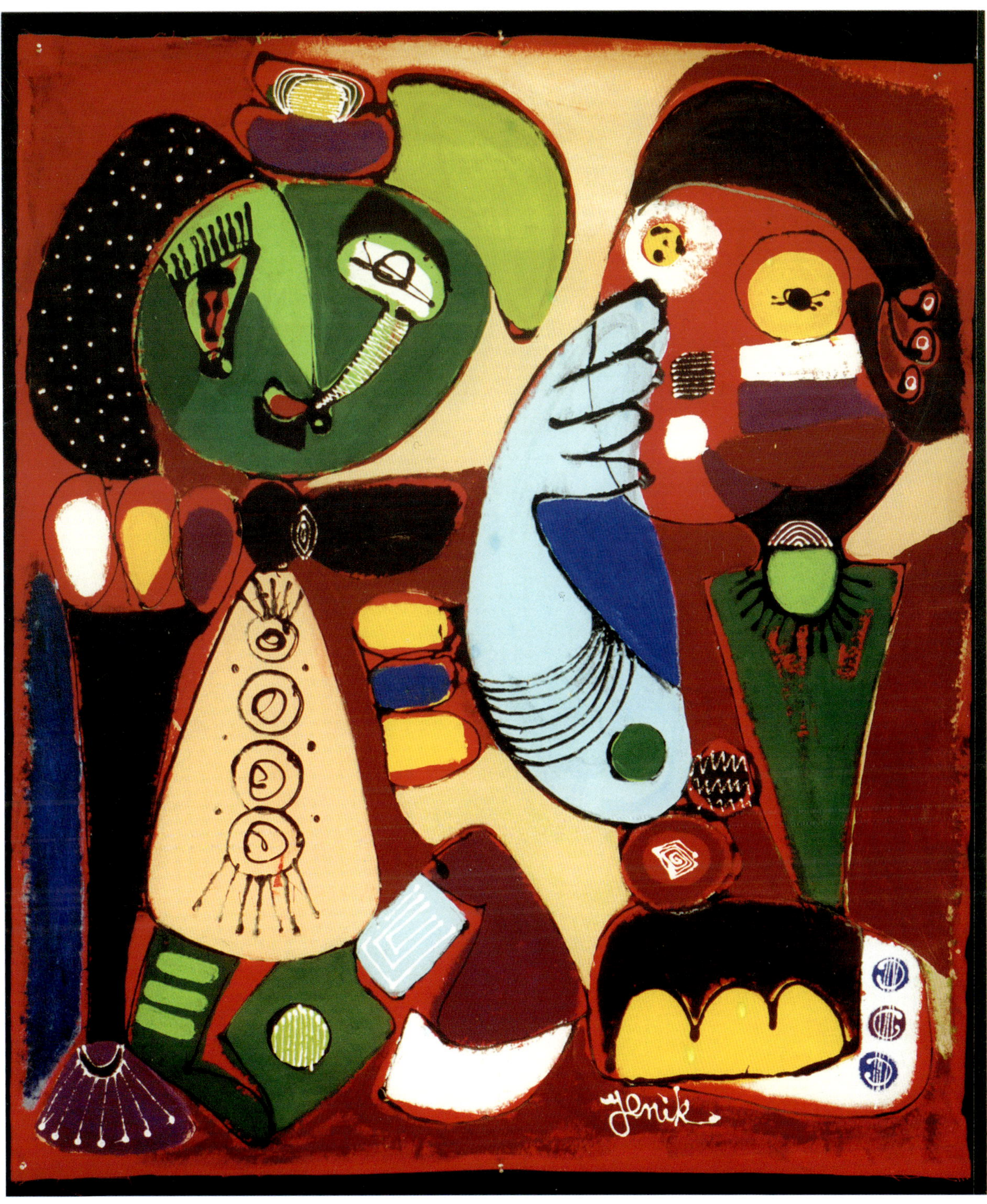

Me & My Friend, Acrylic, 64" x 56"

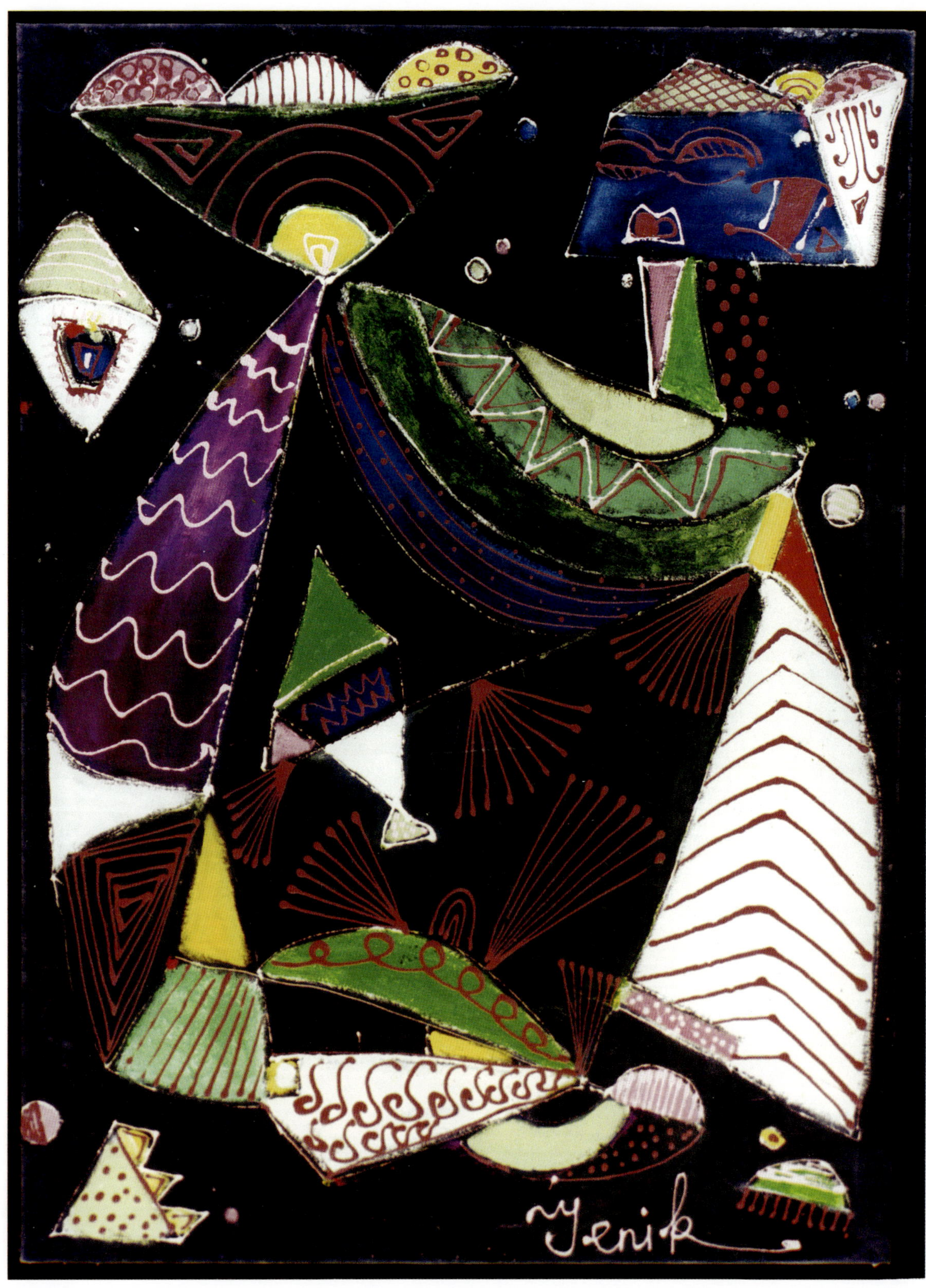

Ceremonial   Acrylic   46" x 40"

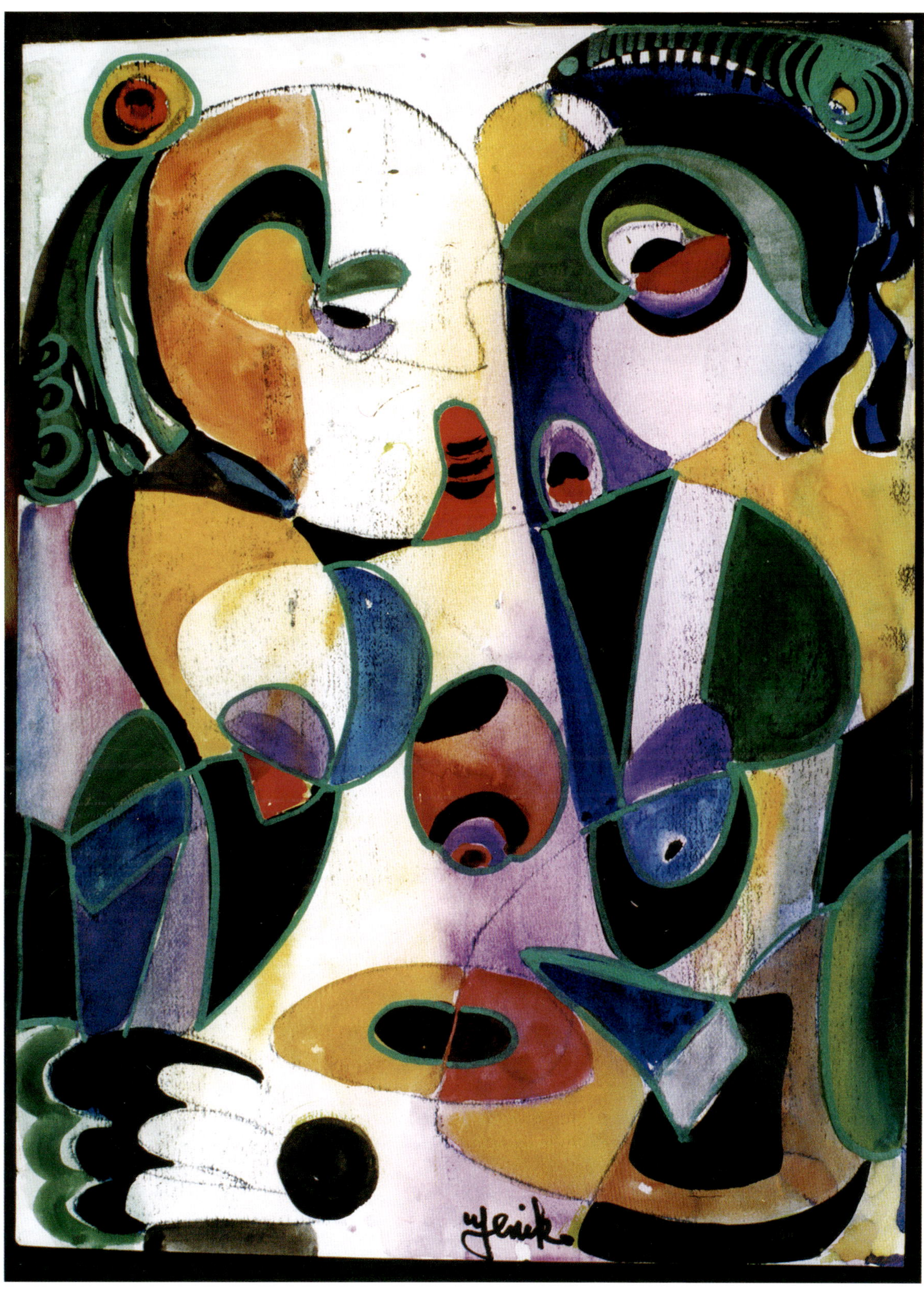

Compassion, Watercolor, 24" x 18"

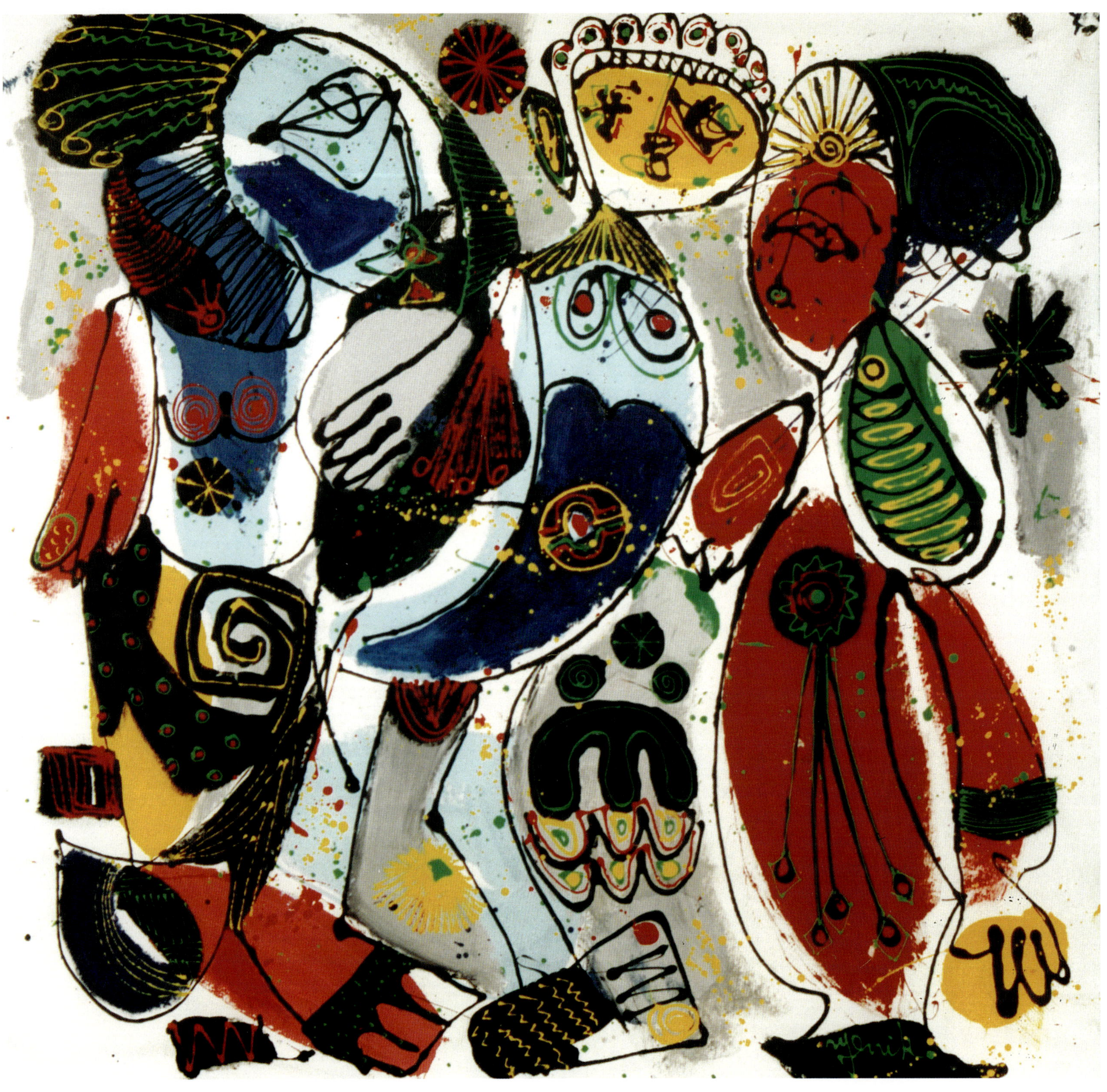

Related Acrylic 56" x 56"

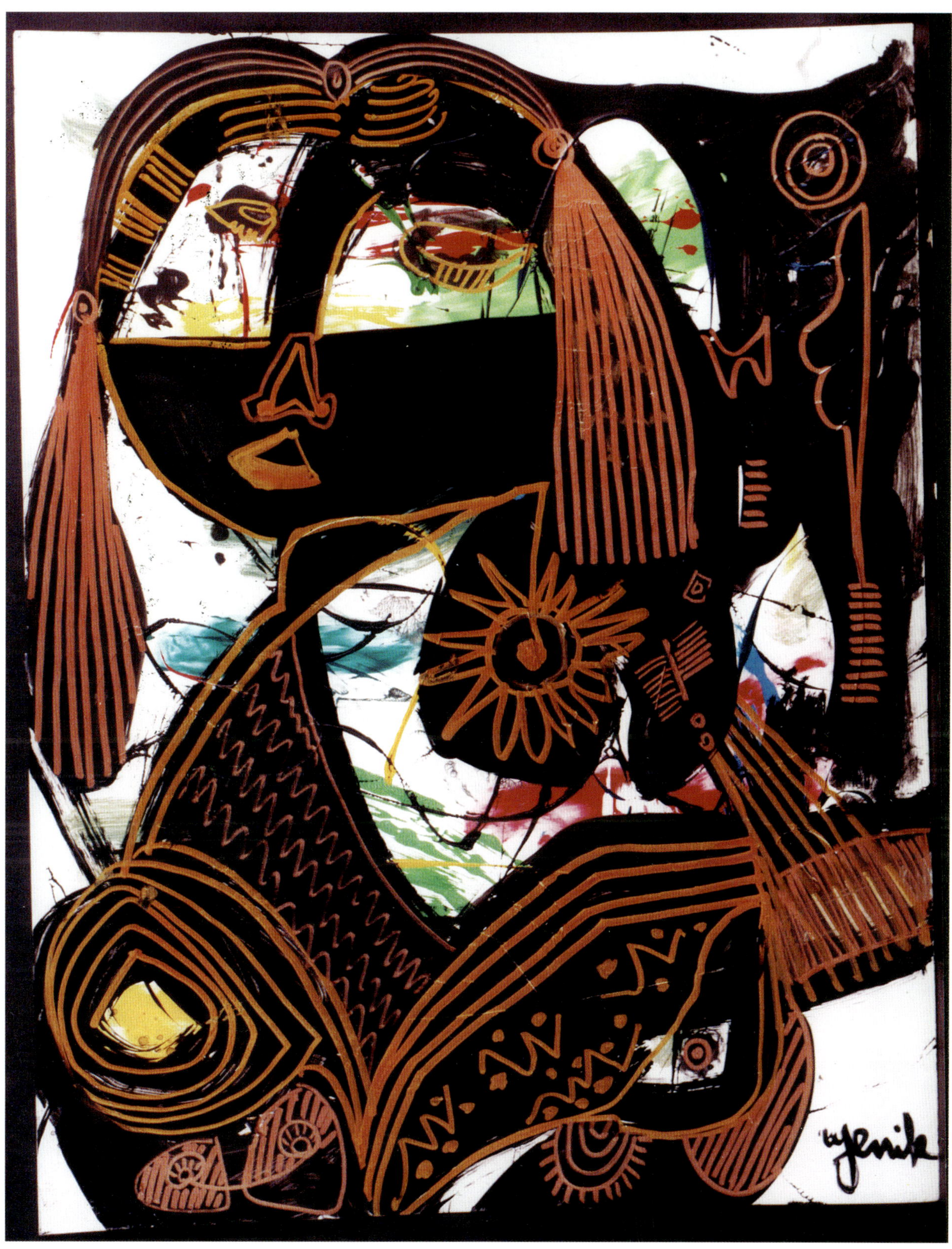

Leila, Watercolor, 28" x 22"

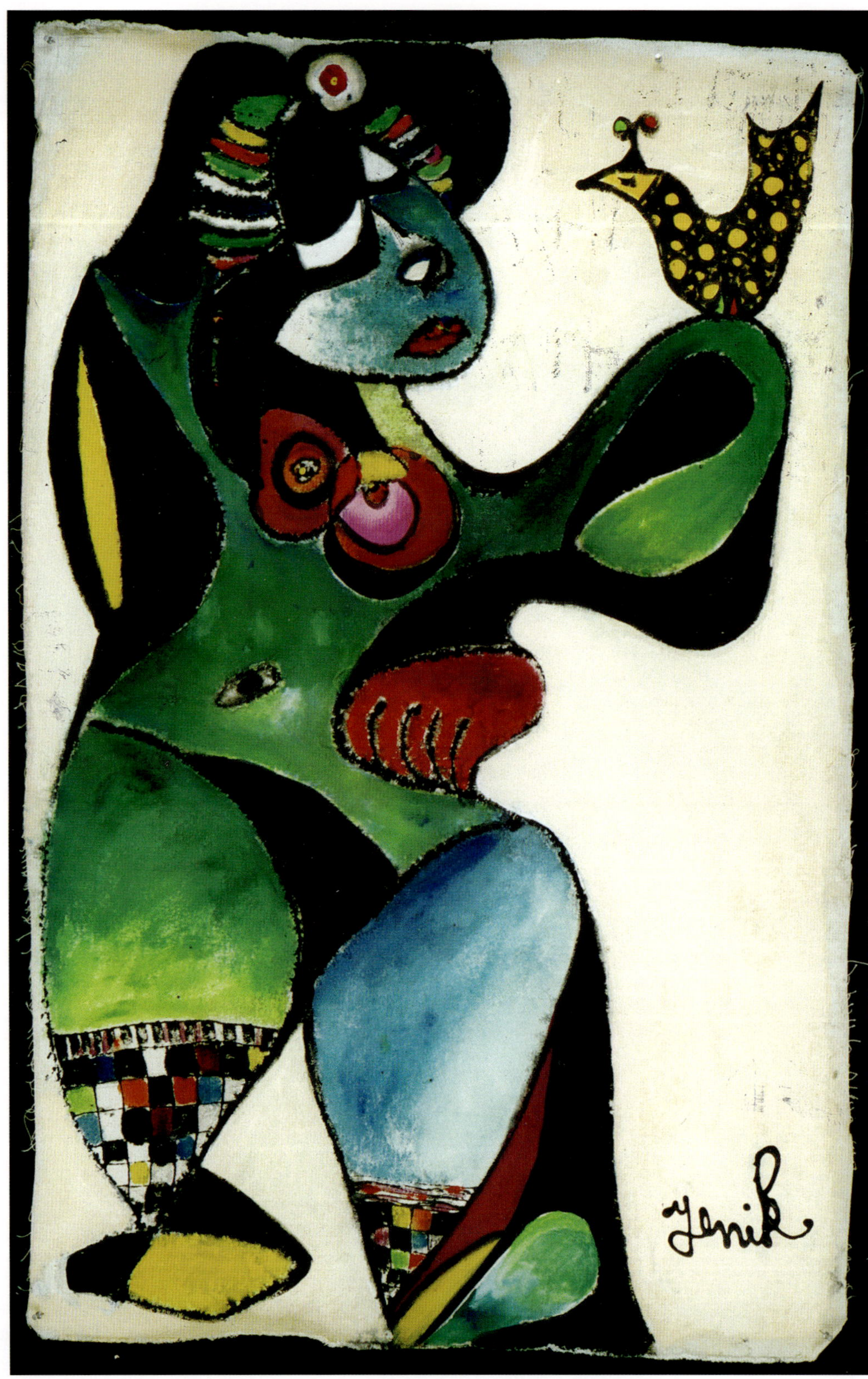

In Her Eye   Acrylic   64" x 40"

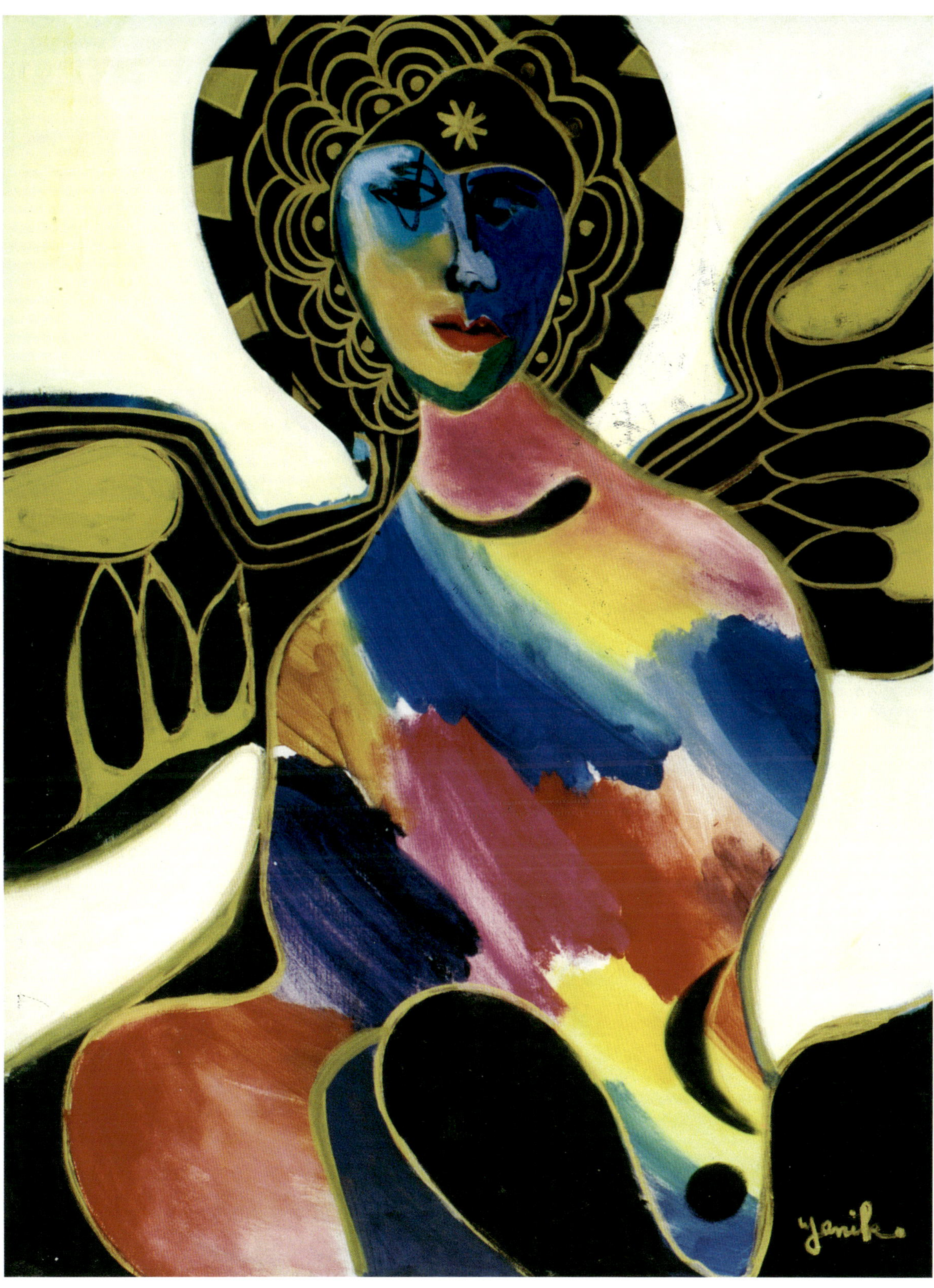

Moniq, Acrylic, 44" x 36"

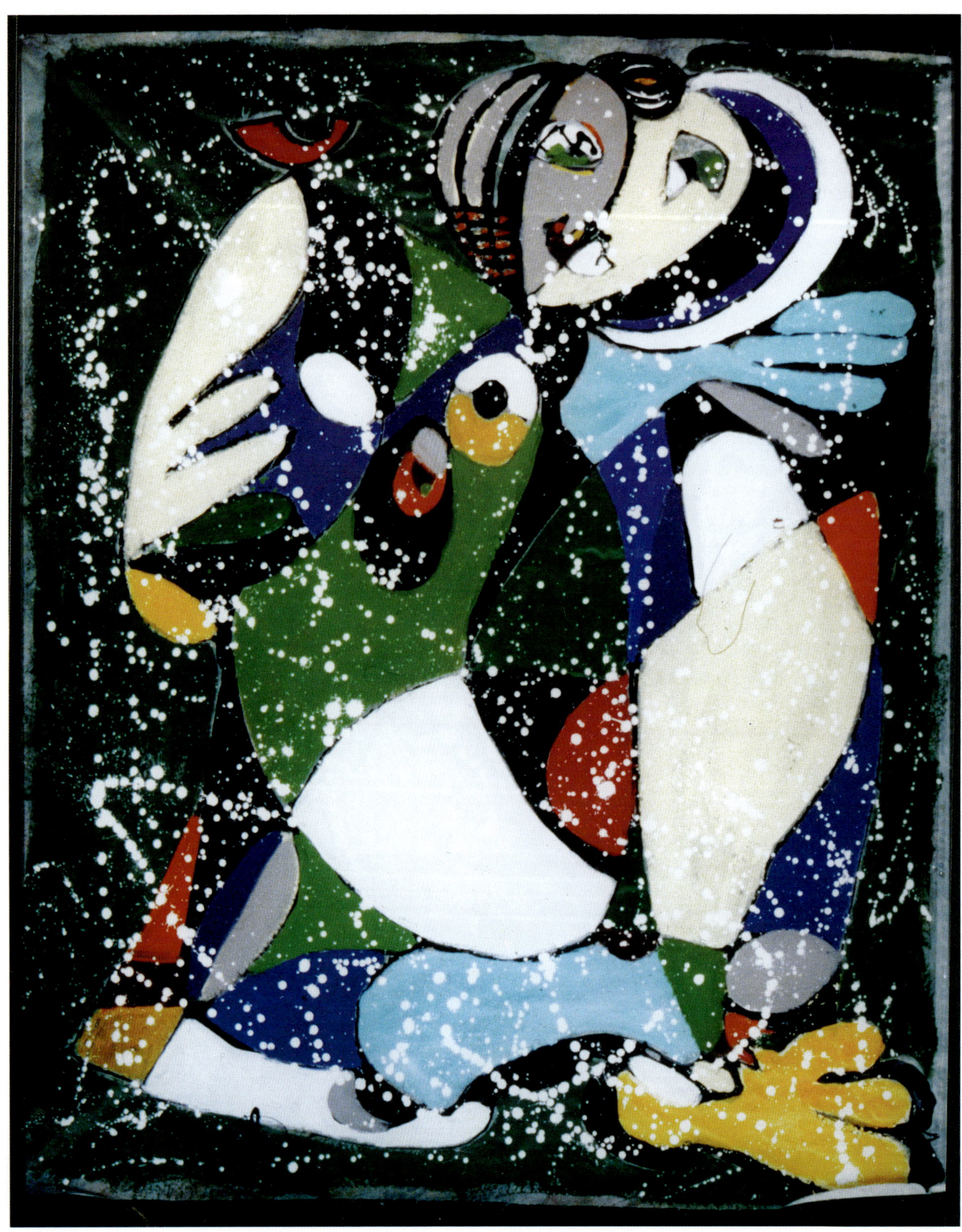

Dancer   Acrylic   64" x 52"

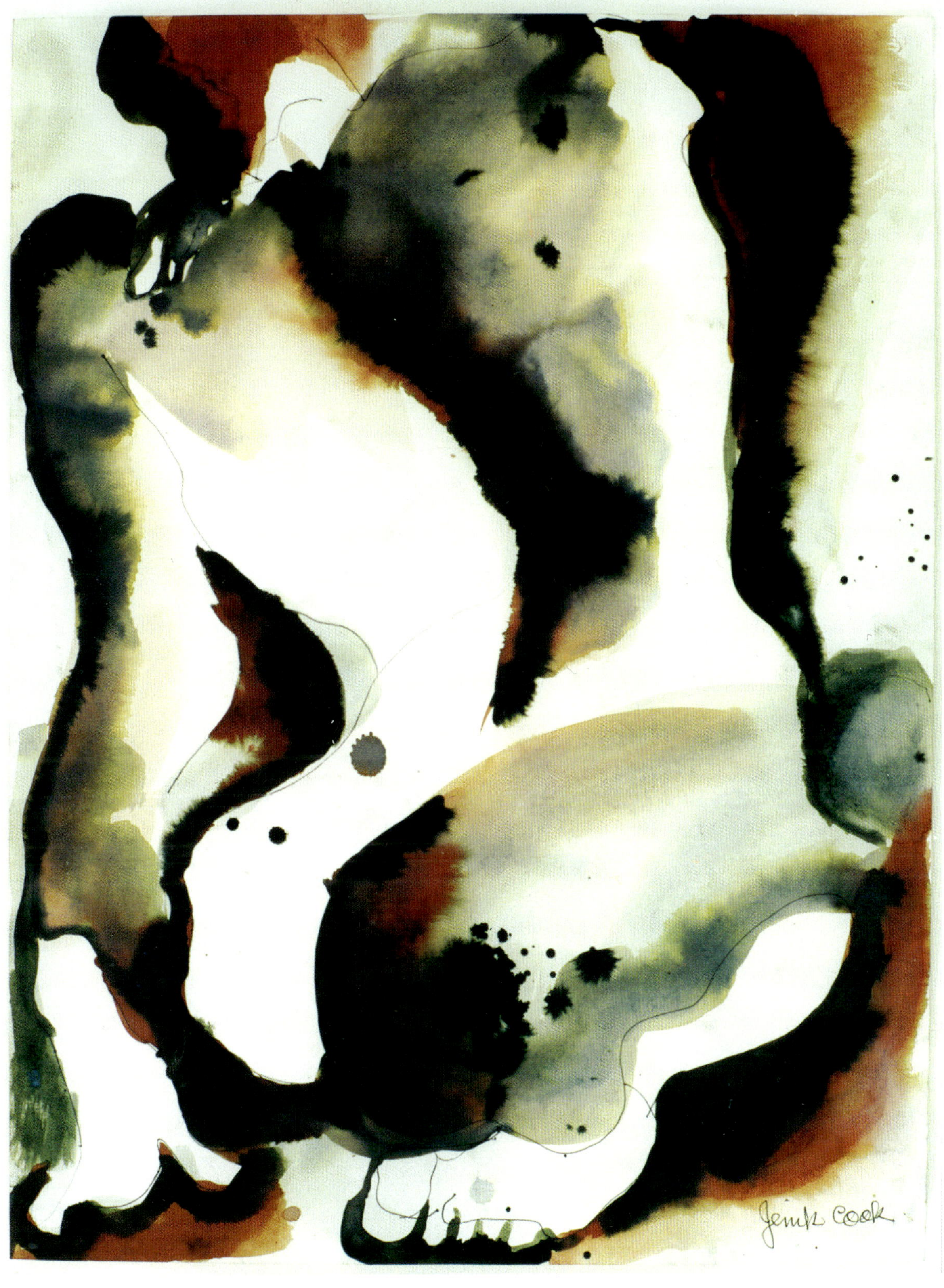

Mututinal   Watercolor   24" x 18"

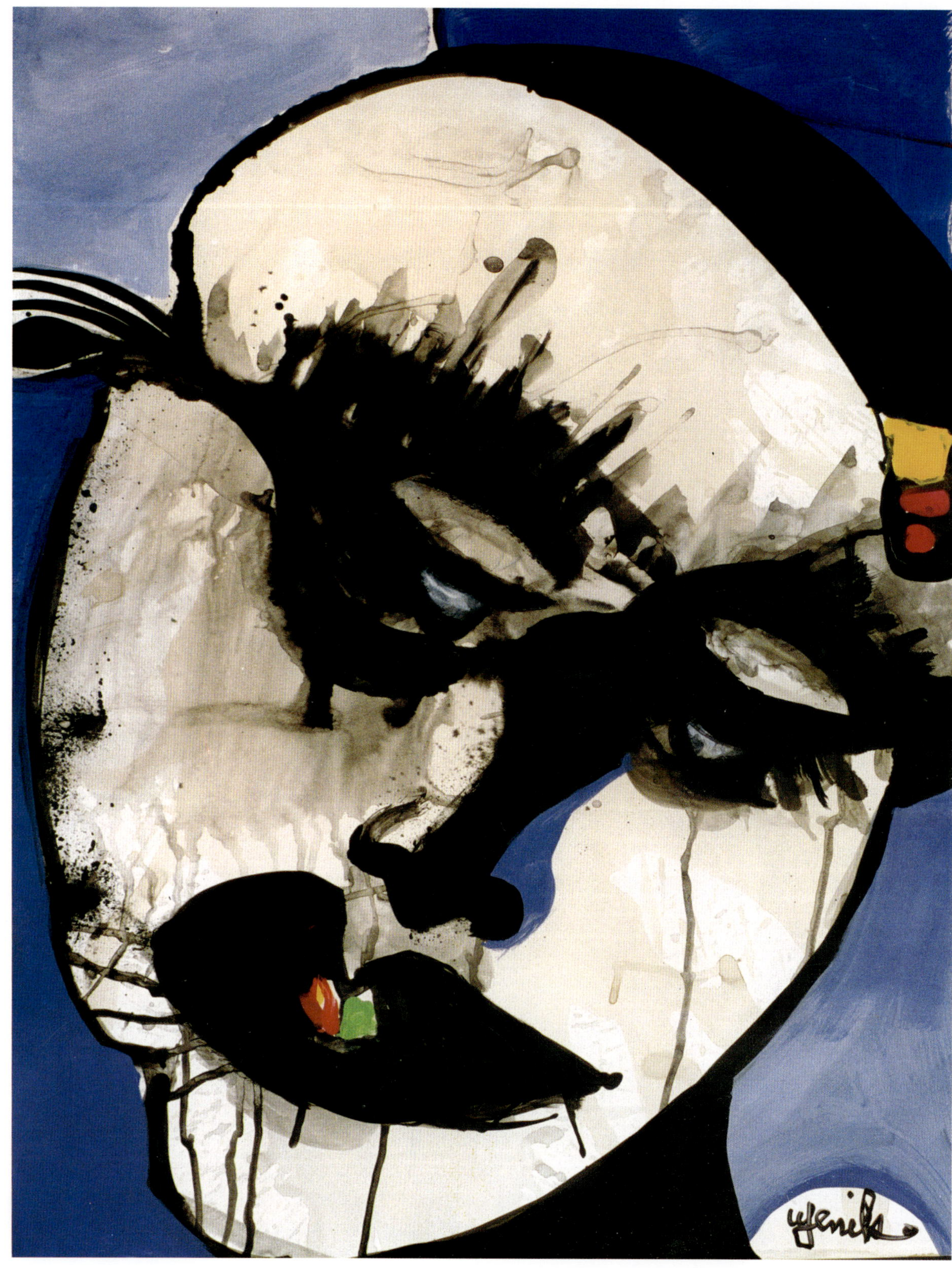

The Sage   Watercolor   28" x 22"

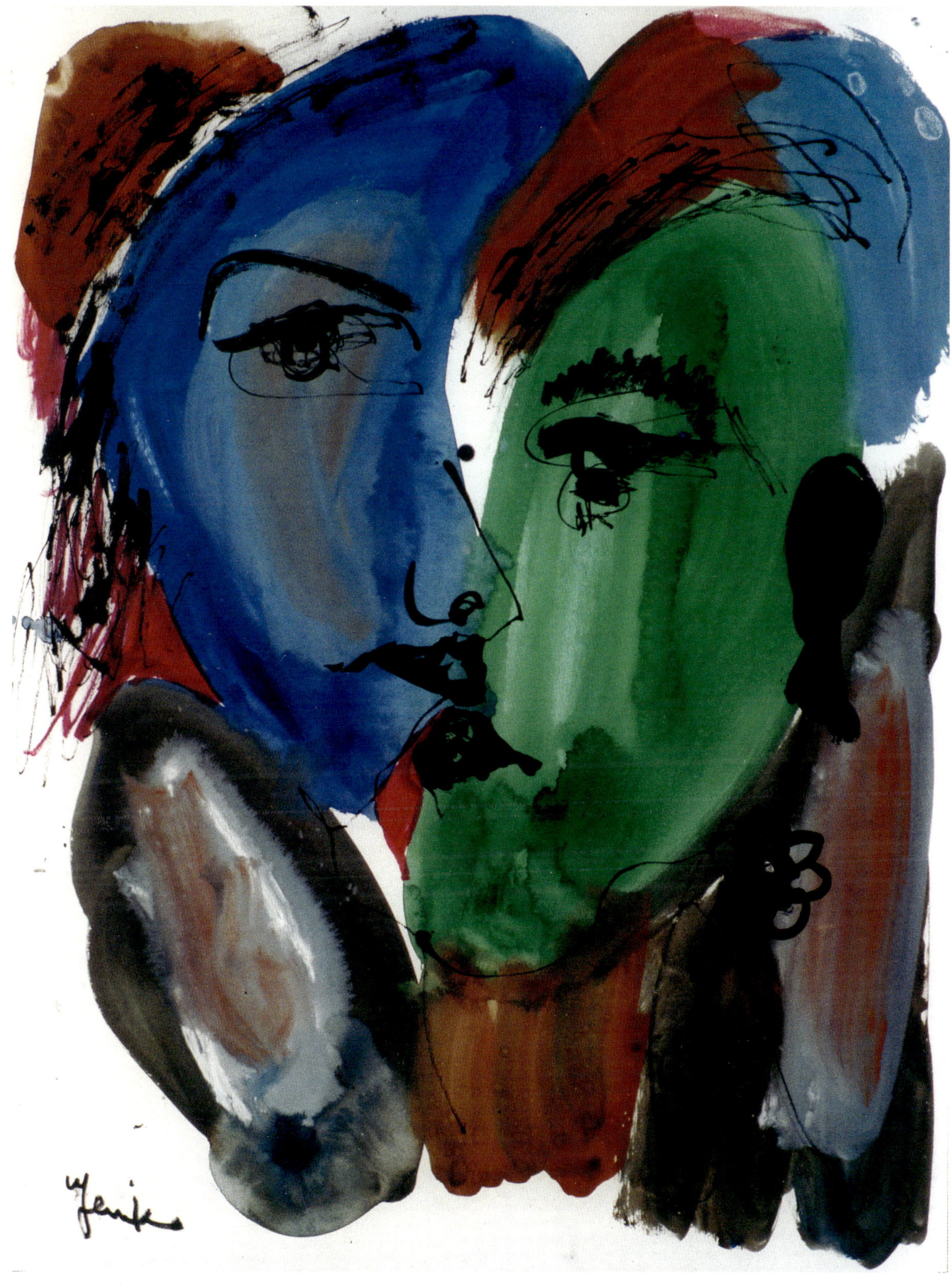

The Kiss   Watercolor   24" x 18"

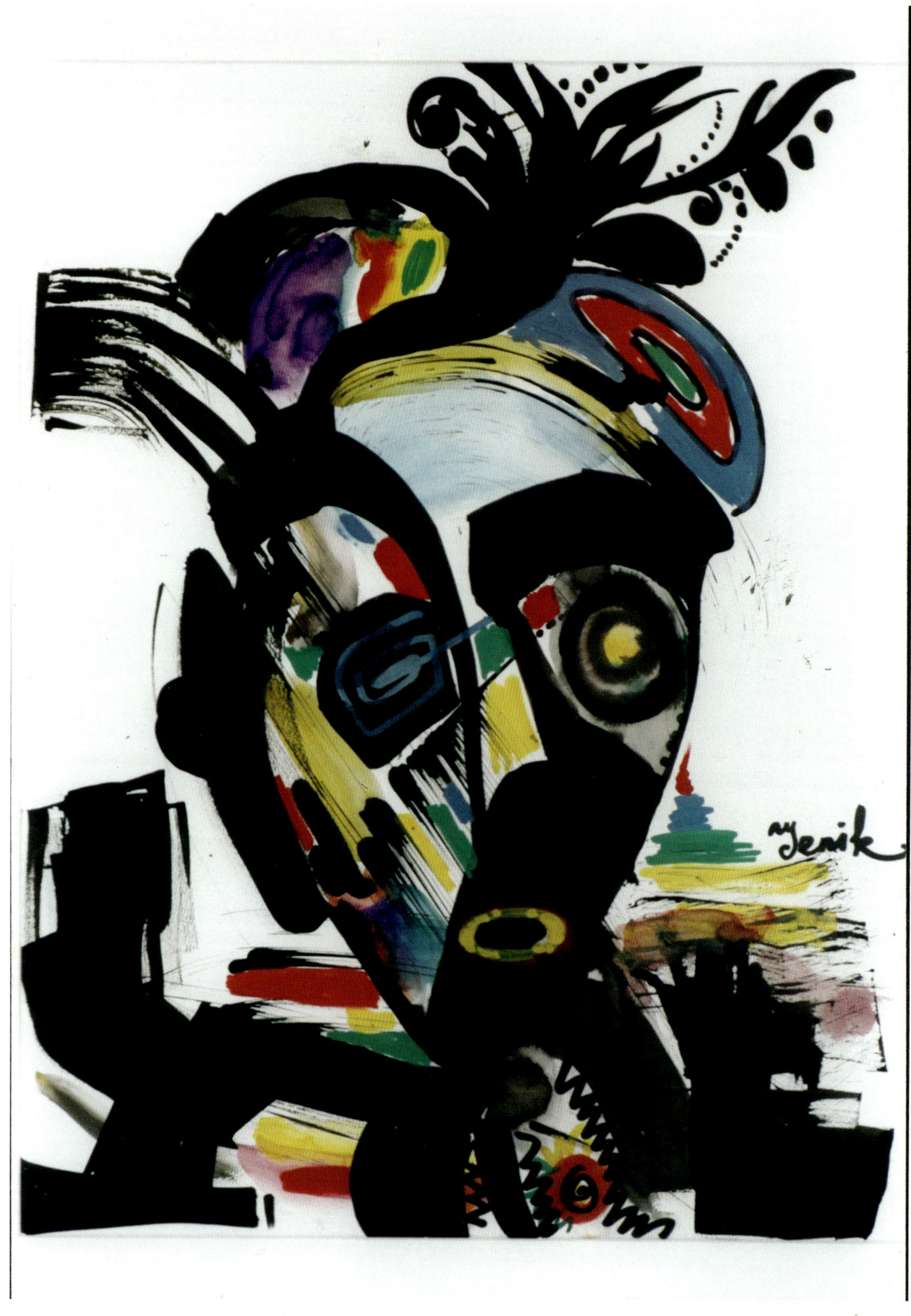

Shaman   Mixed Media   24" x 18"

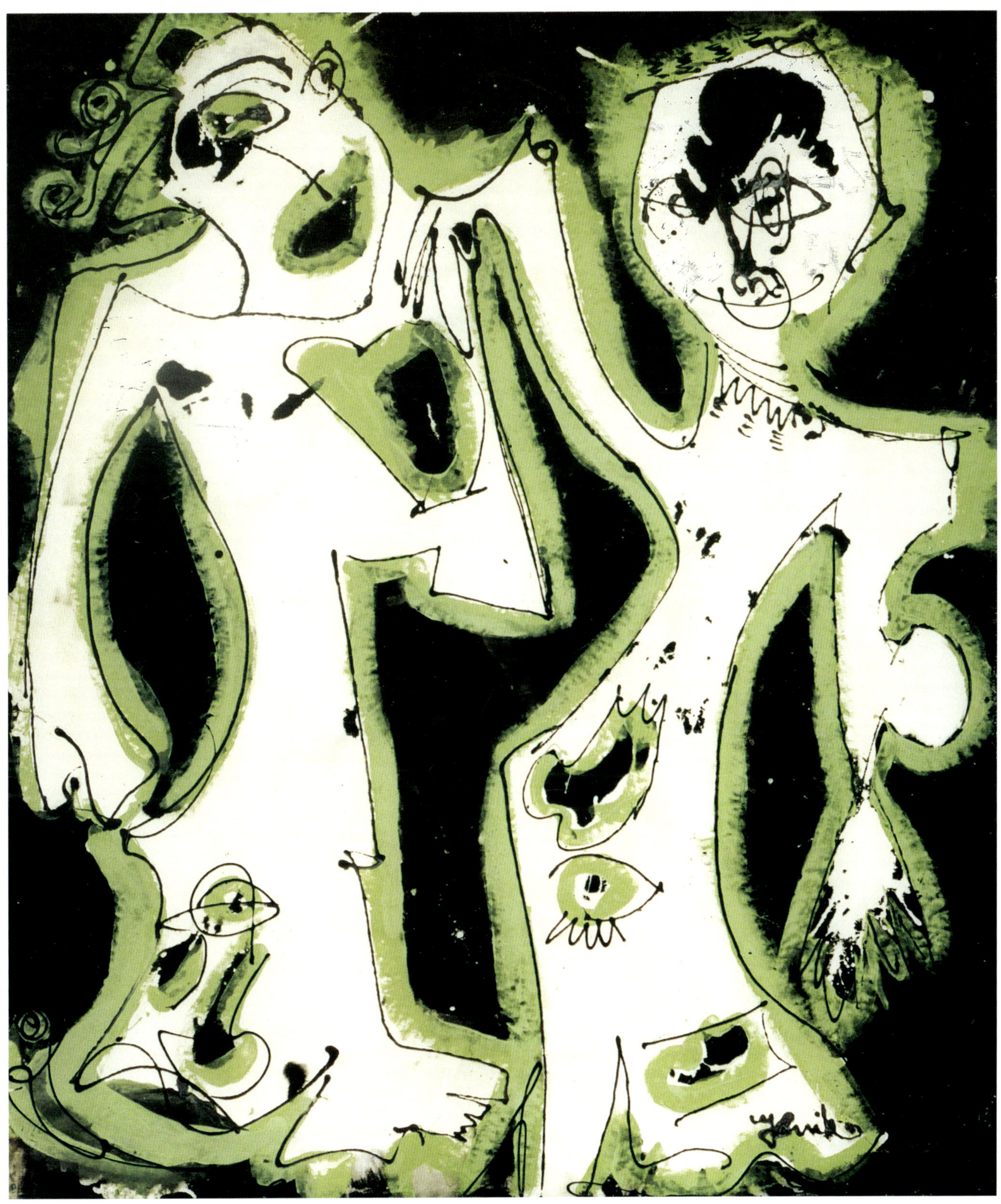

Gaud, Acrylic, 62" x 52"

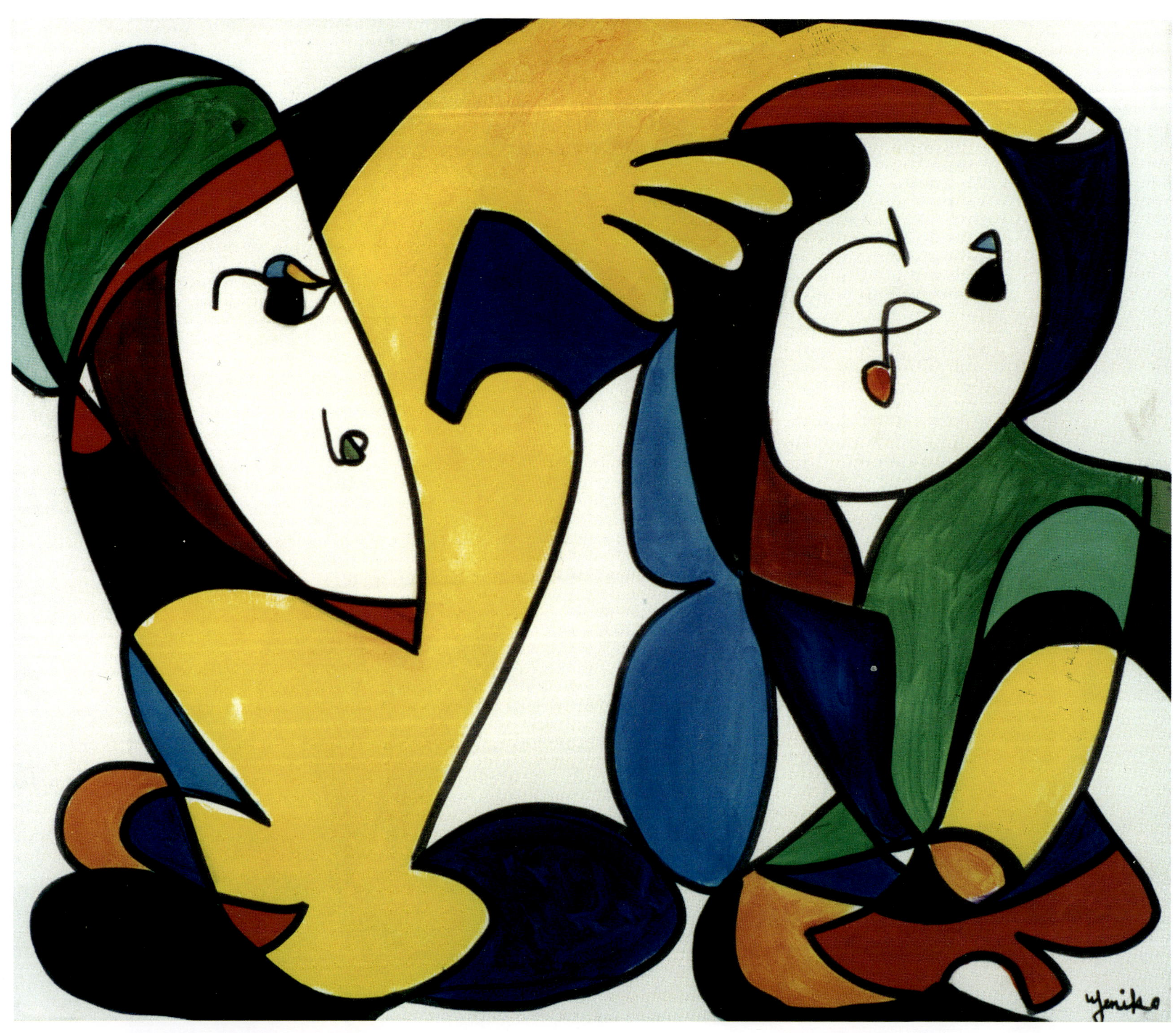

Happiness 32" x 38"

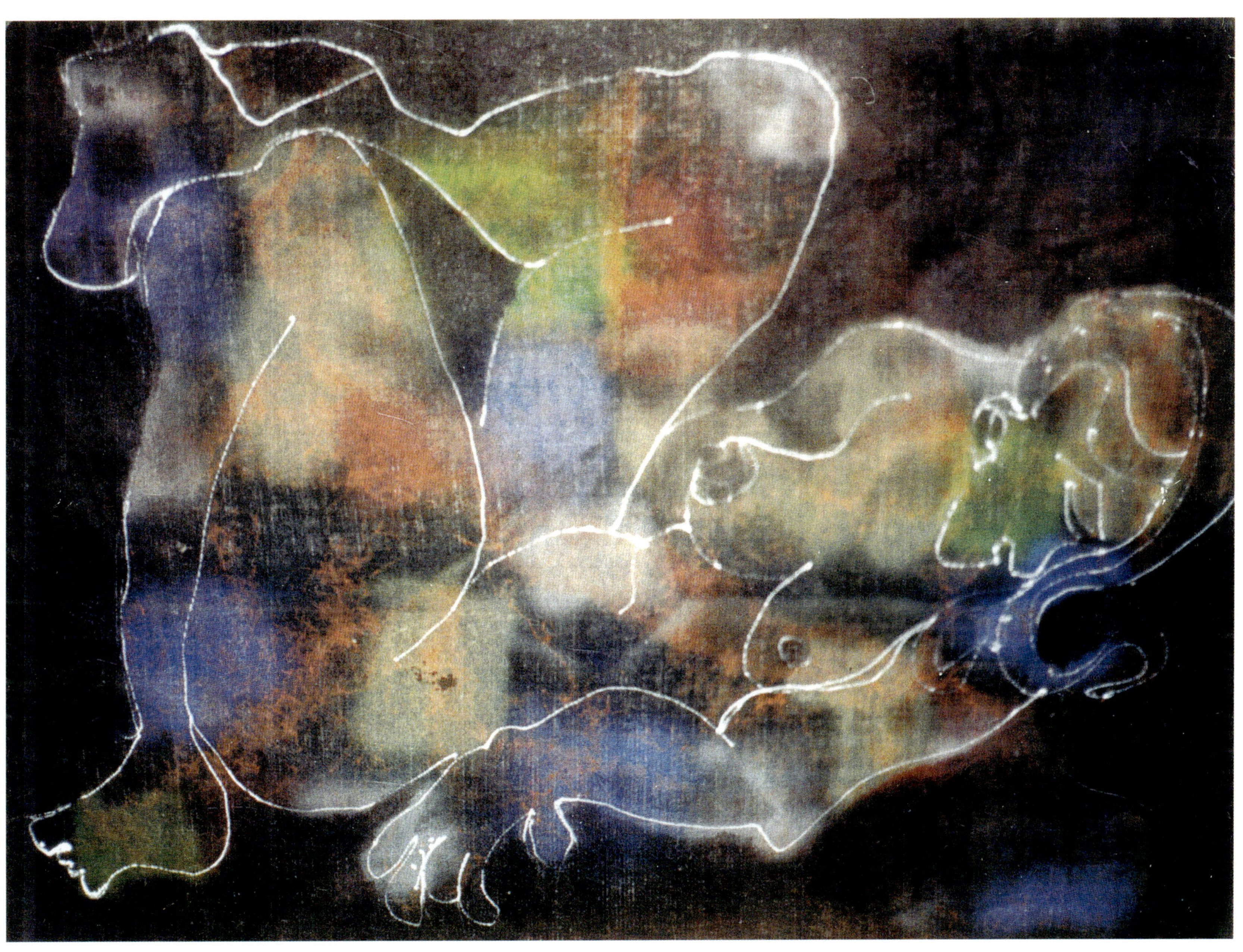

Reclining Nude, Oil, 52" x 64"

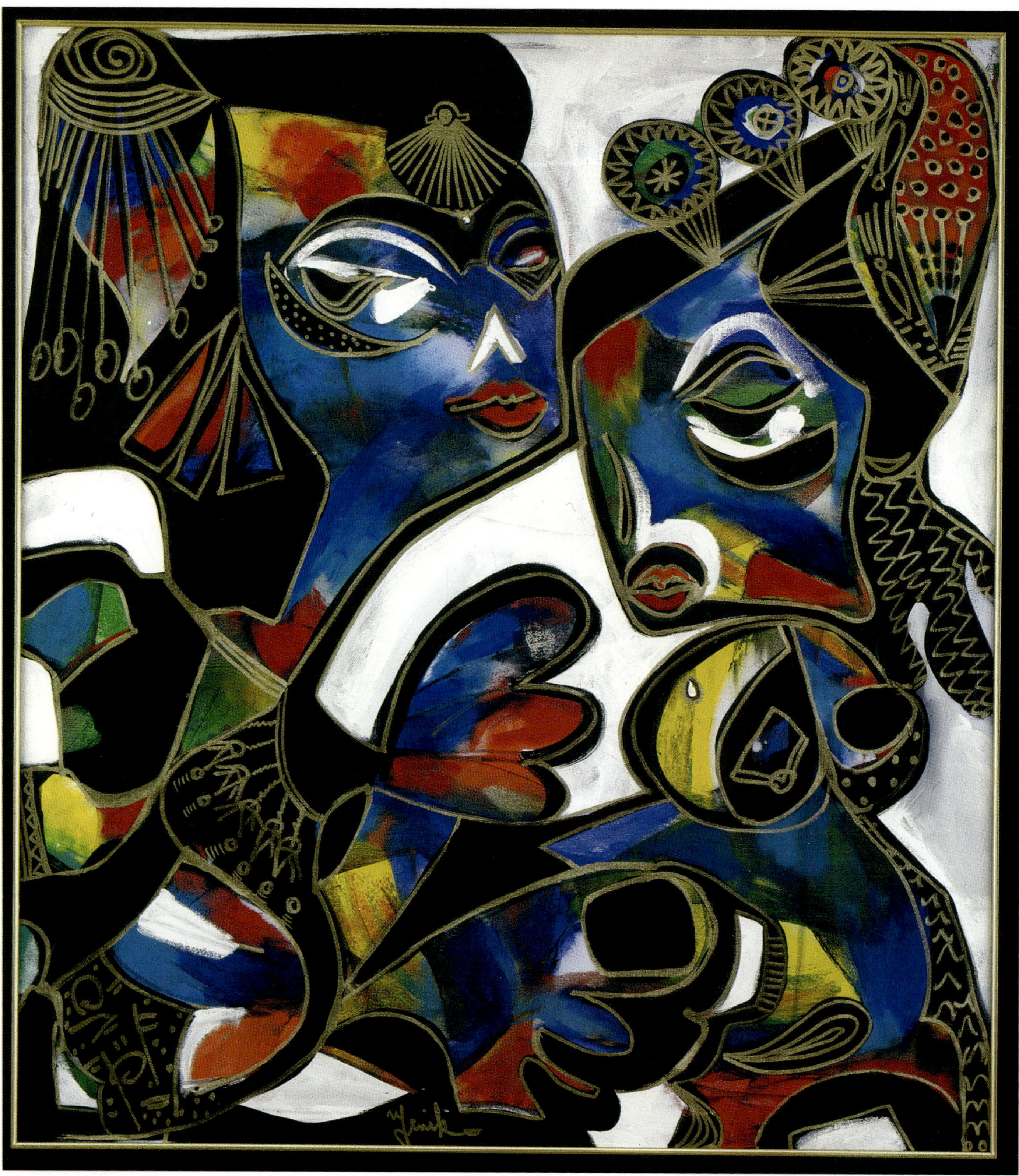

Beloved & Me   40" x 36"

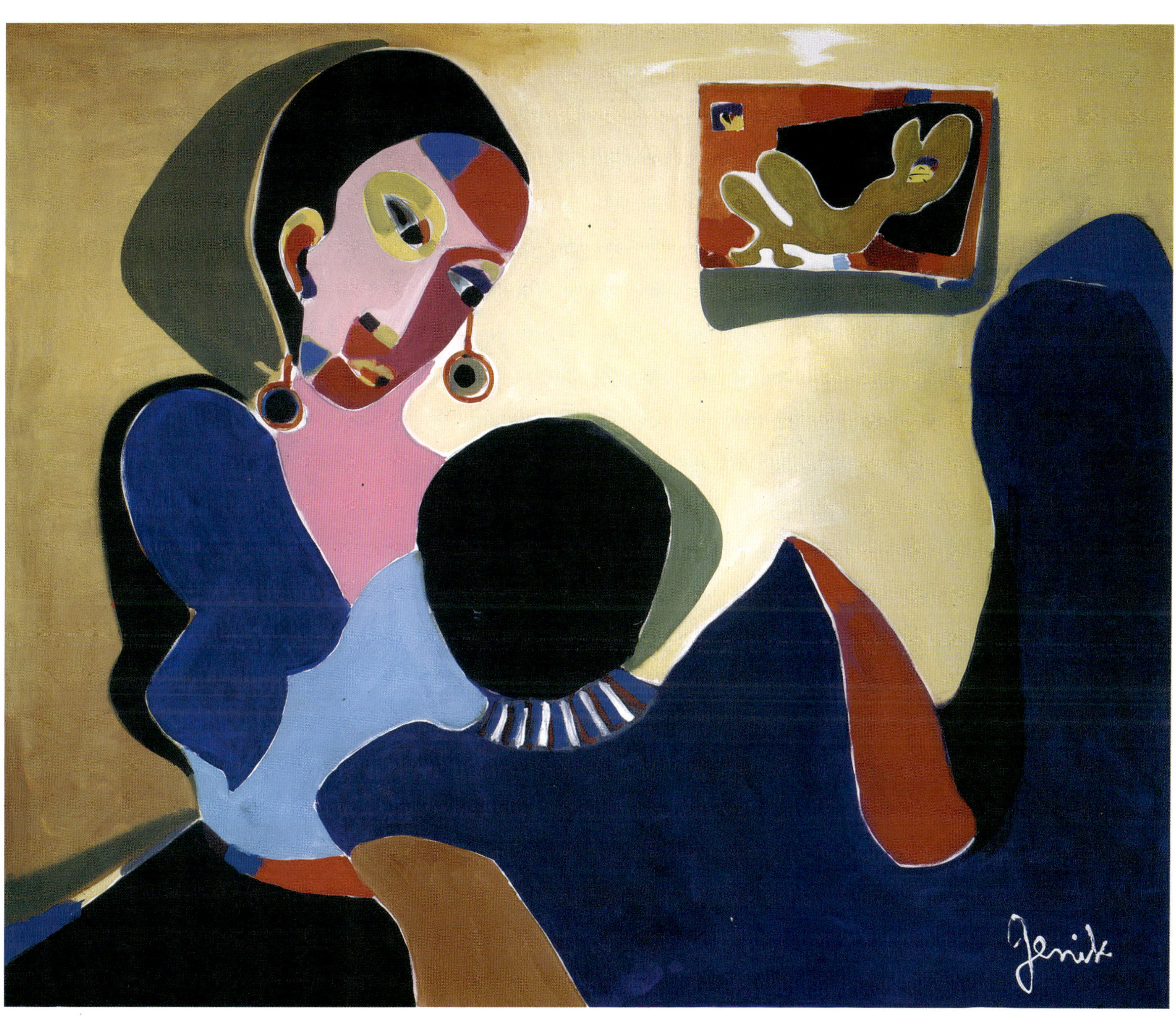

Intimacy, Acrylic, 46" x 56"

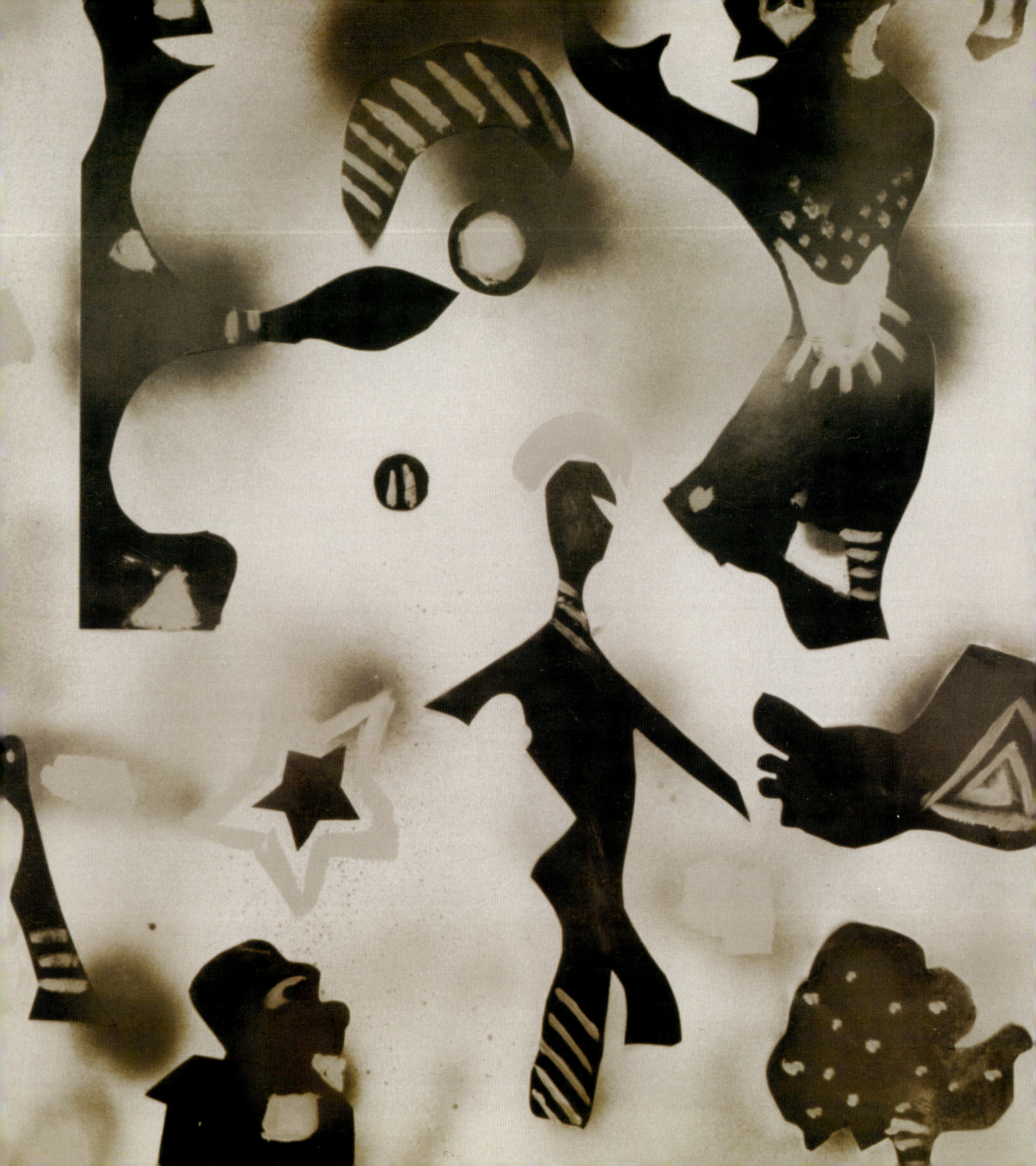

Intimations of creature wonder and worth are starkly reclaimed from simplicity by the heightened impact of wizened angles and contracted tonal range in Jenik's marvelously provocative collage and mixed media work.

MIXED MEDIA COLLAGE

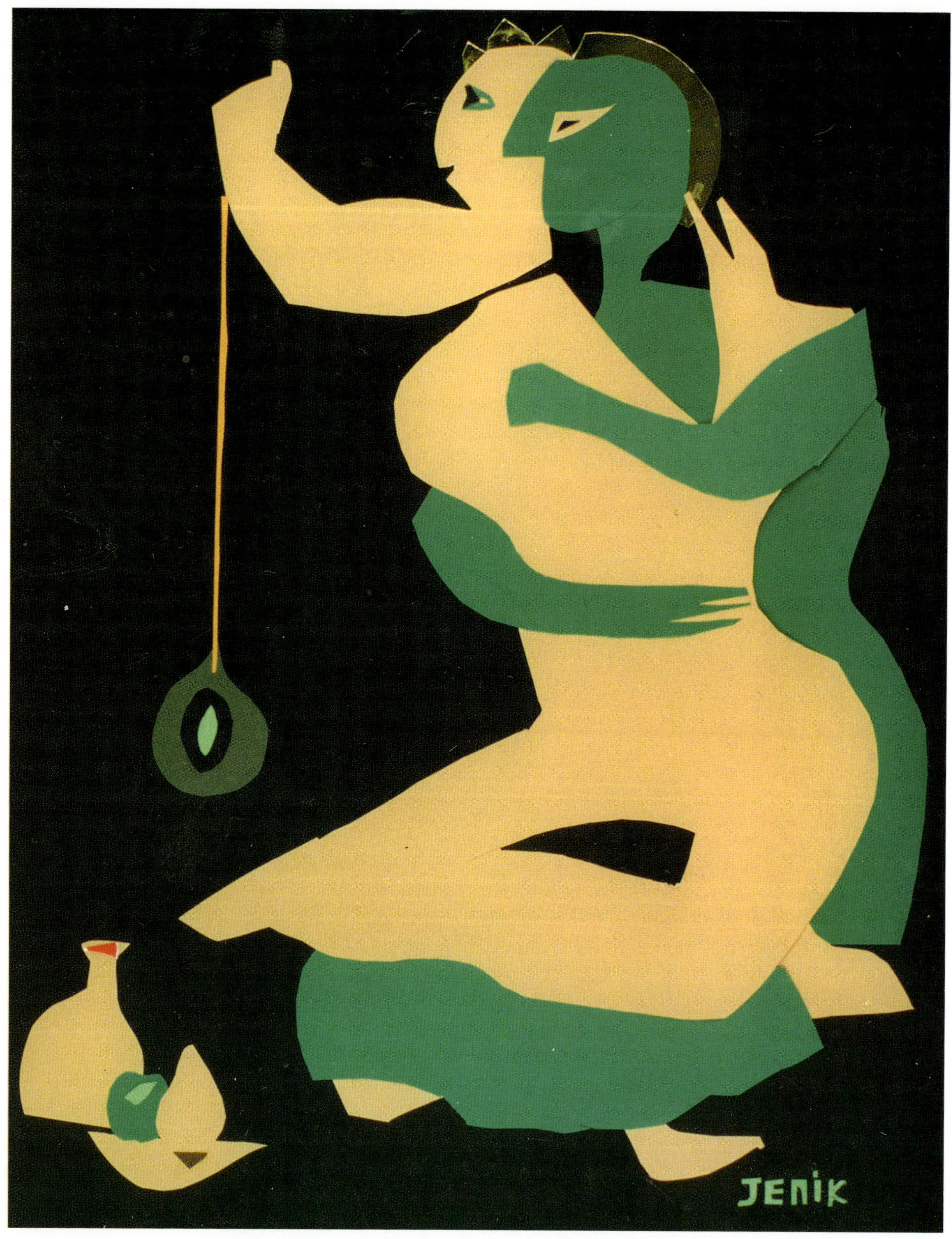

COL No. 1   28" x 22"

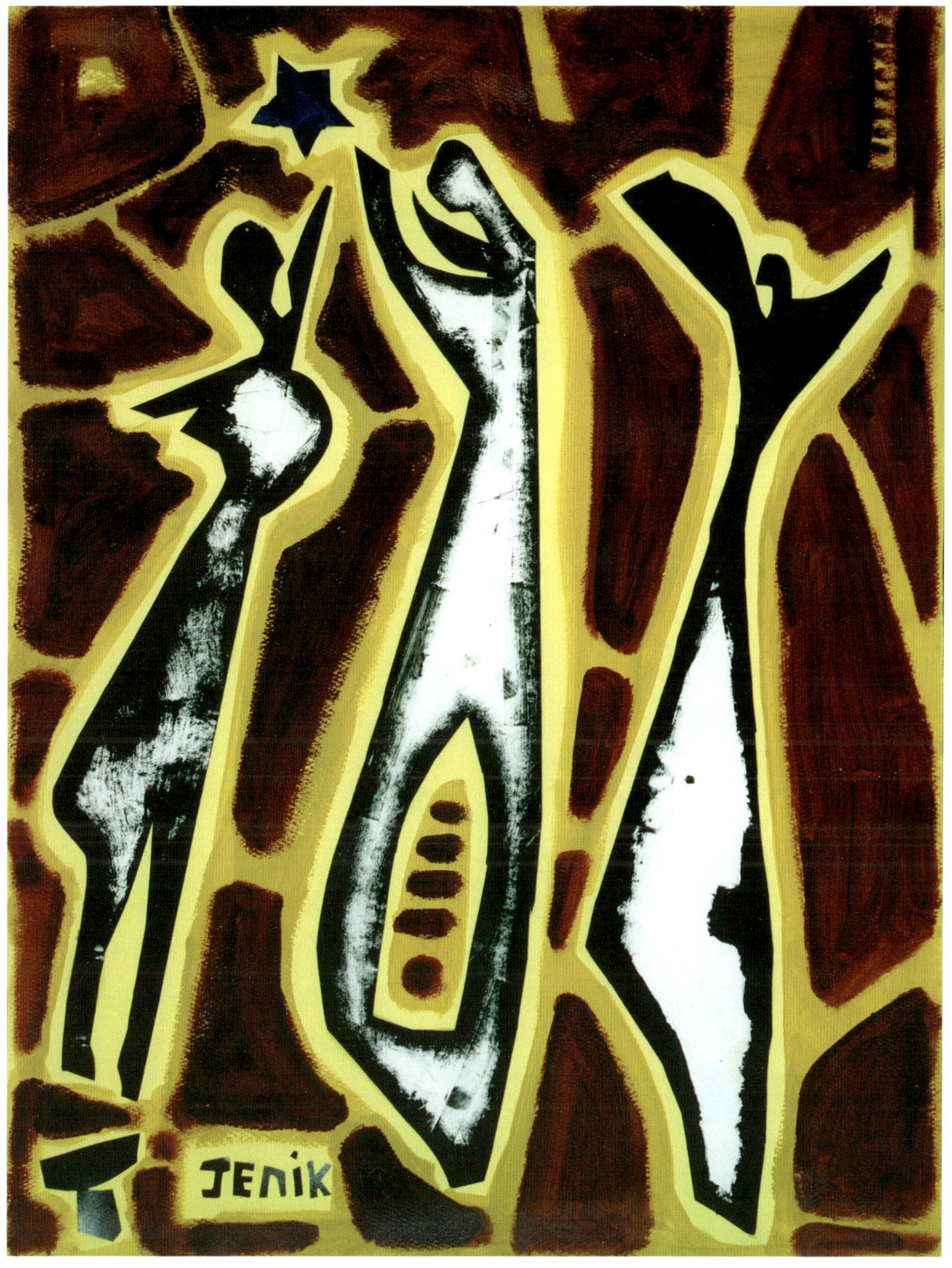

COL No. 5, Mixed Media, 30" x 24"

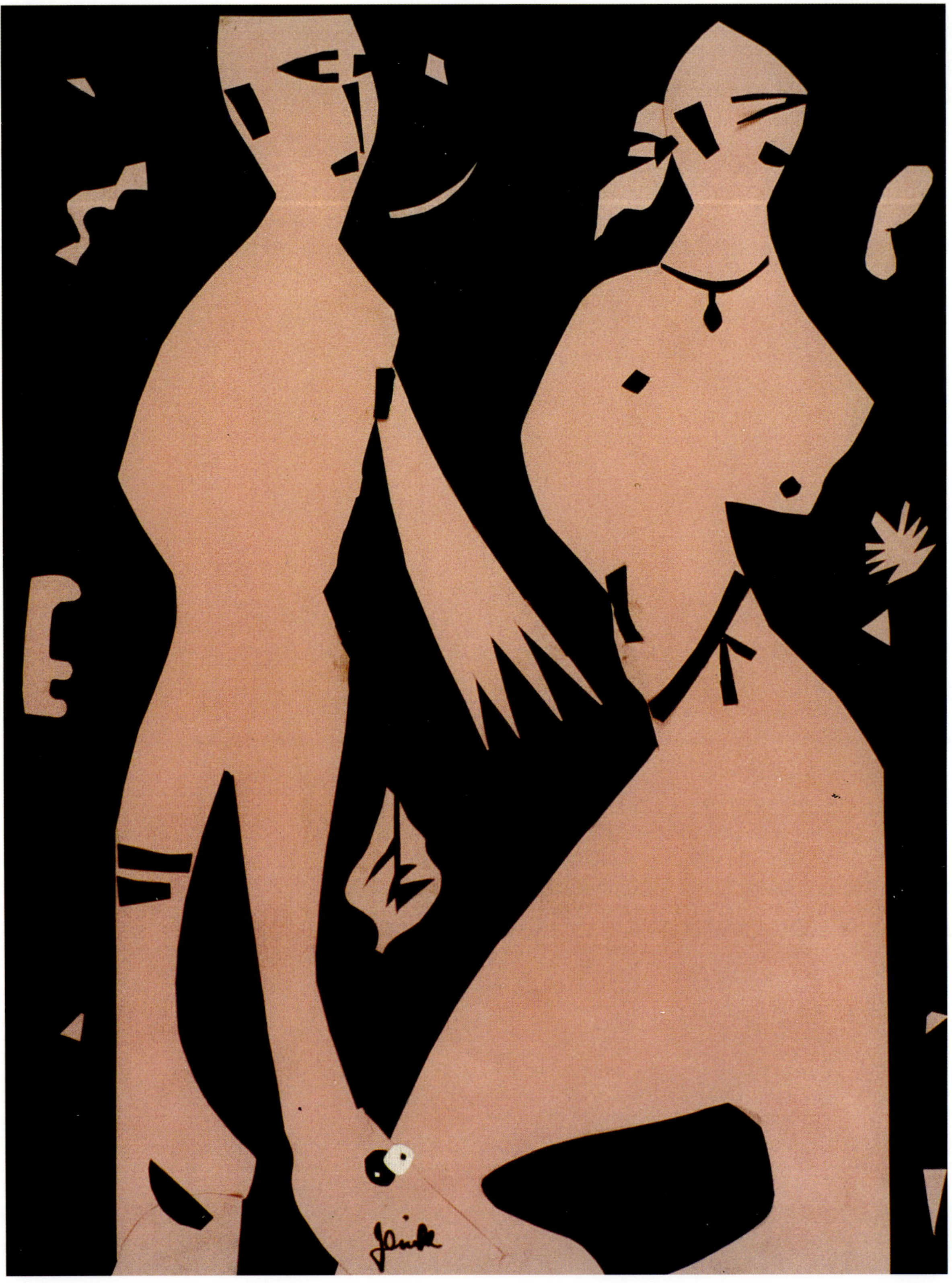

COL No. 9   Mixed media   28" x 22"

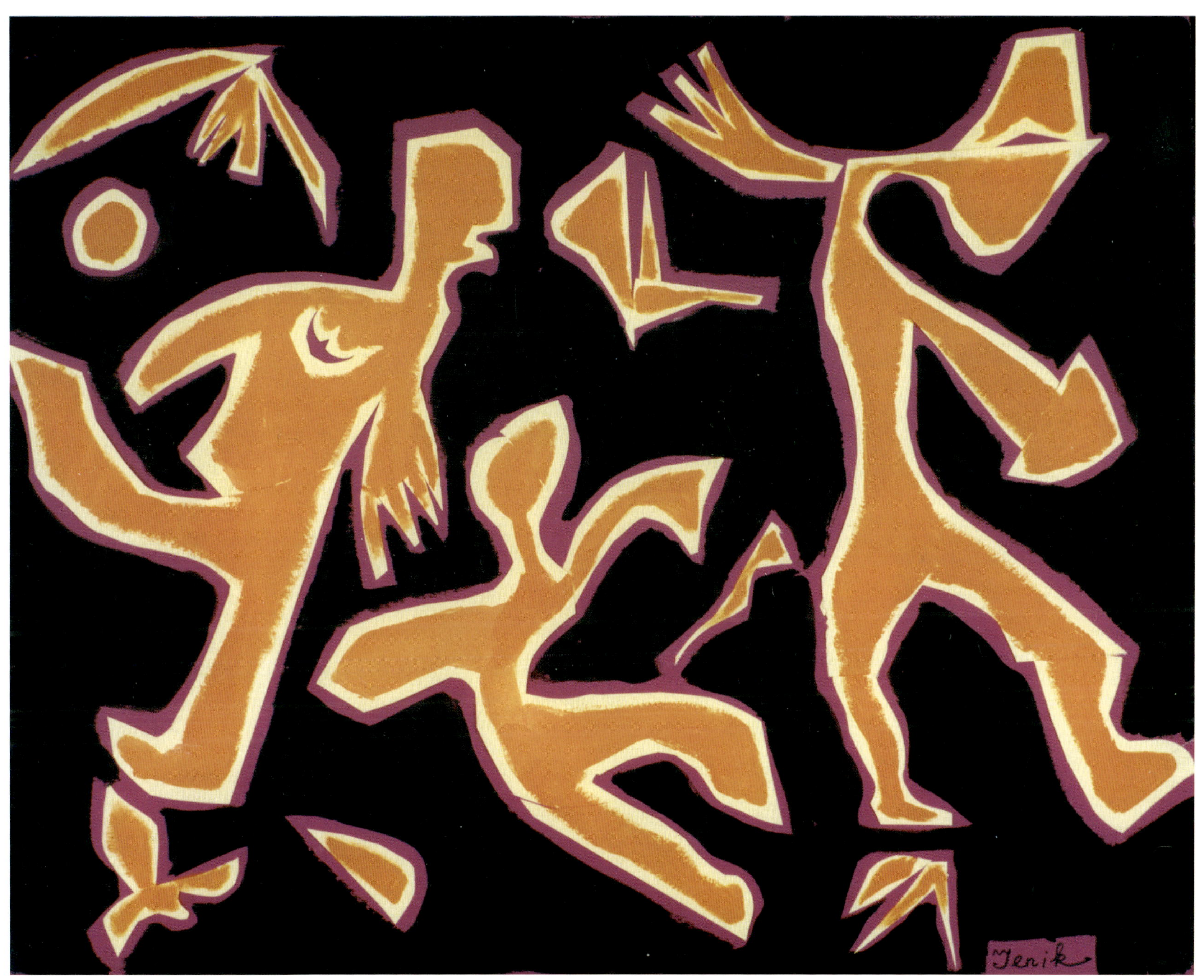

COL No. 8, Mixed Media, 22" x 28"

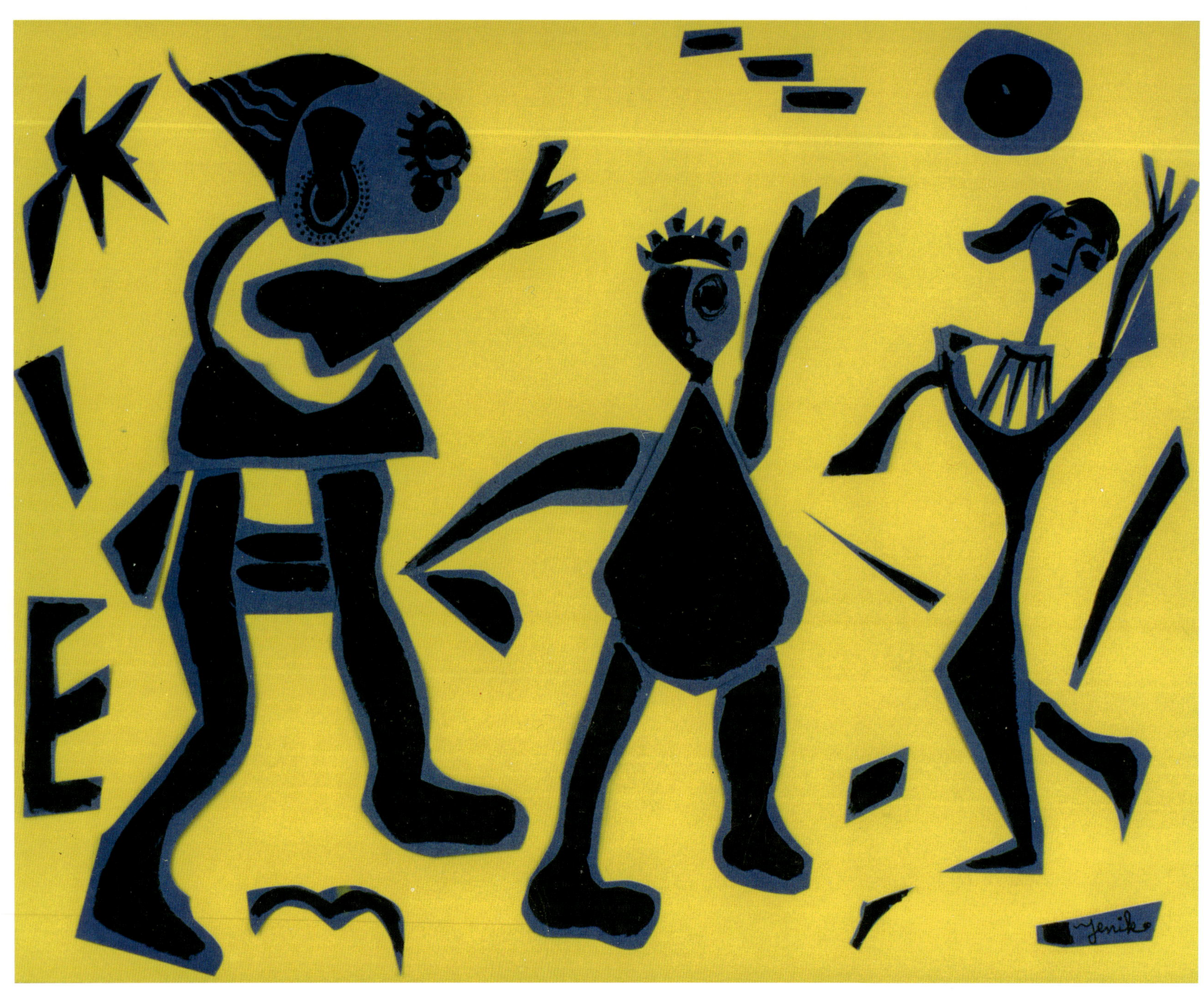

COL No. 11 Mixed media   22" x 28"

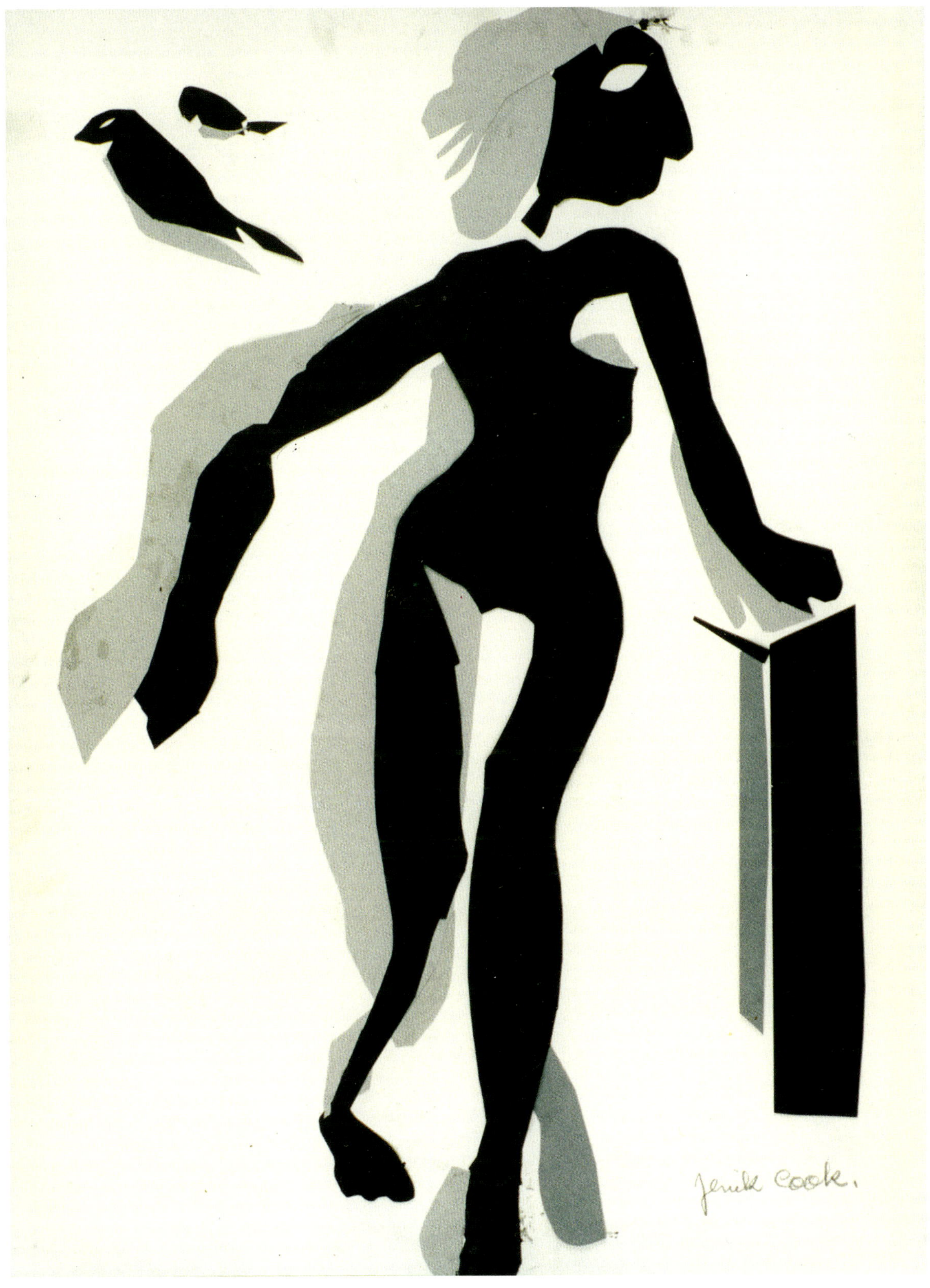

COL No. 19   Mixed media   28" x 22"

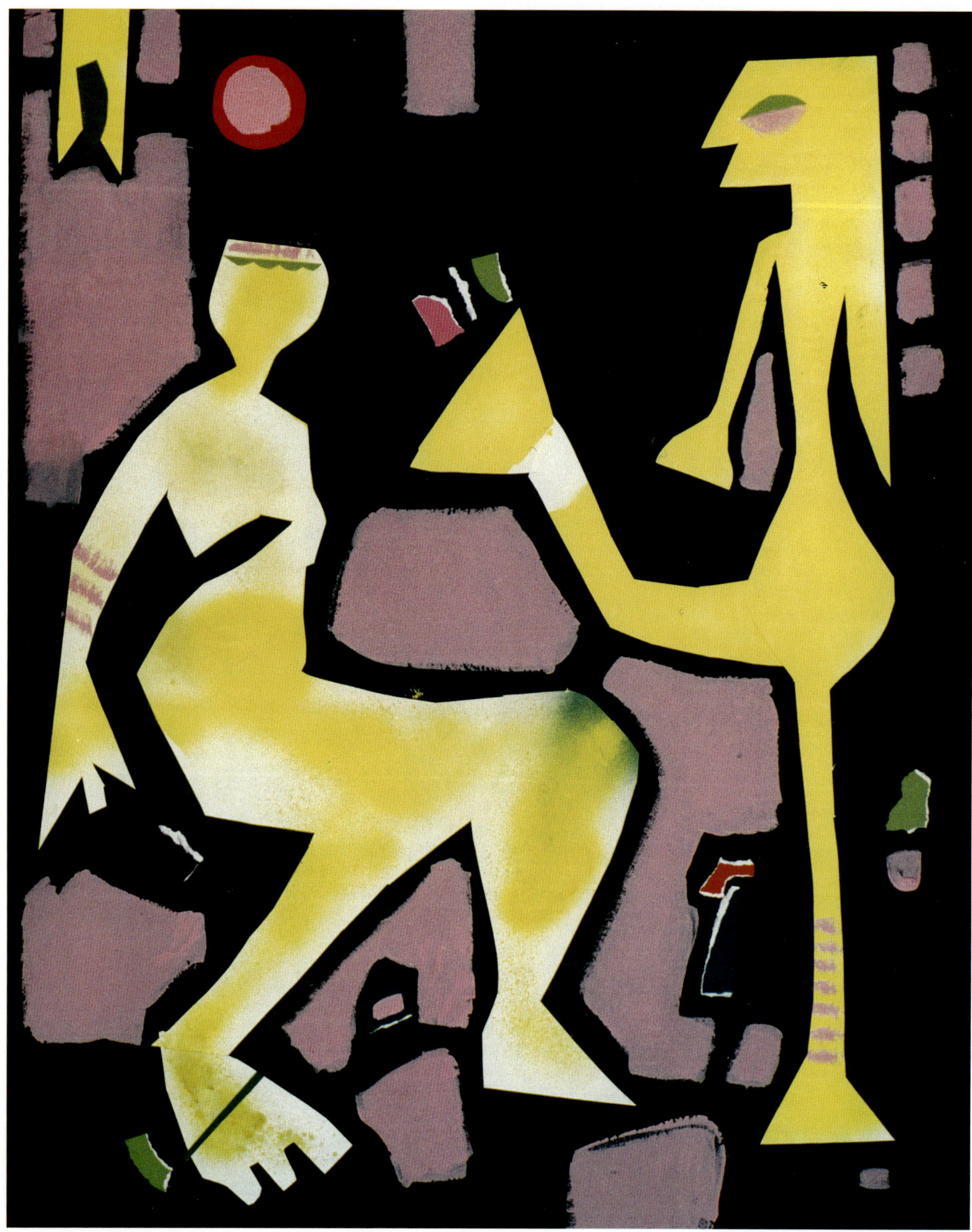

COL No. 6   Mixed media   28" x 22"

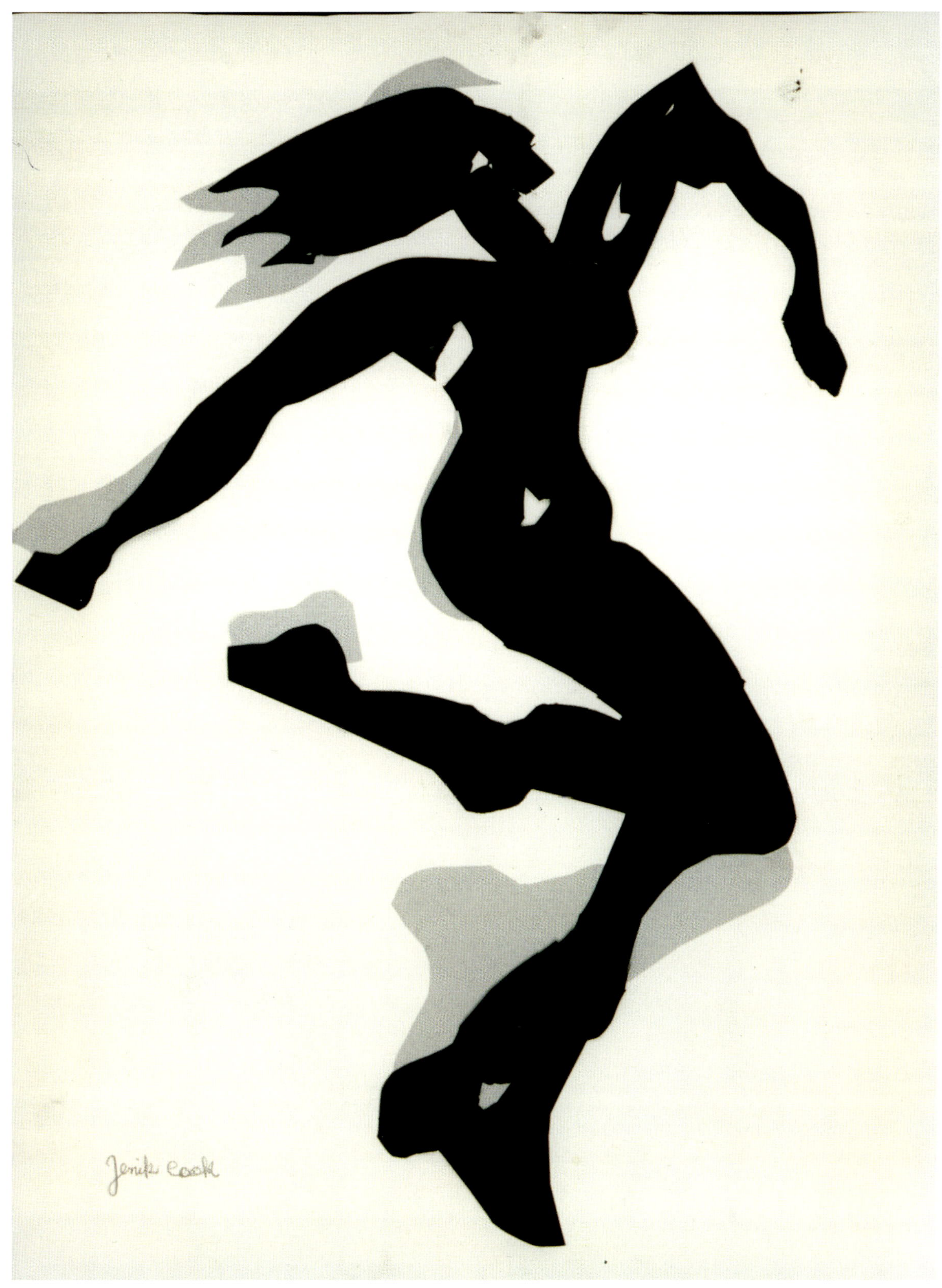

COL No. 18, Black & Gray, 24" x 18"

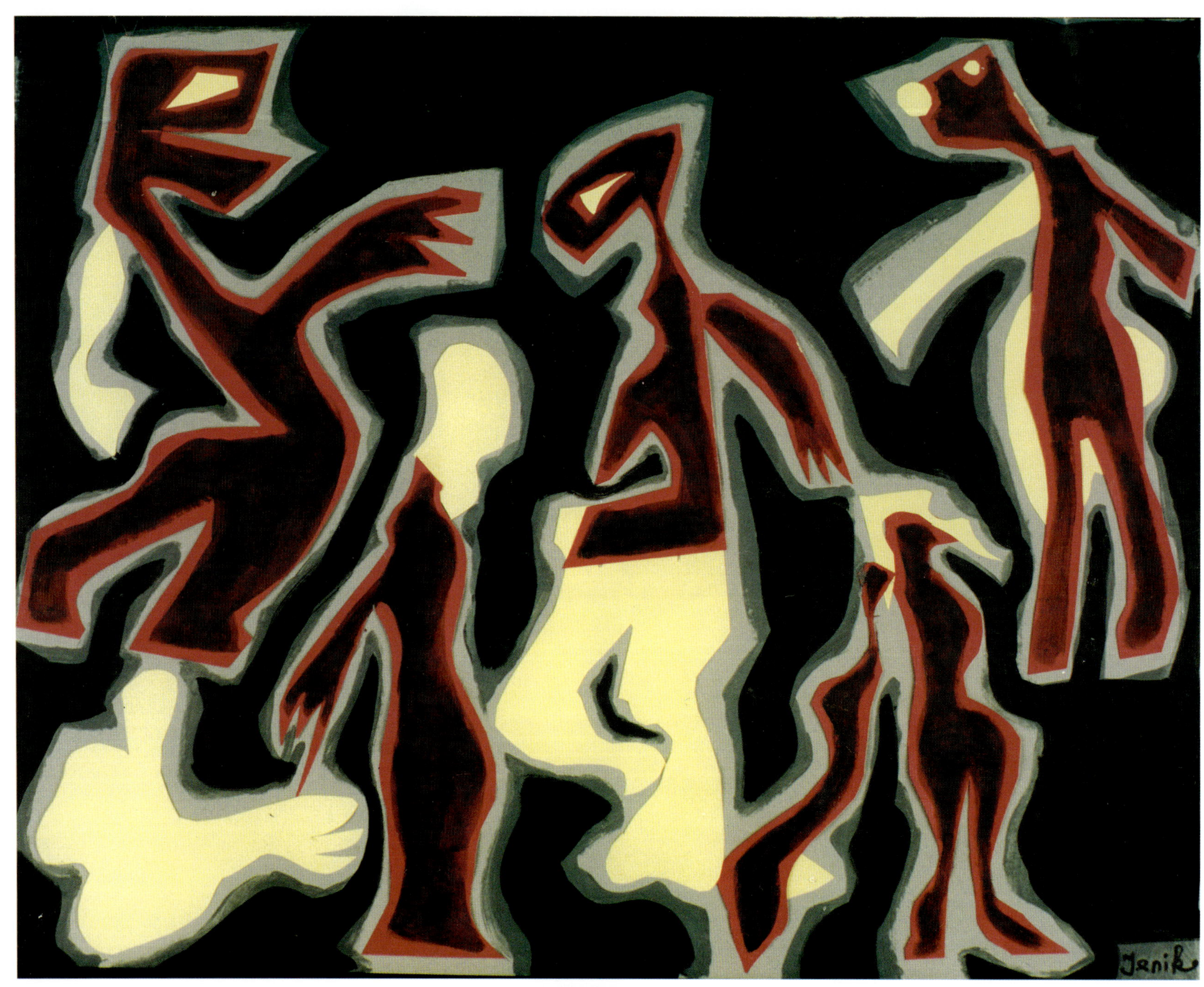

COL No. 4   Mixed media   20" x 30"

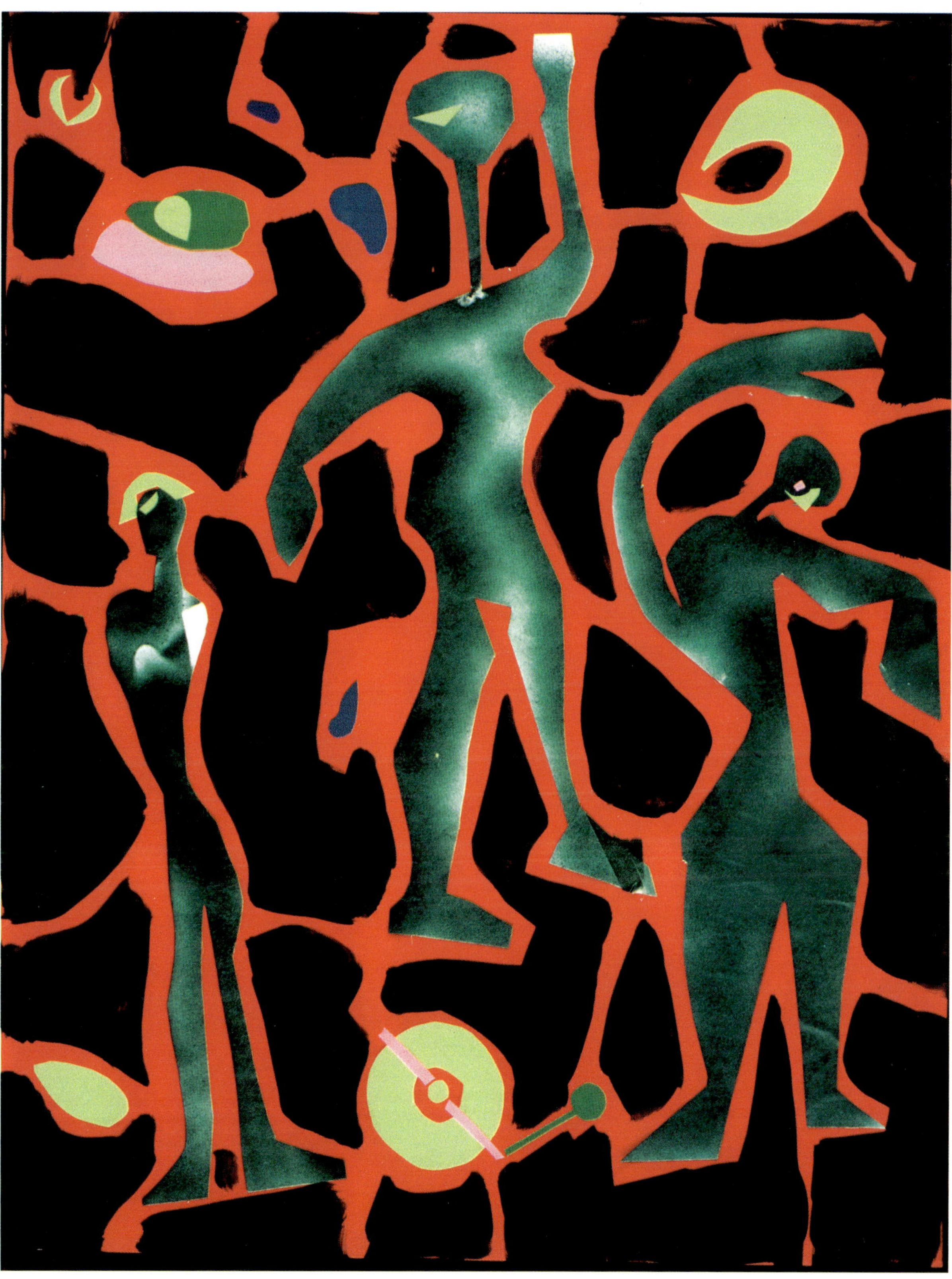

COL. No. 2, Mixed Media, 28" x 22"

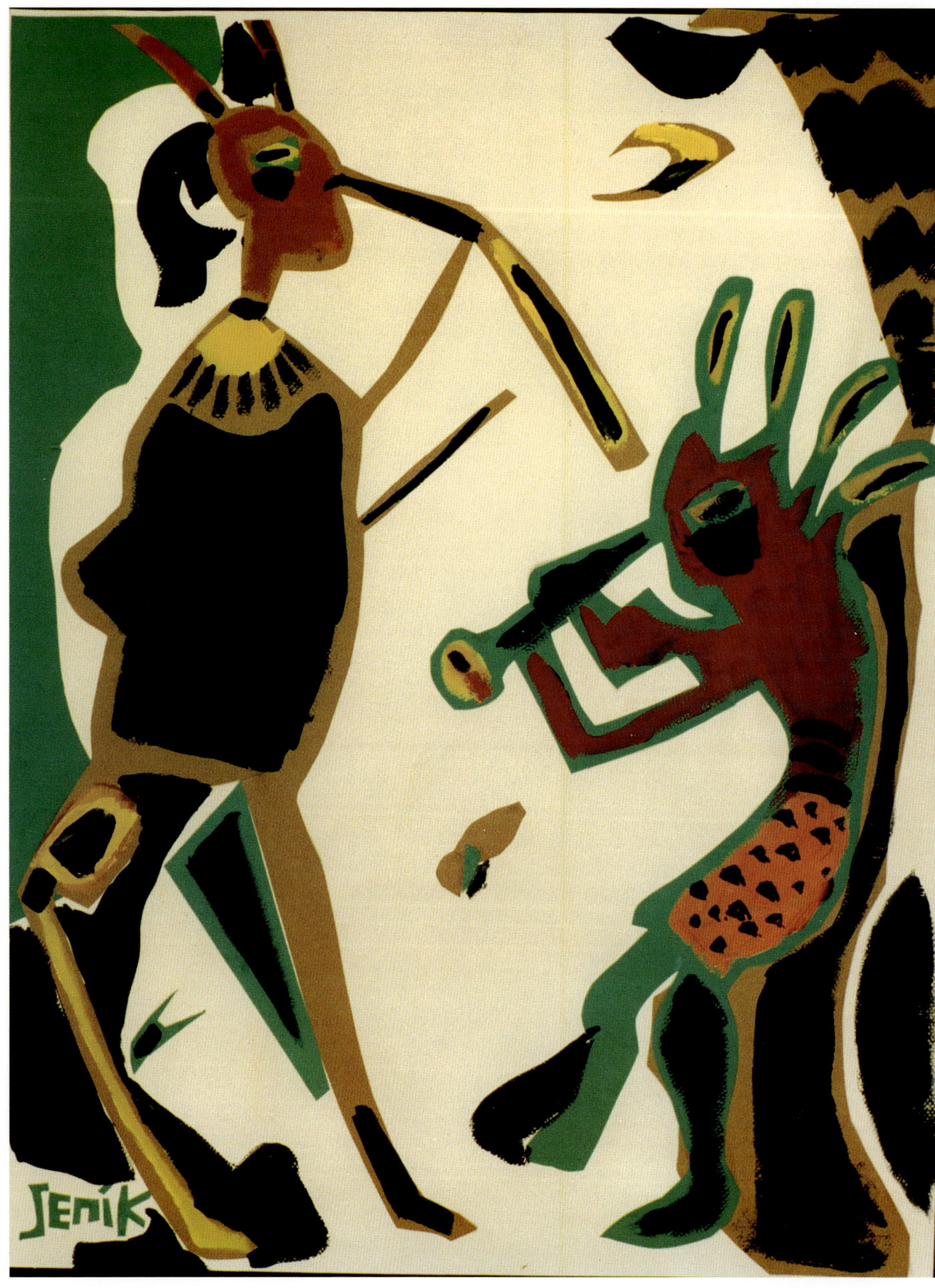

COL No. 3   Mixed media   24" x 18"

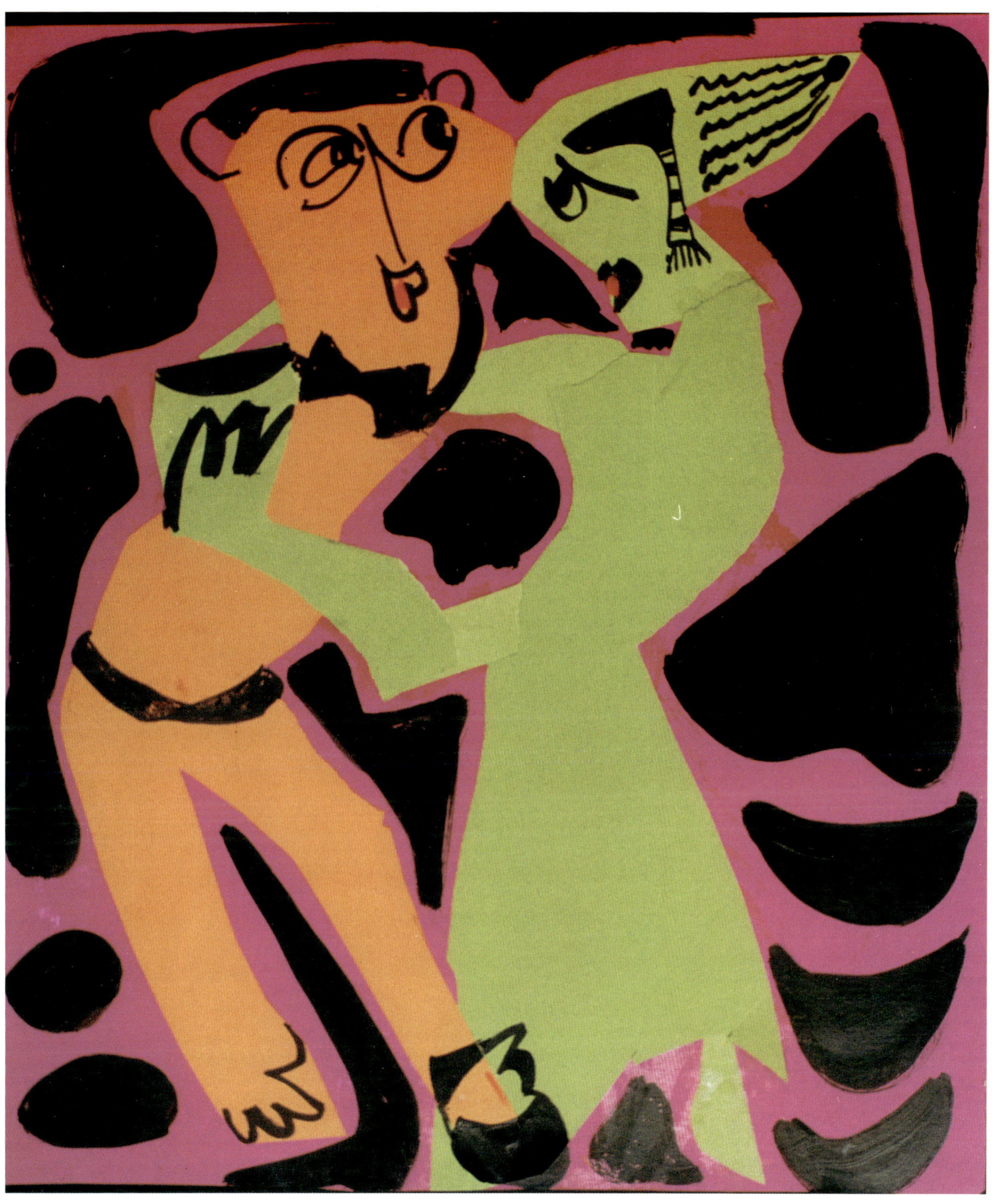

COL. No. 7, Mixed Media, 28" x 22"

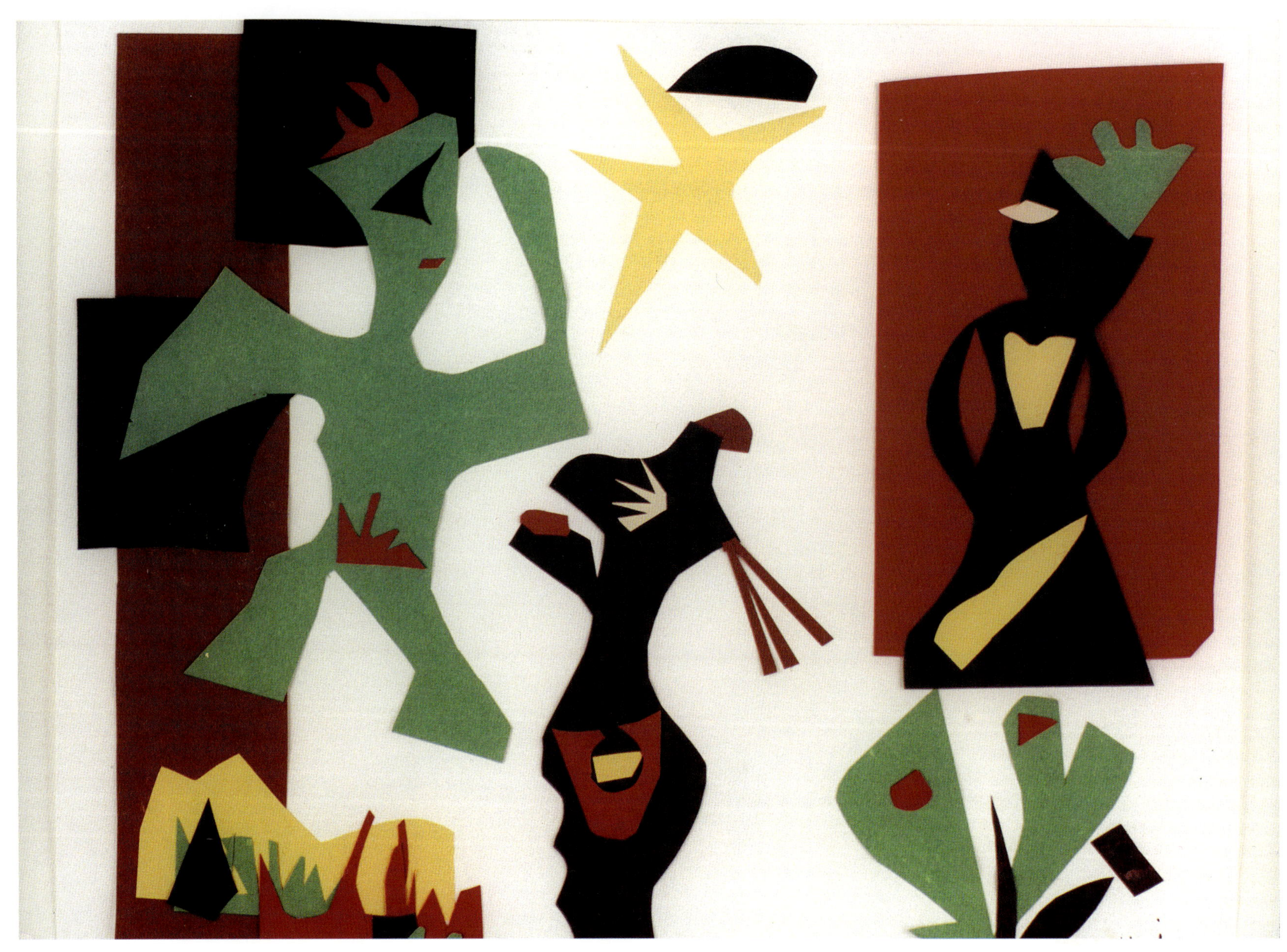

COL No. 10   Mixed media   22" x 28"

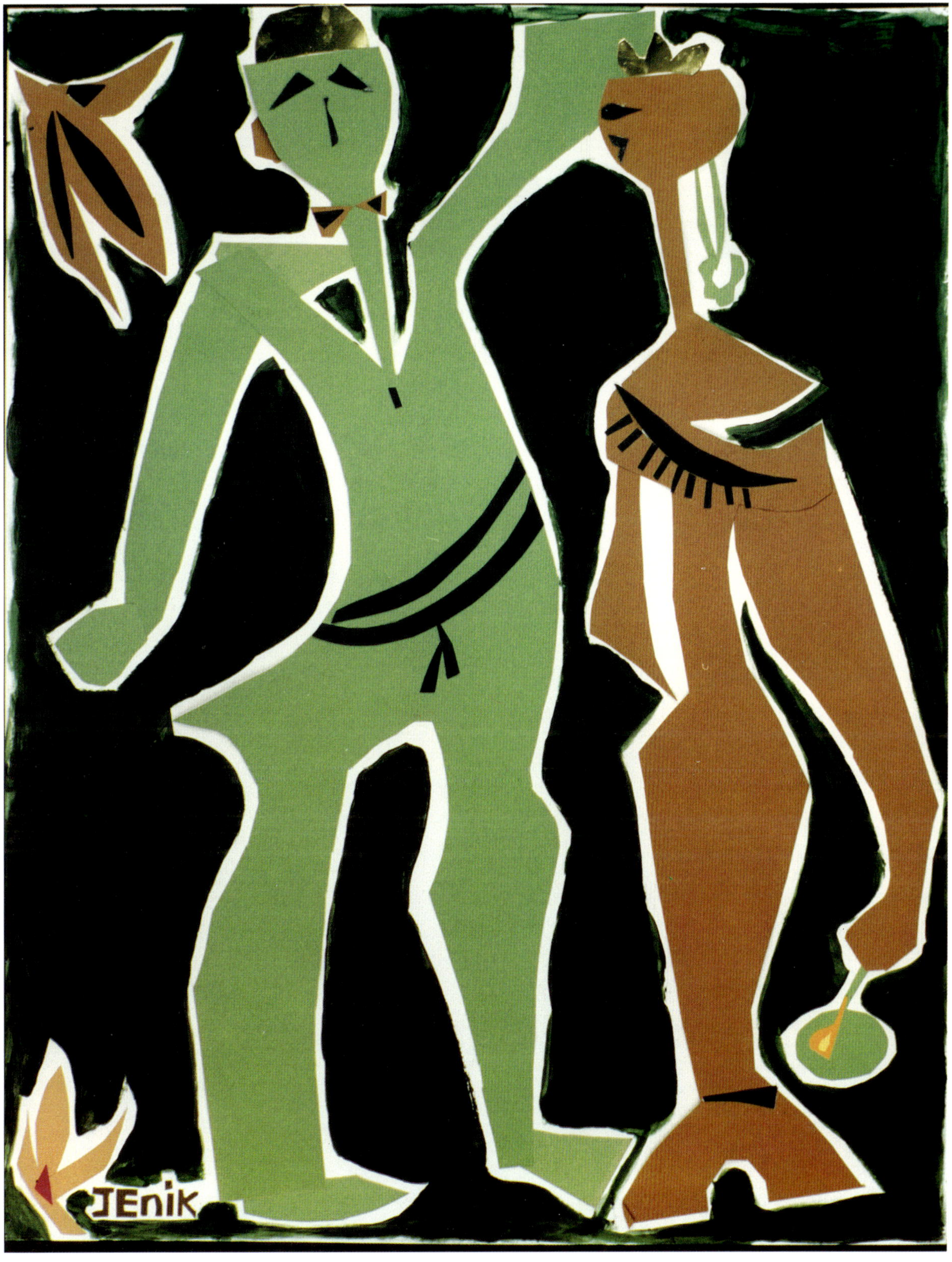

COL No. 12, Mixed Media, 28" x 22"

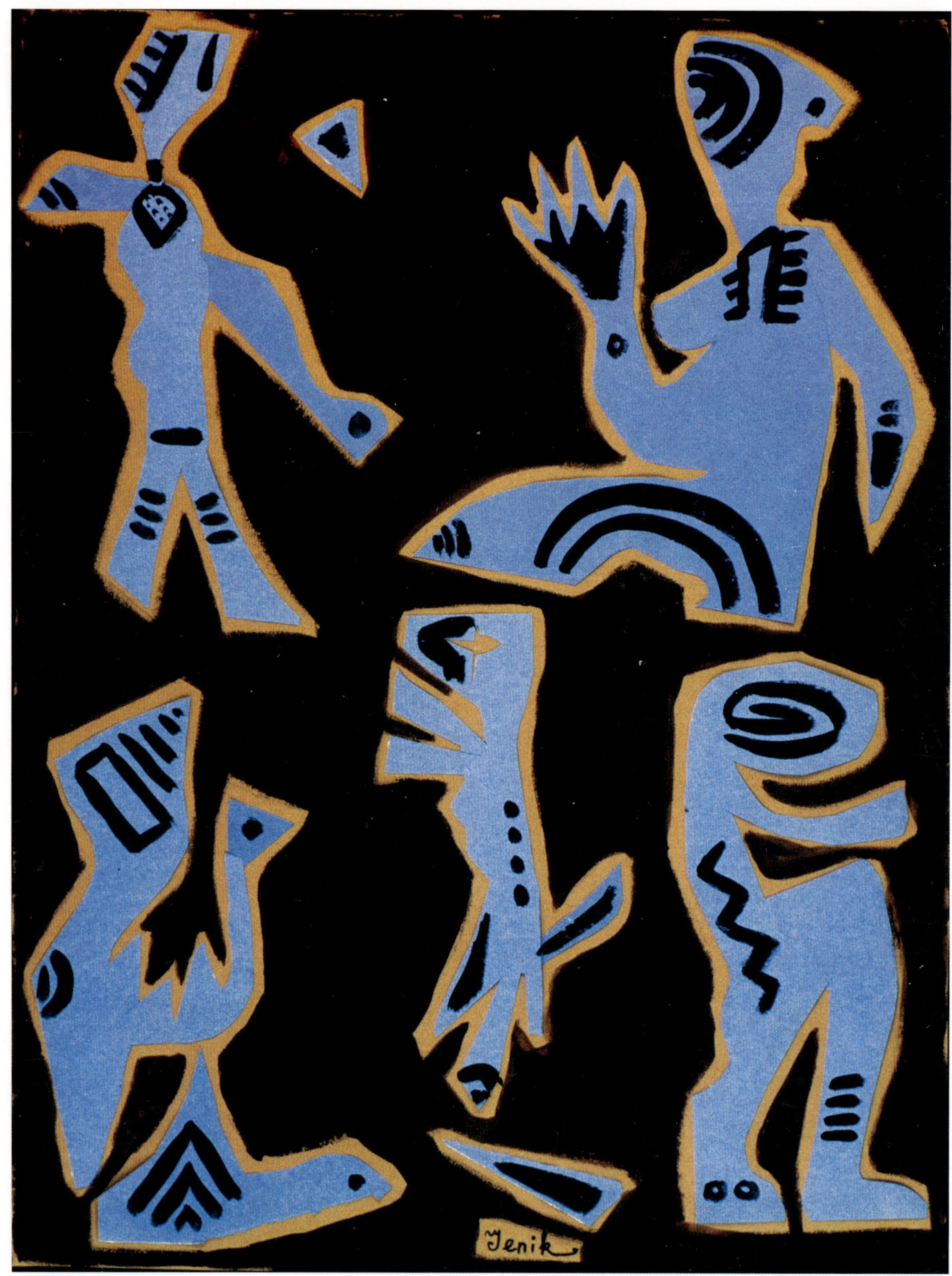

COL No. 13   Mixed media   28" x 22"

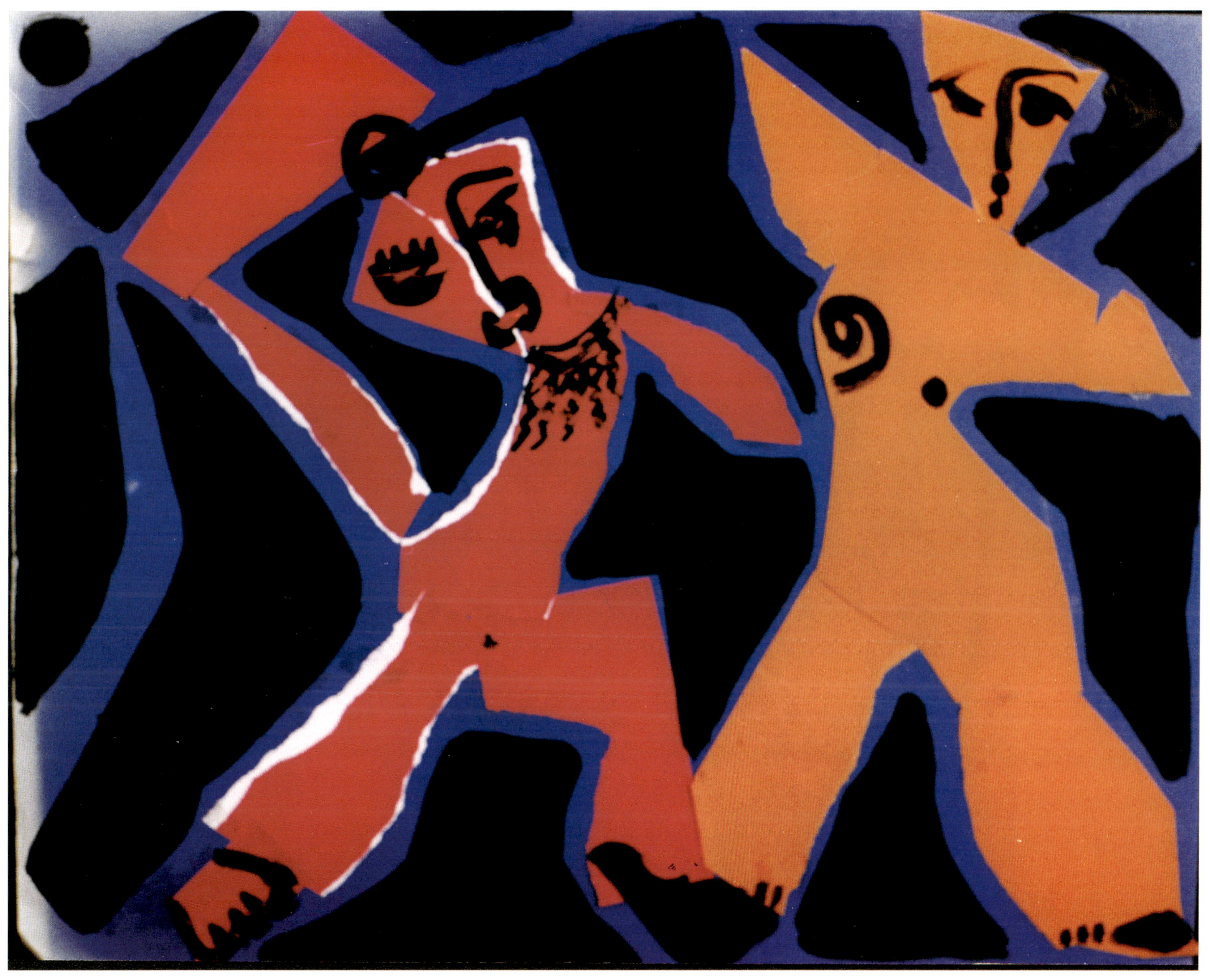

COL No. 14, Mixed Media, 22"x 28"

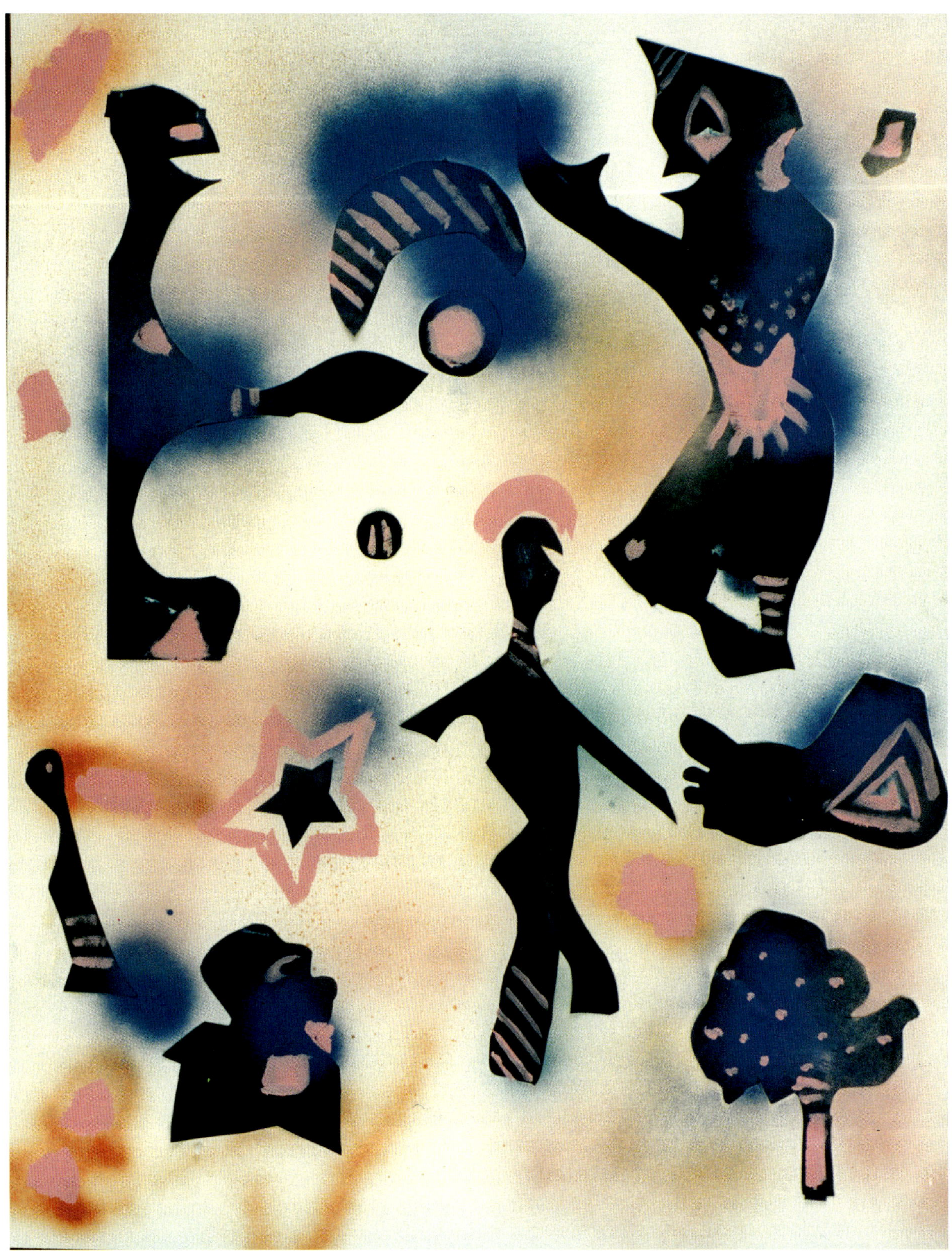

Energized   28" x 22"

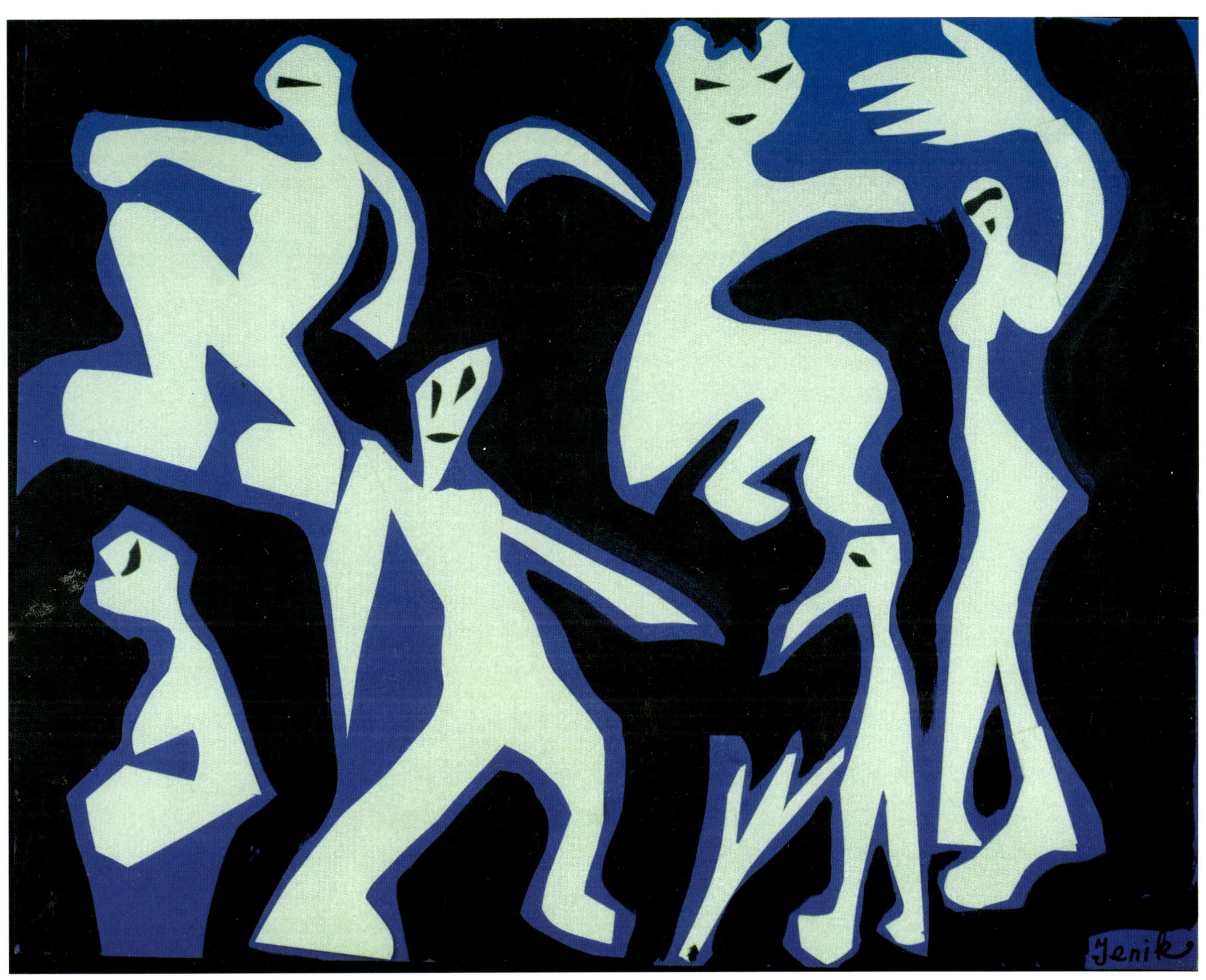

COL No. 17, Mixed Media, 22"x 28"

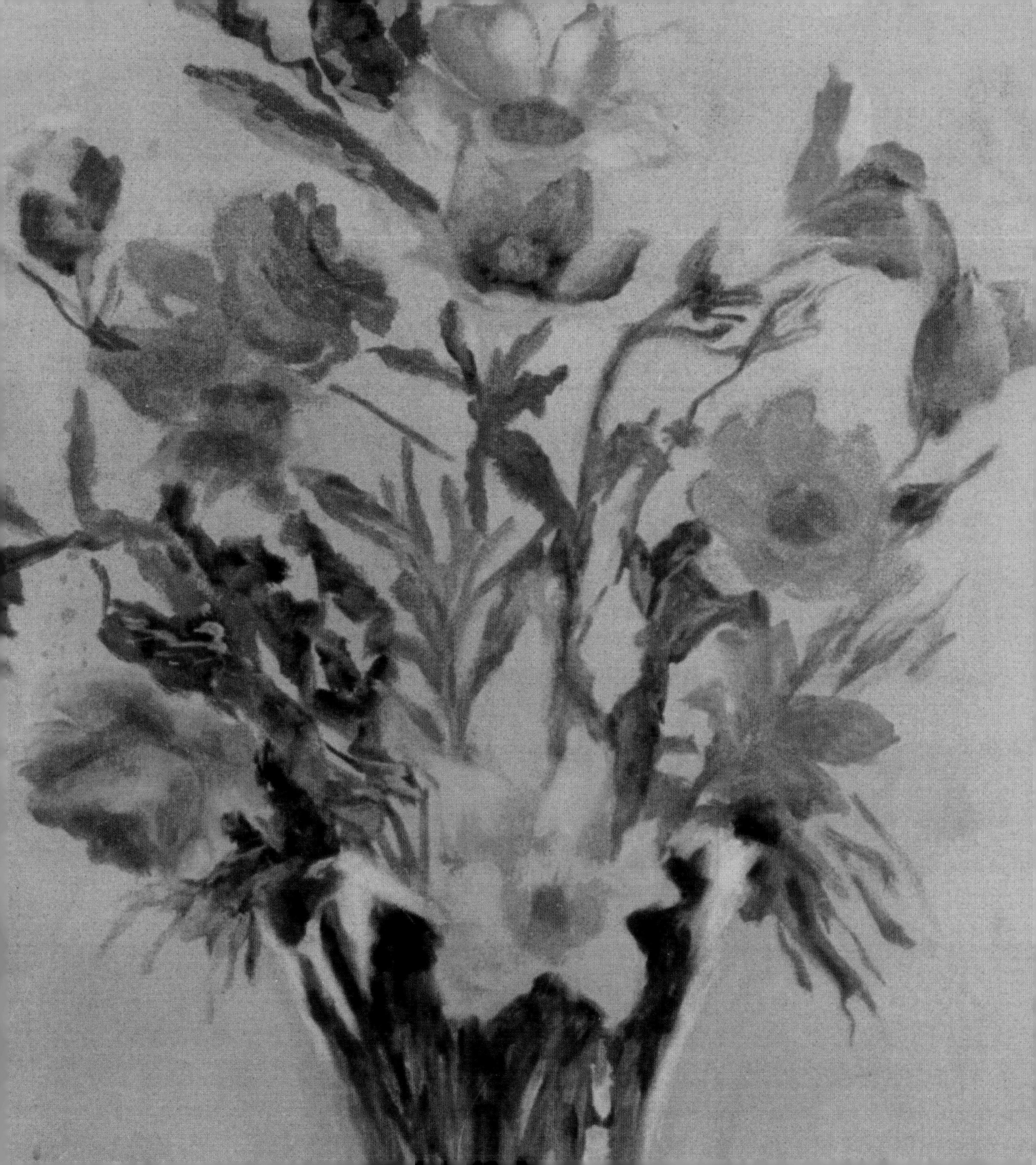

By approaching floral display upon its
diverse and infectious levels of sensation,
Jenik transfers a spirituality of existence into
an identity of color and form.

FLOWERS

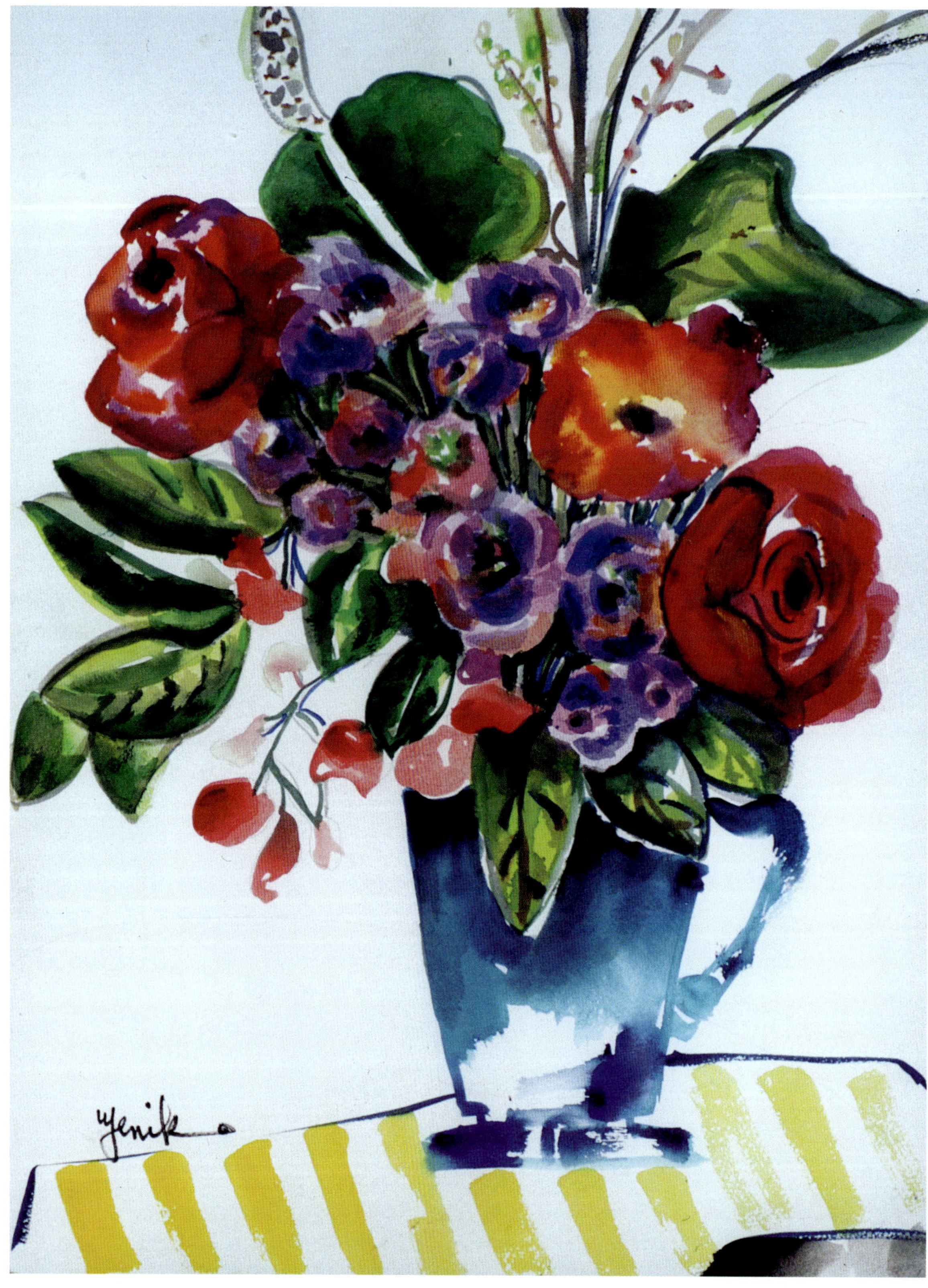

F No. 20   Watercolor   24" x 18"

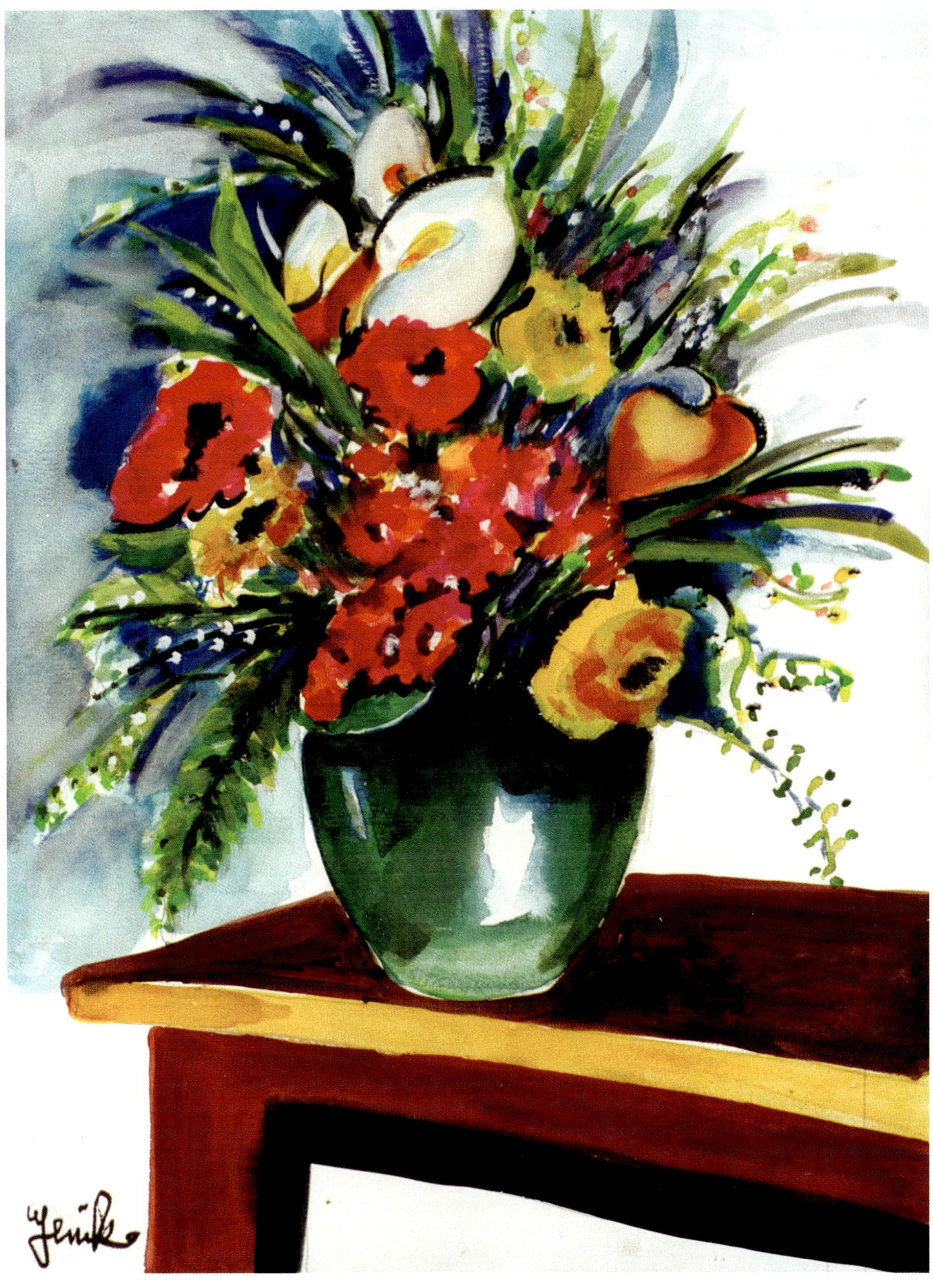

F No. 21, Watercolor, 24" x 18"

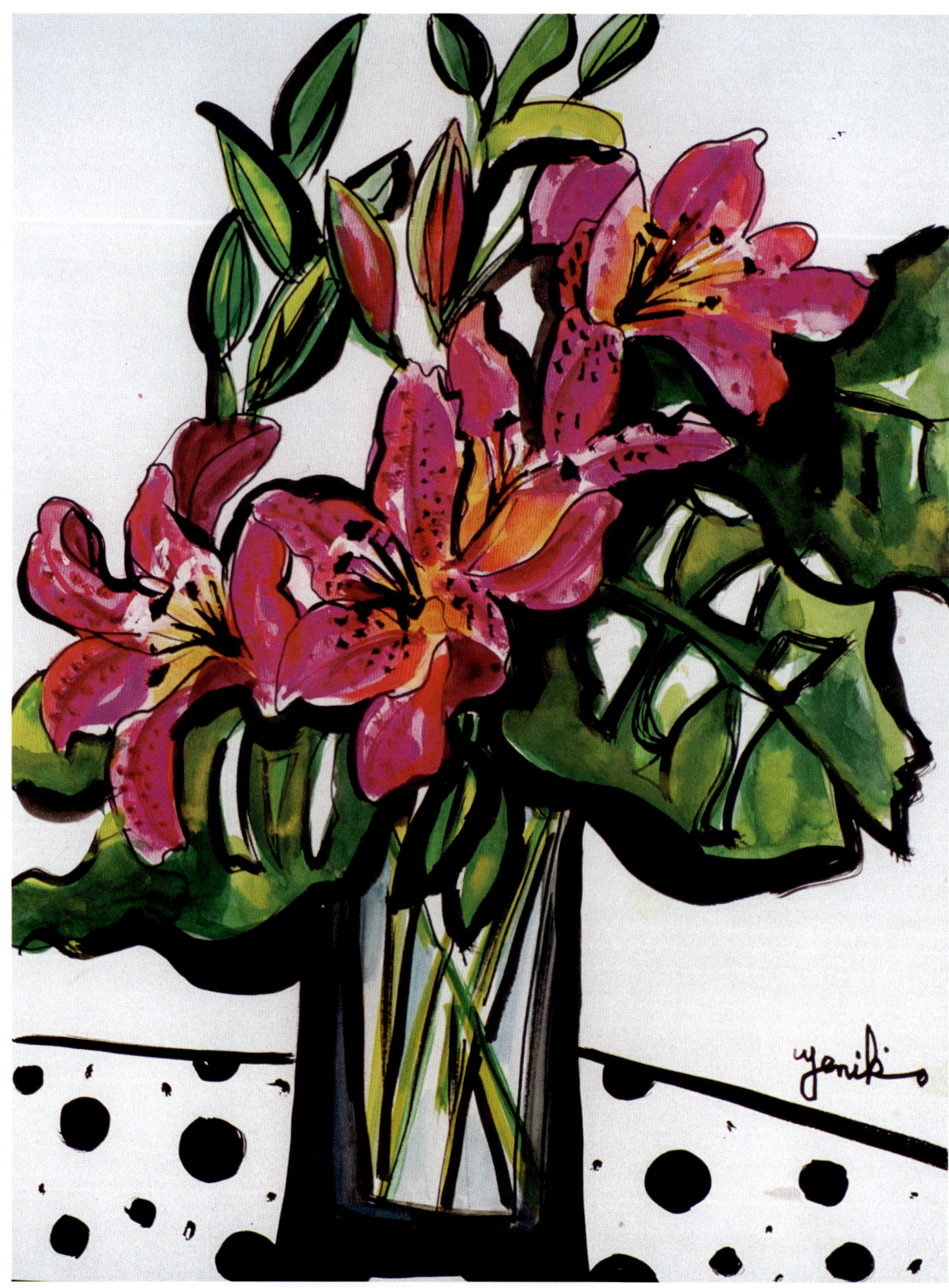

Mergenta Reds   24" x 18"

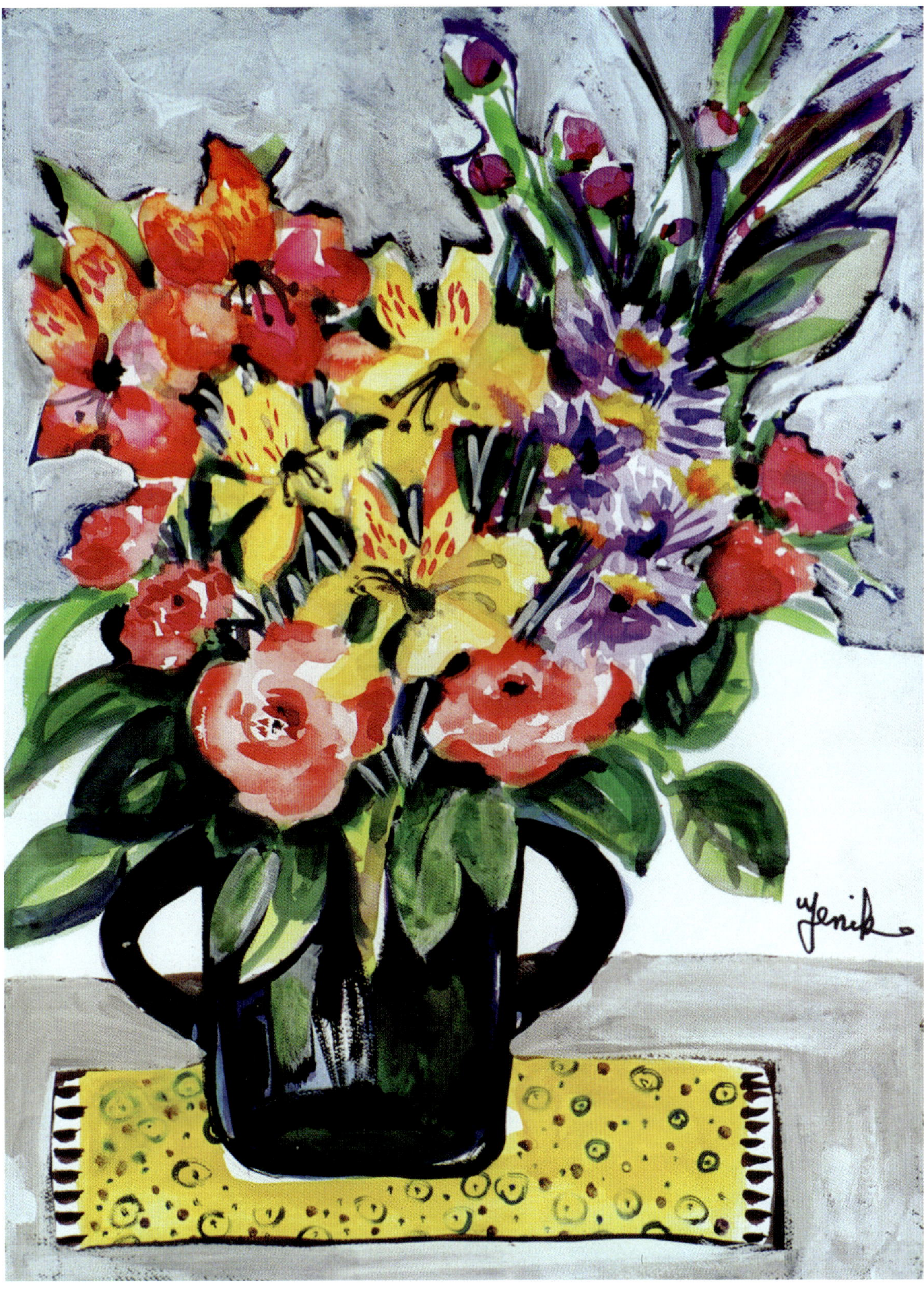

F No. 23, Watercolor, 24" x 18"

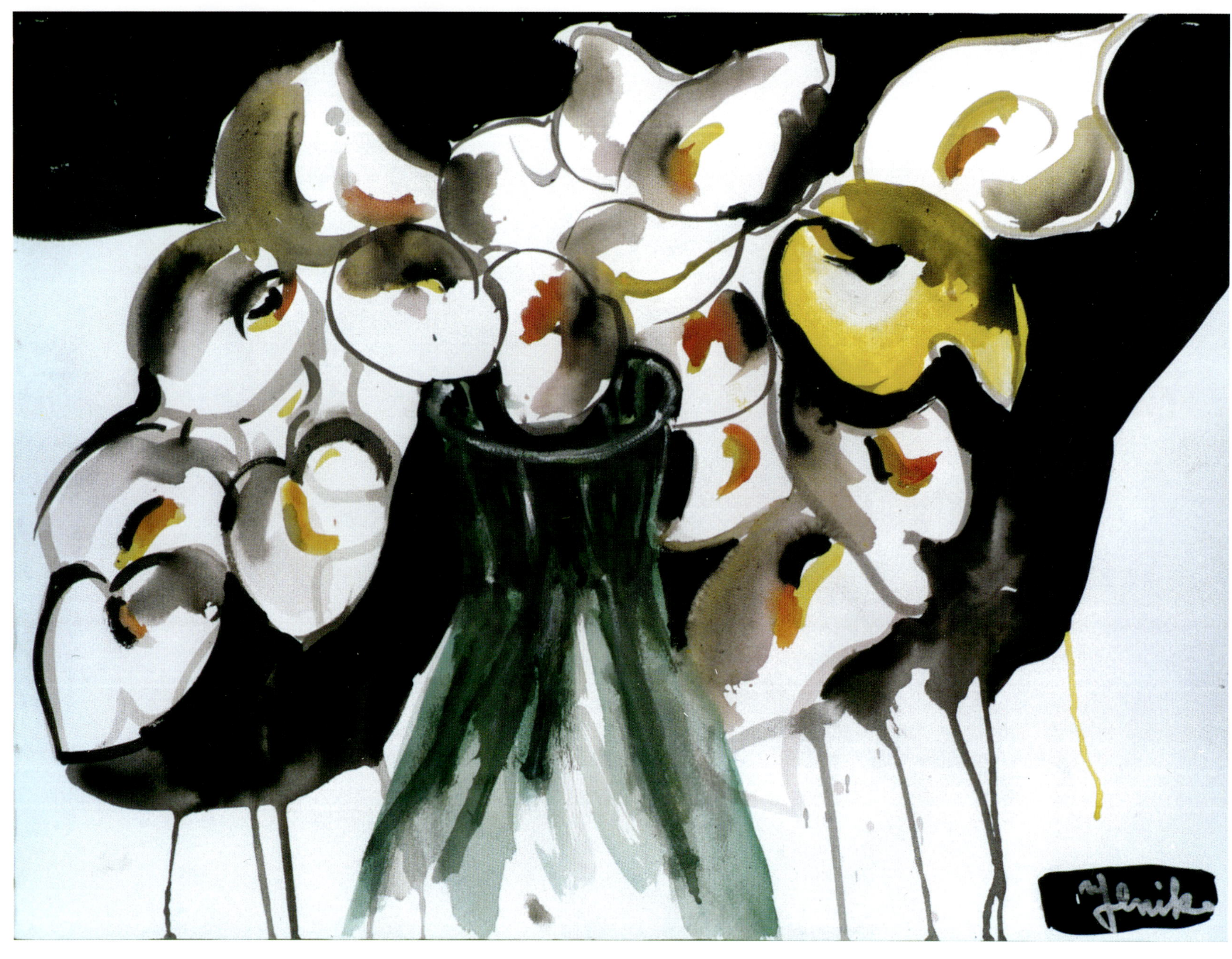

F No. 16 Watercolor 18" x 24"

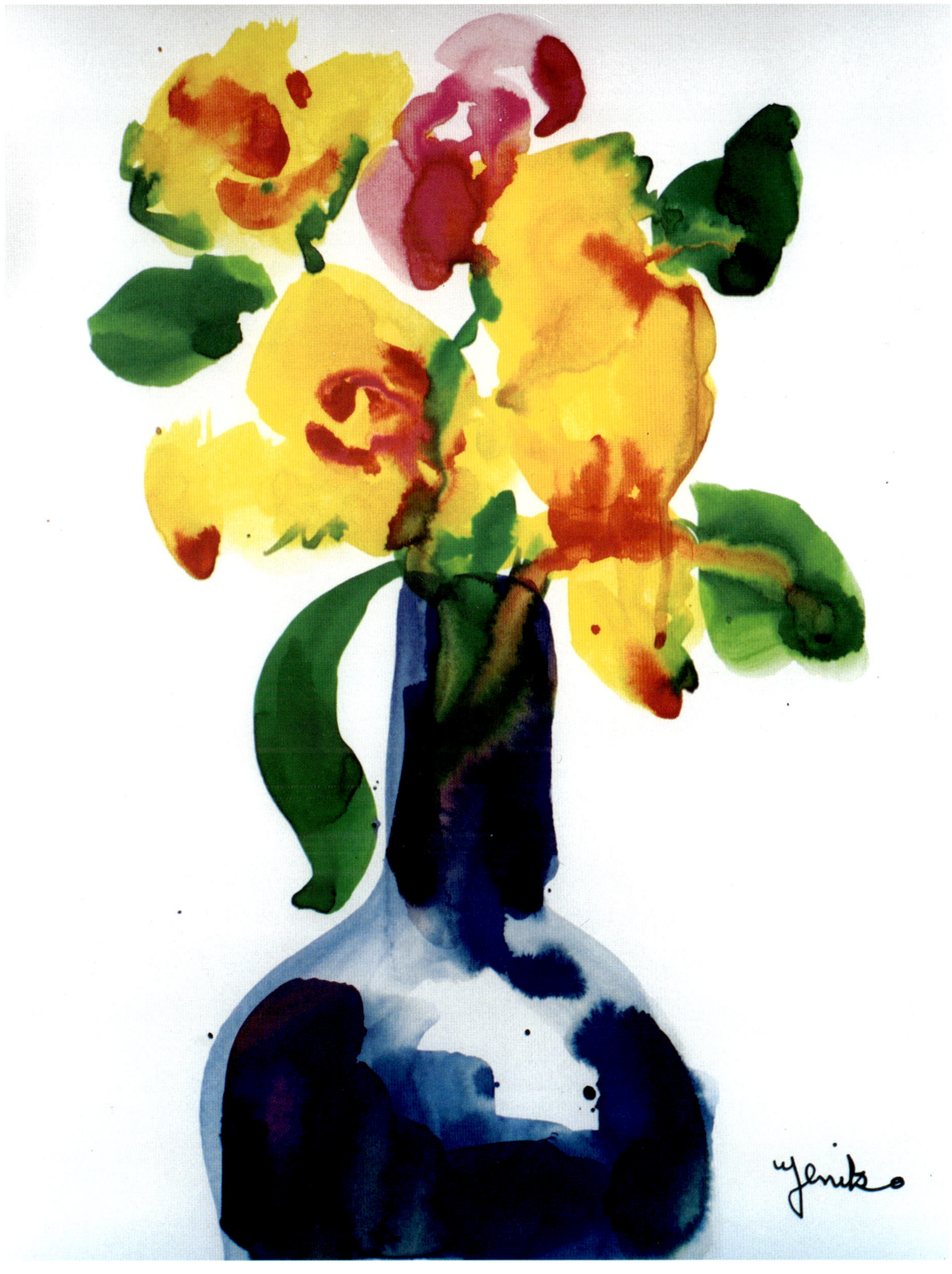

F No. 46, Watercolor, 20" x 16"

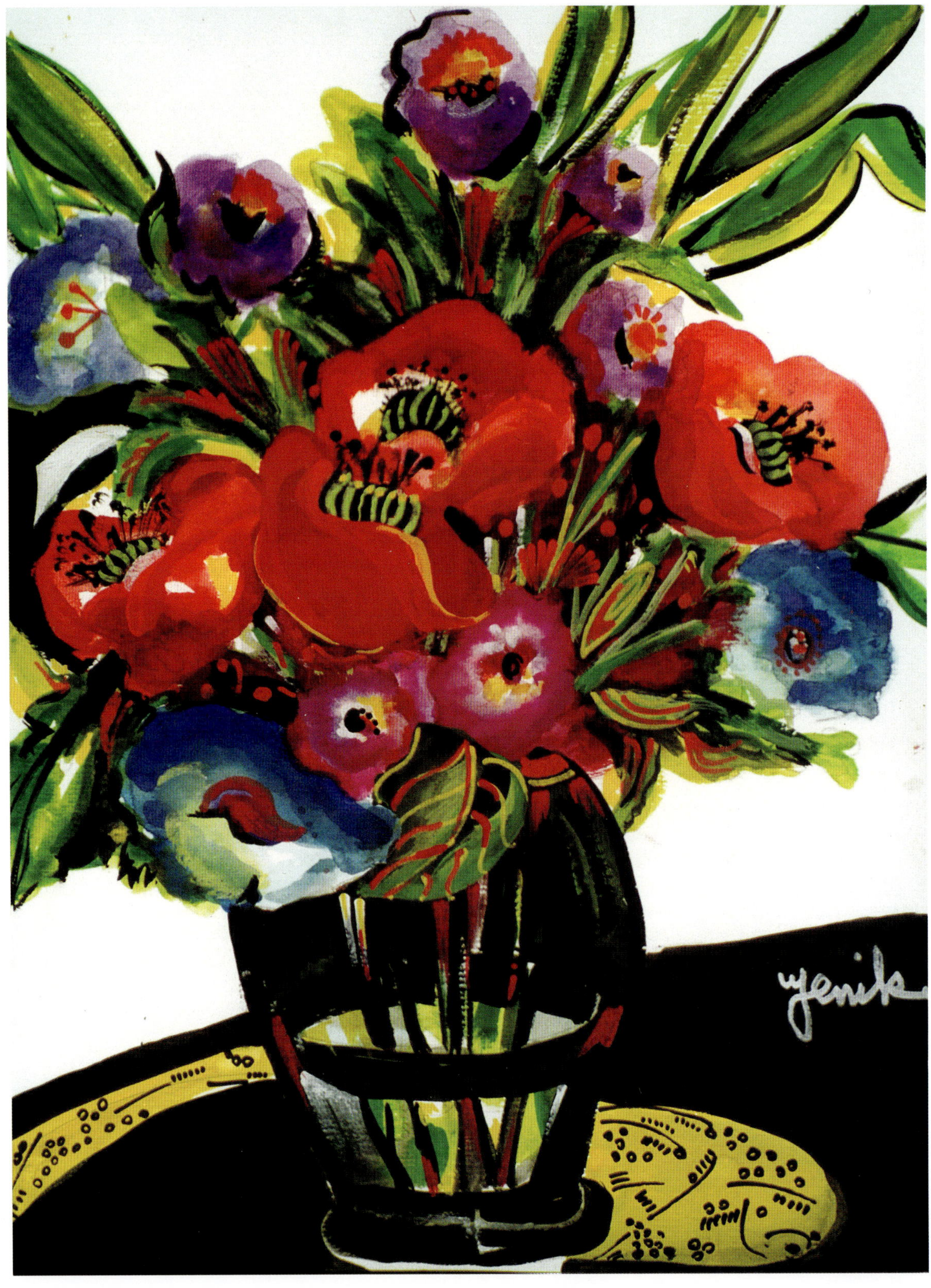

F No. 18   Watercolor   24" x 18"

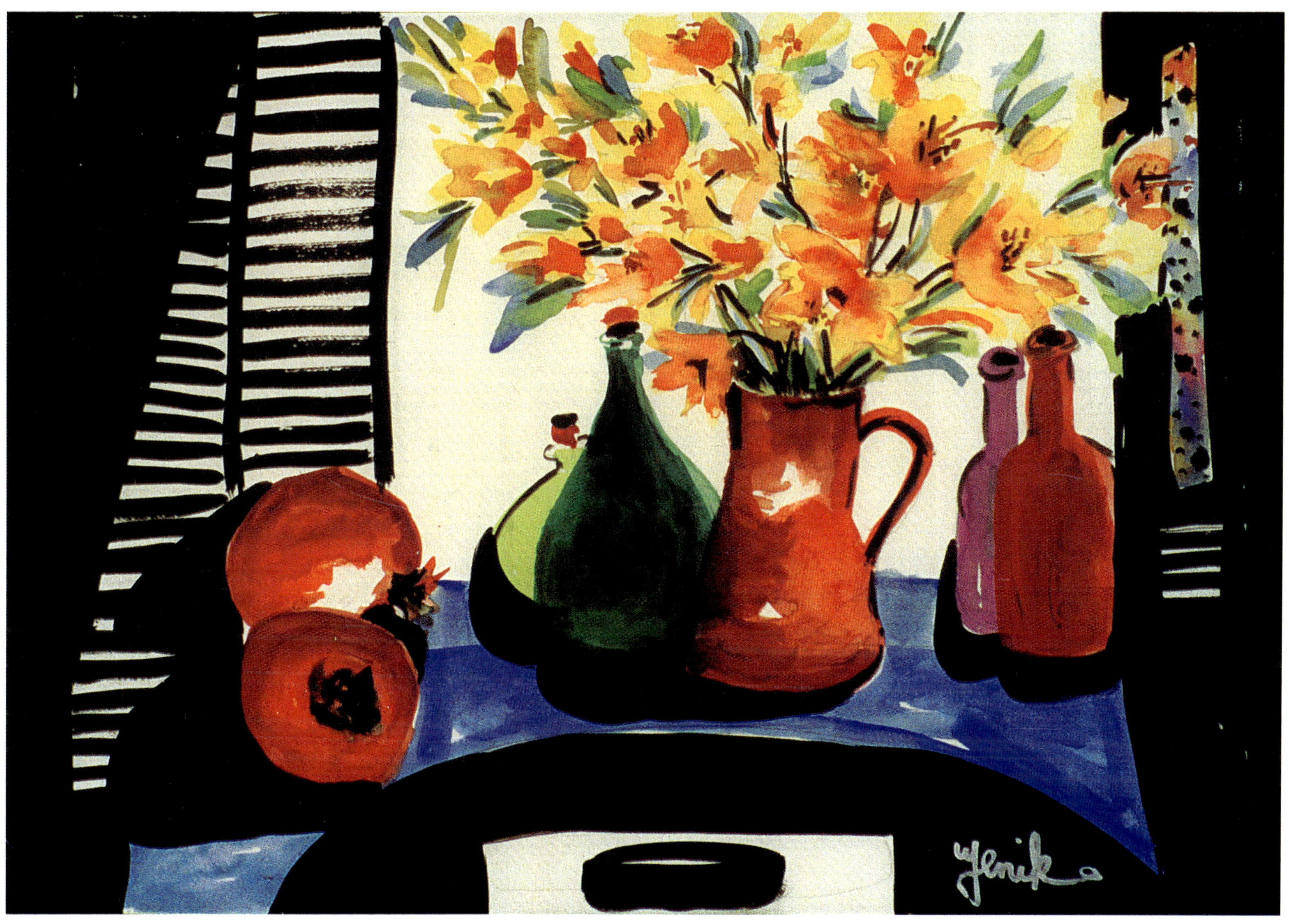

F No. 44, Watercolor, 24" x 18"

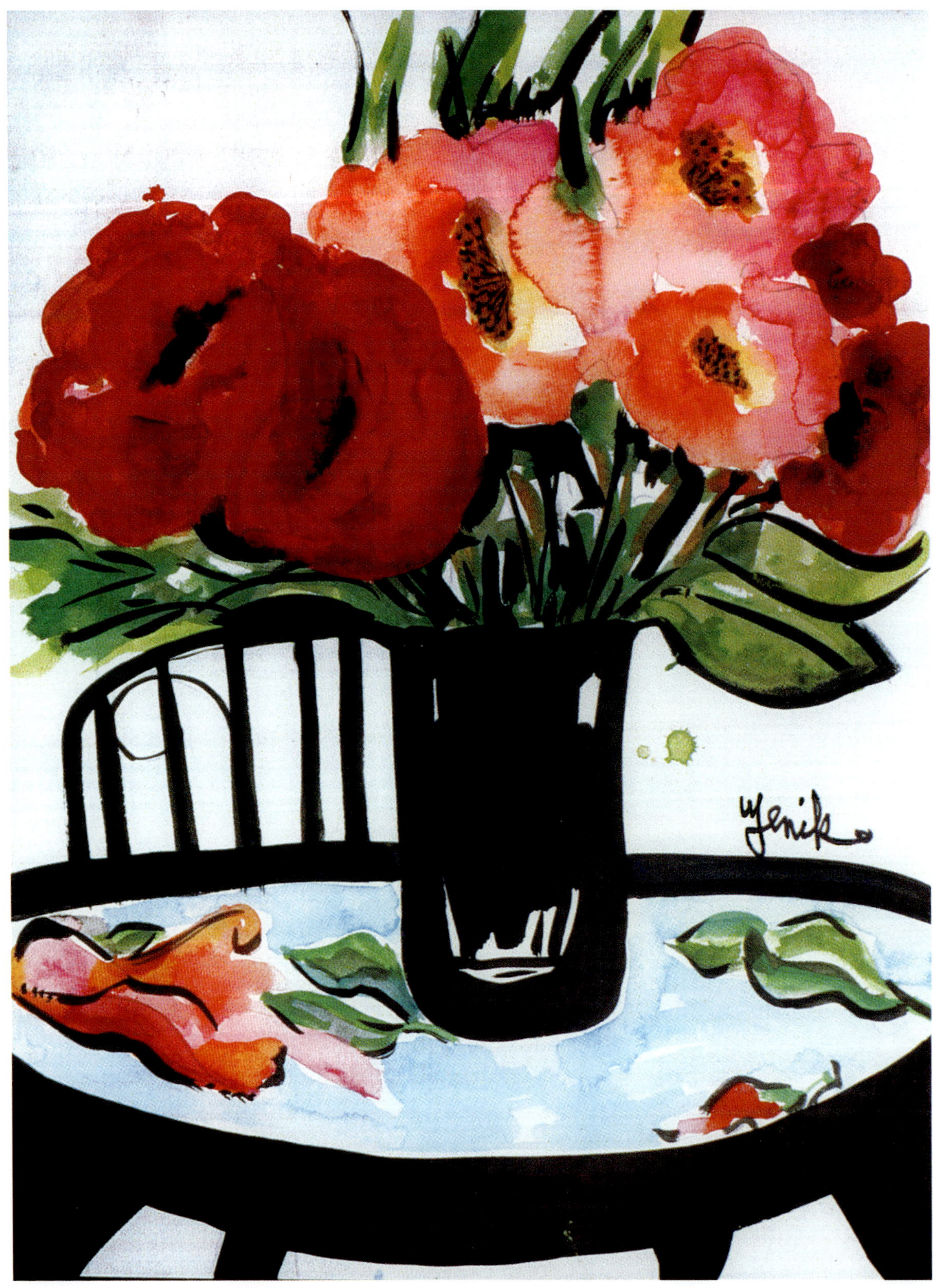

F No. 34 Watercolor 24" x 18"

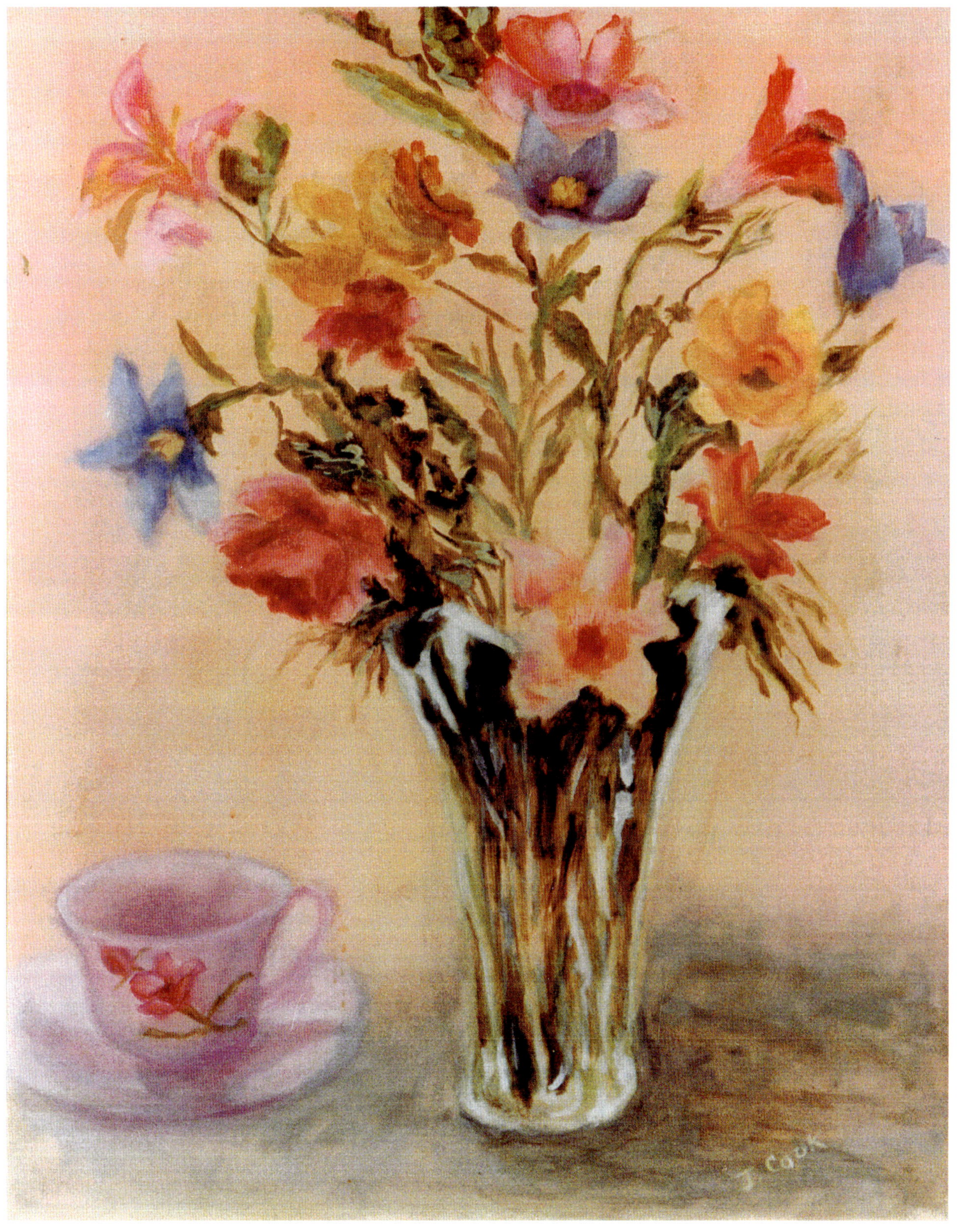

F No. 45, Oil on canvas, 30" x 24"

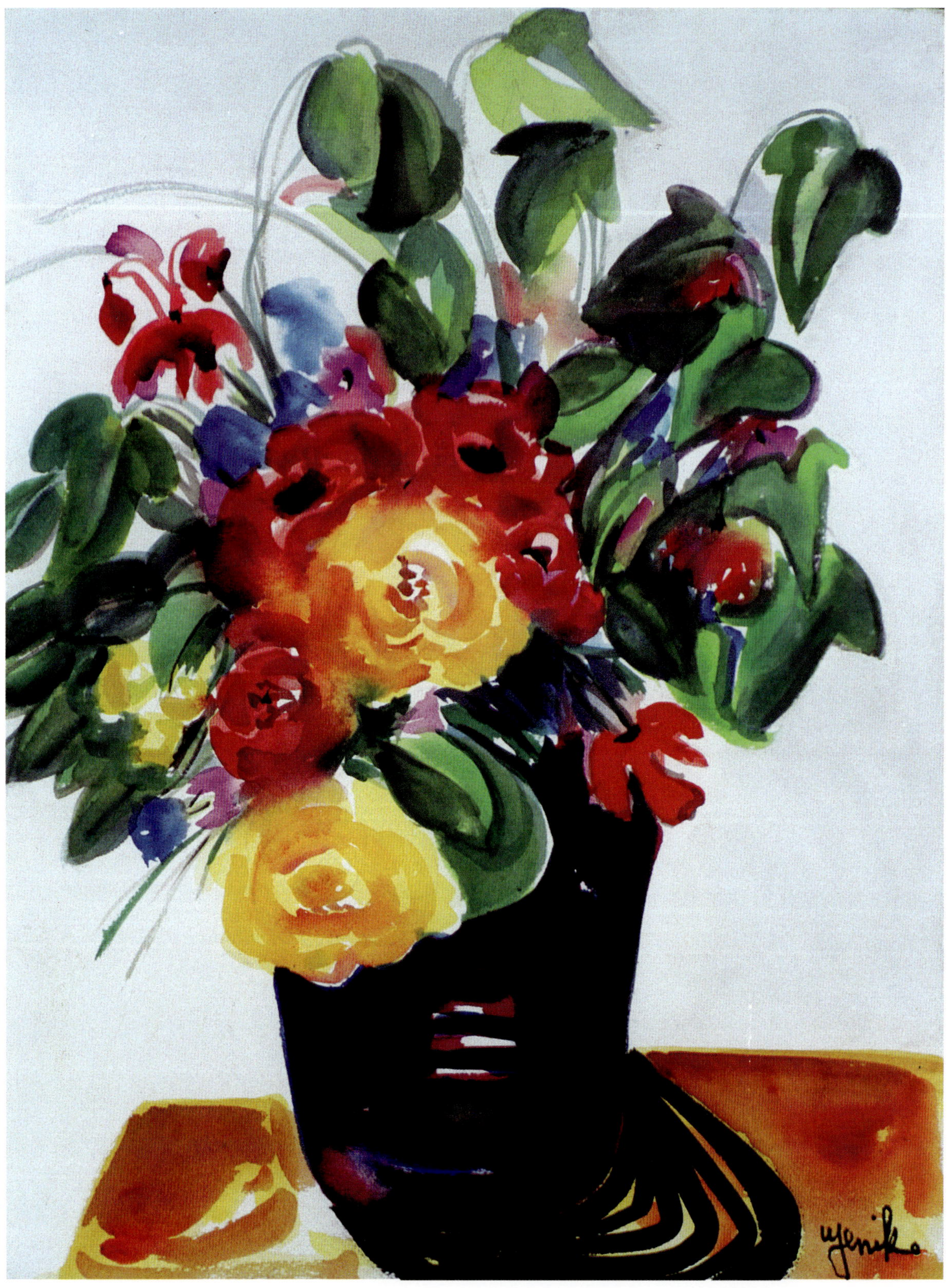

Arrengement   24" x 18"   Watercoior

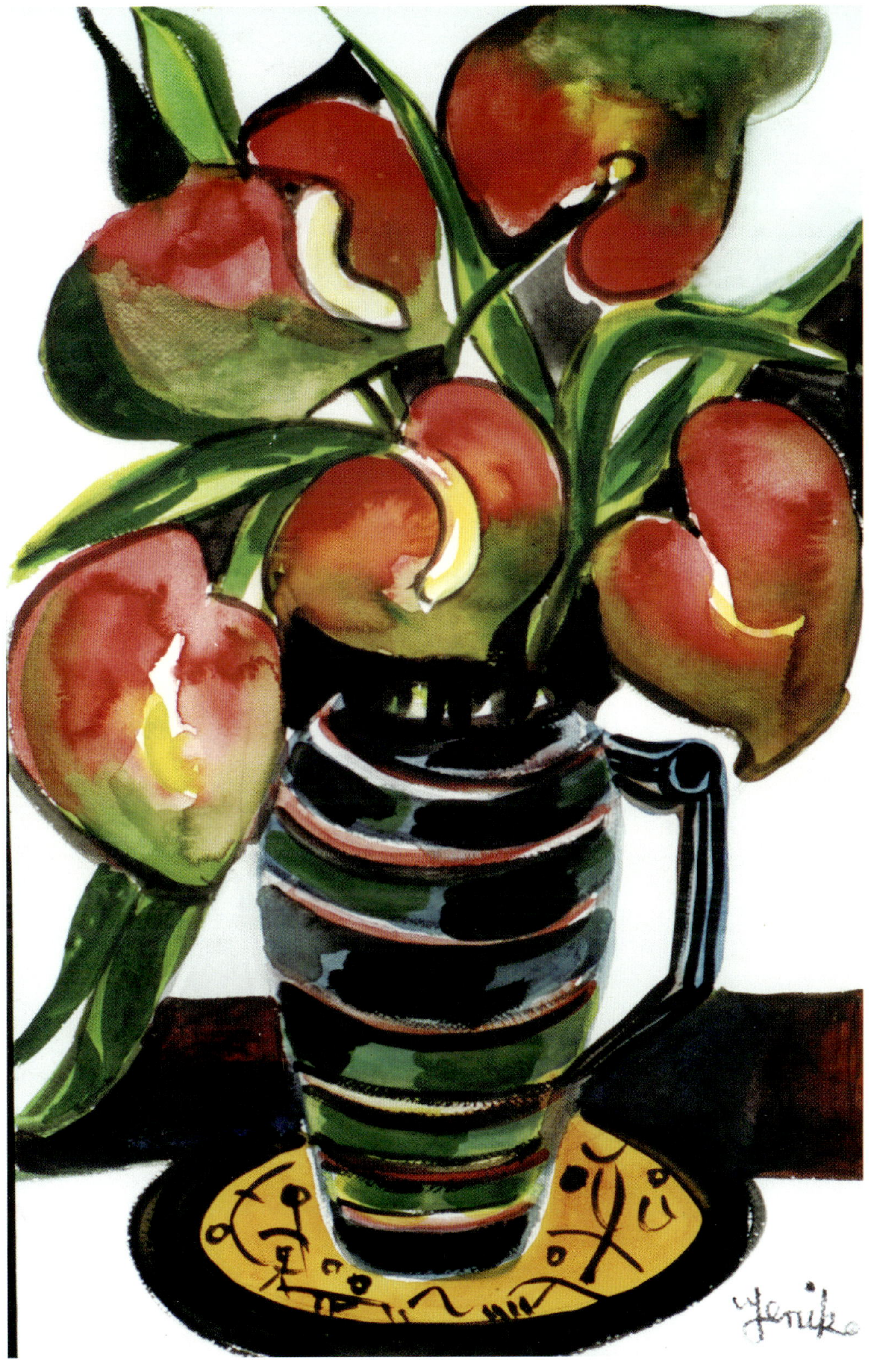

F No. 25, Watercolor, 24" x 18"

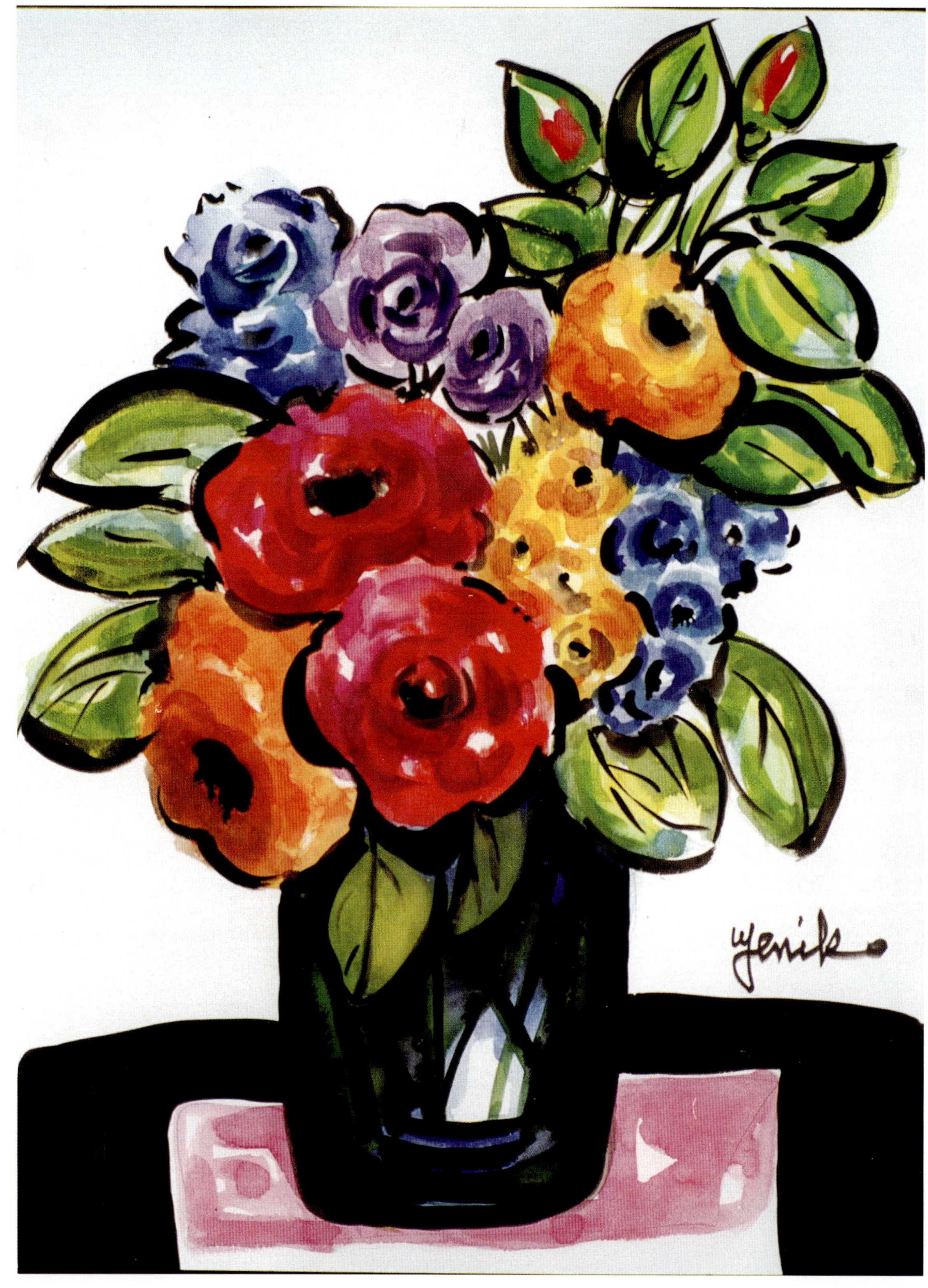

F No. 24   Watercolor   24" x 18"

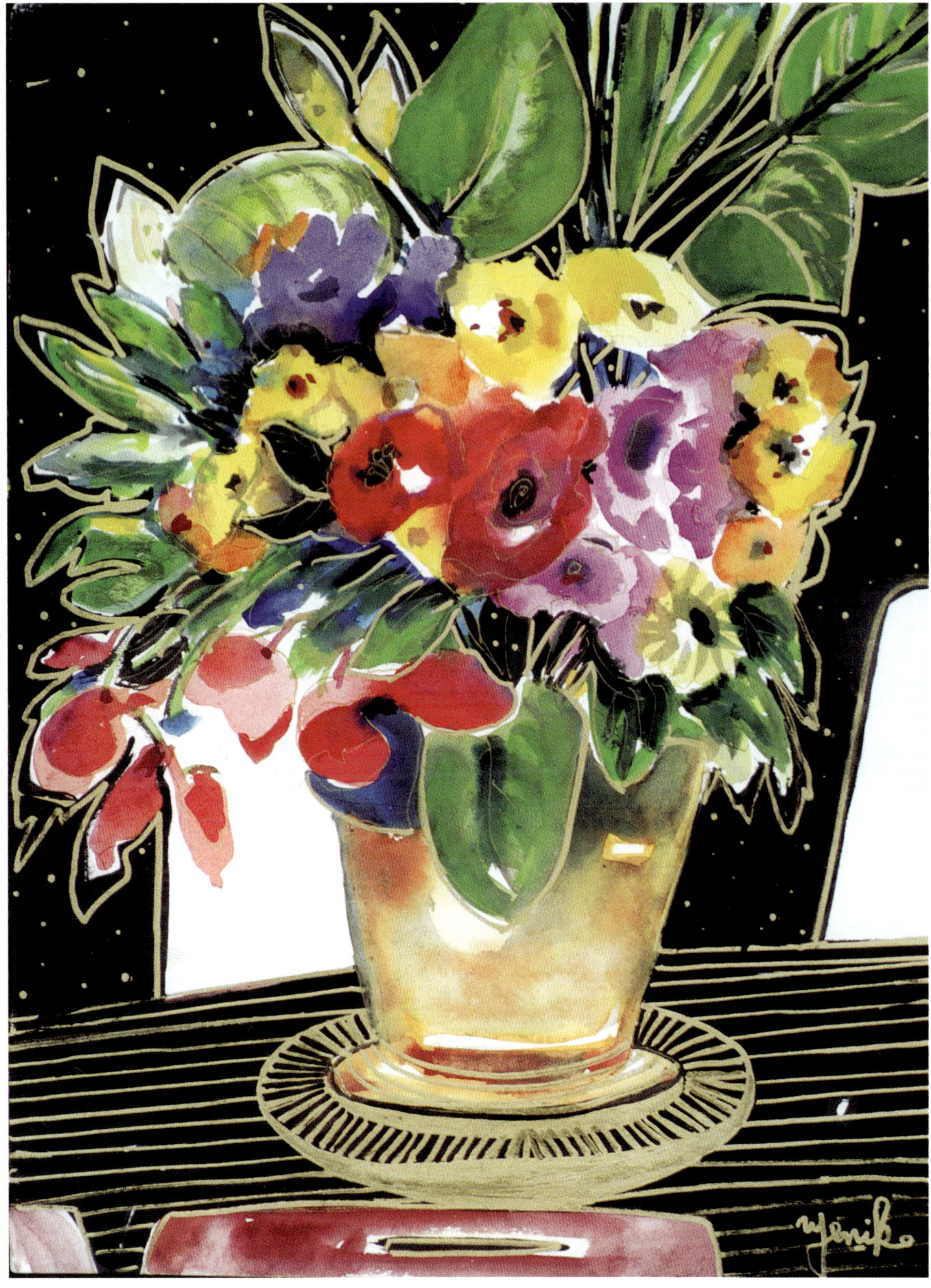

F No. 35, Watercolor, 24" x 18"

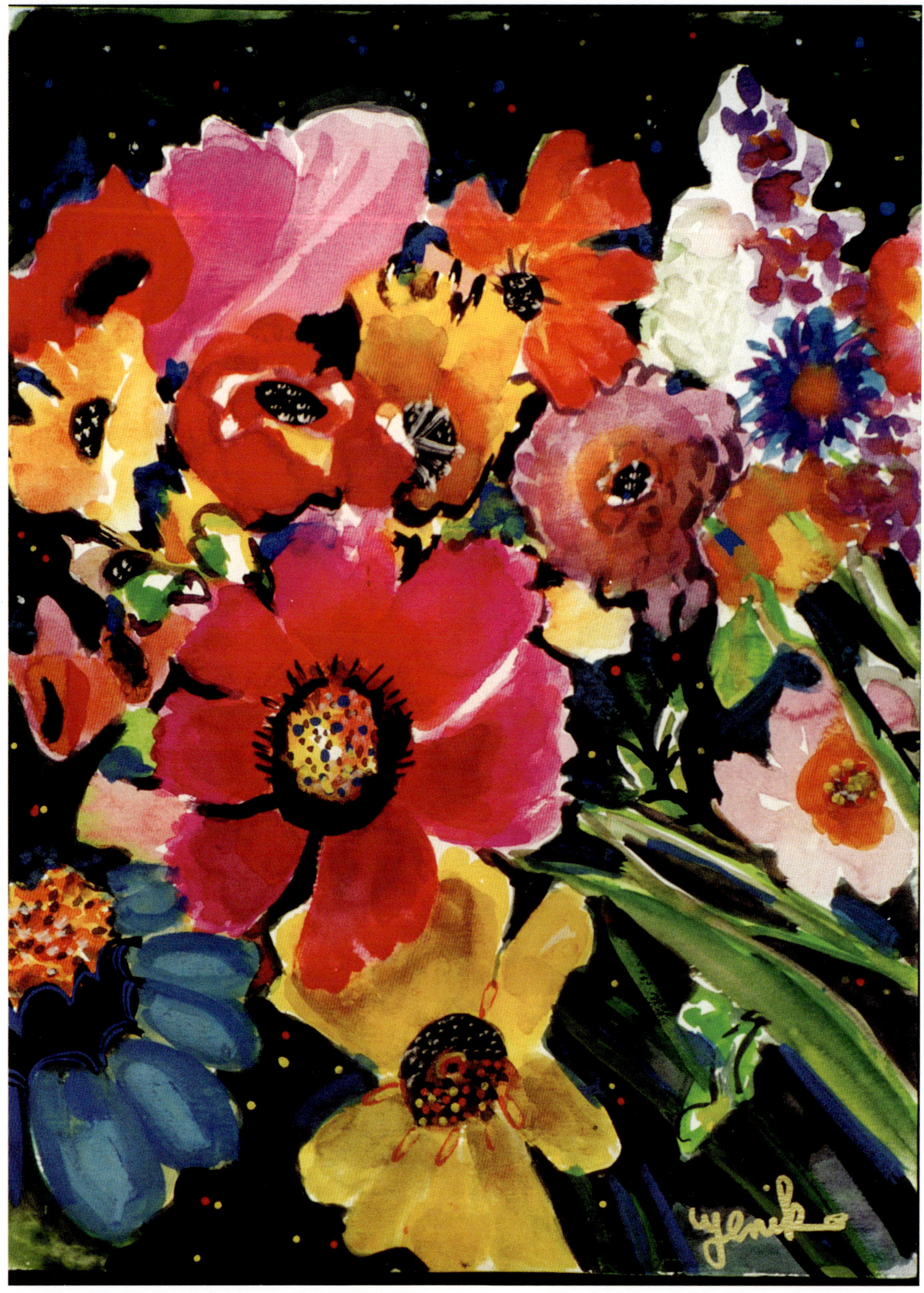

F No. 19   Watercolor   24" x 18"

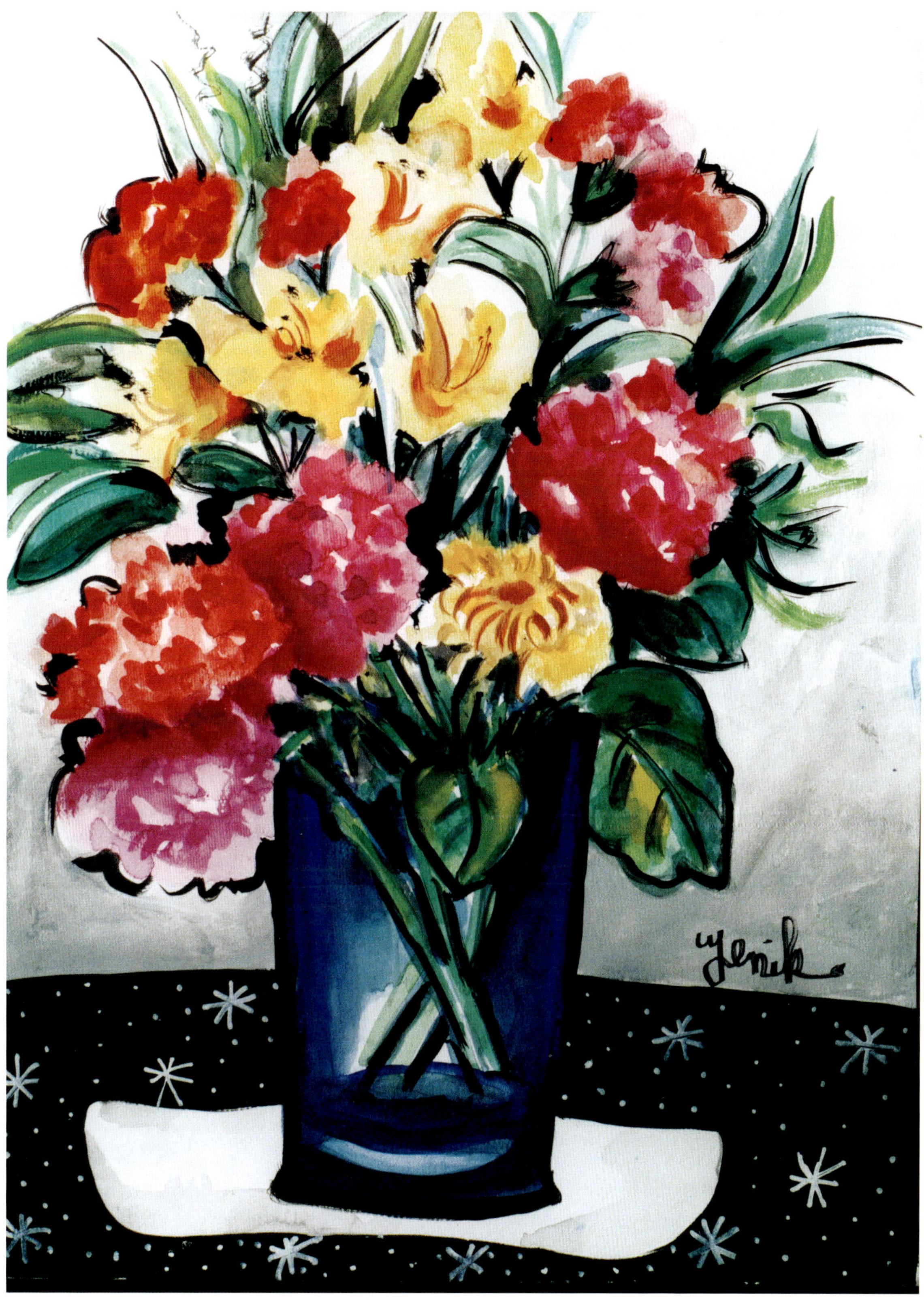

F No. 8, Watercolor, 24" x 18"

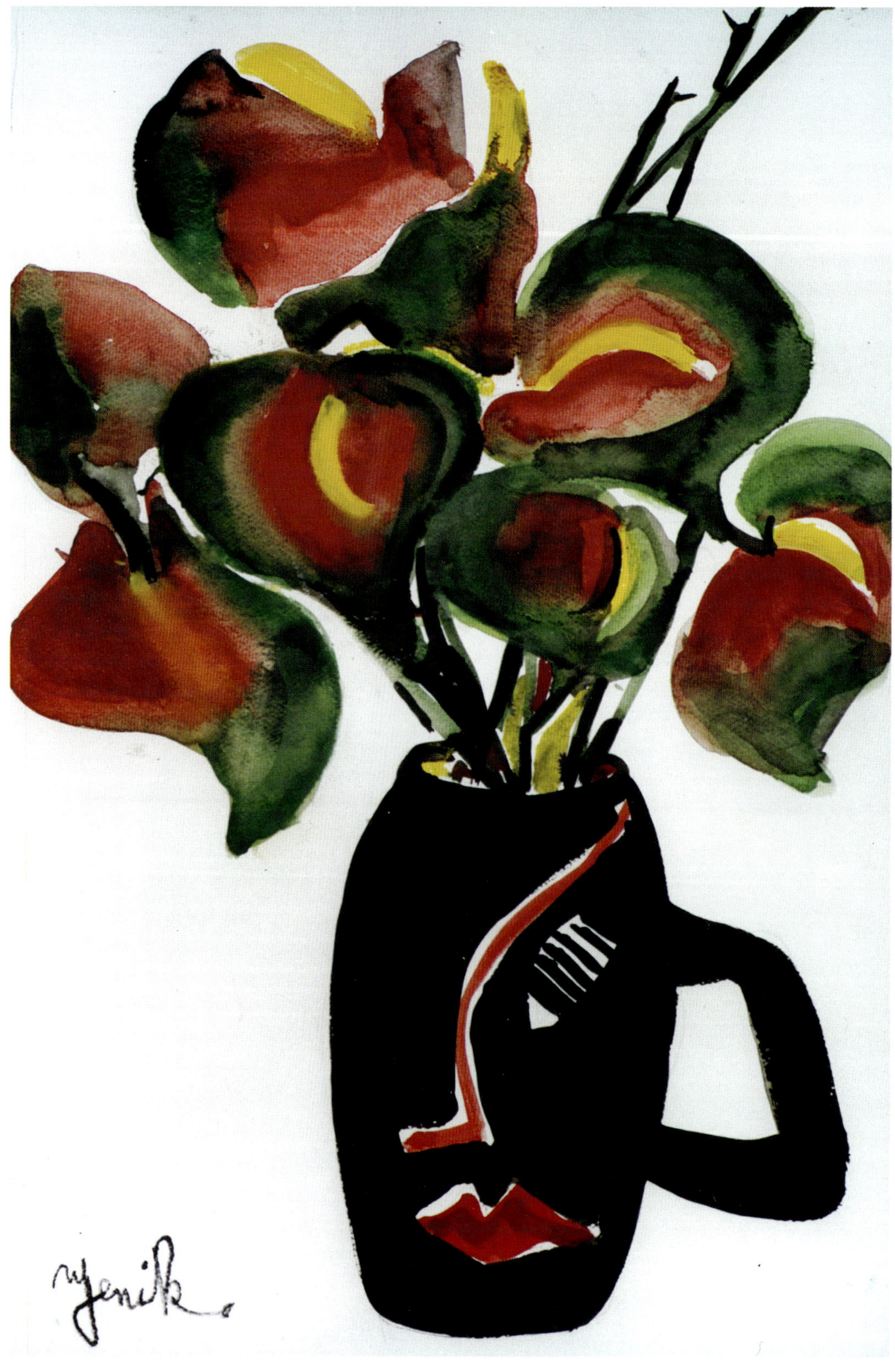

F No. 5   Watercolor   24" x 18"

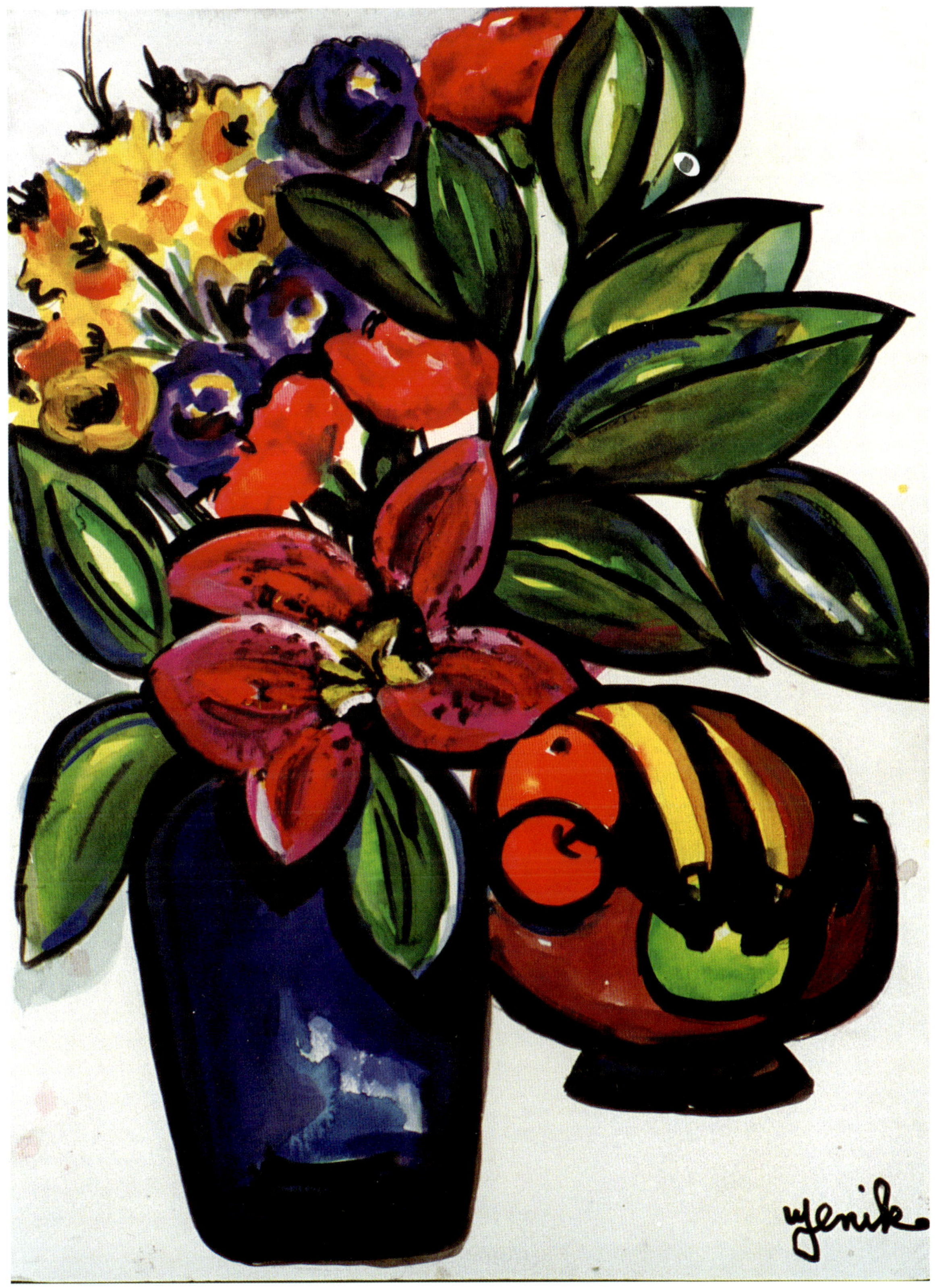

F No. 2, Watercolor, 18" x 24"

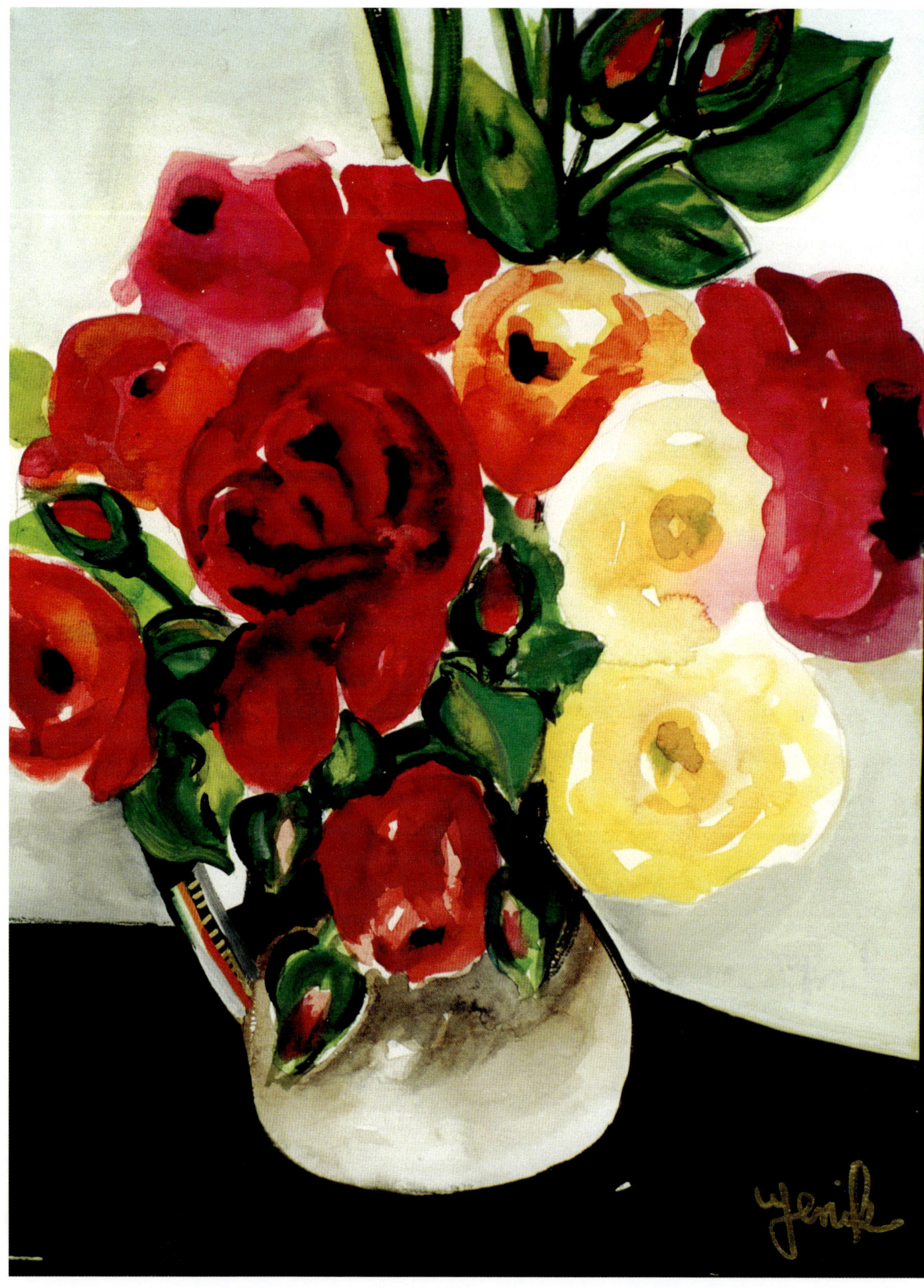

Roses Are   24" x 18"

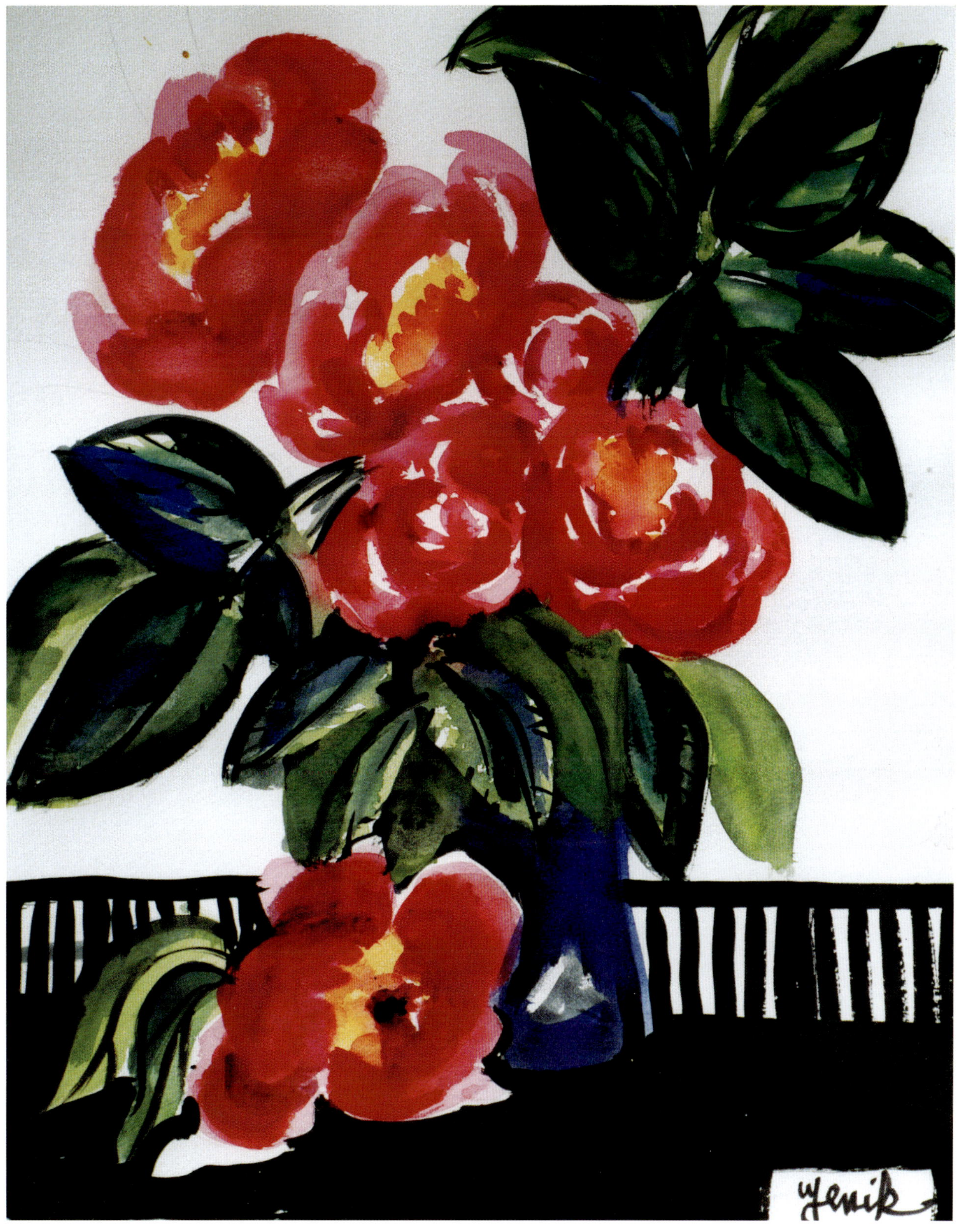

F No. 29, Watercolor, 24" x 18"

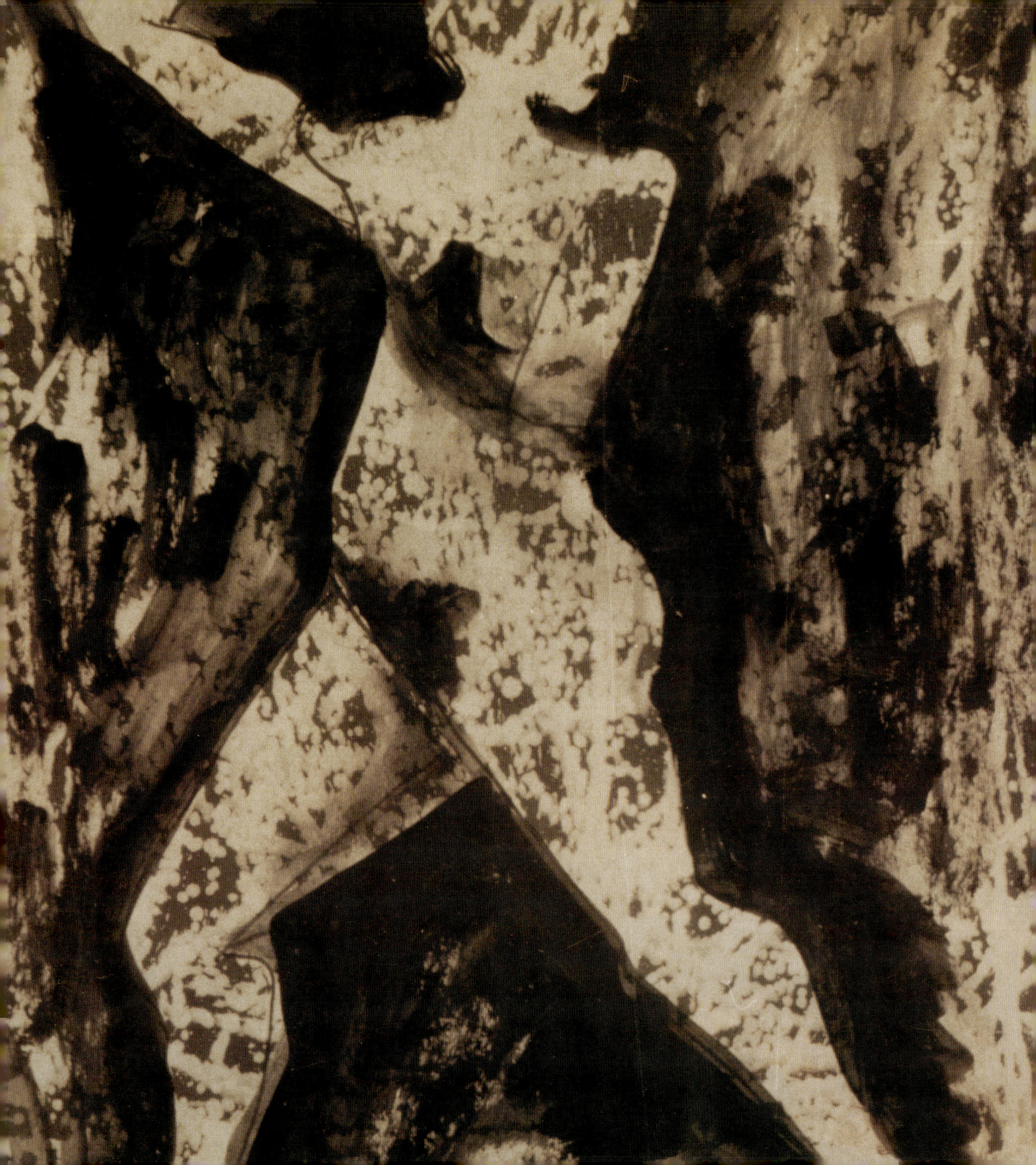

Although essentially figurative by nature, the smudged categorical boundaries of a certain plurality of Jenik's paintings venture by varying degrees into terrains of Objective Expressionism.

Expressive Figuration

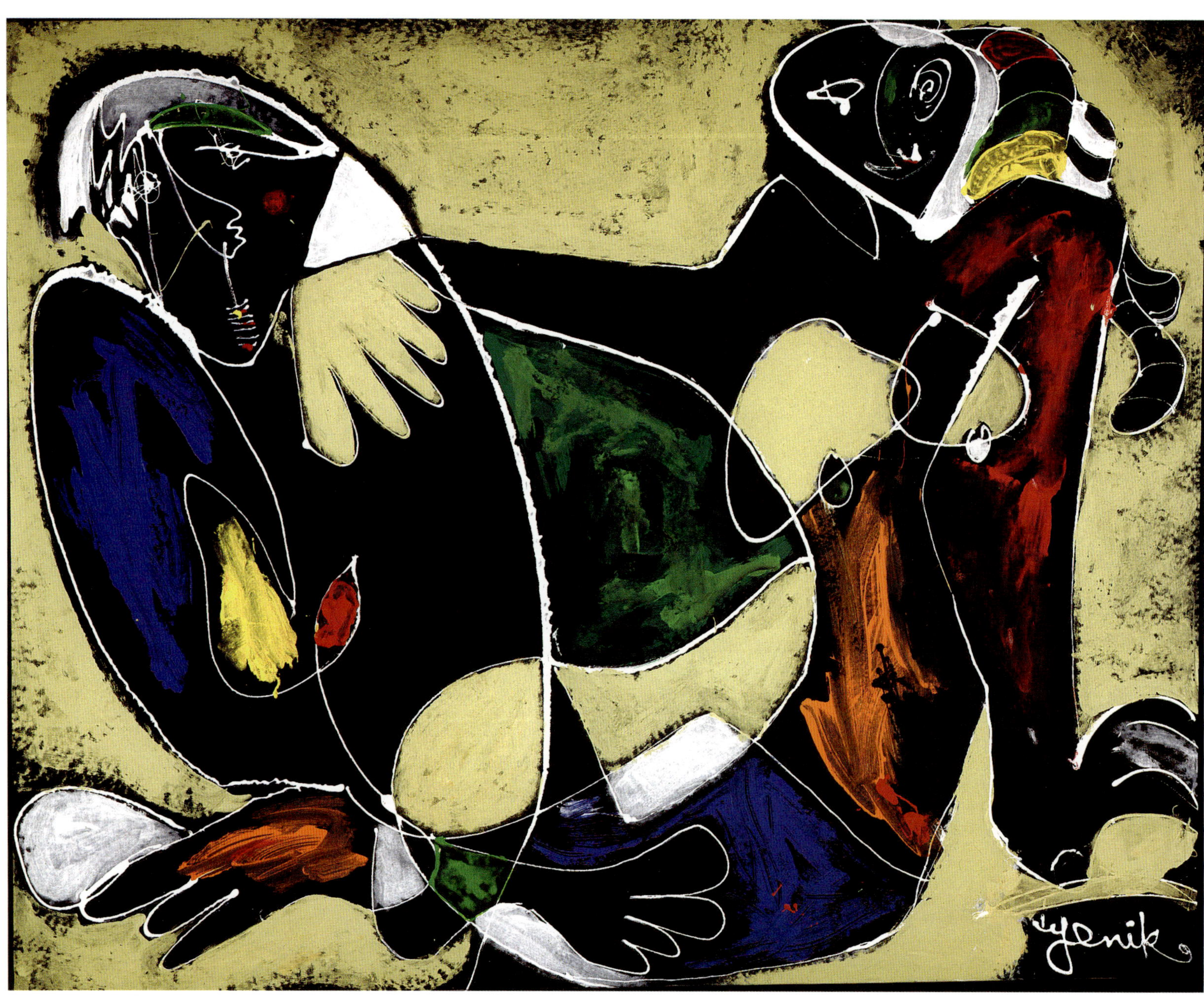

Inseparable Acrylic   54" x 74"

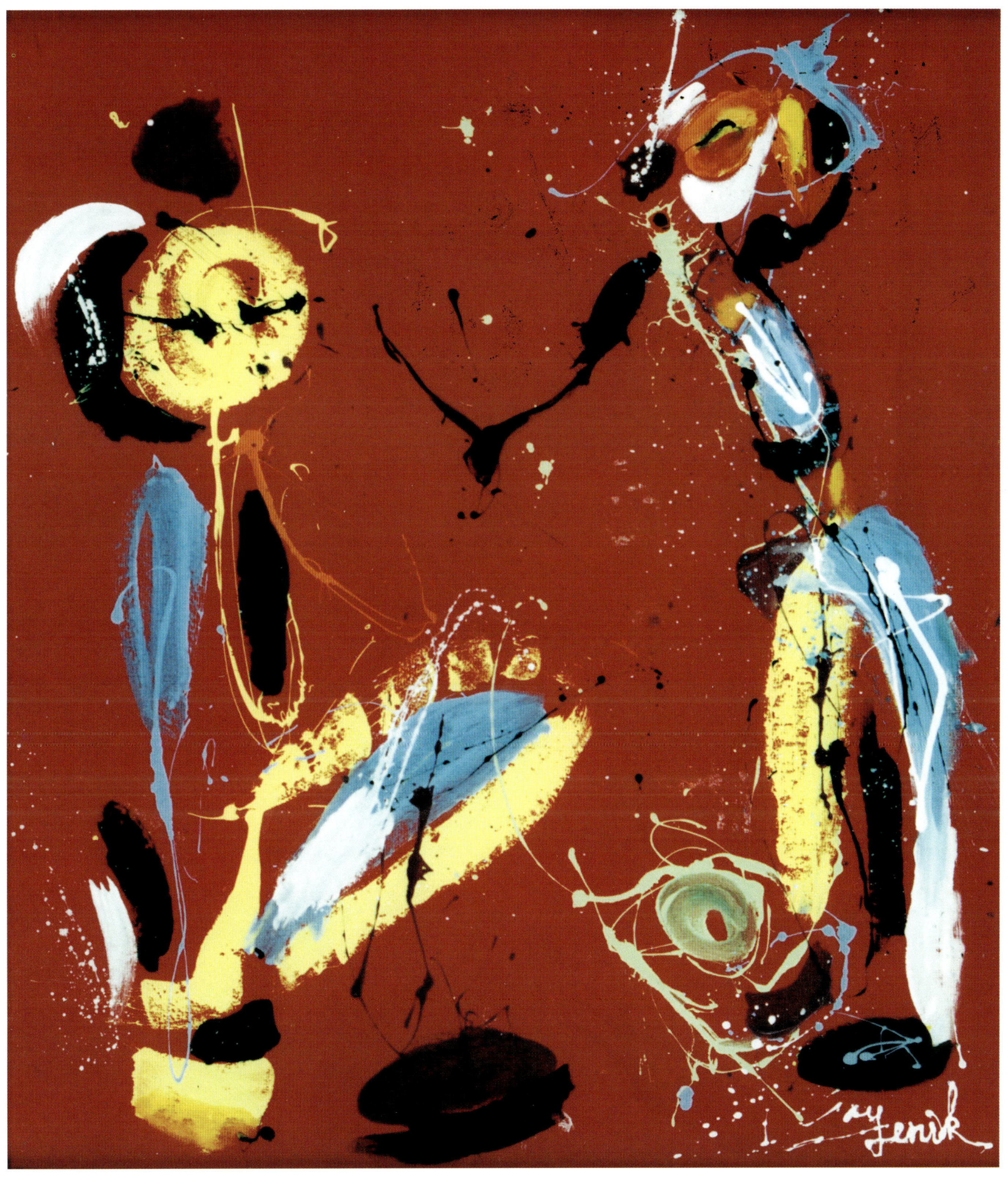

Bonjour   Acrylicon silk   58" x 54"

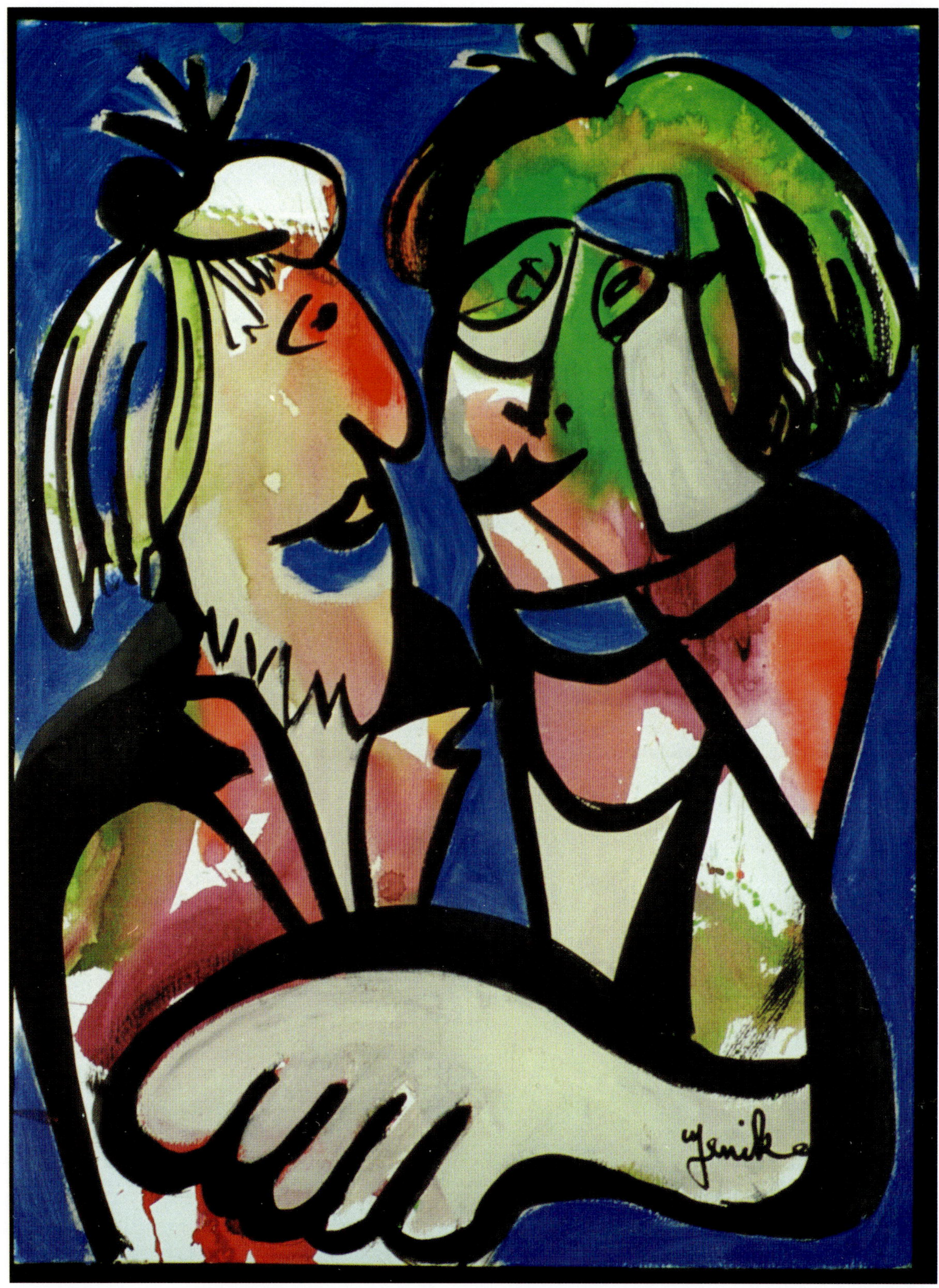

Reaching Out   24" x 18"

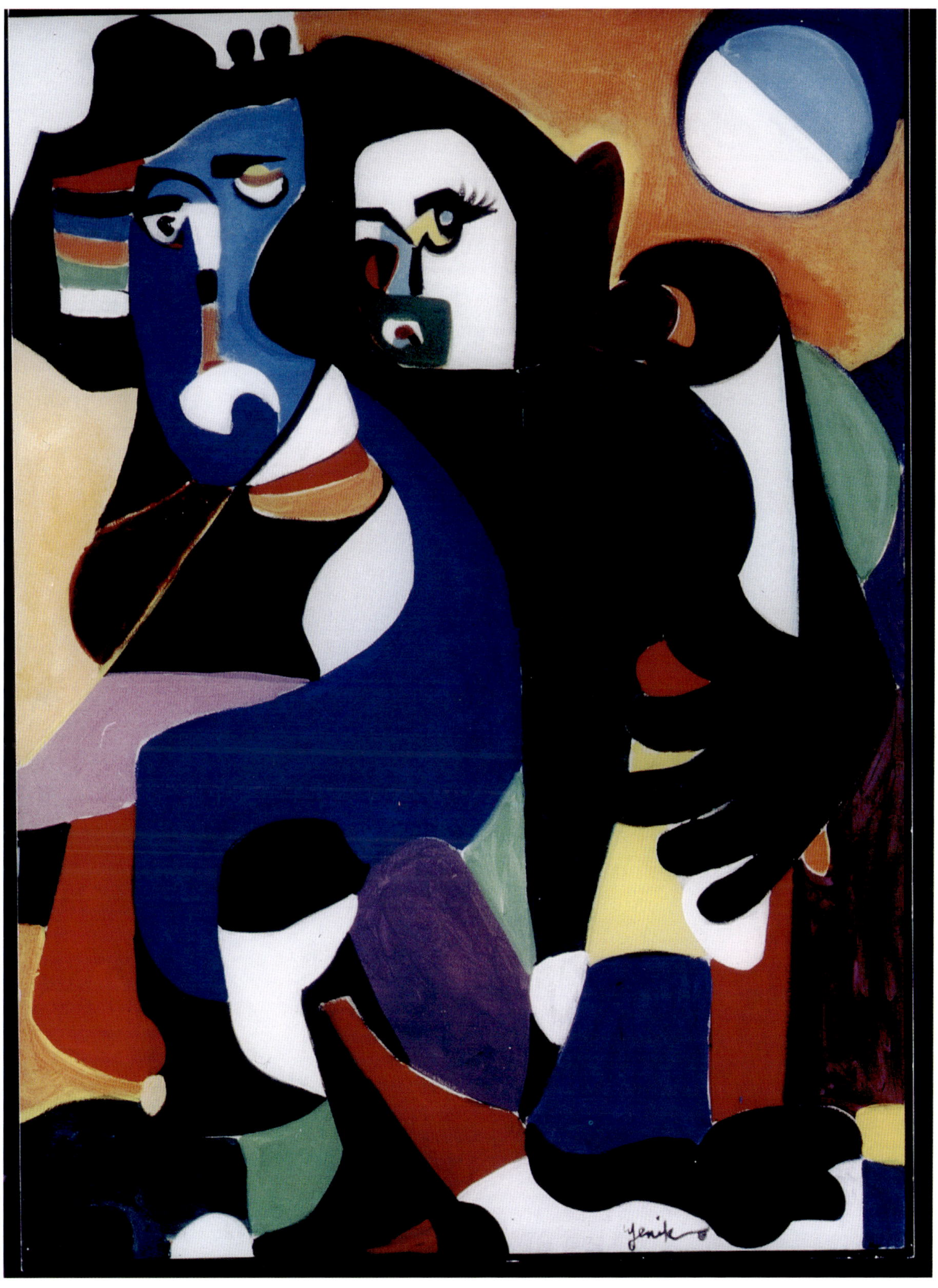

Supportive 46" x 38"

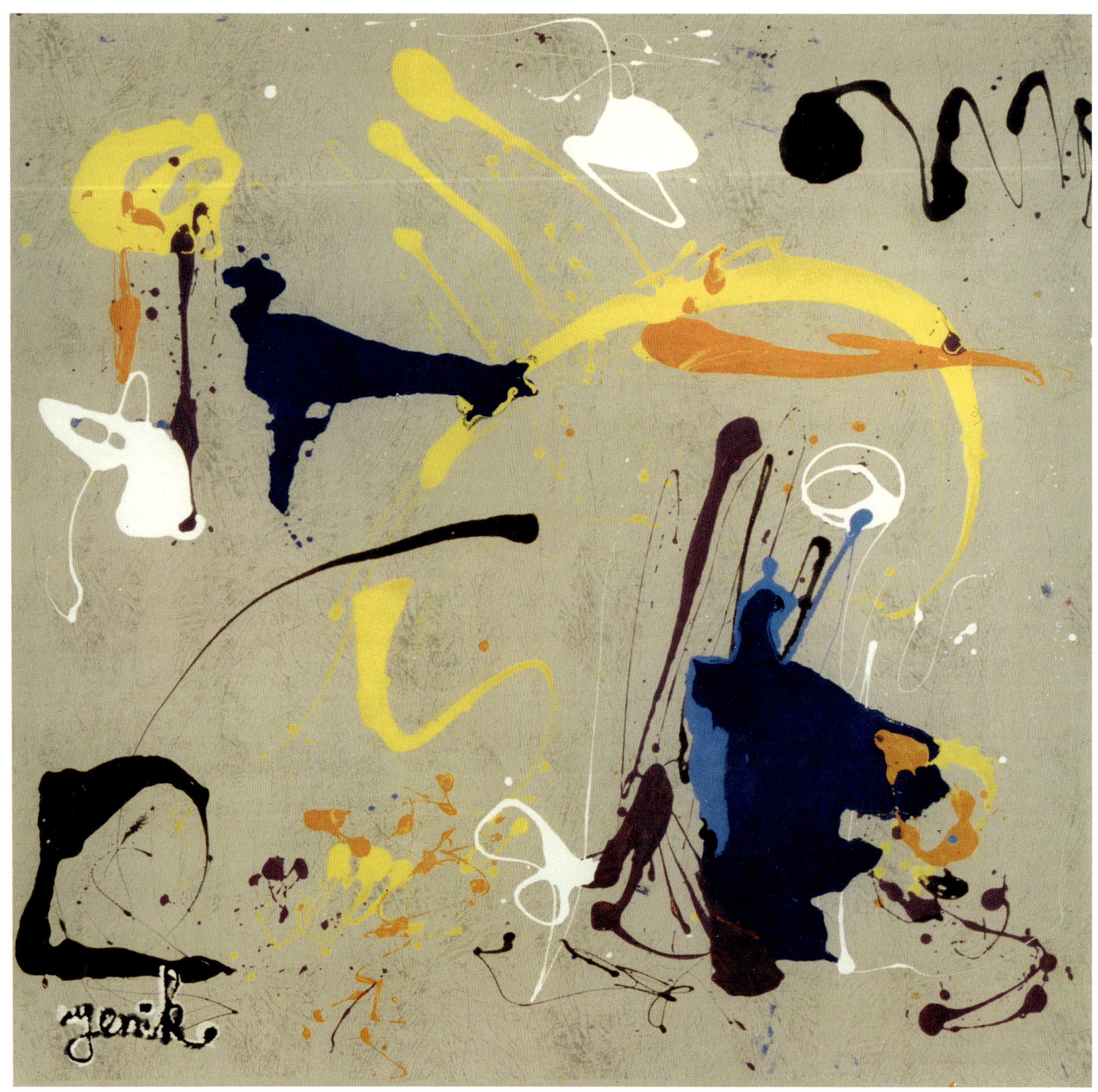

Untitled No 67   Acrylic   48" x 52"

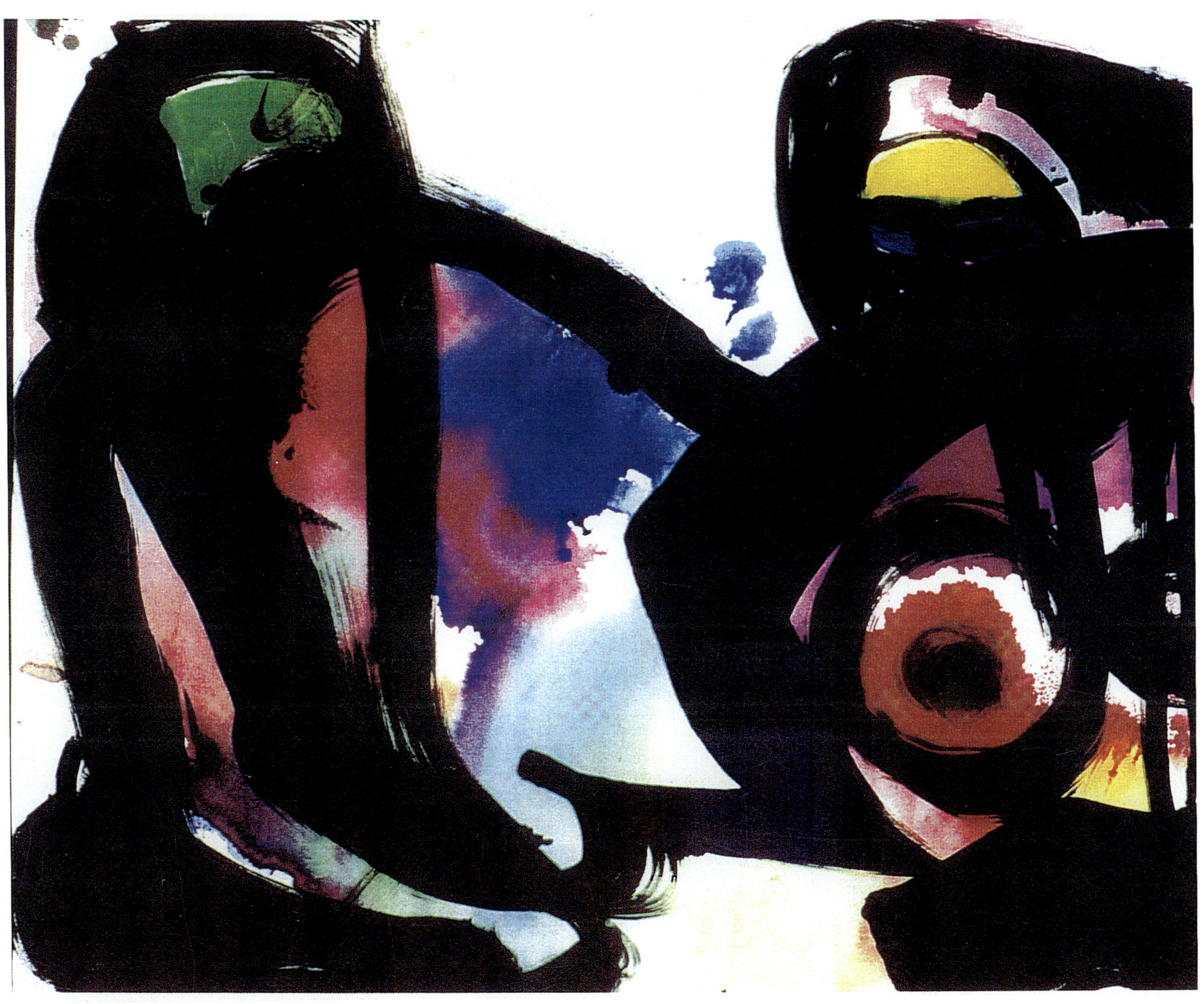

Reclined   18" x 24"

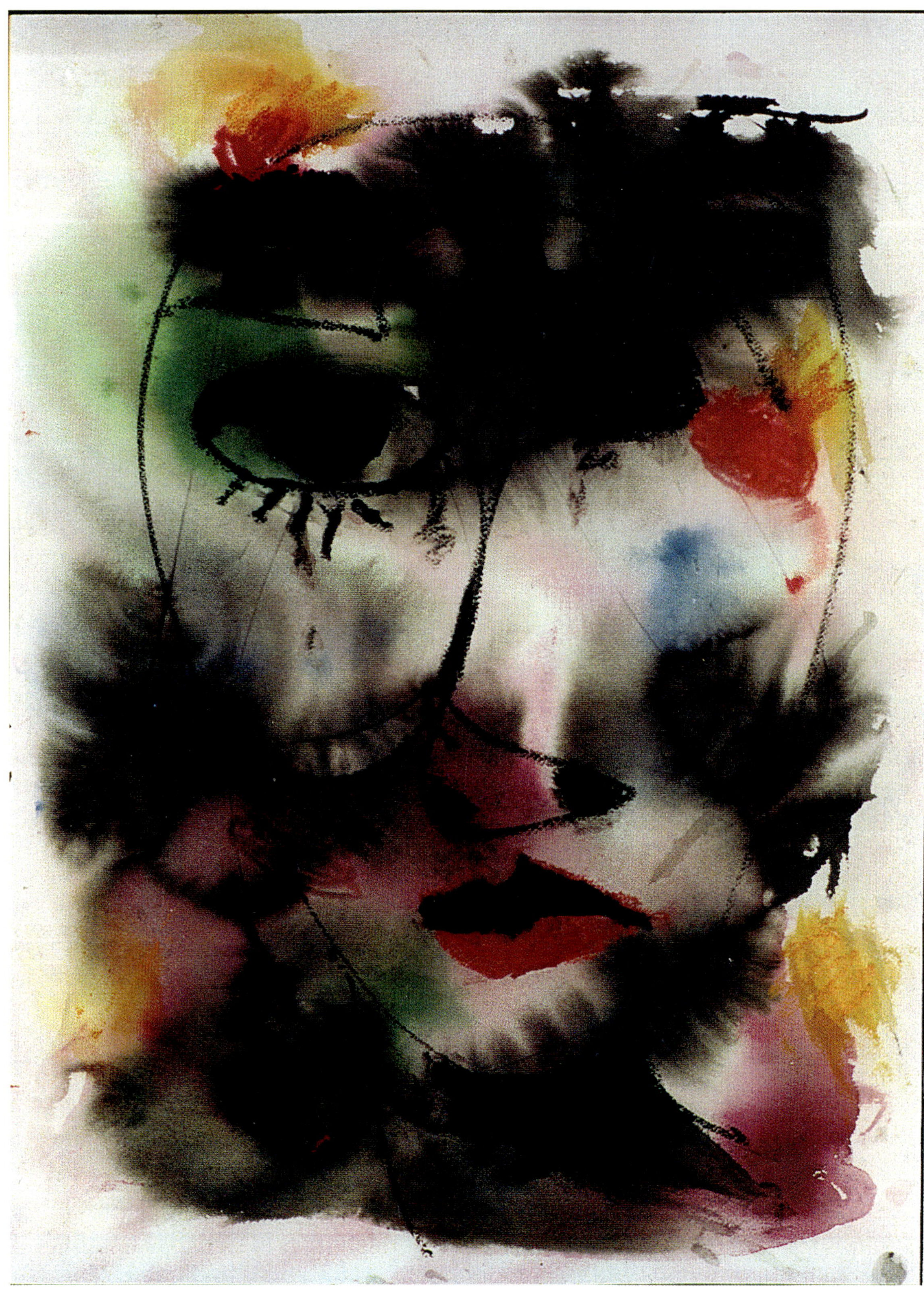

Misty   24" x 18"

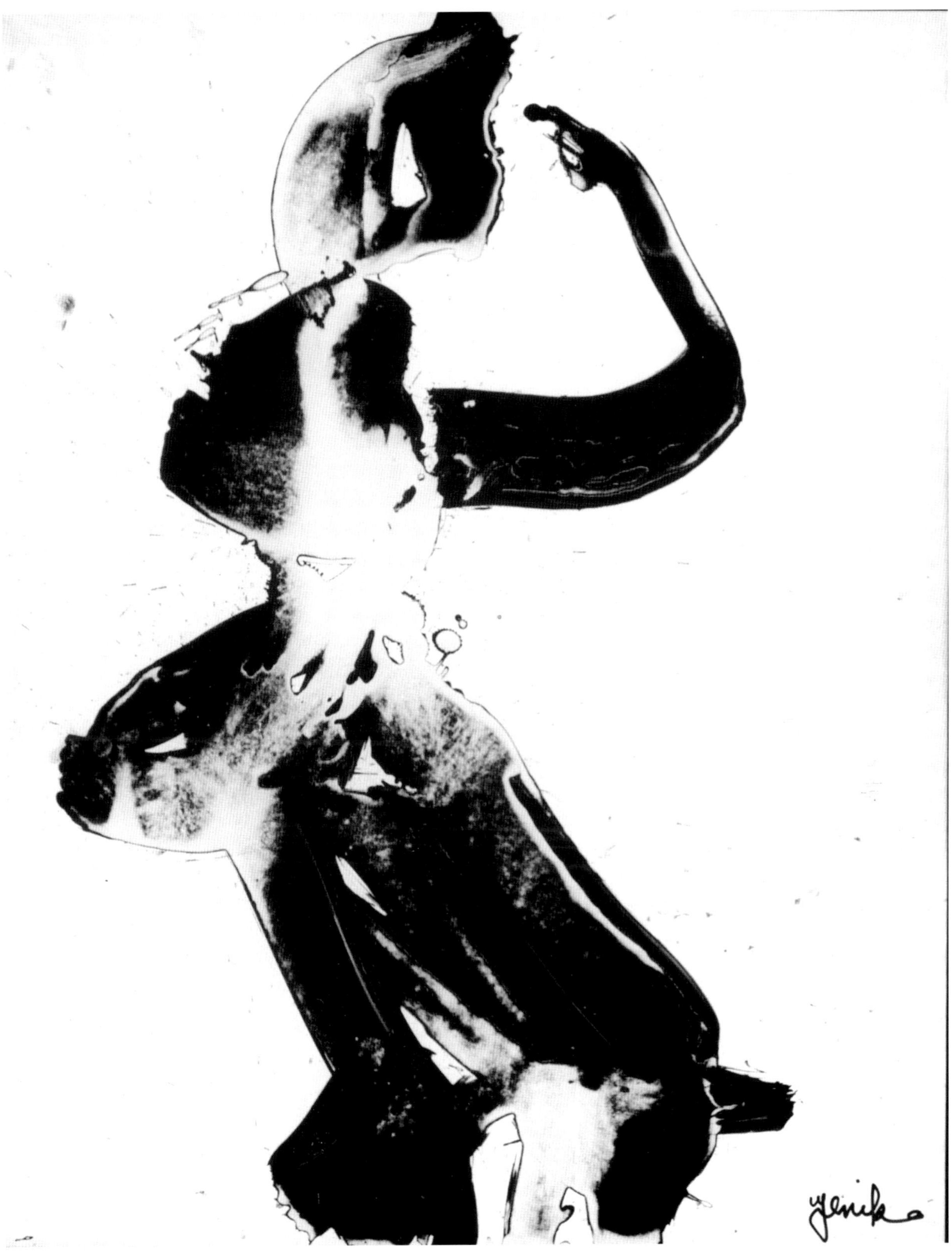

The Window of the Soul   Black Ink   28" x 22"

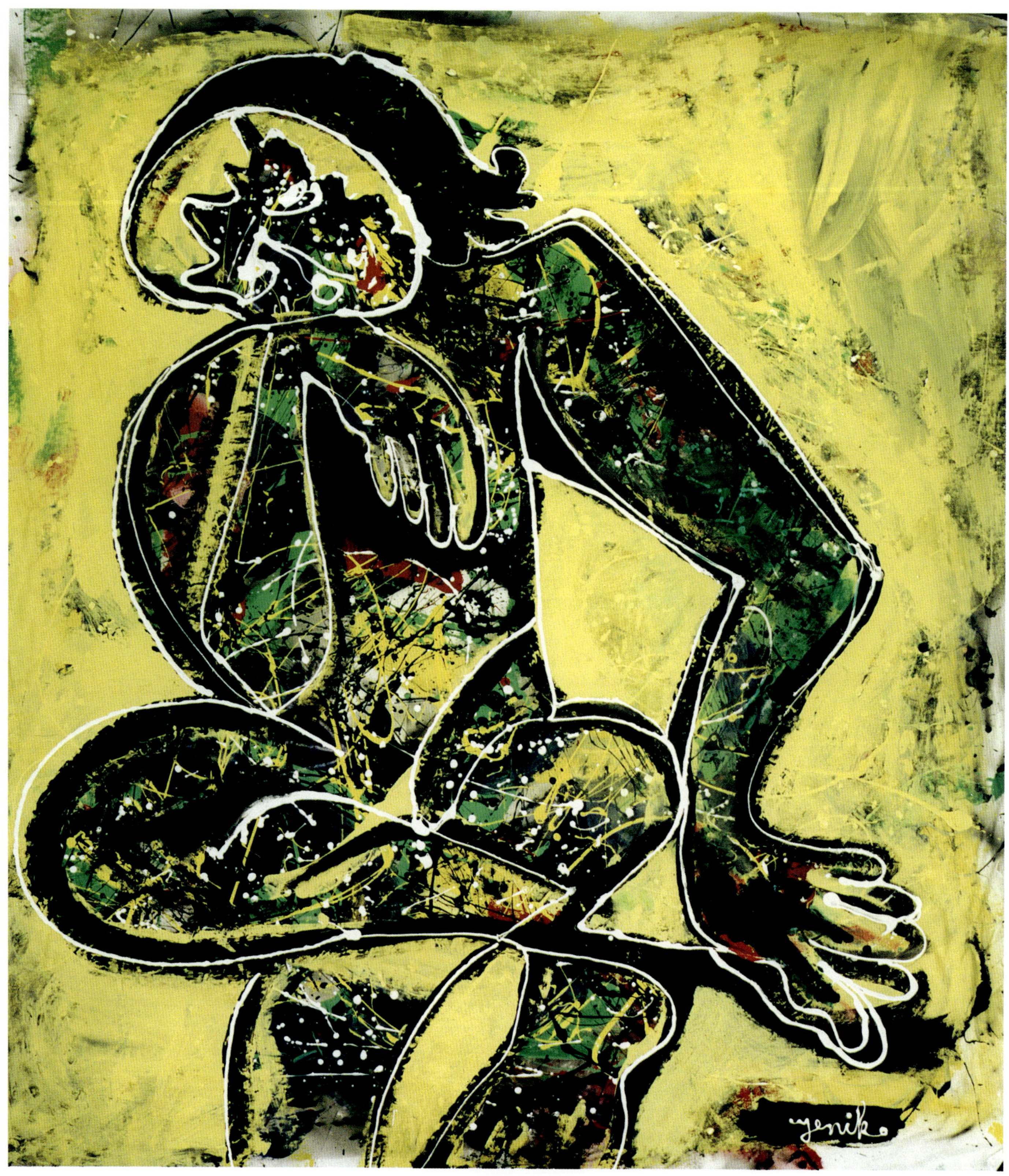

Introvert   68" x 62"   Acrylic

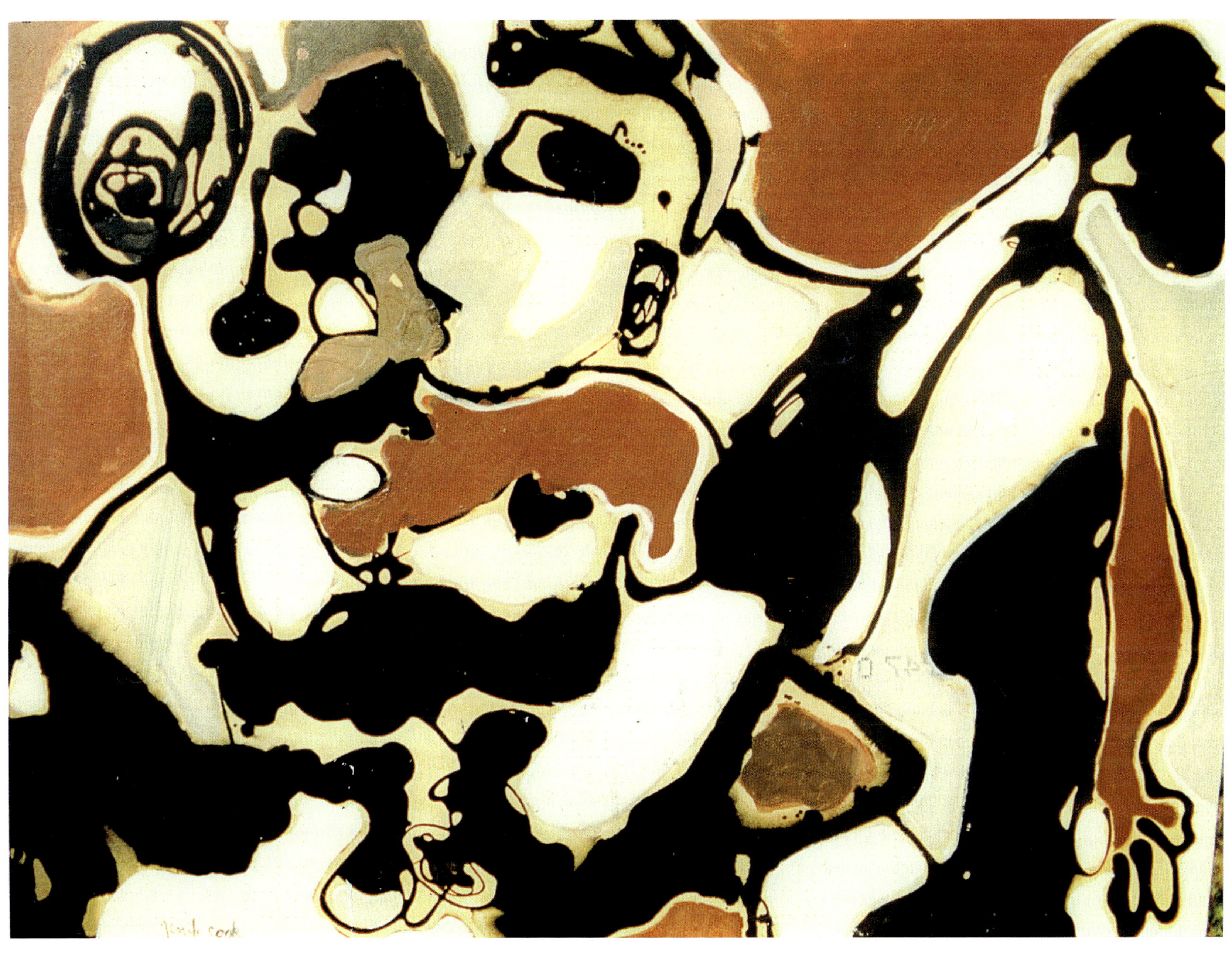

Whisper   36" x 30"

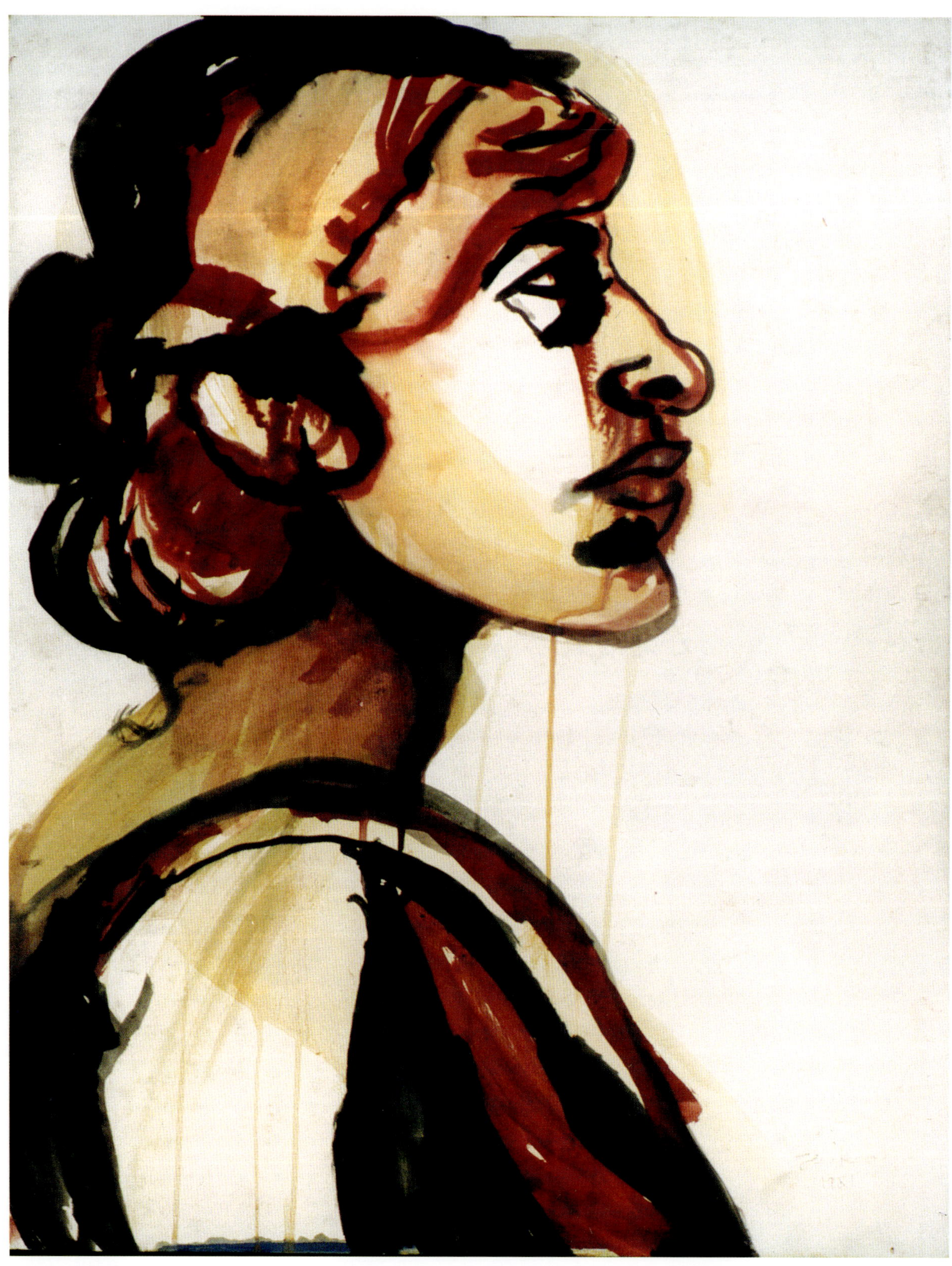

Macy   Mixed media   28" x 22"

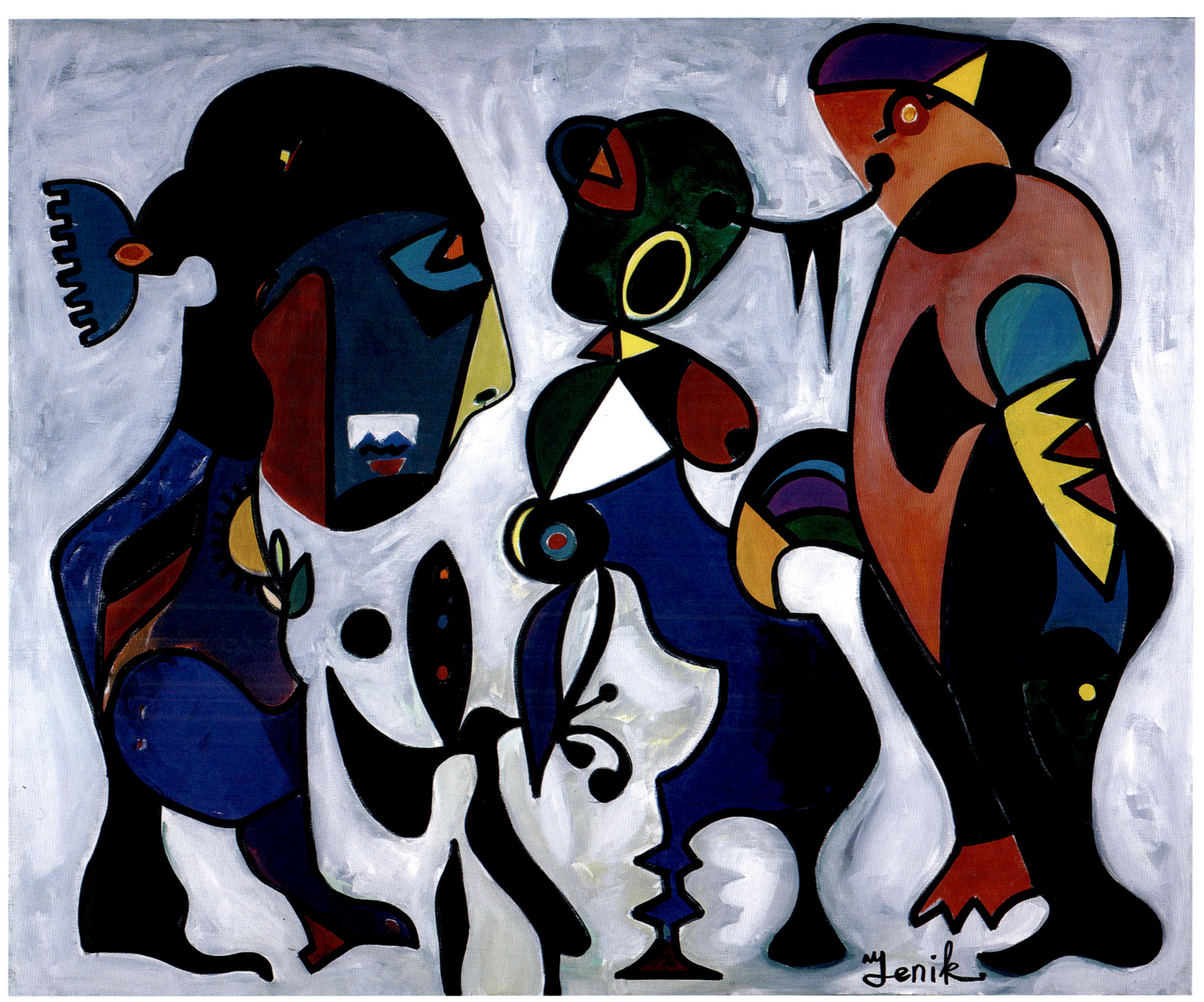

Unconcious Memory   48" x 60"

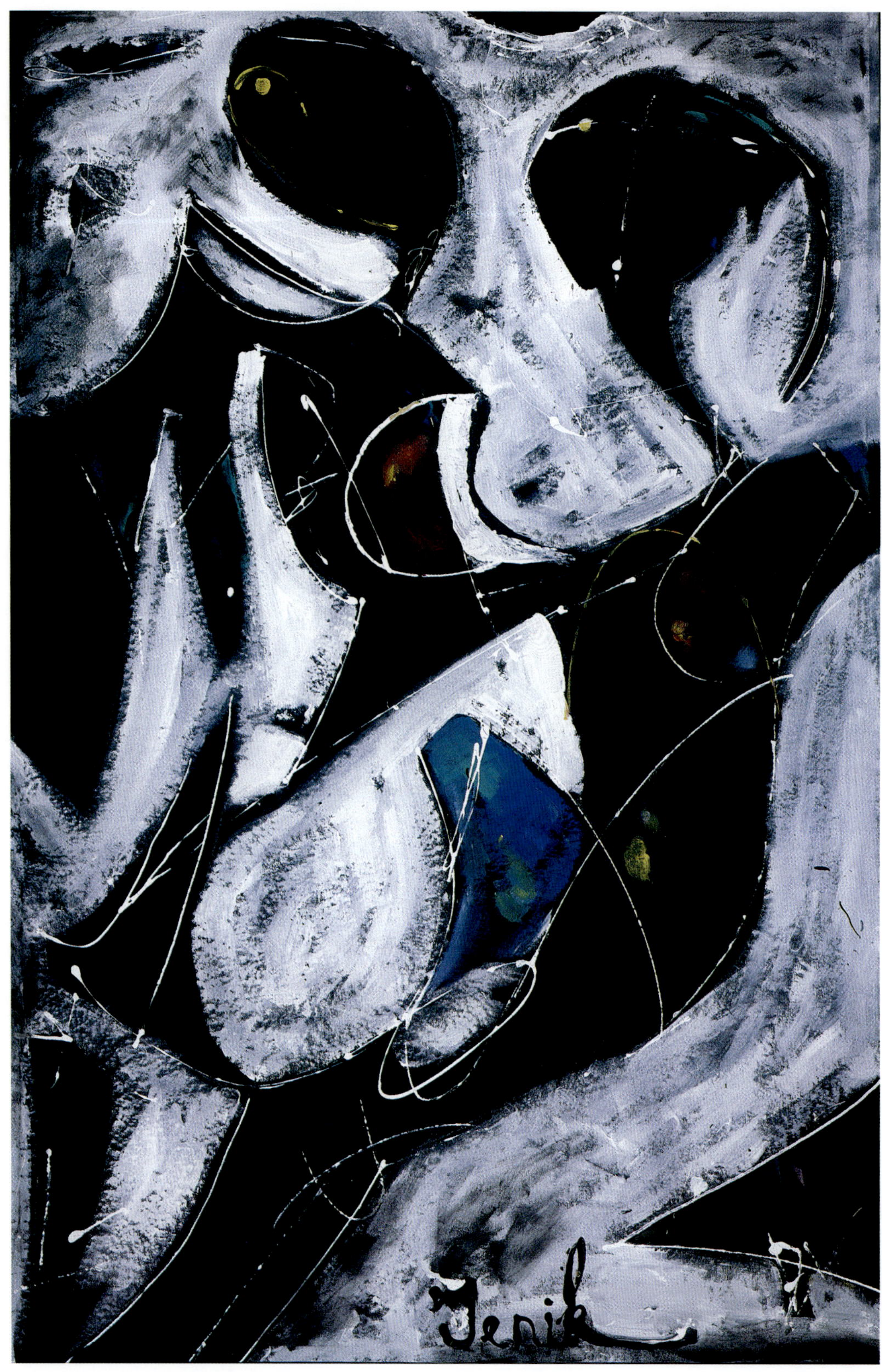

Living in the Light   34" x 46"

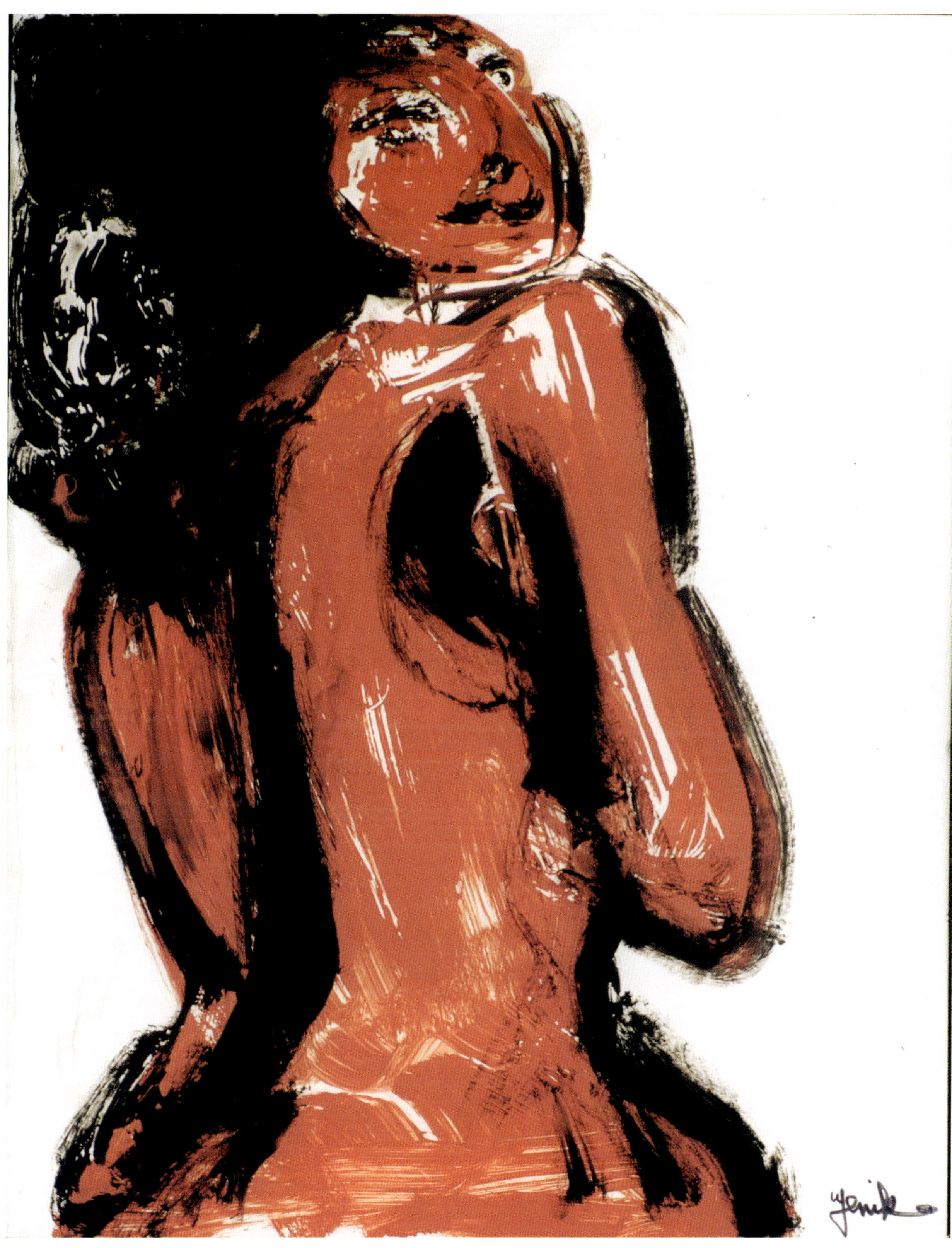

Rita, Acrylic, 28" x 22"

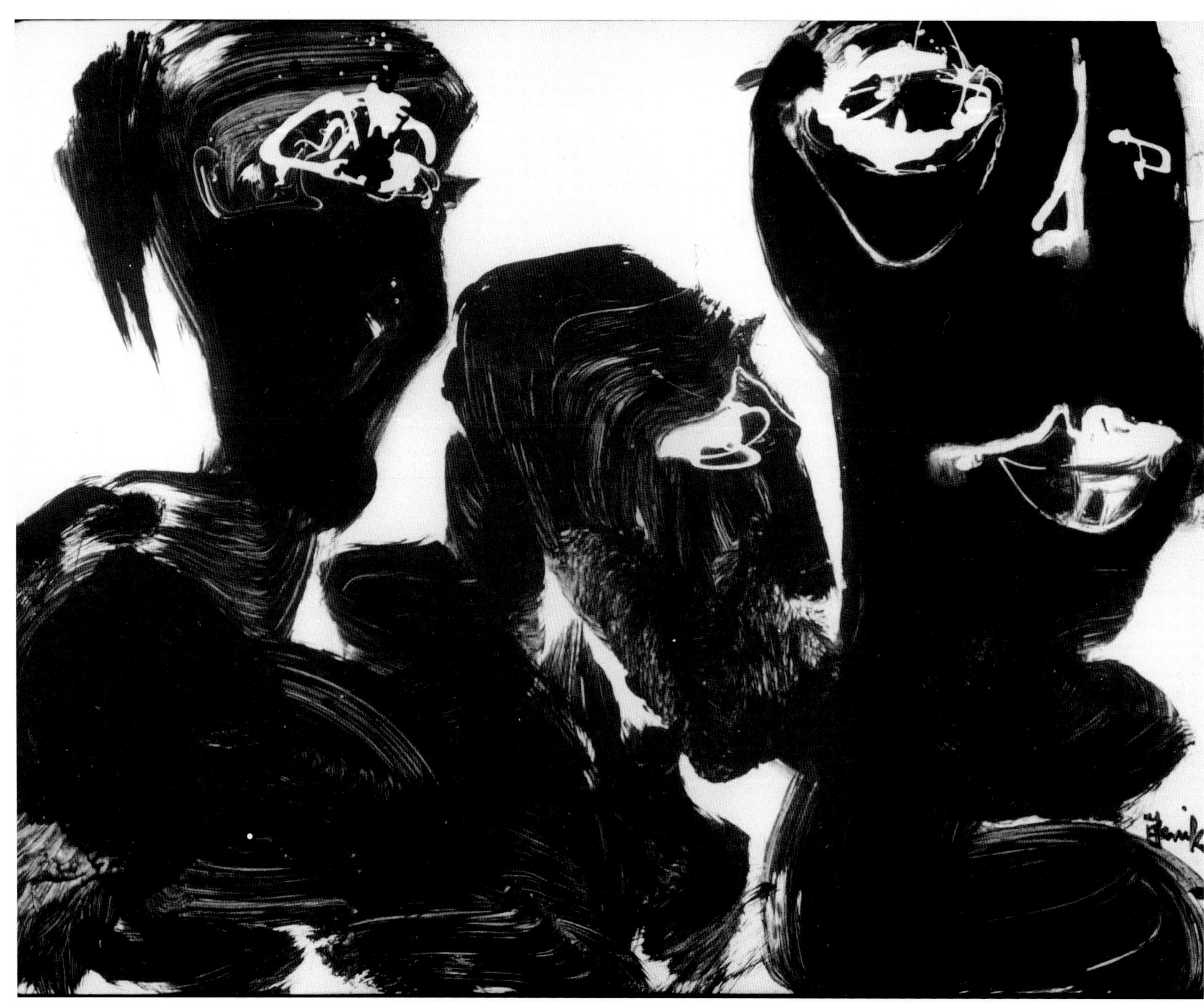

On the Move   22" x 28"

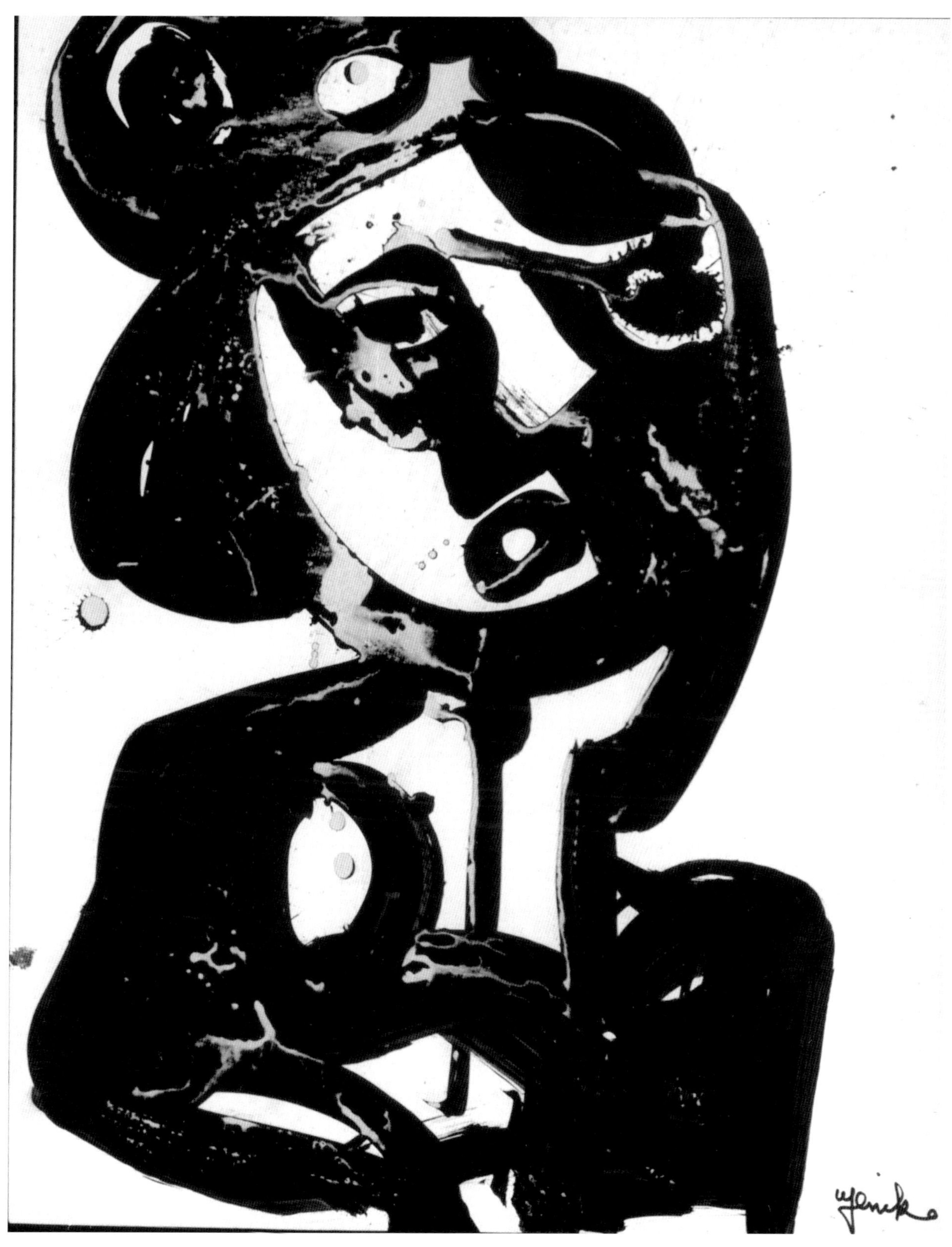

Aravic, Acrylic, 28" x 22"

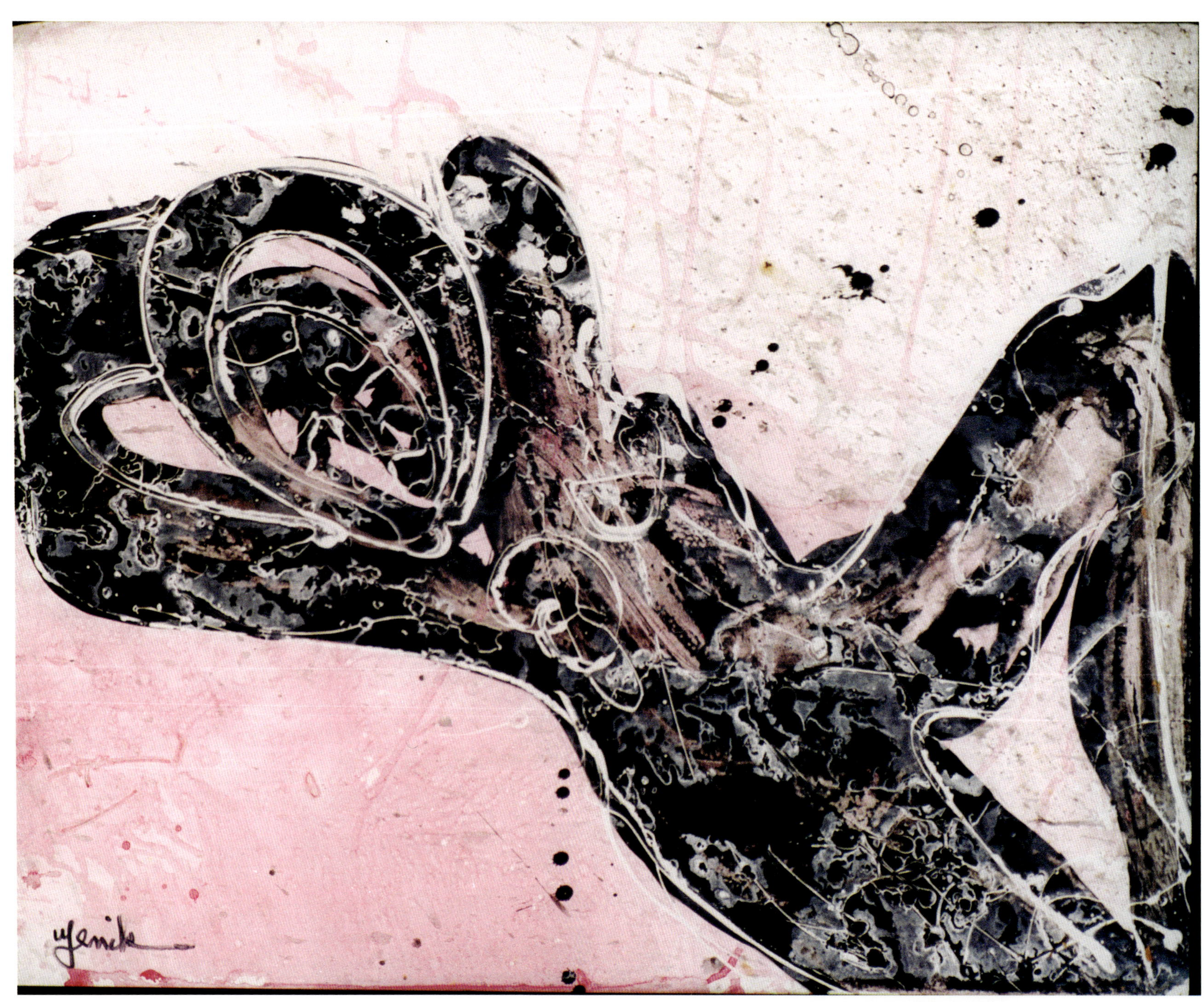

Dafna   Mixed media 24" x 18"

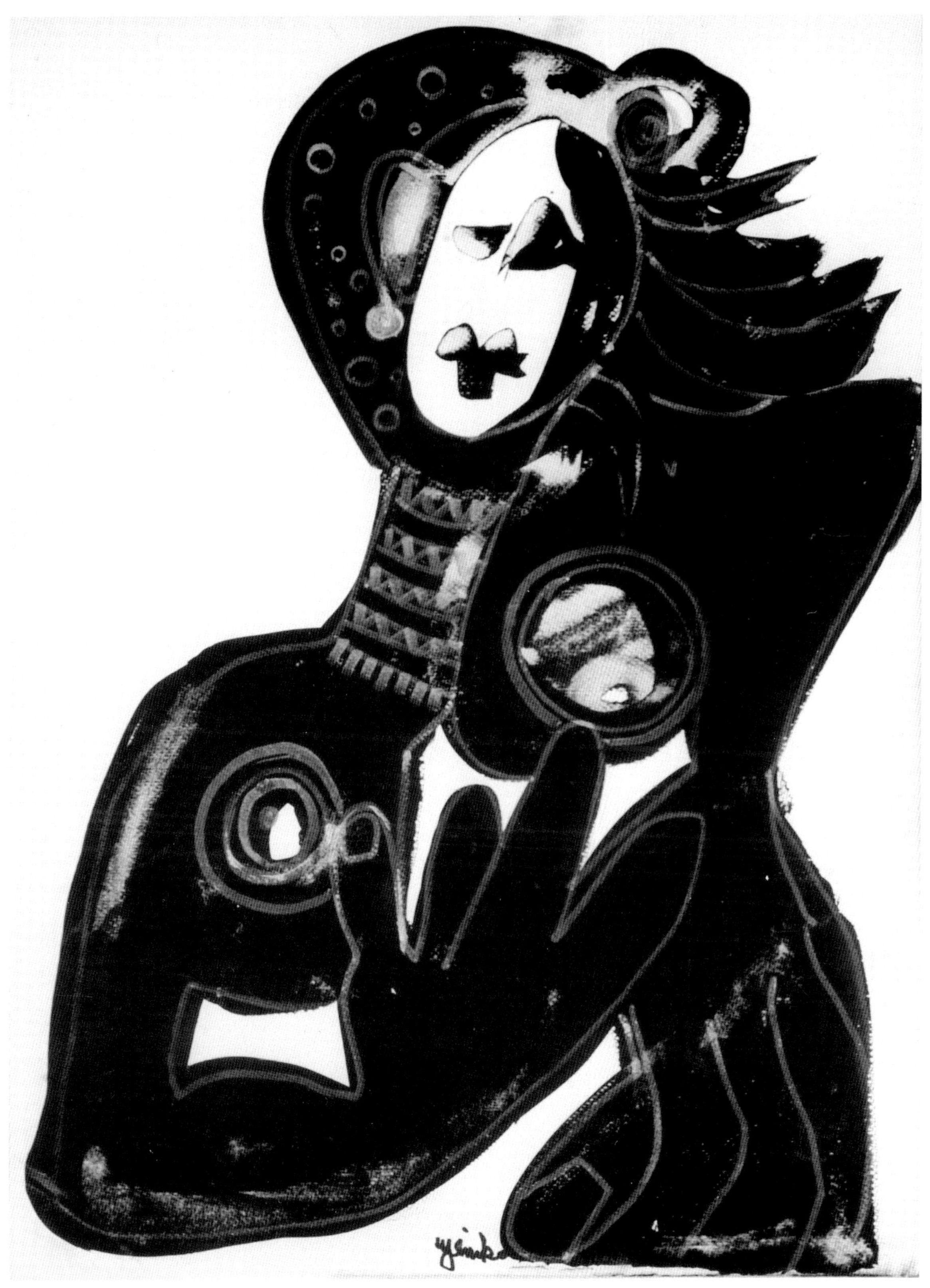

A Touch, Ink / Acrylic, 24" x 18"

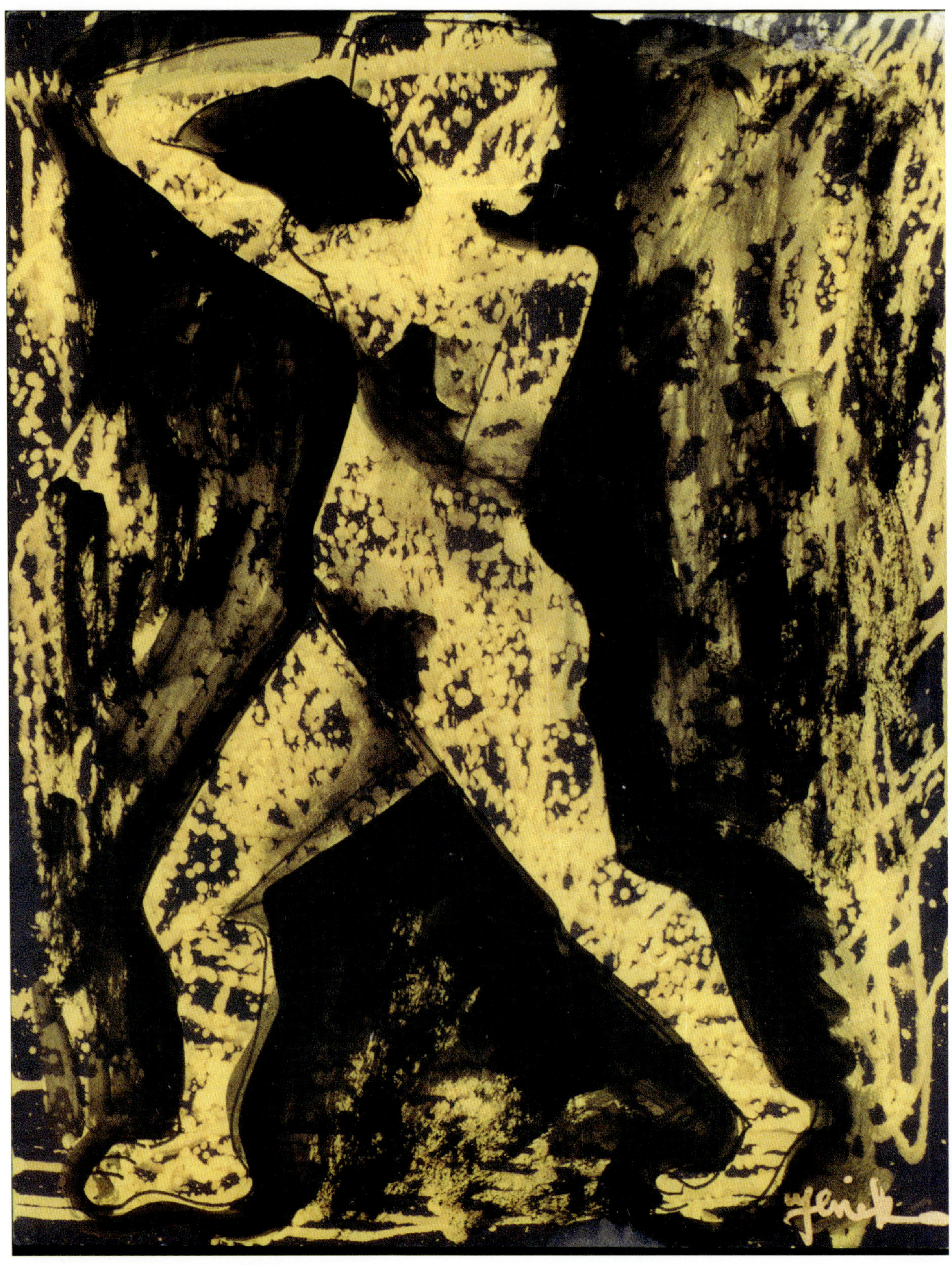

Nadia   28" x 22"

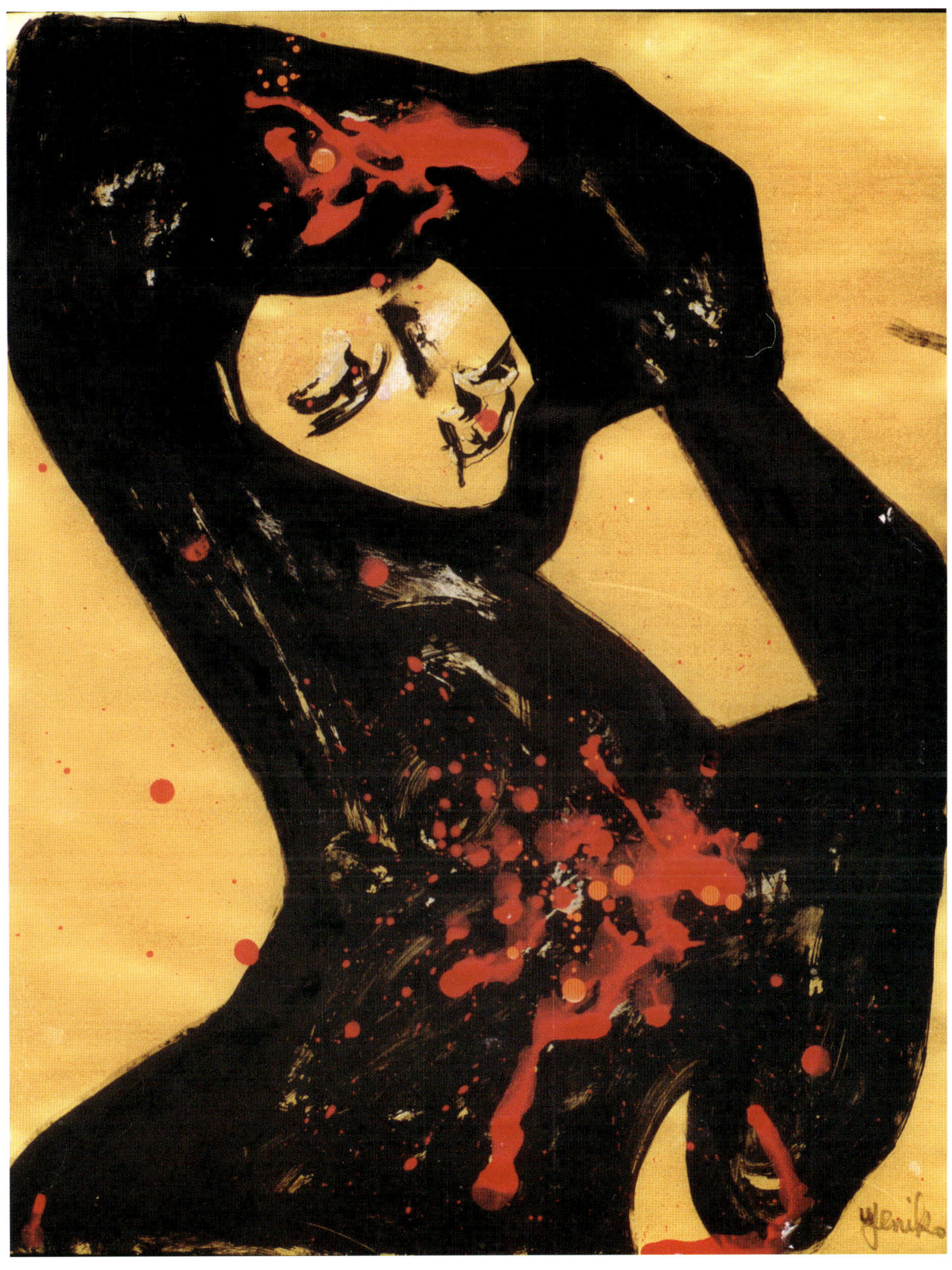

Zola, Acrylic / Ink, 28" x 22"

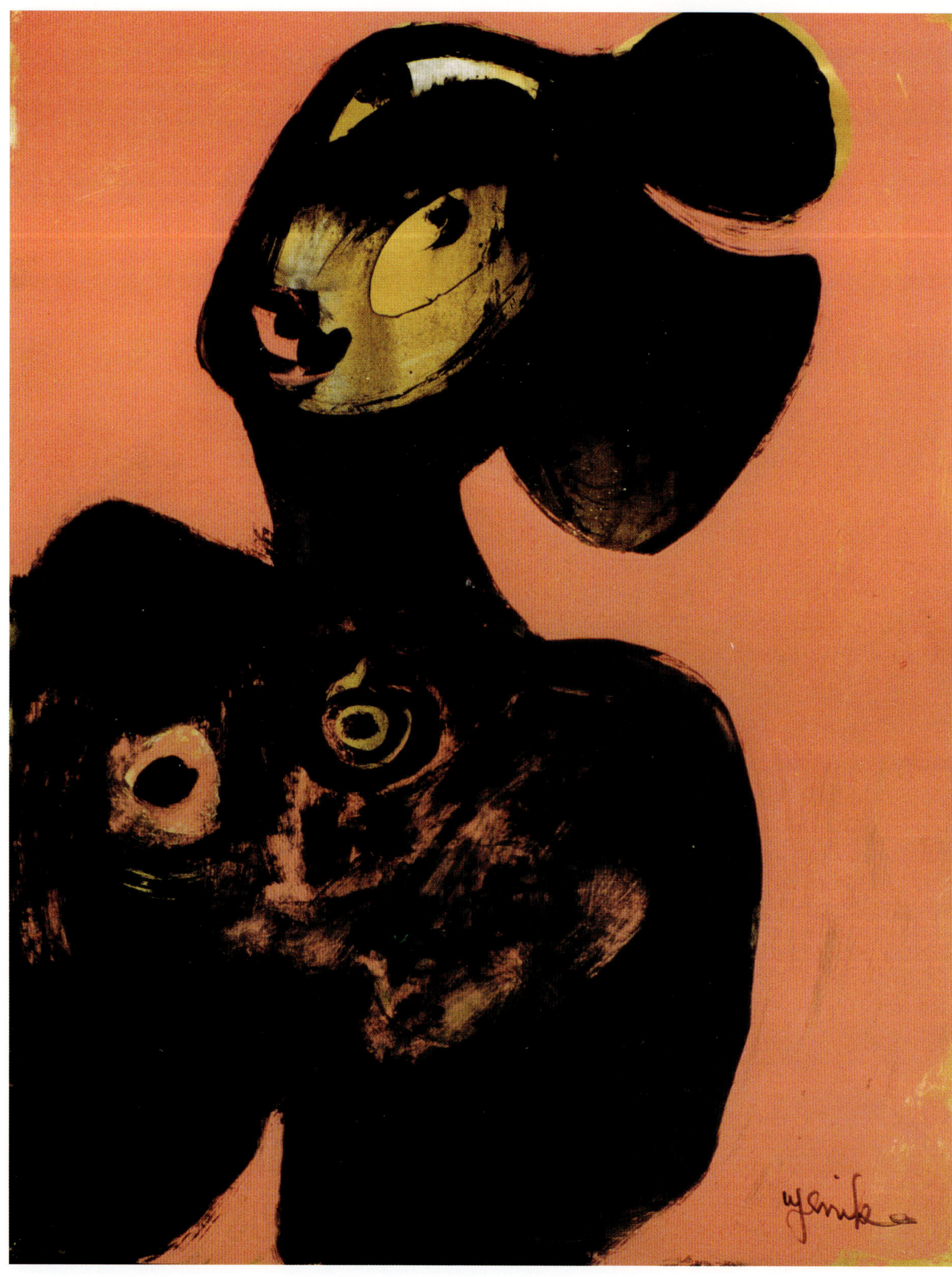

Nobar   Mixed watercolor   28" x 22"

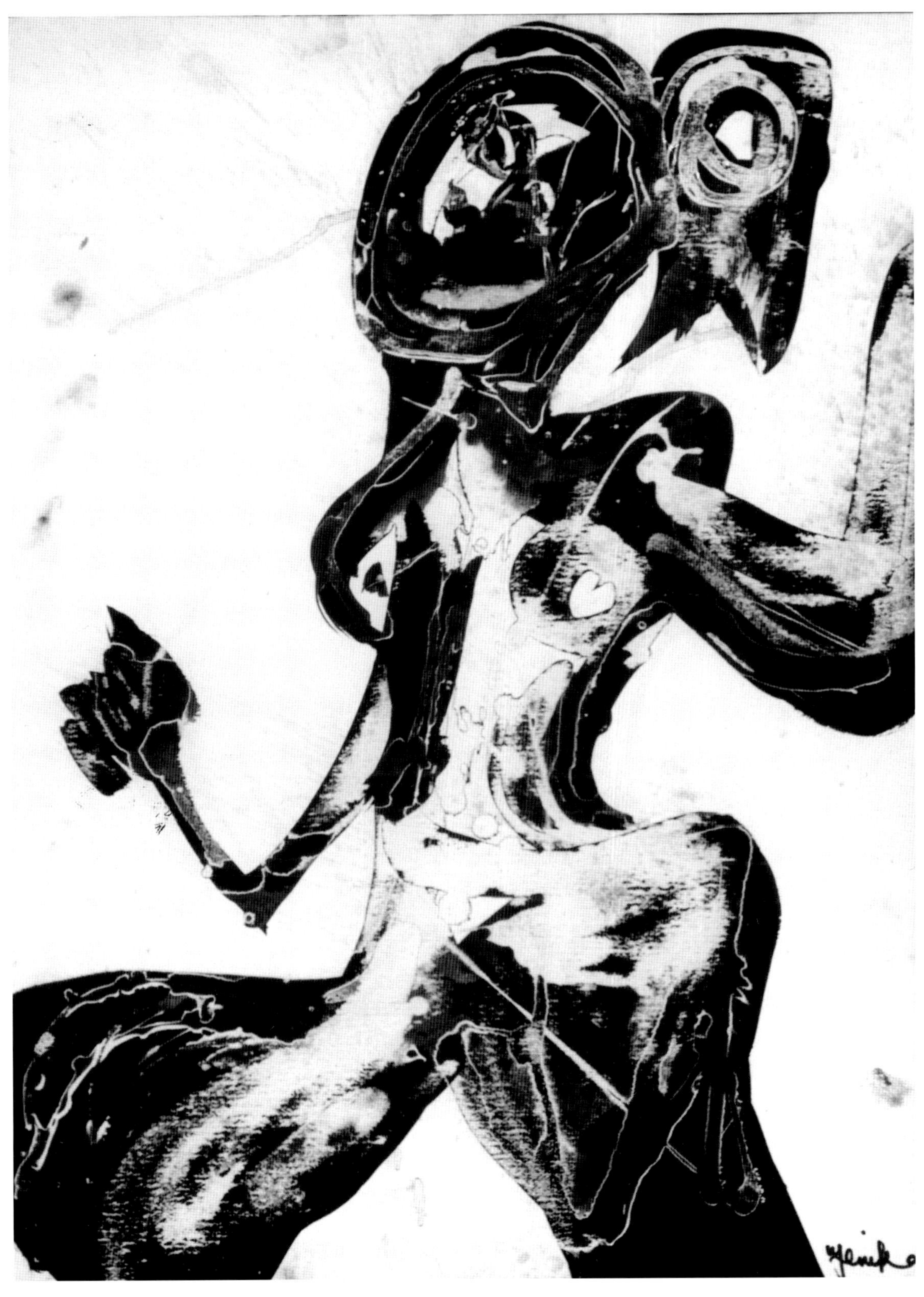

Farnaz, Watercolor, 28" x 22"

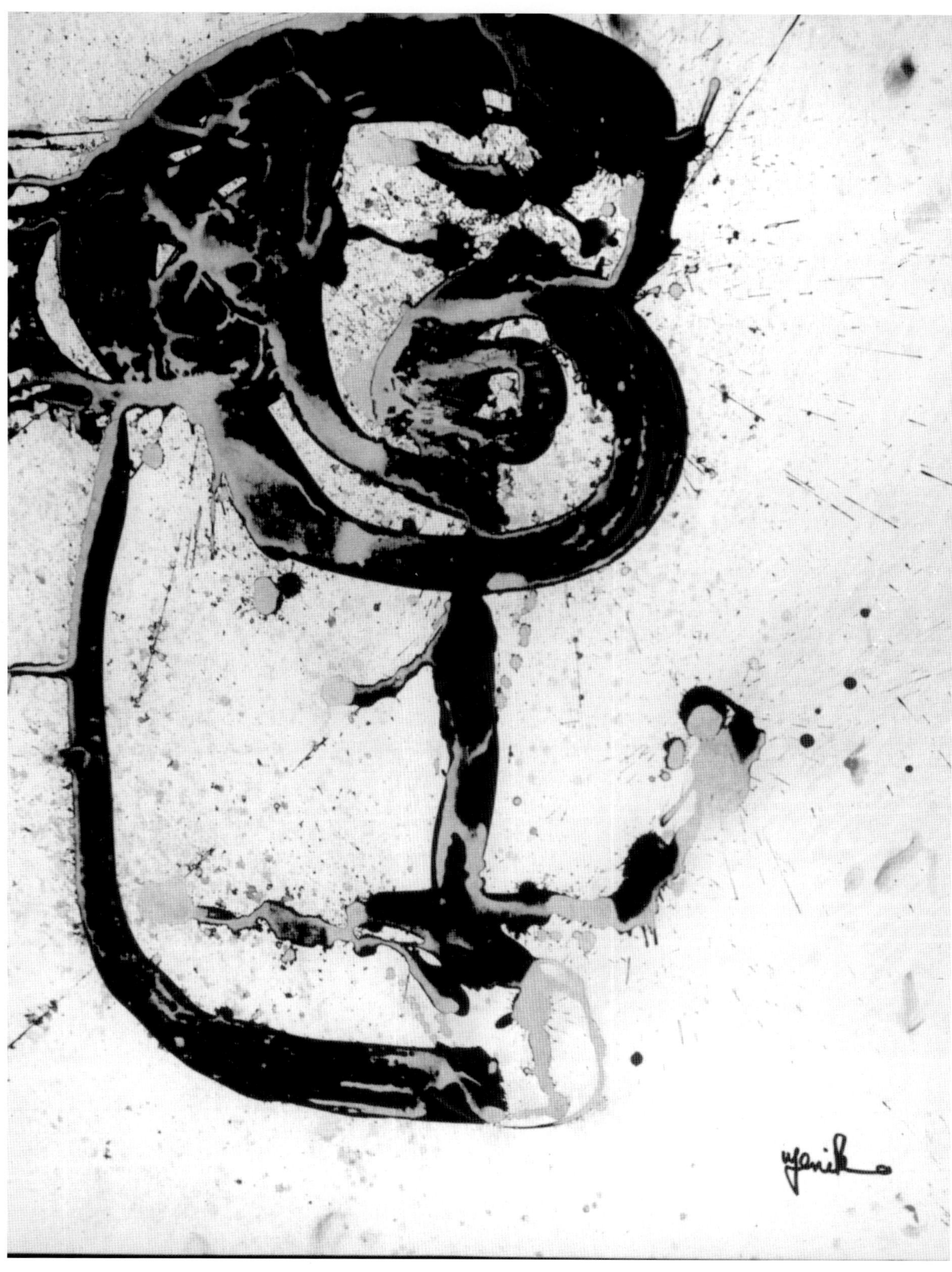

Emerging Serpent   28" x 22"

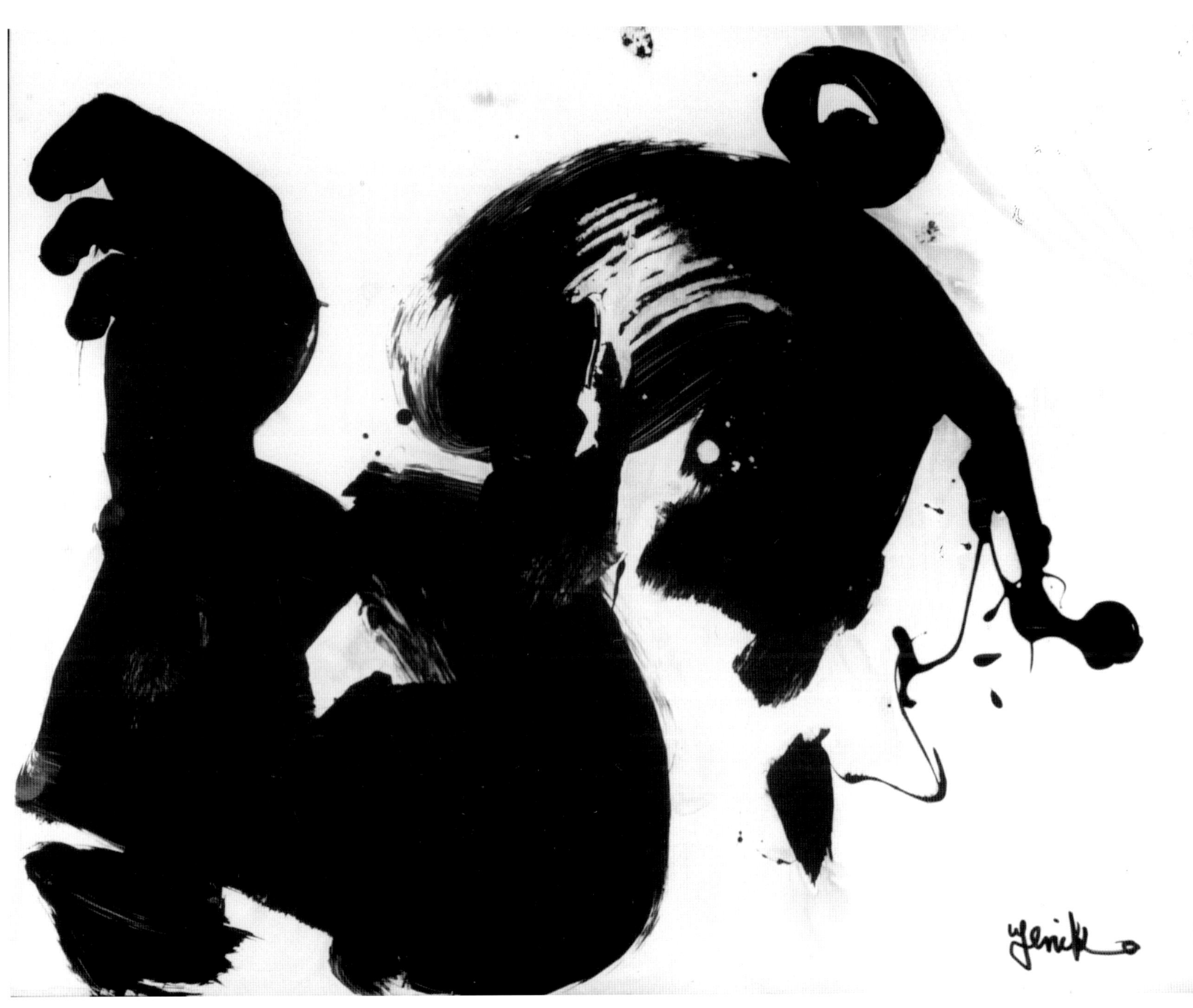

Day Dreaming, Acrylic, 28" x 22"

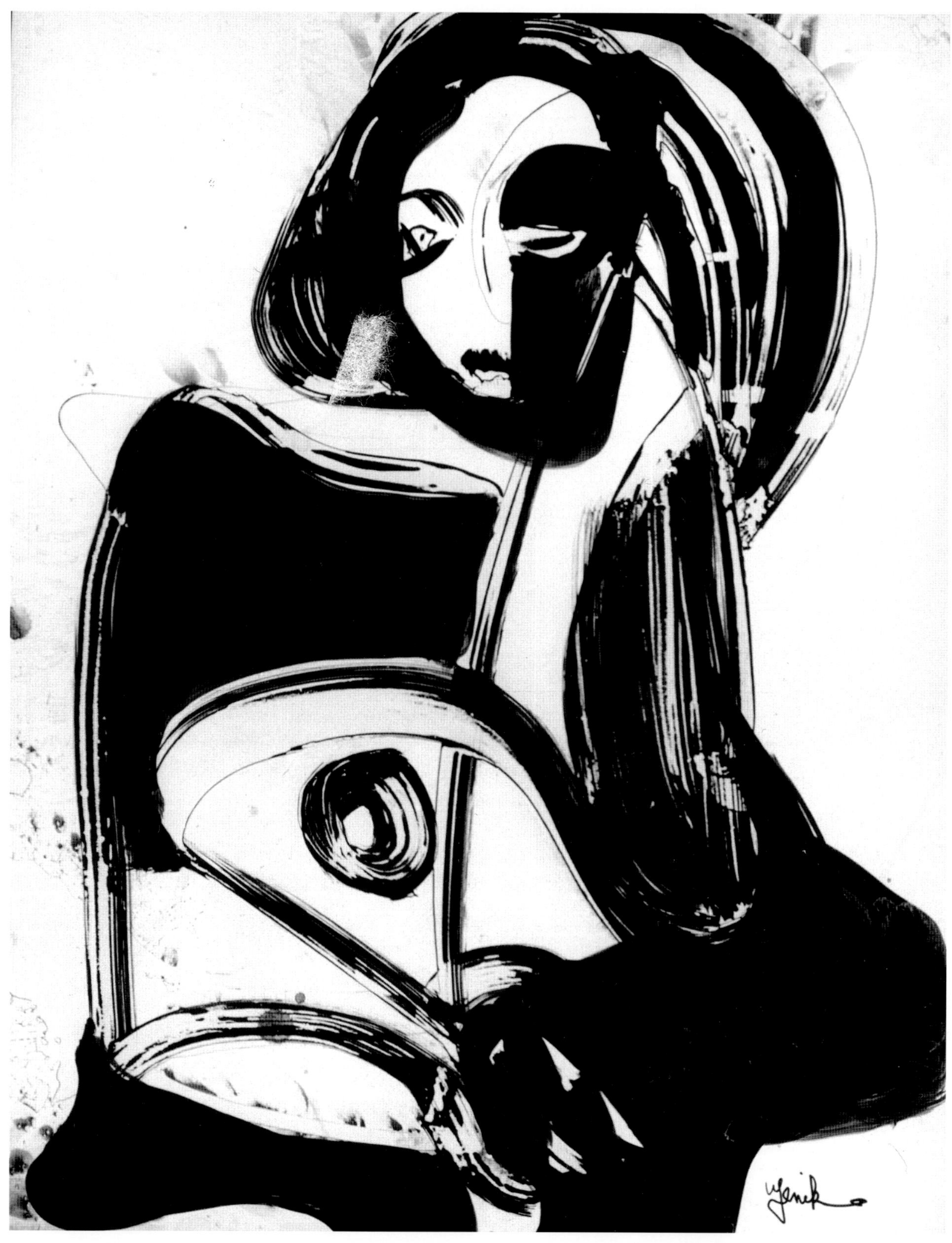

Meditation   Acrylic   28" x 22"

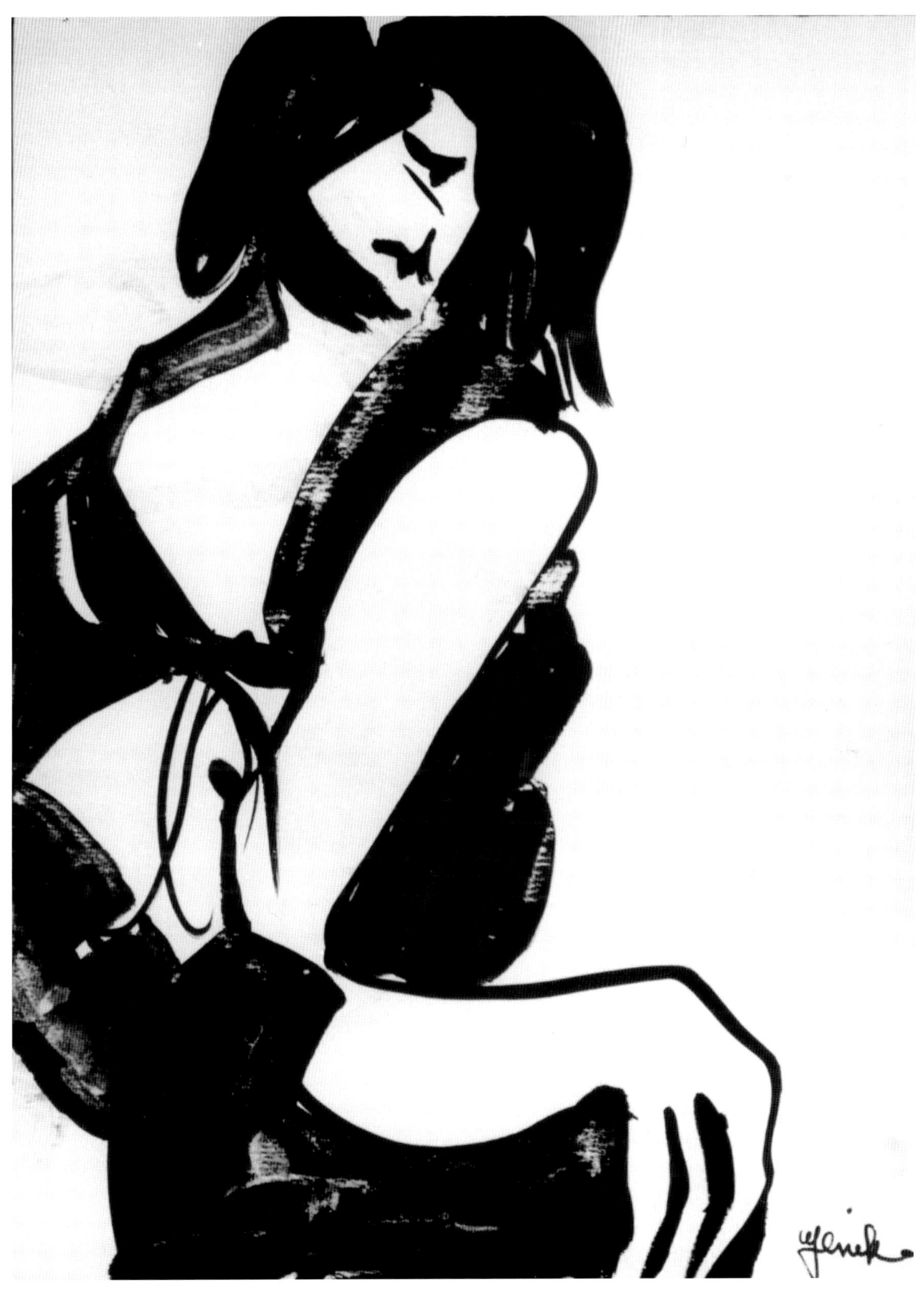

Kyla, Ink, 24" x 18"

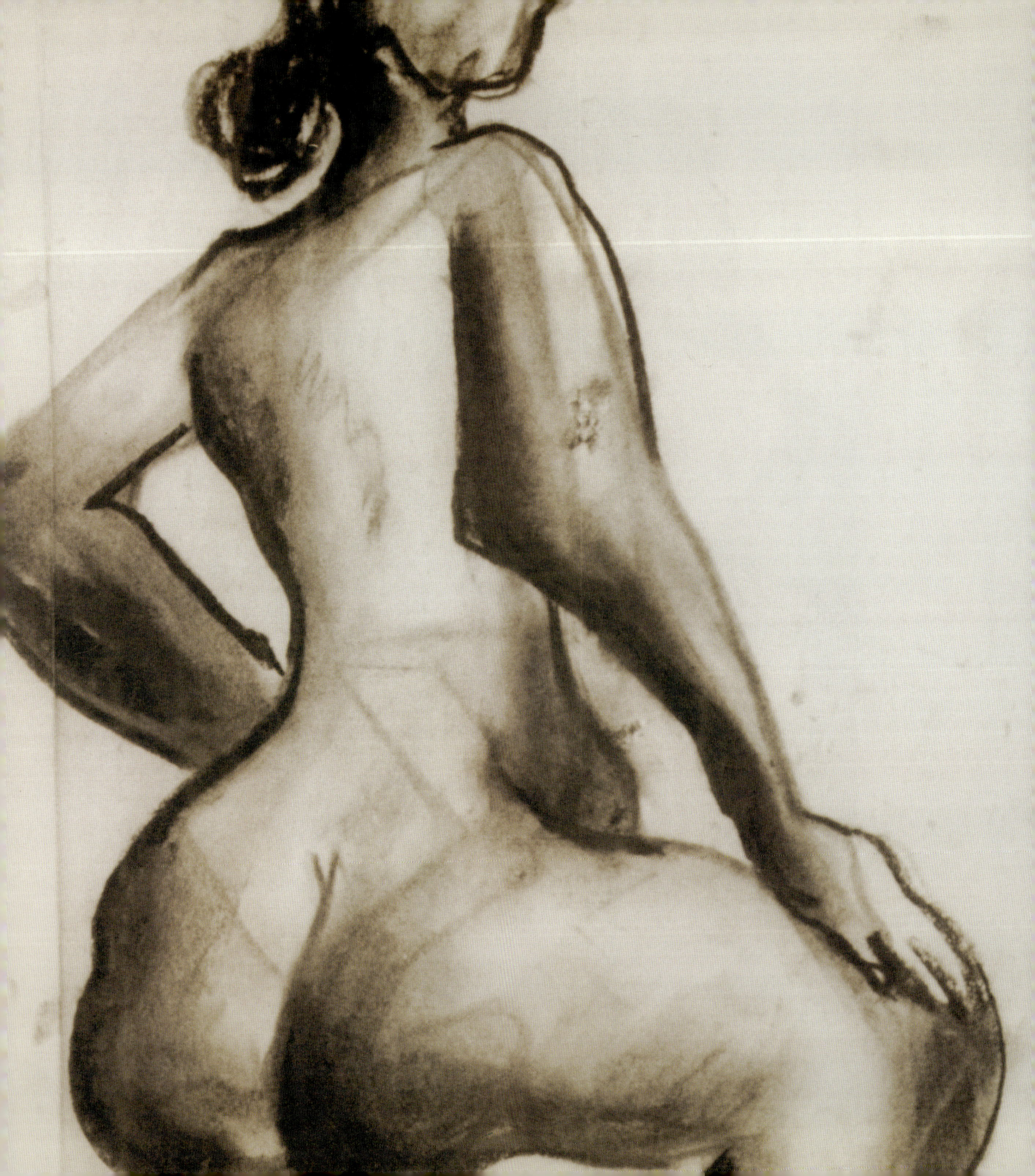

As "gesture" is generally understood in the world of art, beyond the movement which creates the mark, it represents the essential qualities of what is seen or felt by the artist. In drawing, an activity foundational to many artists, we see by an admirable economy of line and tone in these examples (including a modest self-portrait), and in the Black and White studies which follow, how the capture of gesture is observed in Jenik's fundamental approach.

Drawing &
Black and White

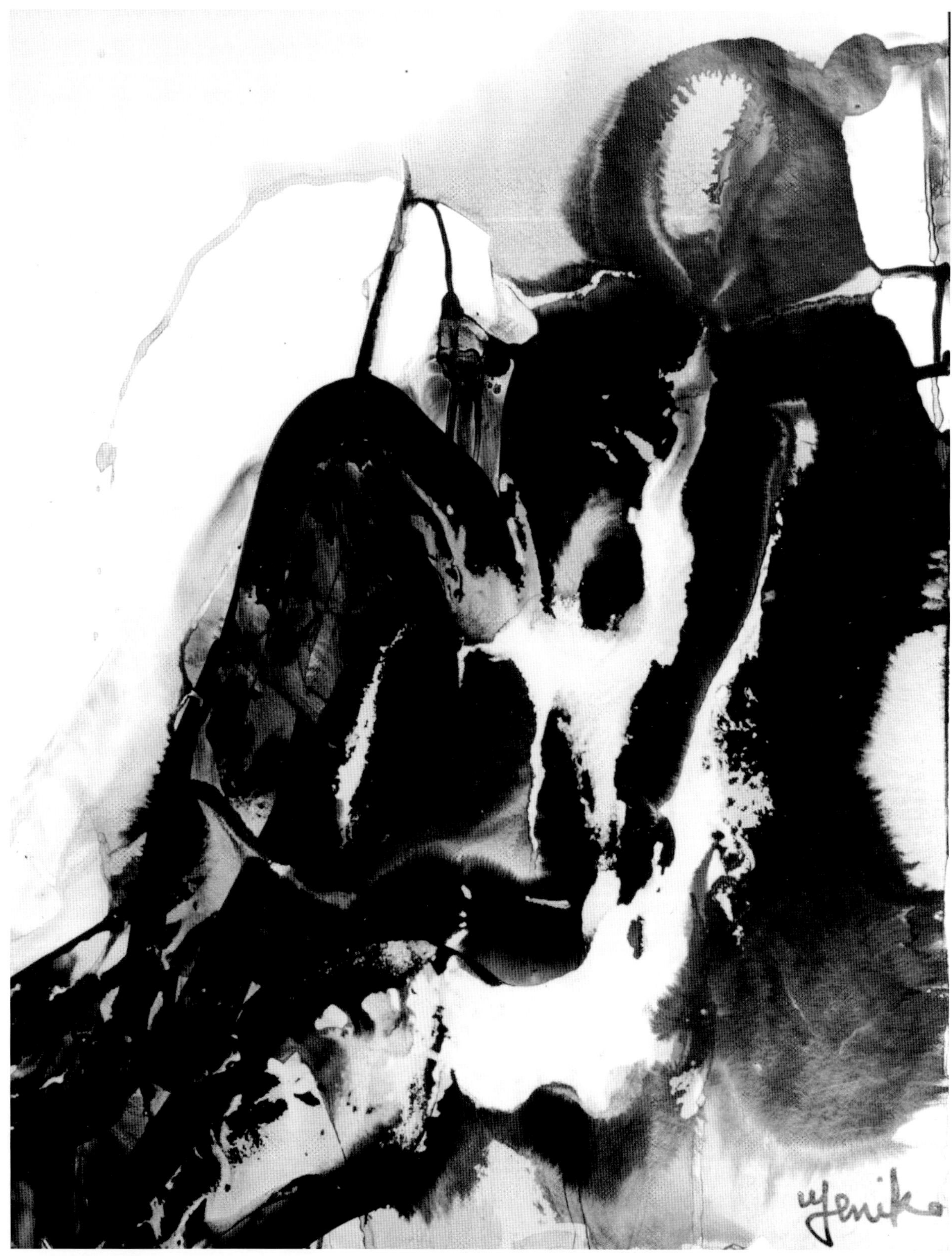

Black & White No. 14   Black Ink   28" x 22"

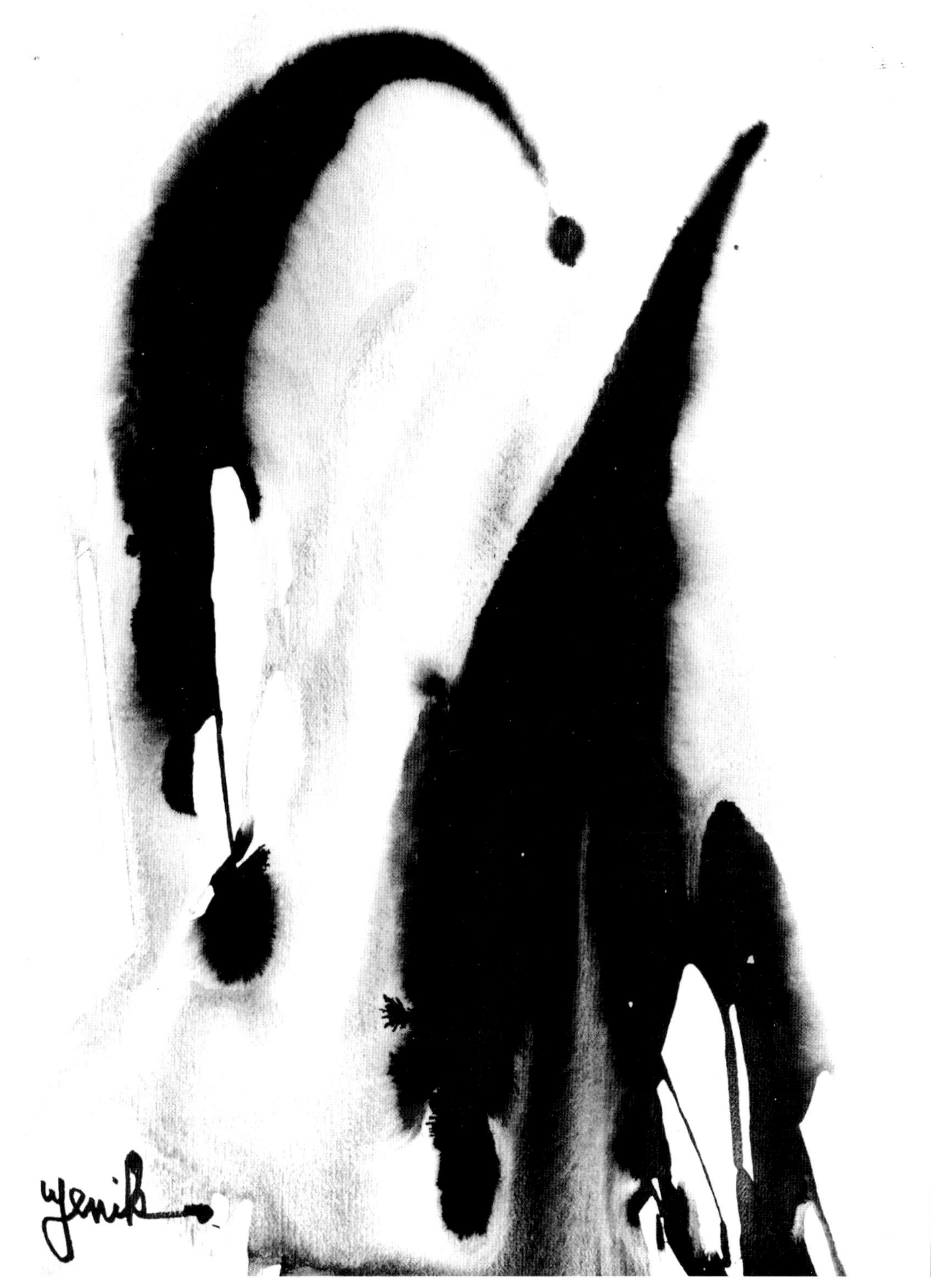

B&W No. 16, Black Ink, 24" x 18"

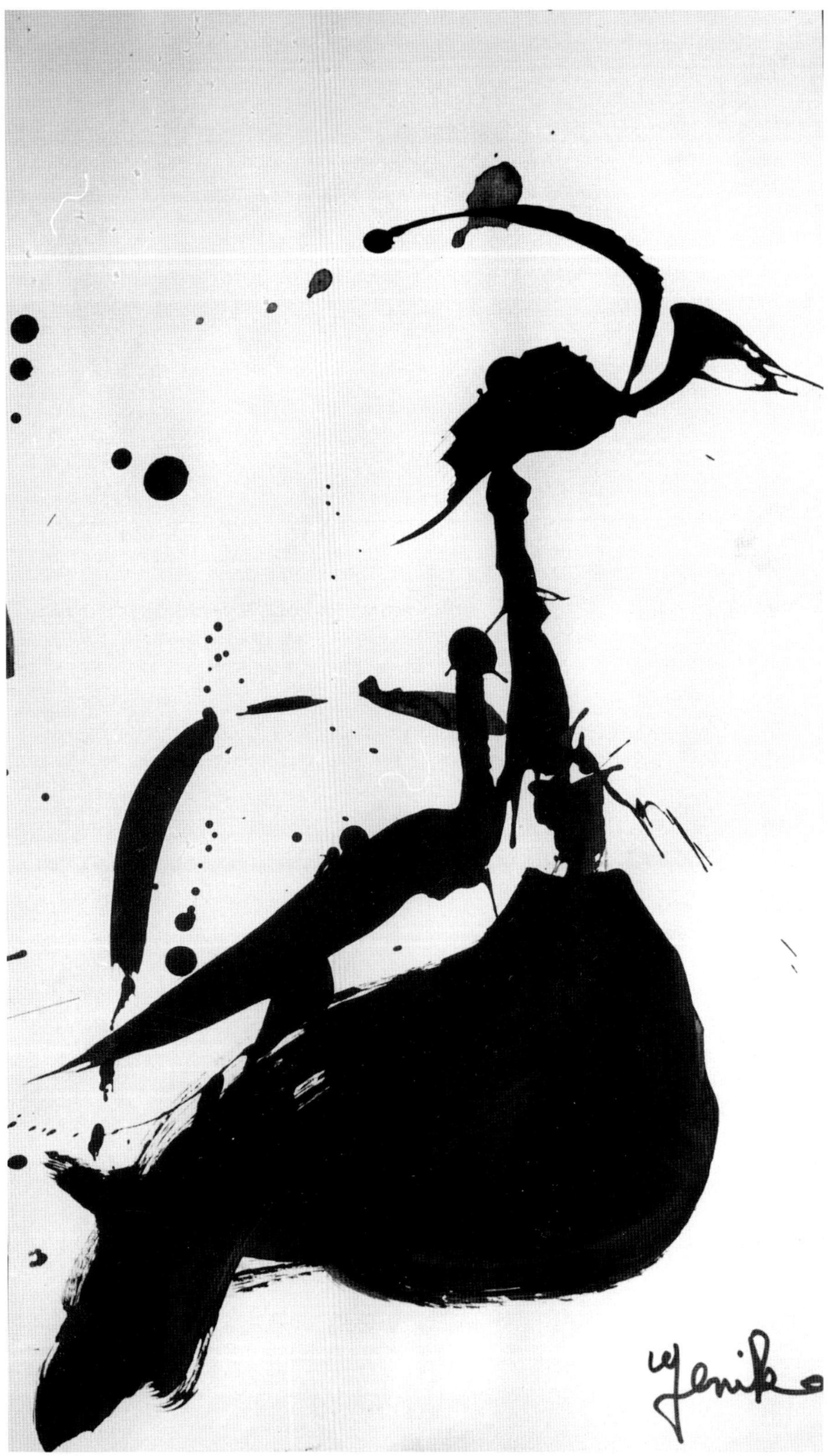

Untitled

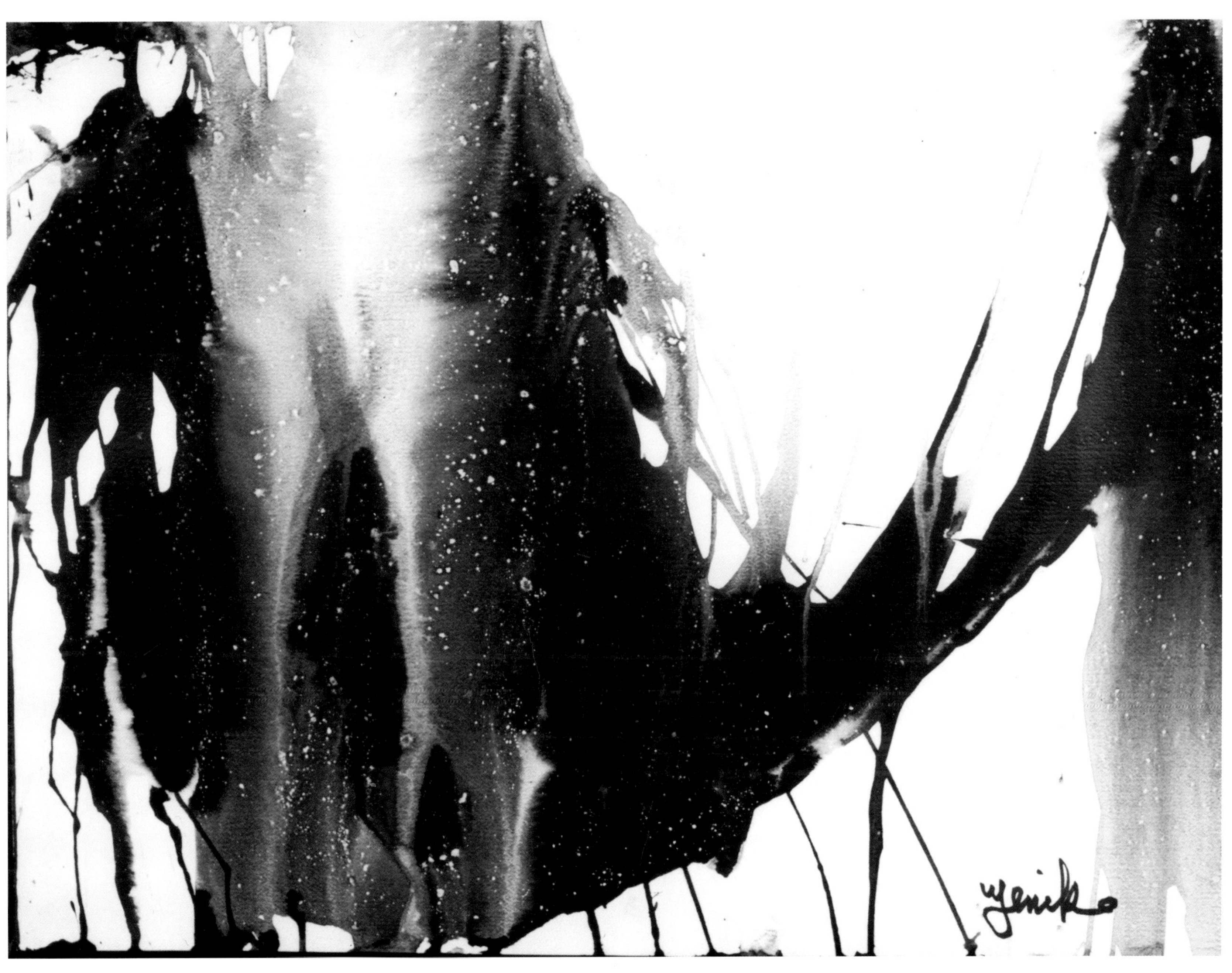

B & W No. 5, Black Ink, 30" x 24"

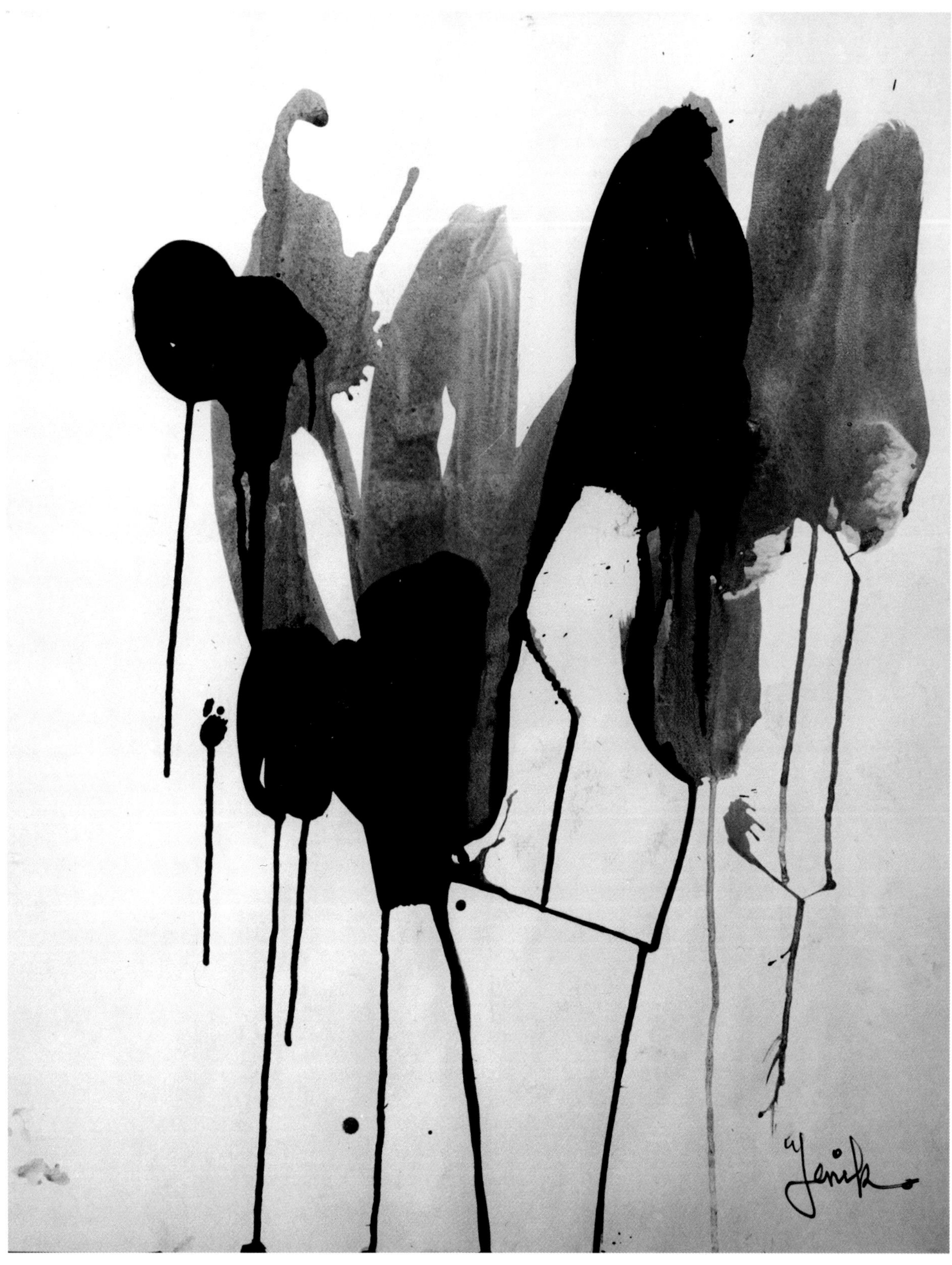

B & W No. 9   Ink   30" x 24"

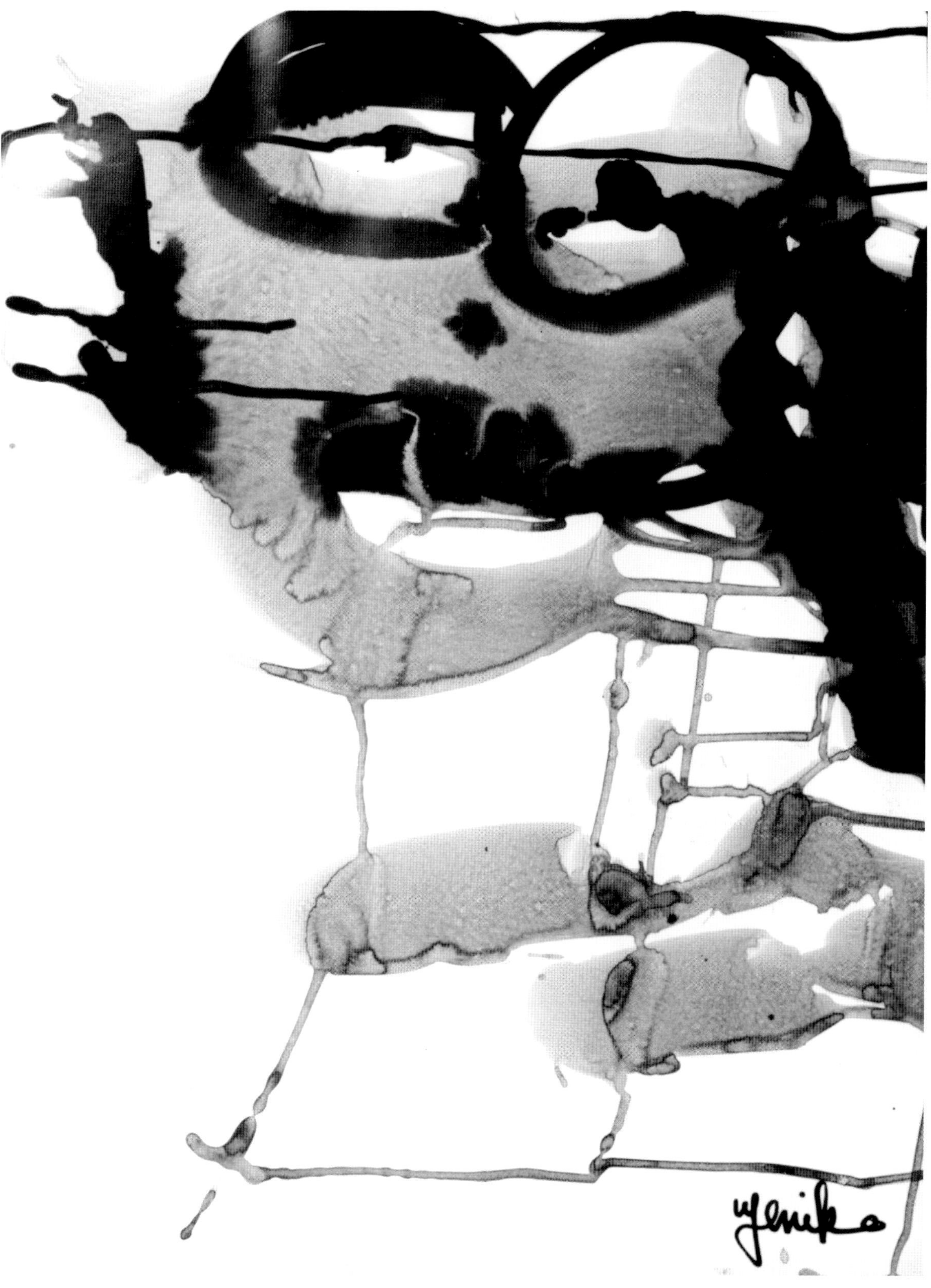

Serop 22" x 16"

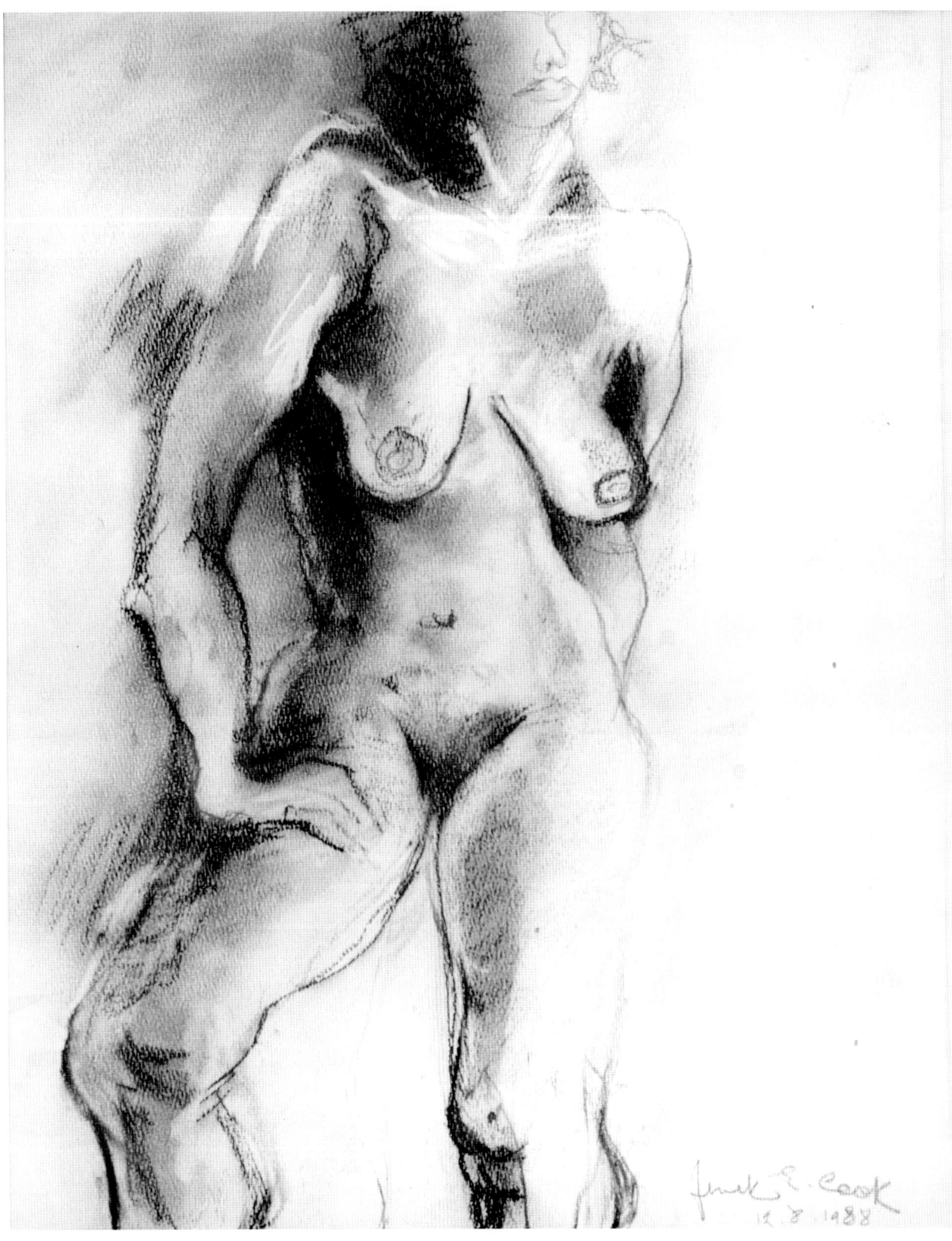

Ello Crayon 24" x 18"

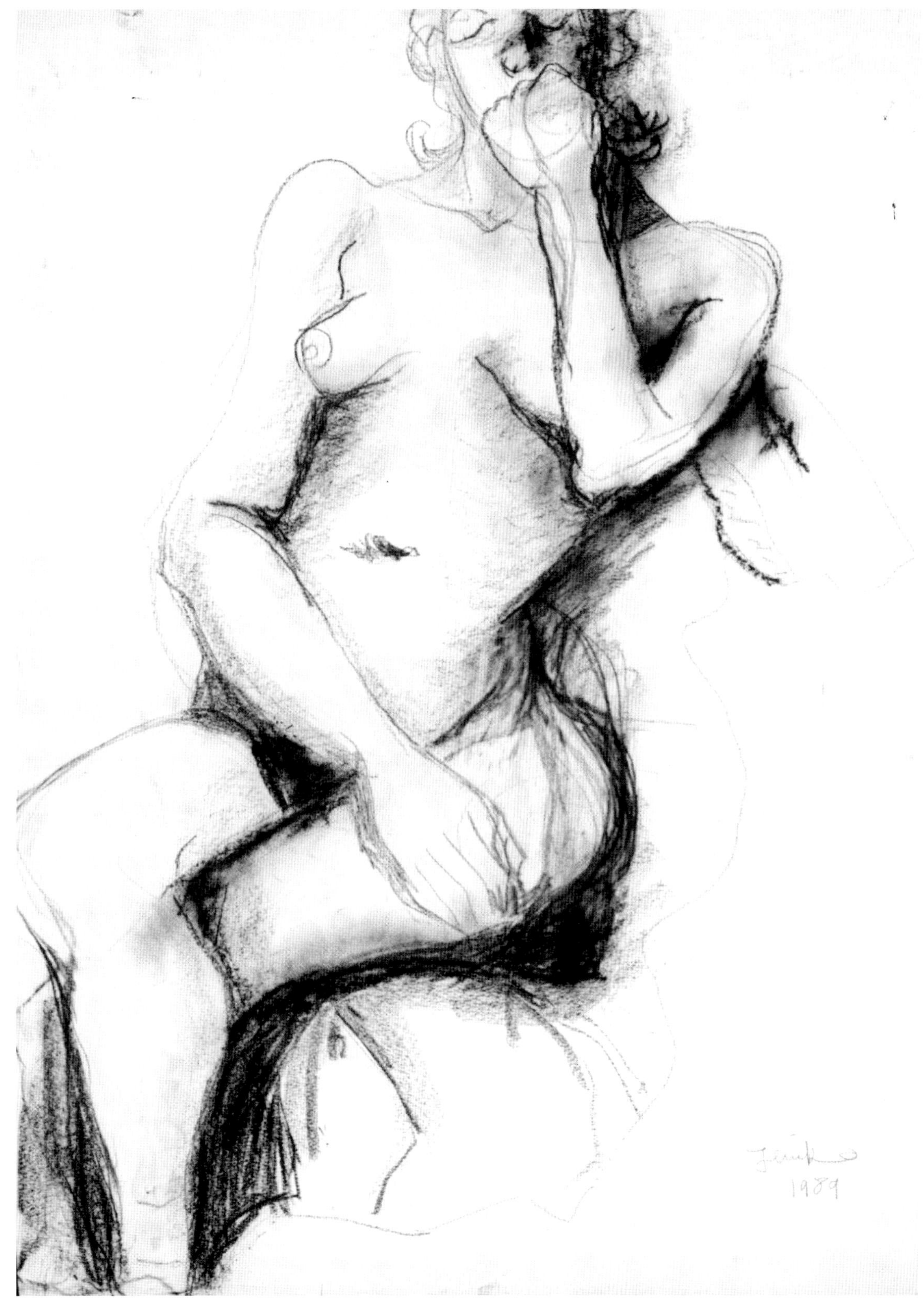

Joie   Crayon 24" x 18"

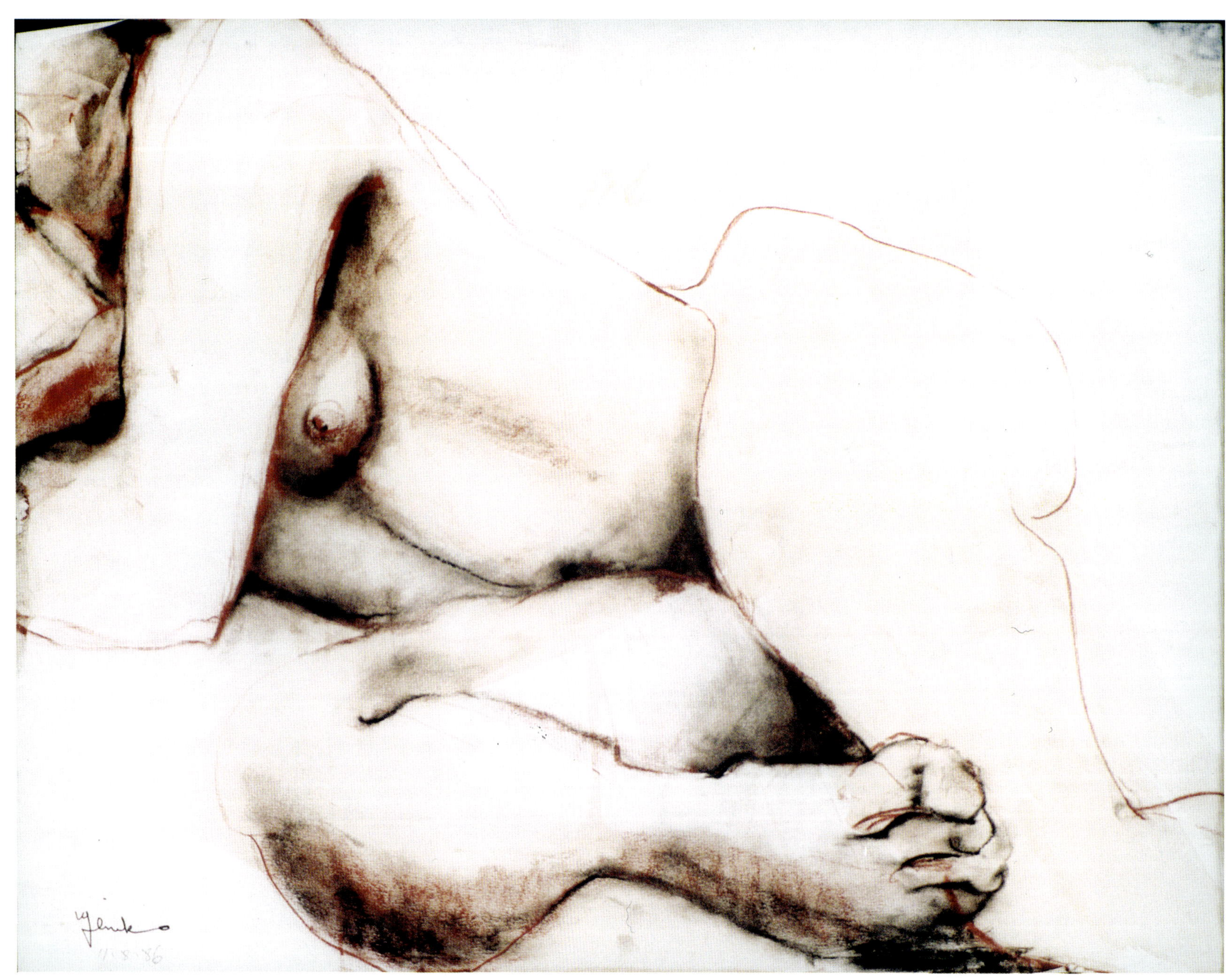

Reclining Ink wash 24" x 18"

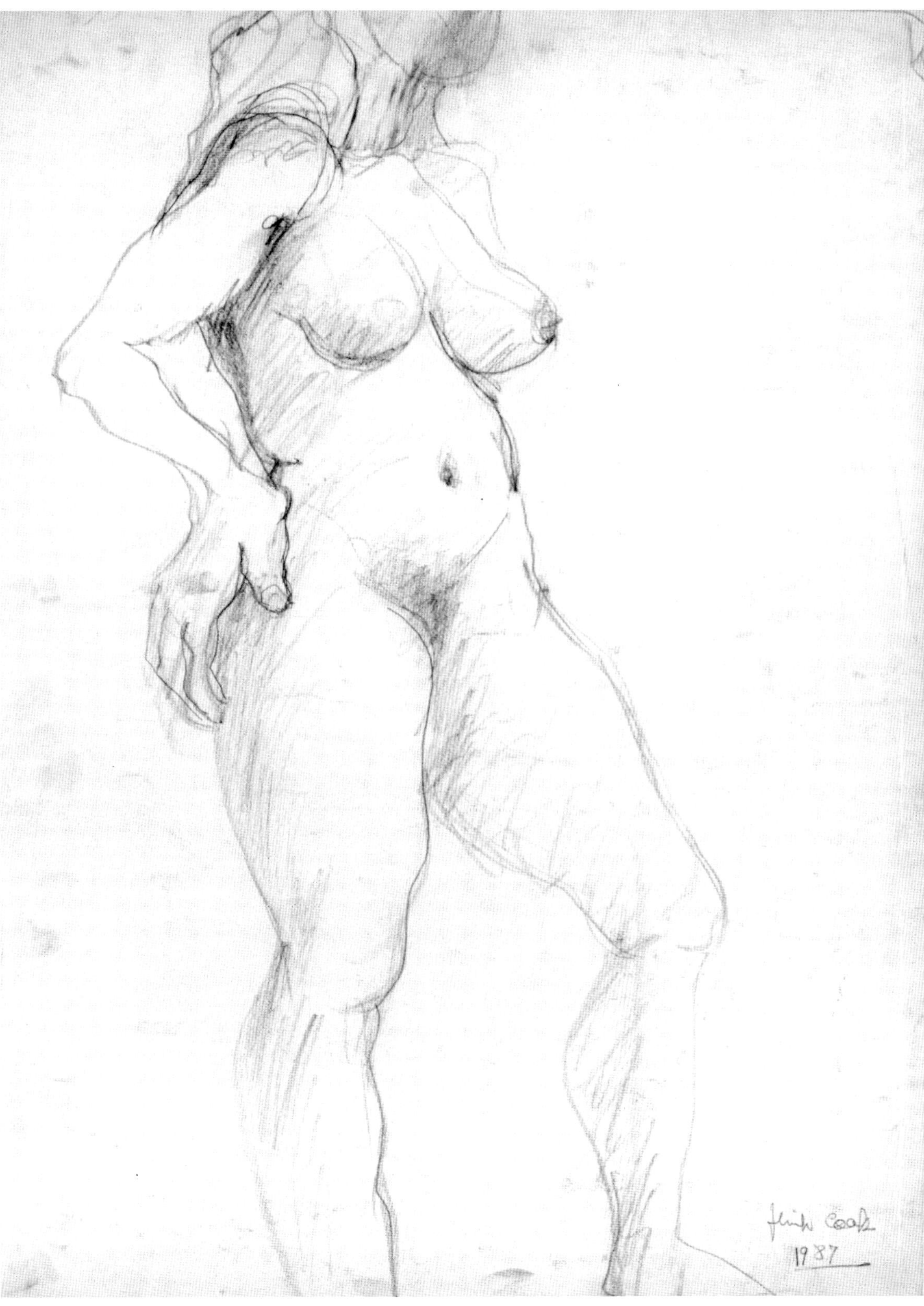

Laura   Pencil   28" x 22"

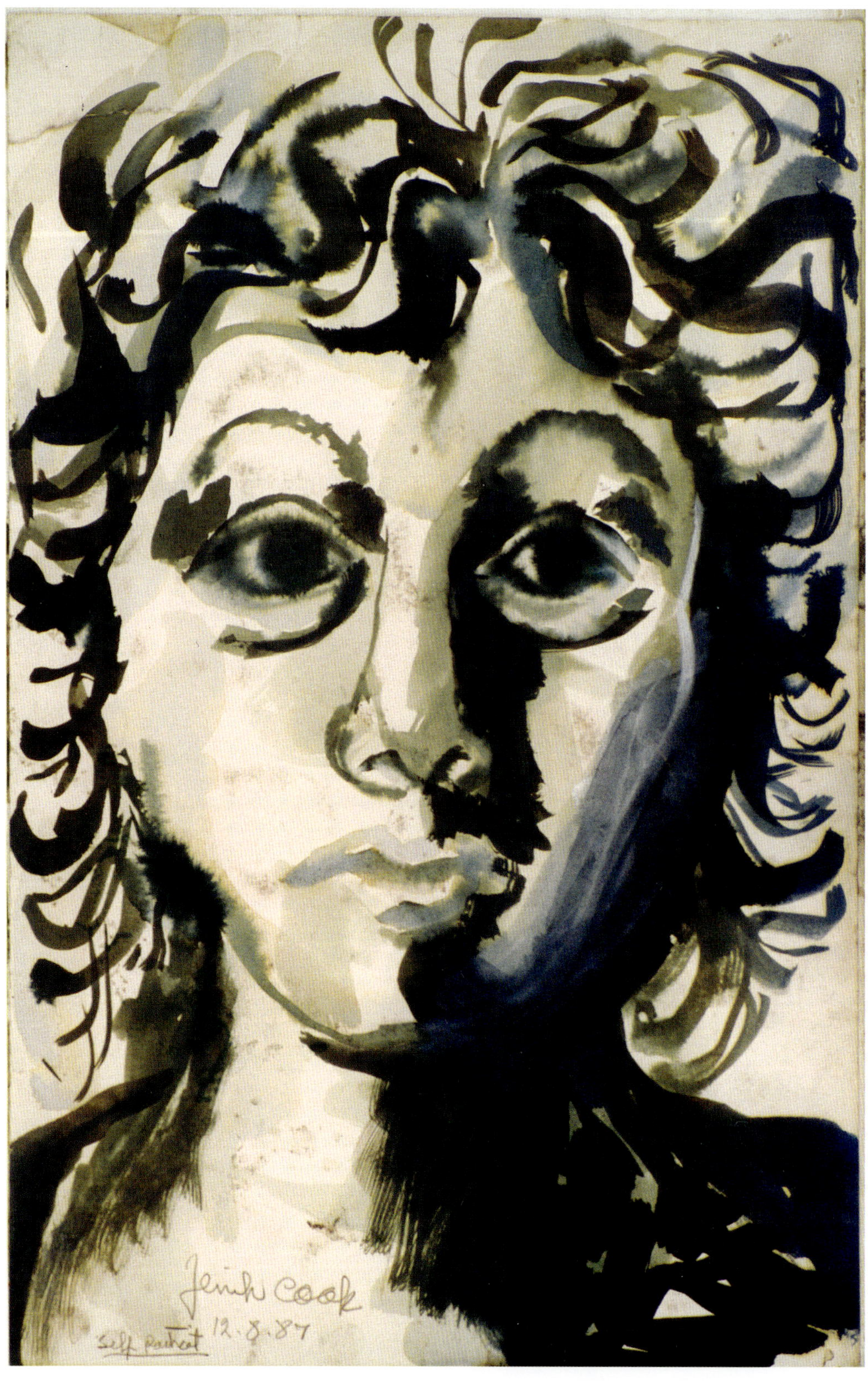

Jenik   Ink   16" x 12"

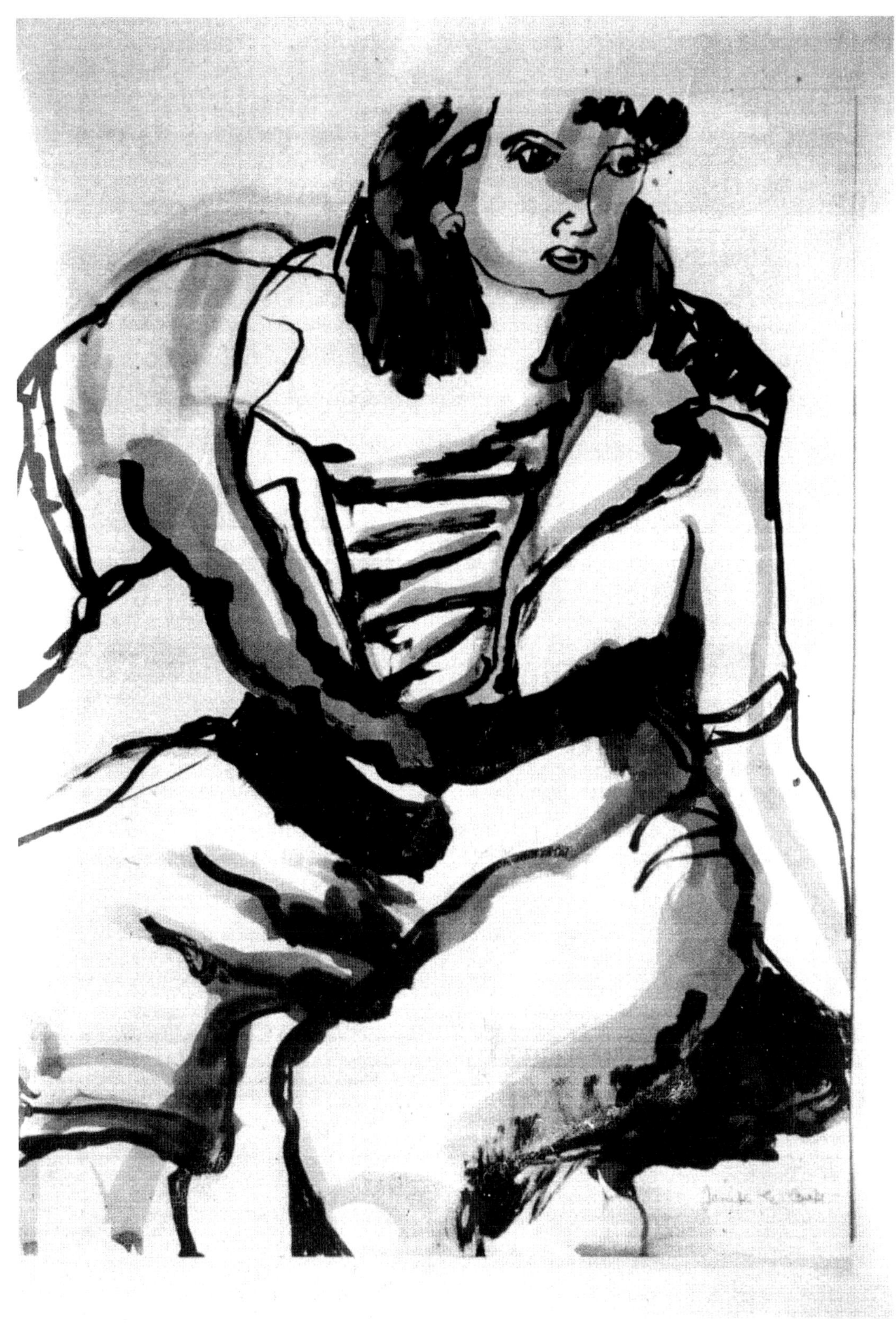

Cathy   18" x 24"

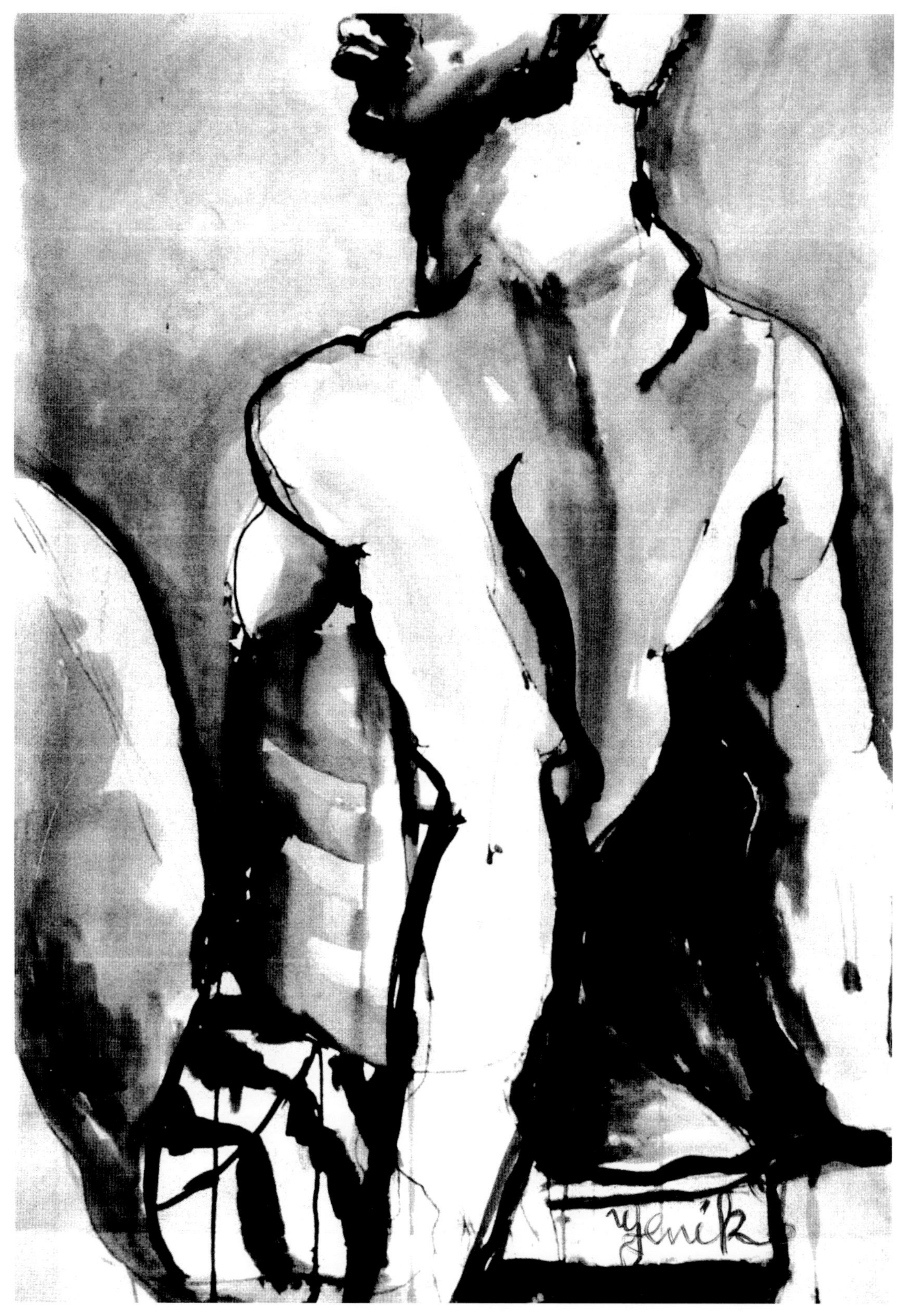

B & W No. 33   Mixed media   28" x 22"

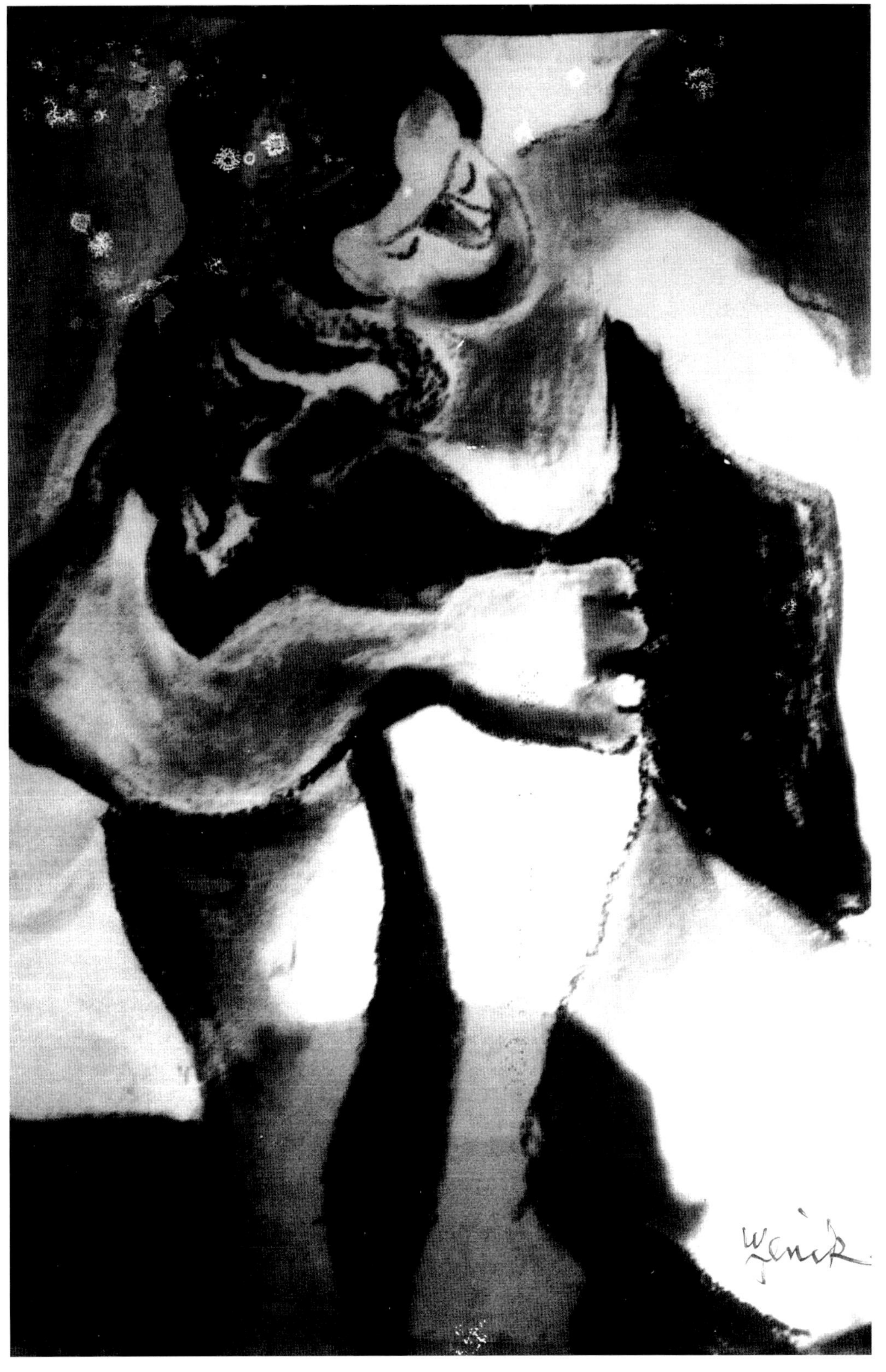

B & W No. 27   Wash & charcoal   24" x 18"

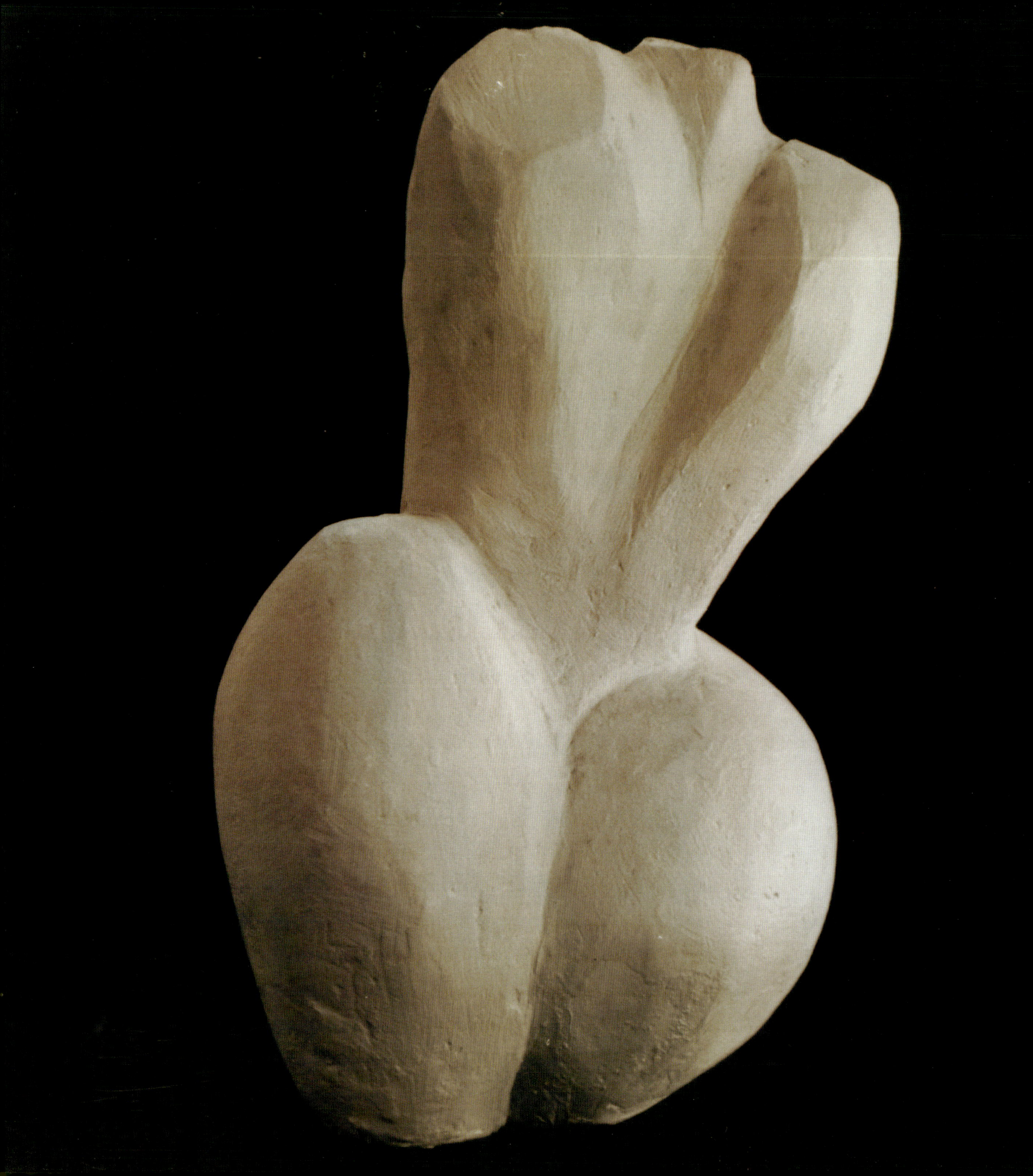

When light-hearted wile persuades material, pliant or severe,
into allusions of human presence, we gain an acquisition of
reference which resounds at the core of our collective identity.
The examples of Jenik's approach to sculpture which follow
reflect various aspects of her benignly individualistic posture.

Sculpture

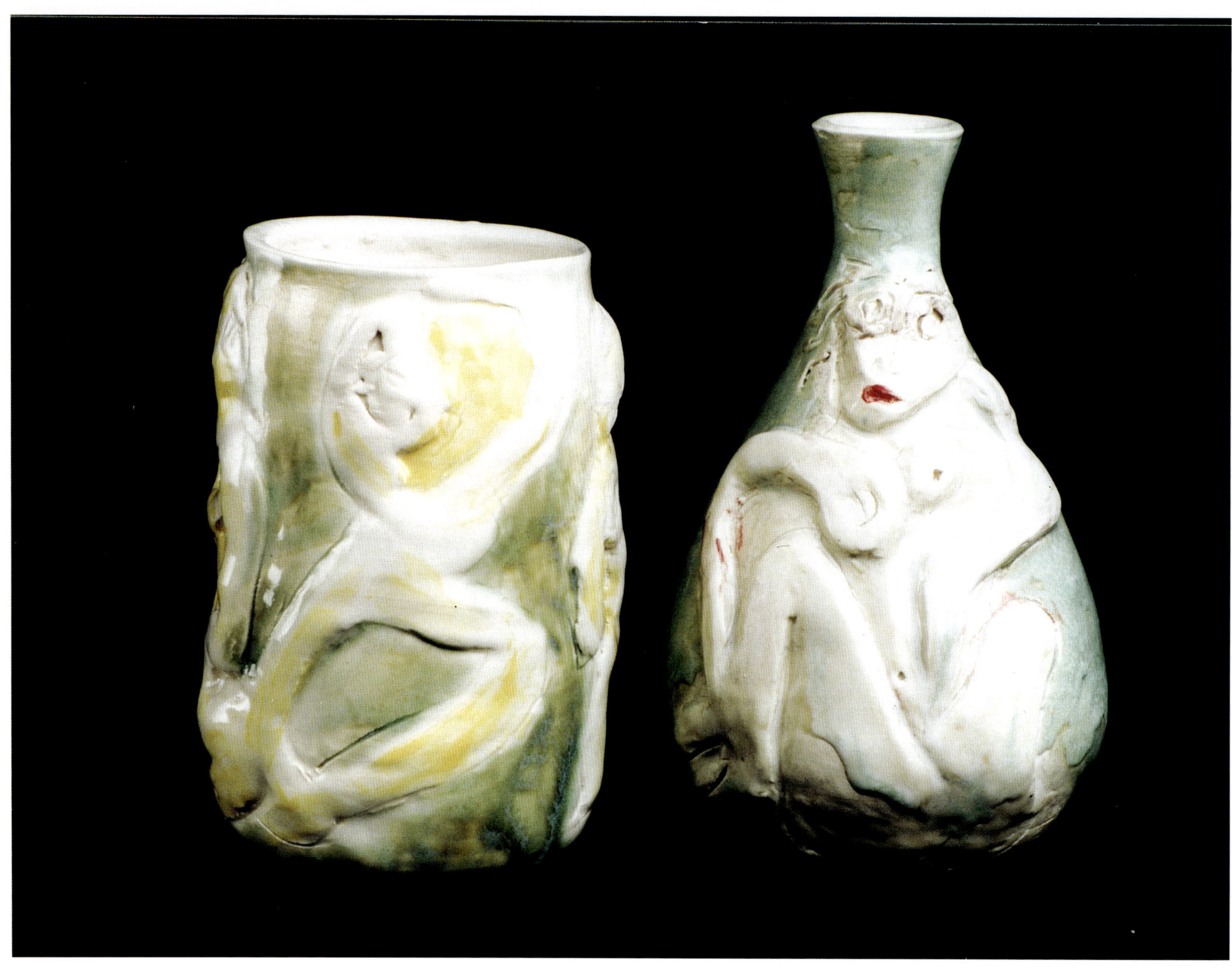

Untitled 6" x 12"   Untitled 8" x 14"

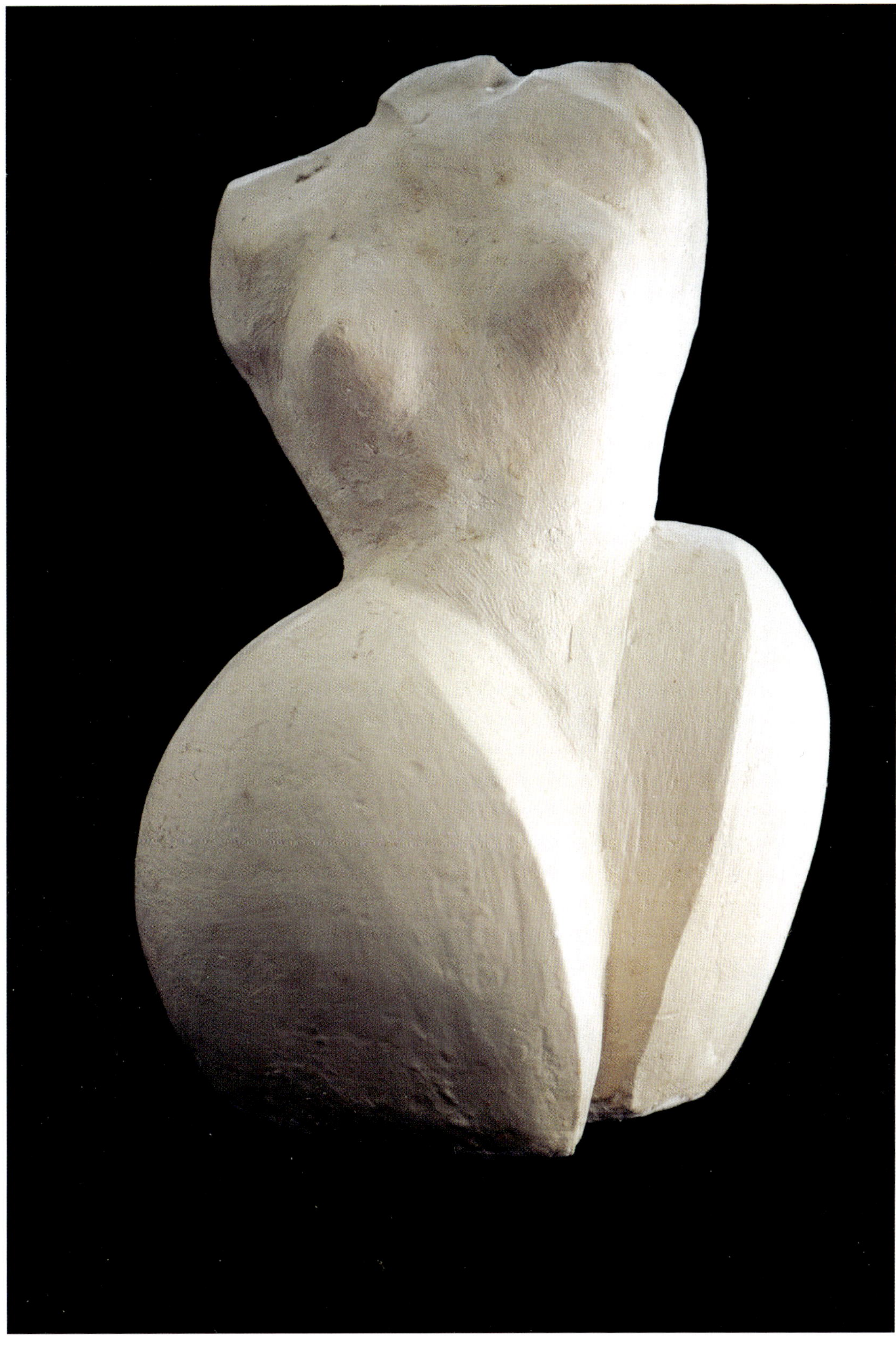

Untitled   Clay   17" x 30"

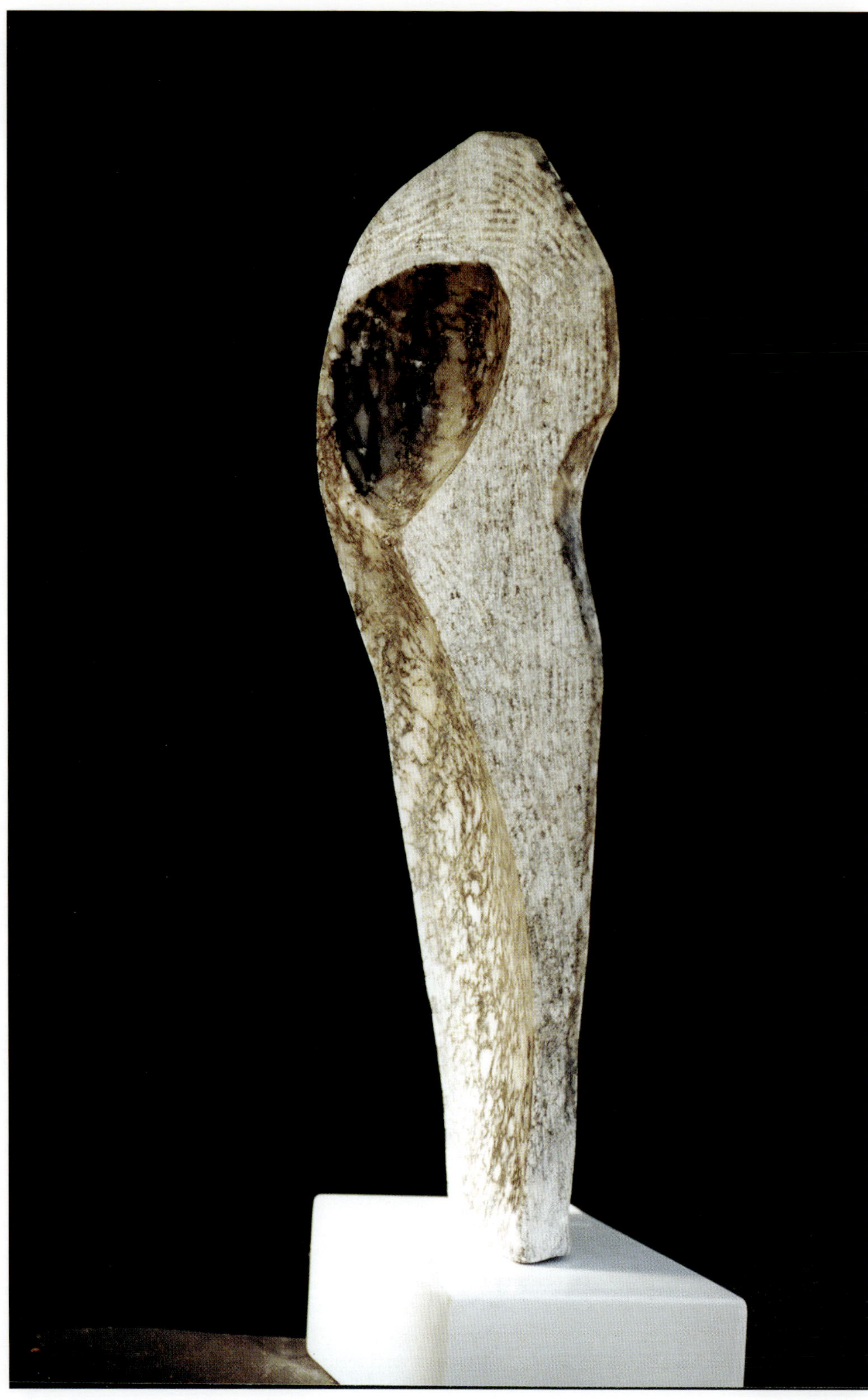

Untitled Stone 16" diameter

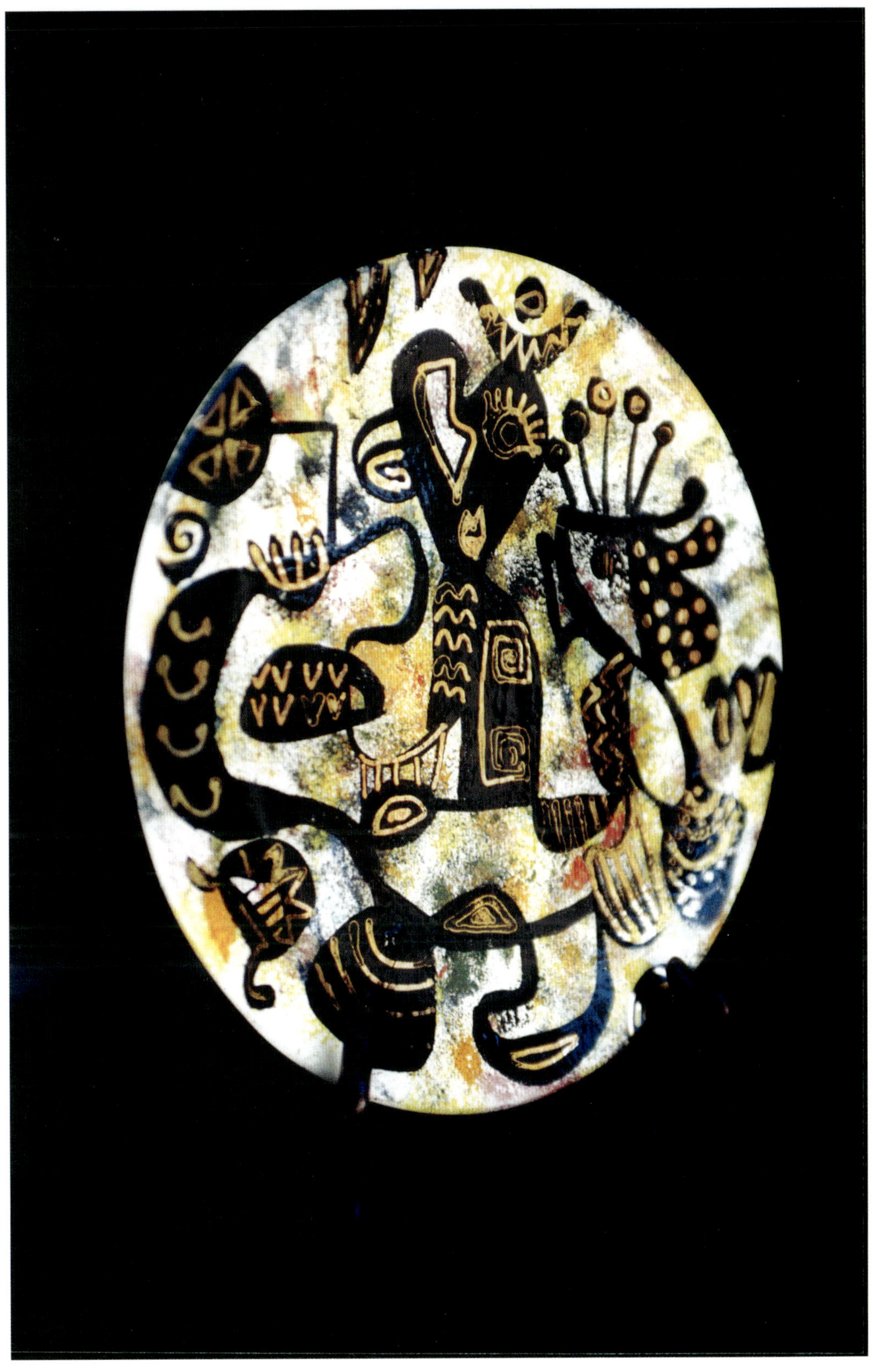

Plate, Low fire, 16" diameter

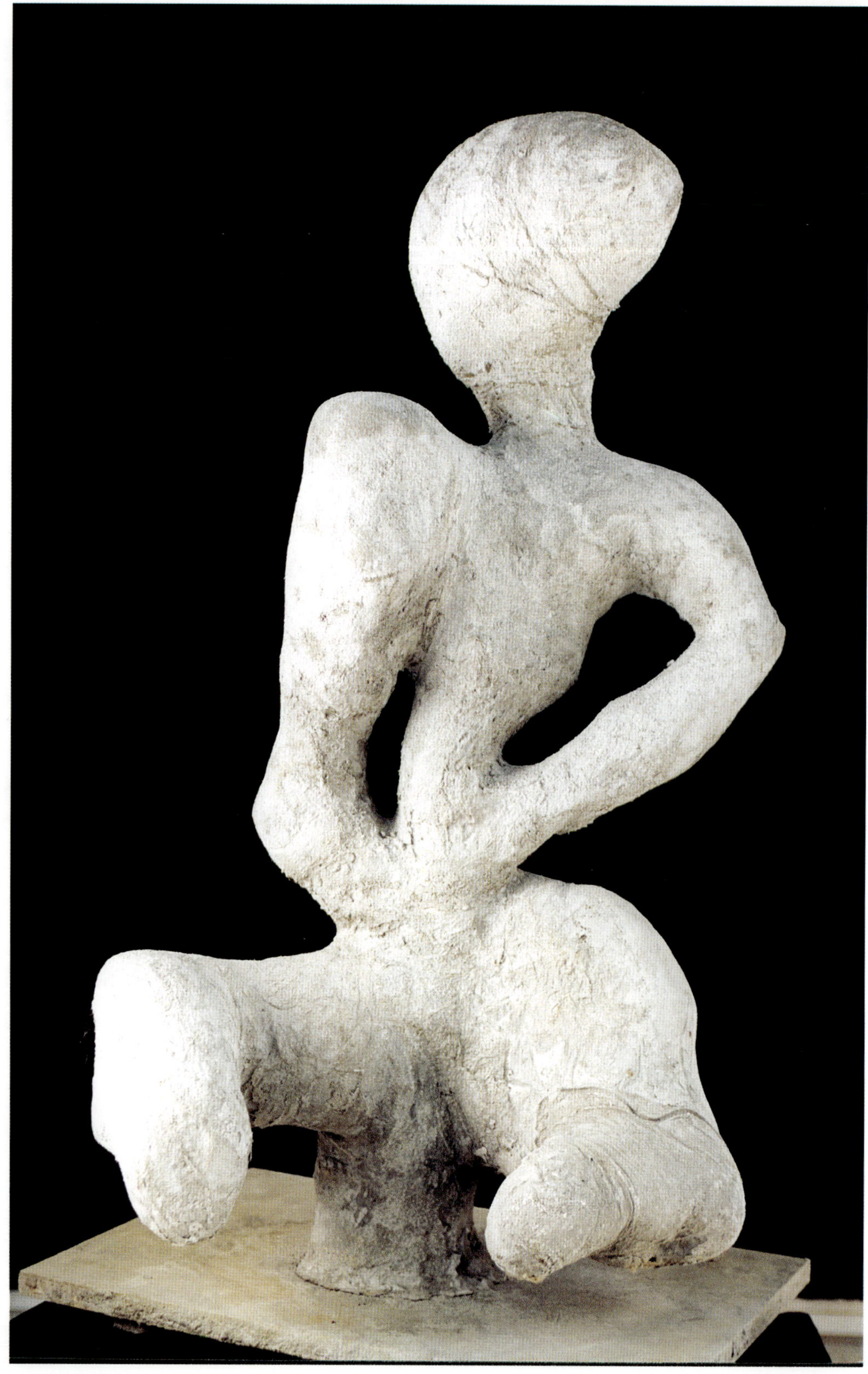

Untitled Cement 38" x 42"

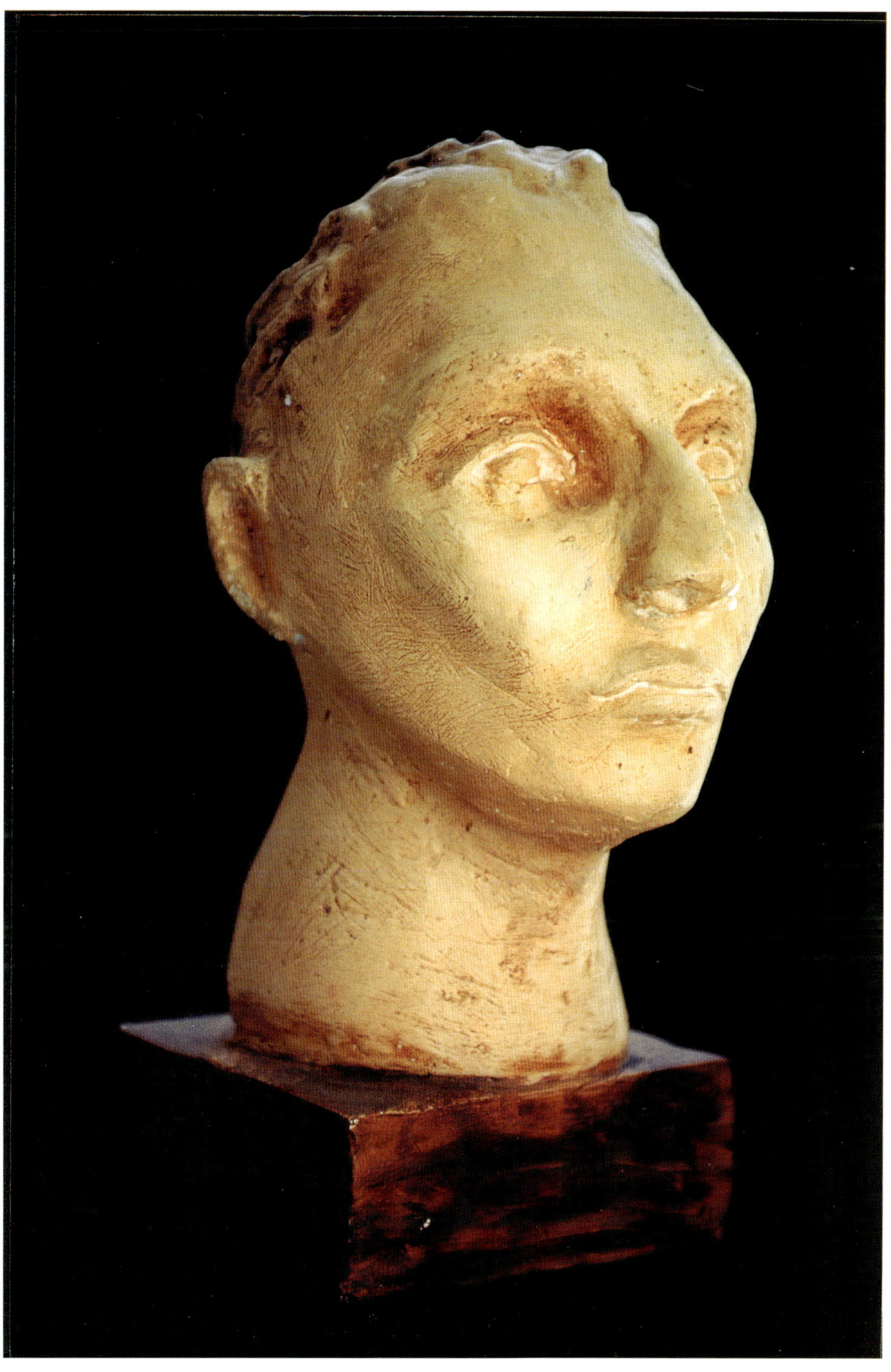

3/4 of Face, Plaster, 15" hight

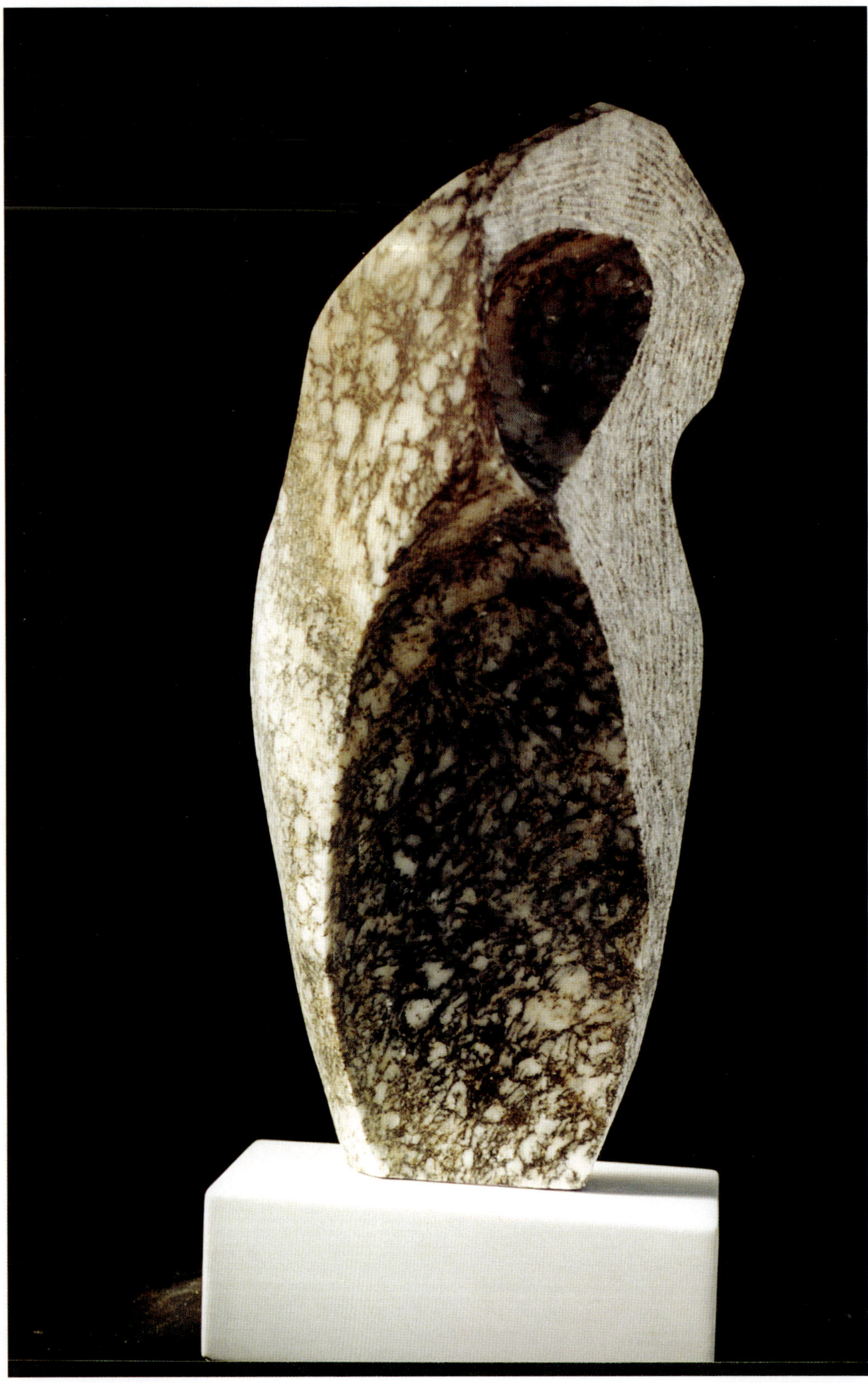

Untitled   Stone   20" x 22"

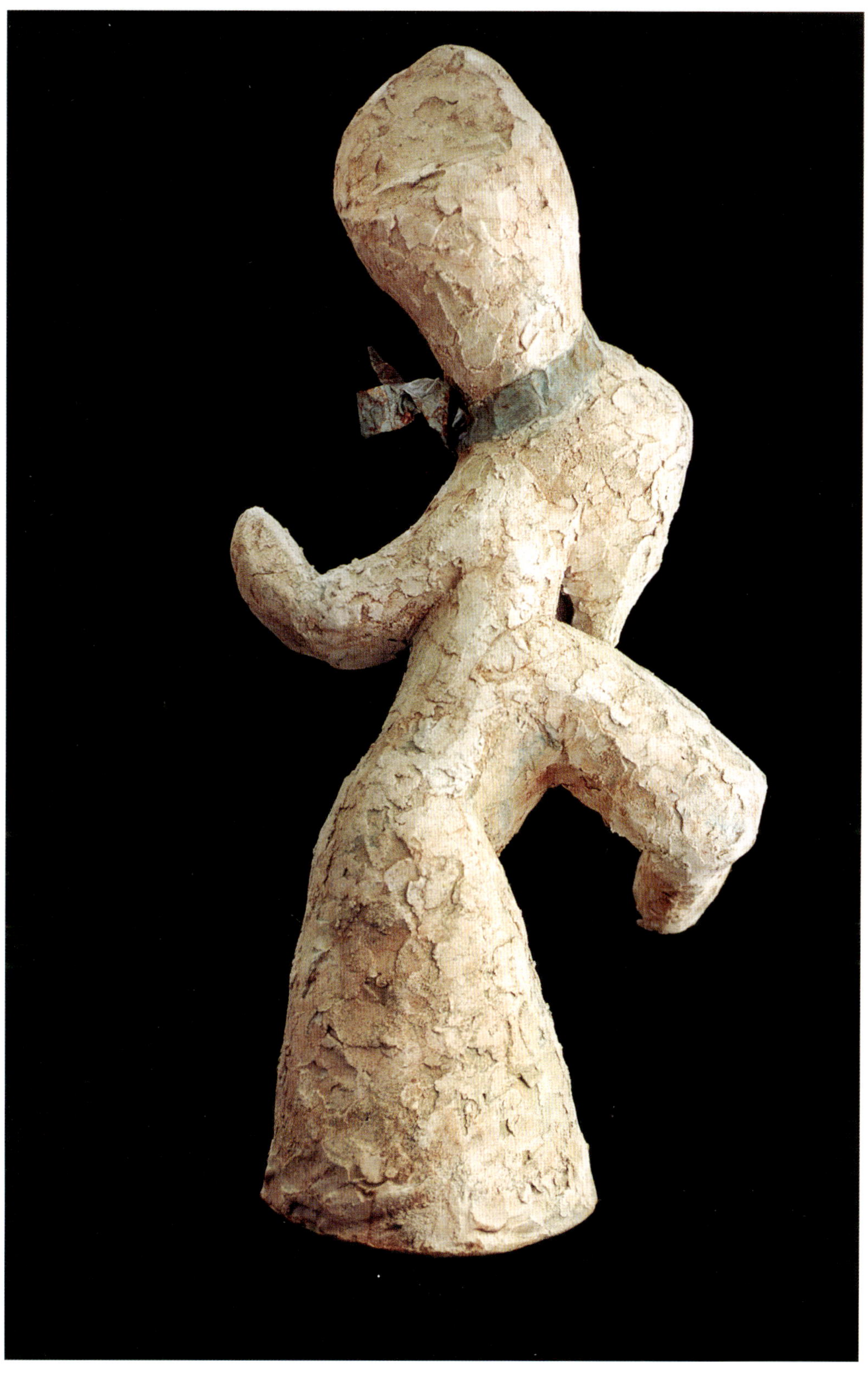

Untitled, Cement, 27" hight

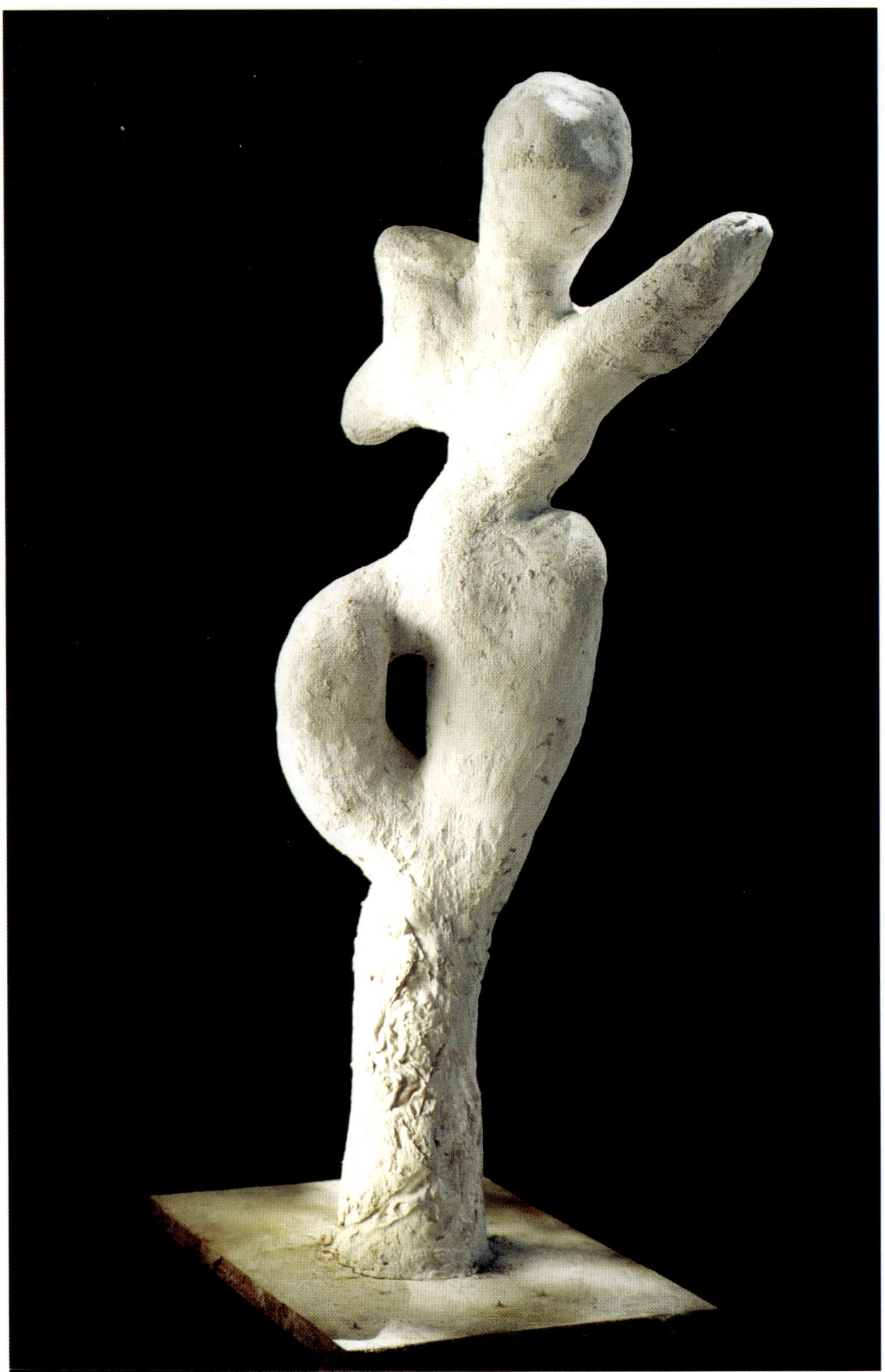

Untitled Cement 35" x 35"

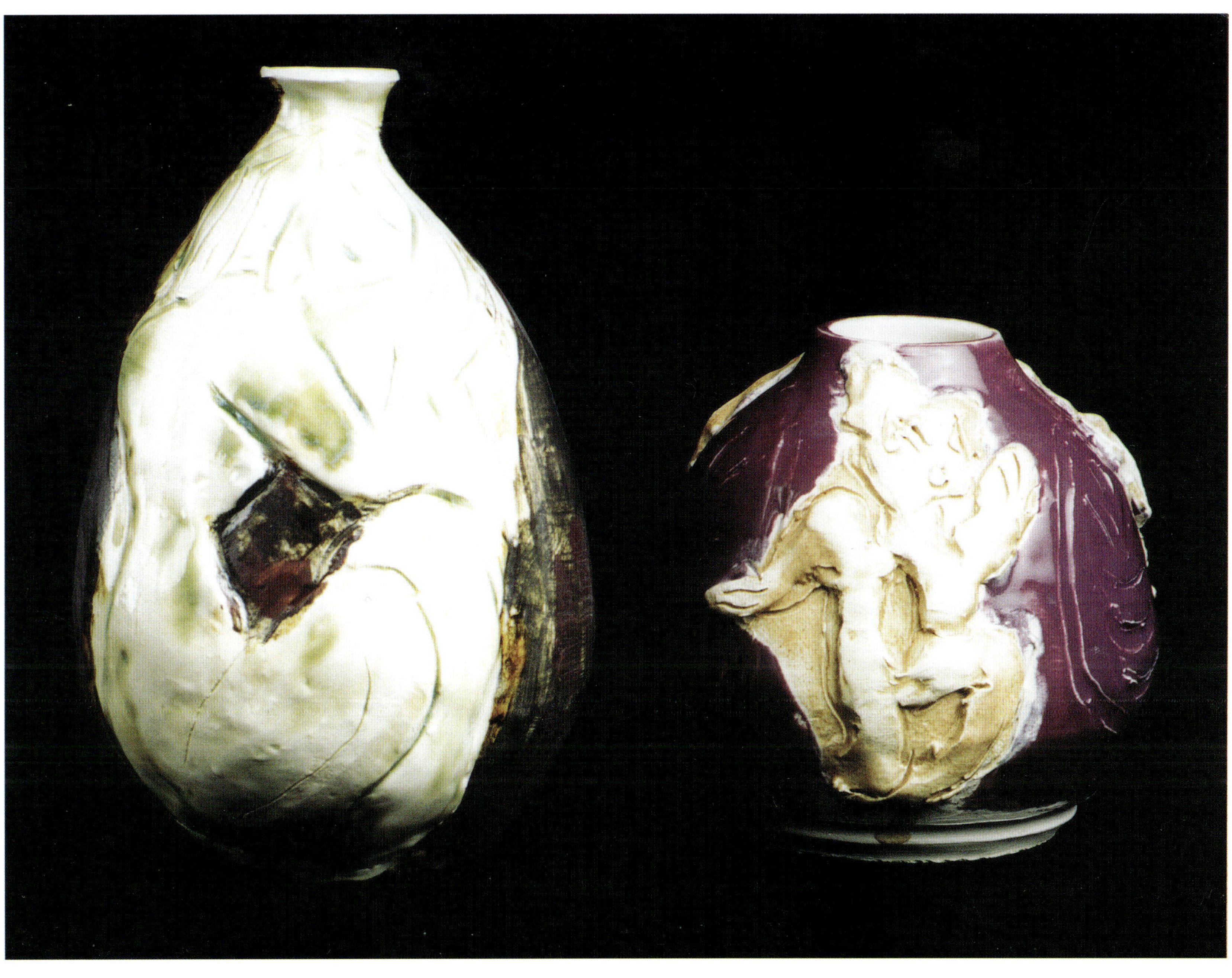

Untitled 8" x 16"   Untitled 6" x 18"

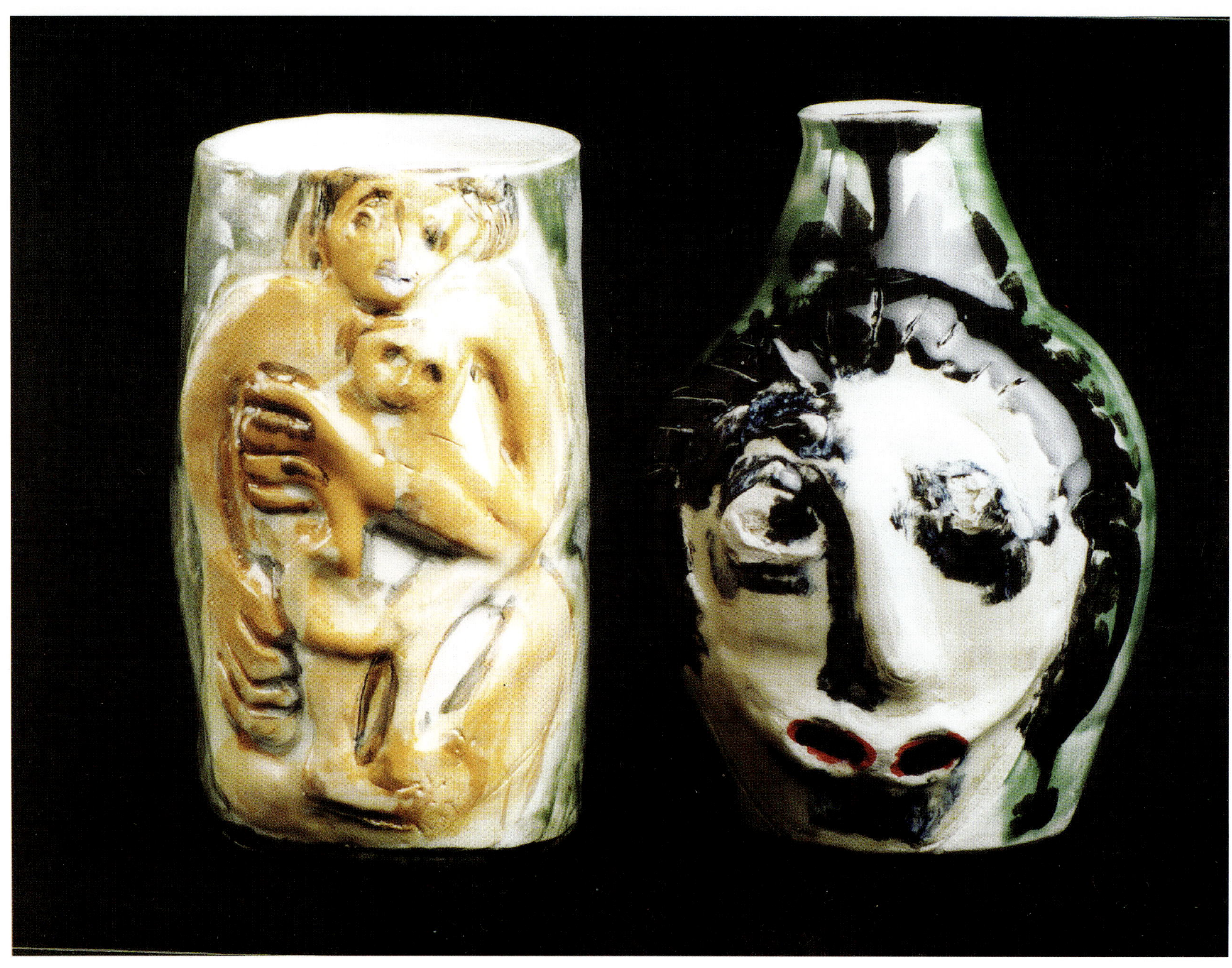

Untitled 7" x 13"   Untitled 8" x 16"

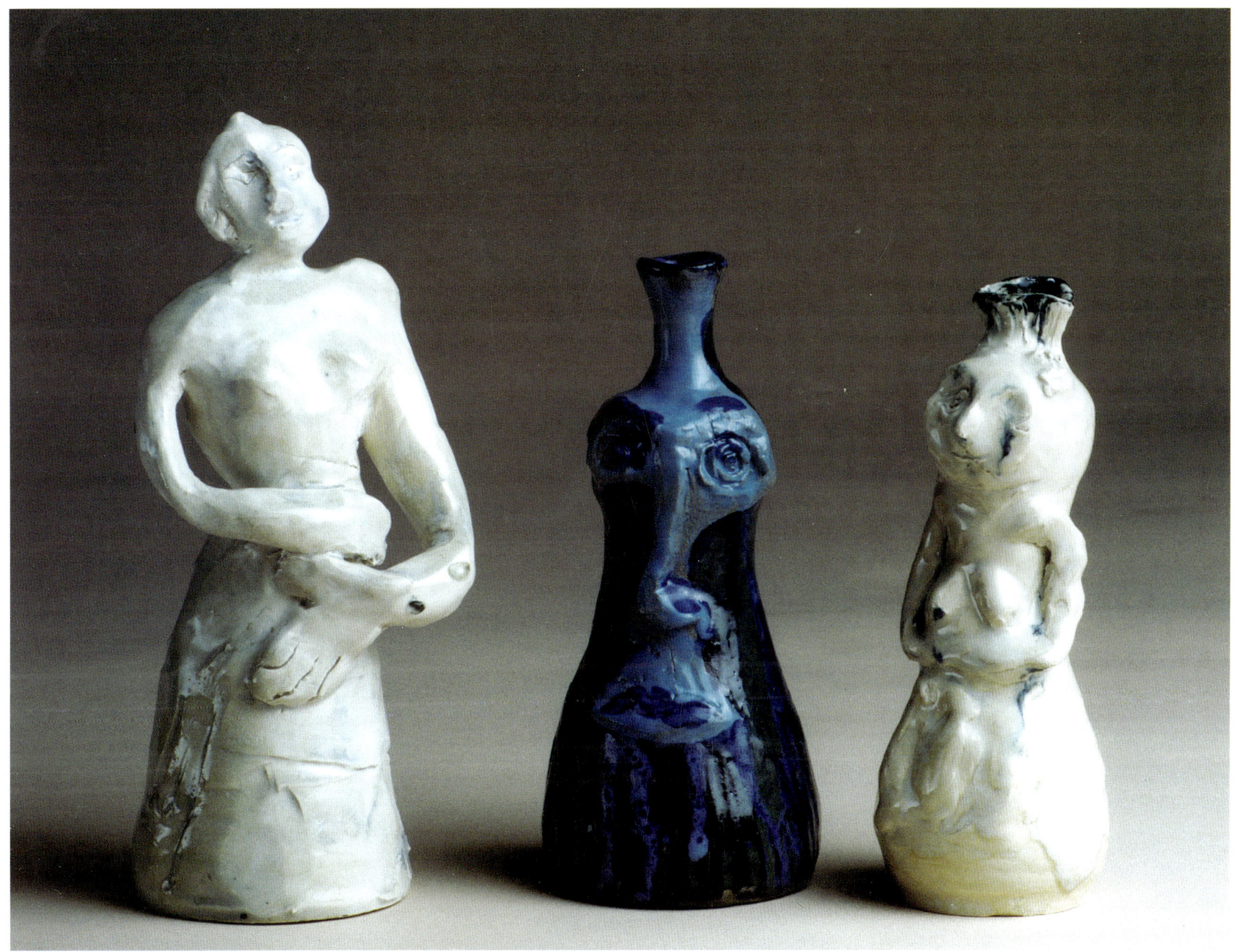

Untitled 14" x 16"   Untitled 7" x 12"   Untitled 7" x 9"

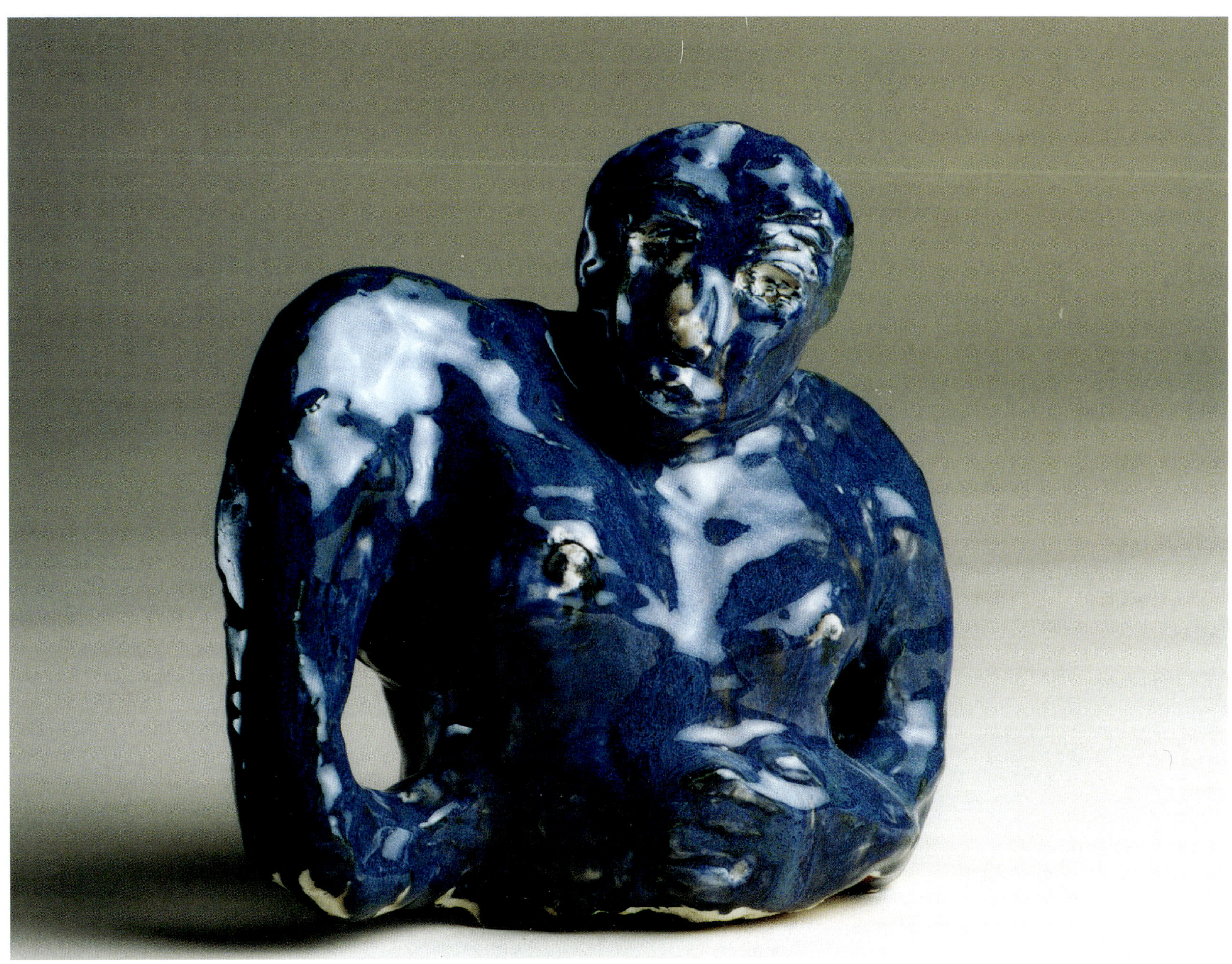

Untitled Clay 7.5" x 19"

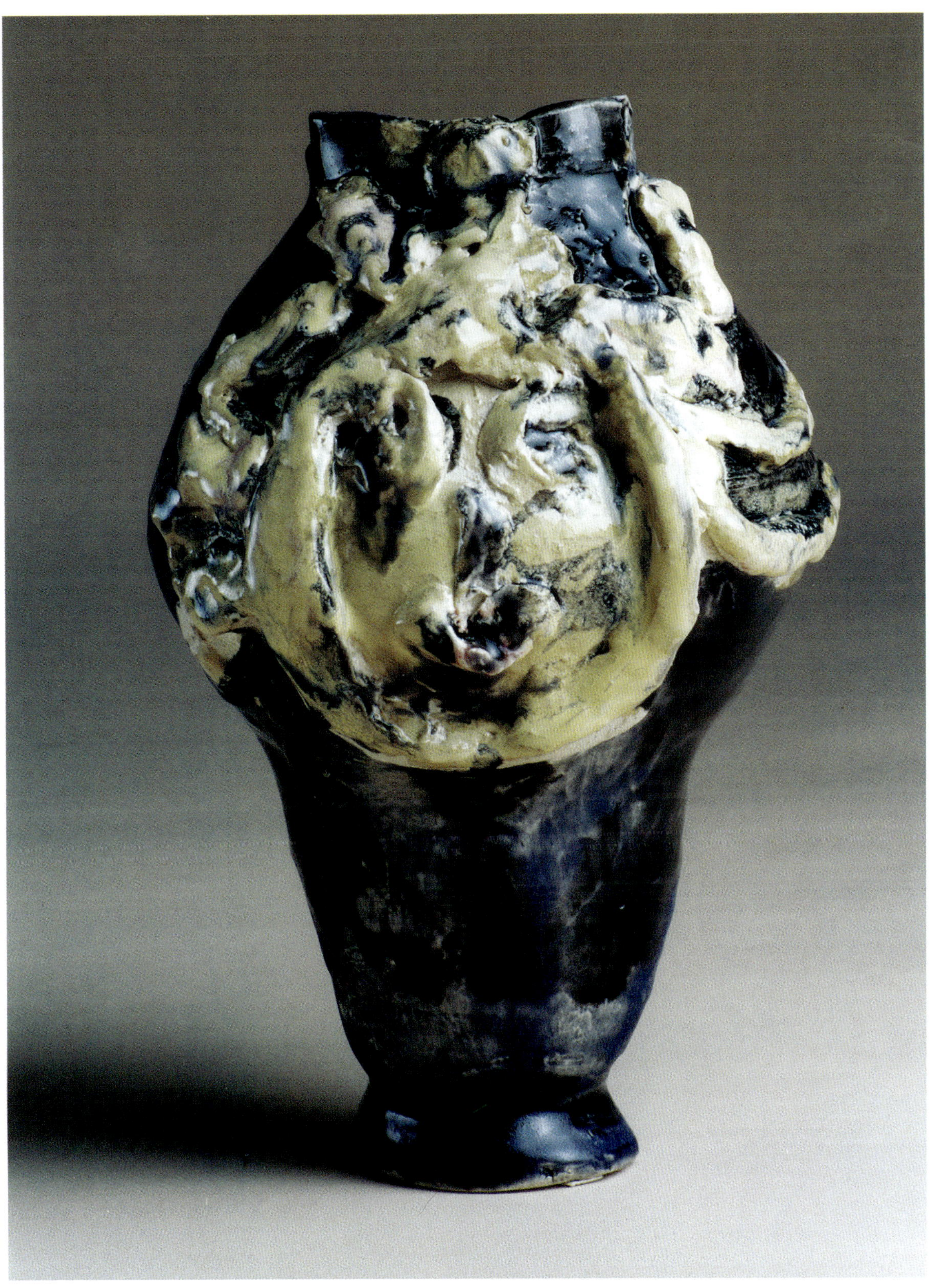

Untitled Clay 10" x 20"

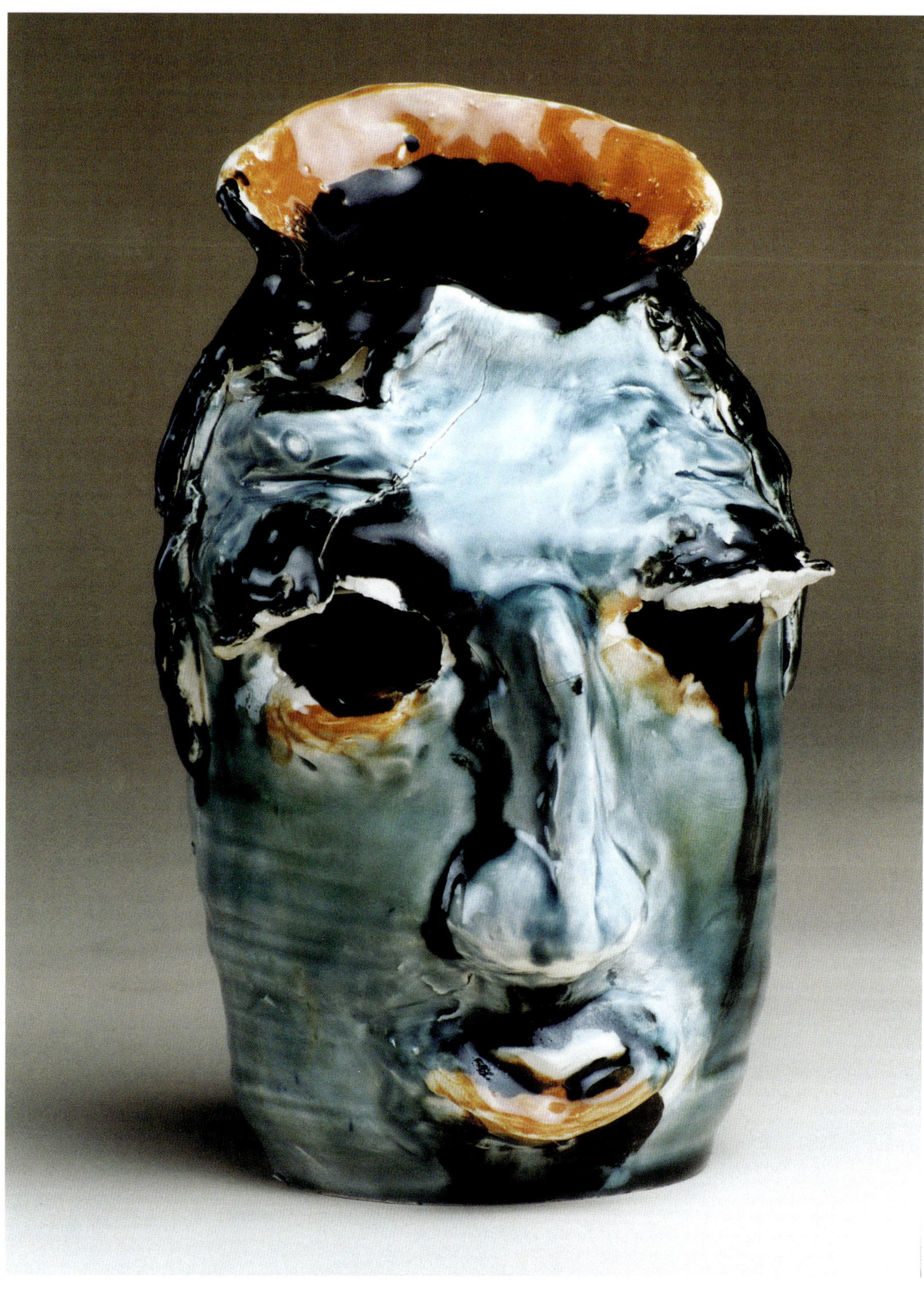

Untitled   Clay   10" x 18"

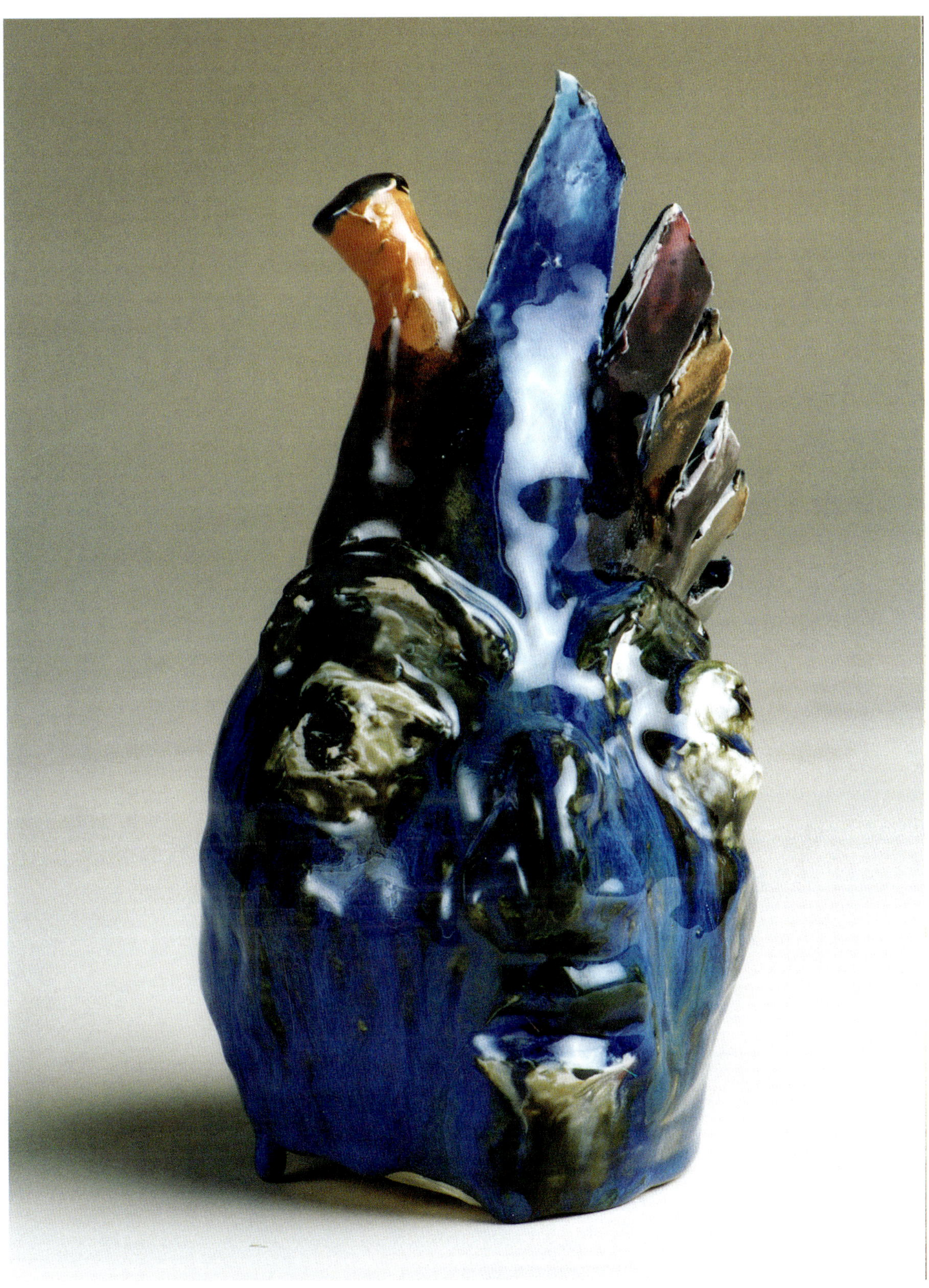

Untitled Clay 14" x 16"

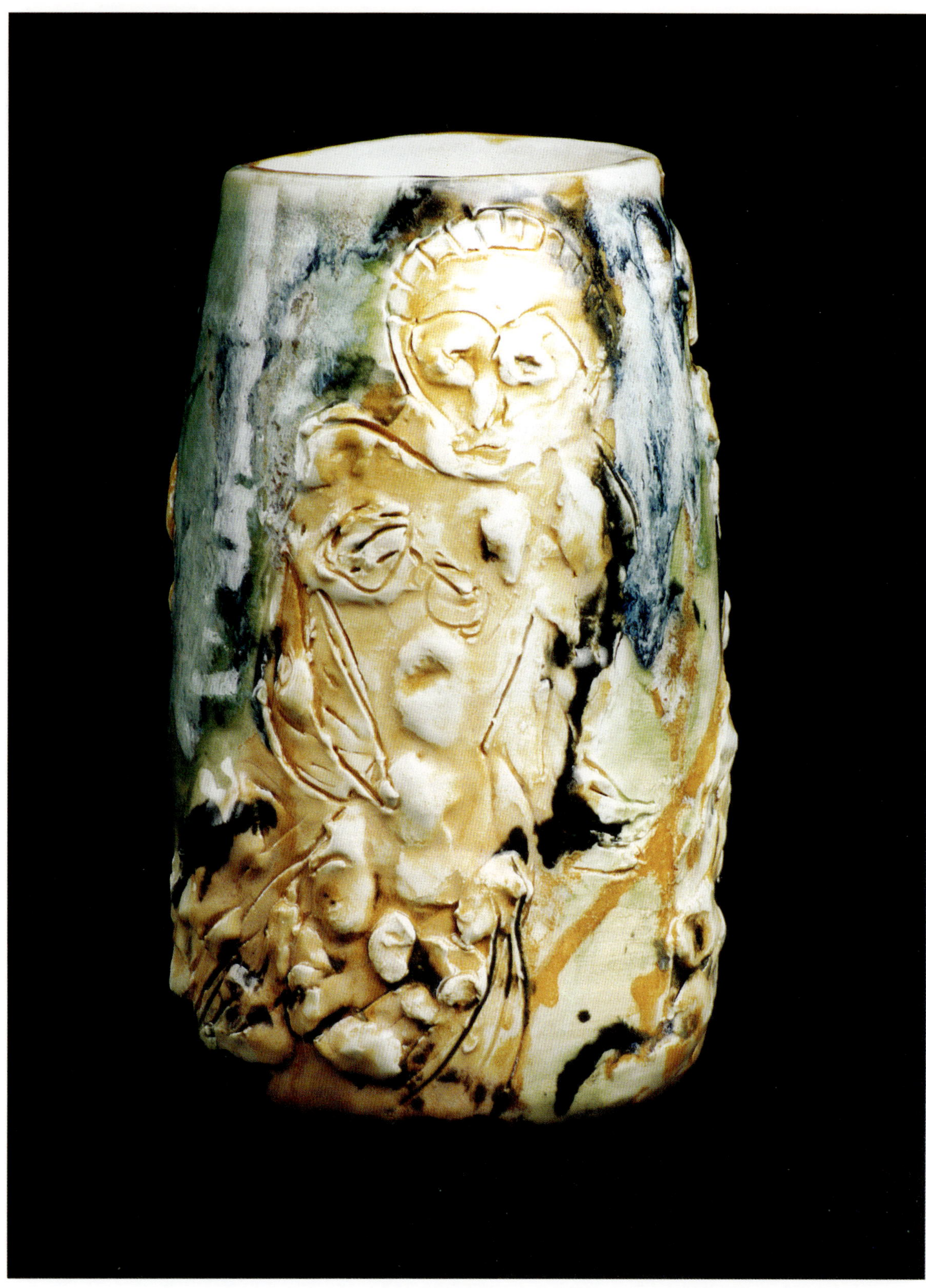

Untitled   7" x 14"

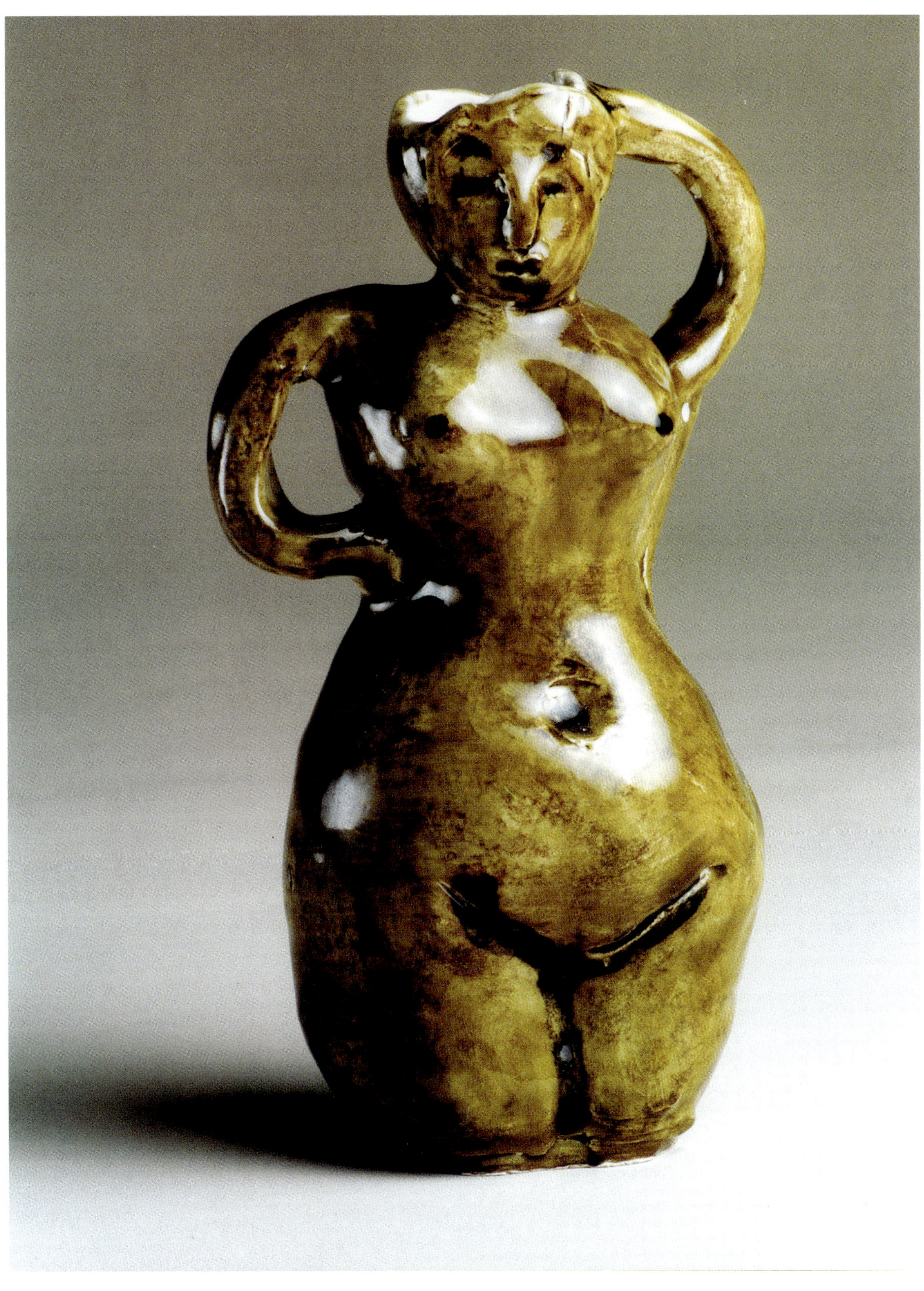

Untitled Clay 9" x 12"

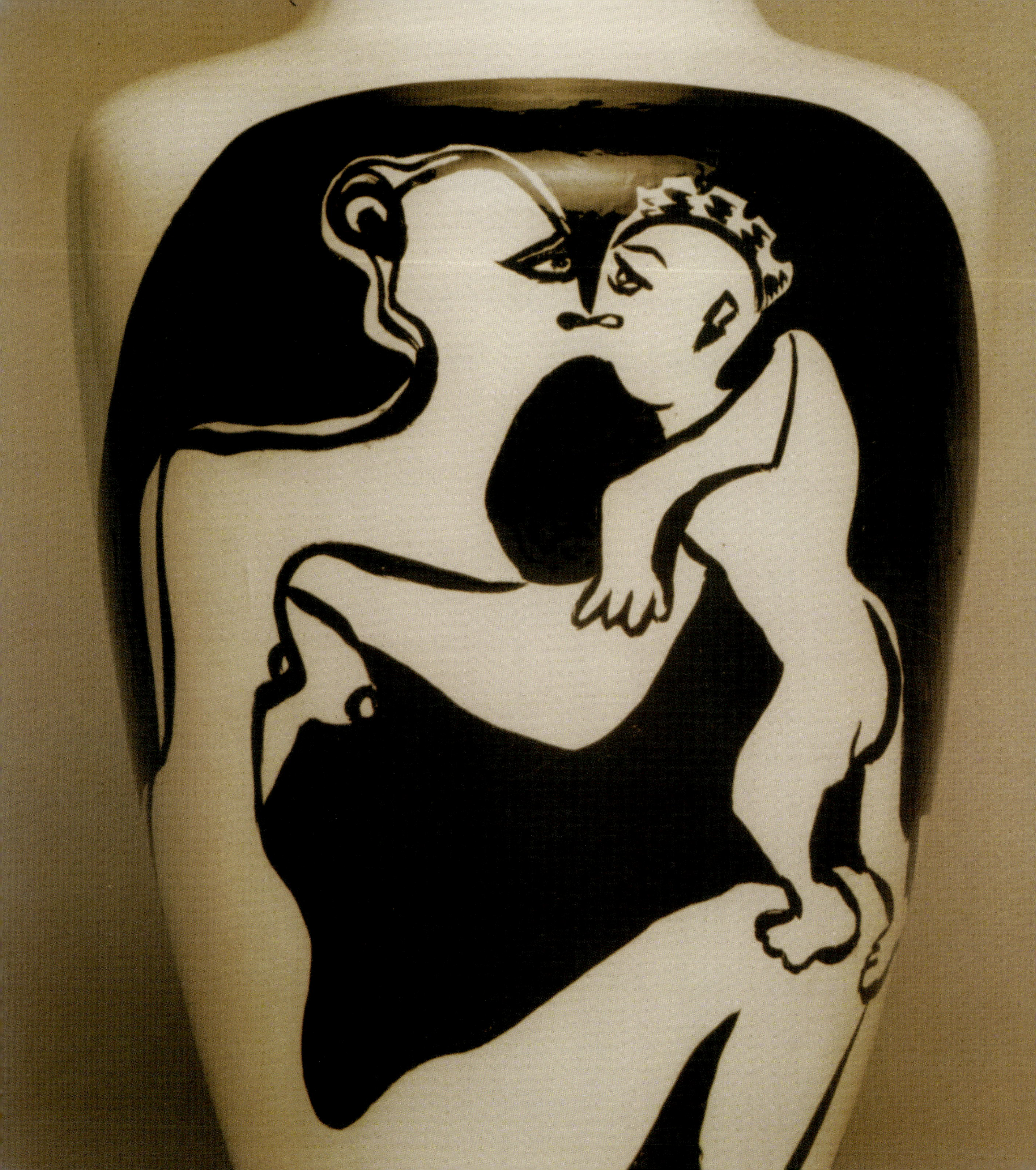

Turning her distinct *coup d'œil* to the surface curvatures of an art with roots lost in the mists of time, Jenik applies her apportionments of image with the same lust of guided freedom which distinguishes her work on canvas or paper. Adjustment more than concession tends to characterize her address to texture and substance in achieving the overall effect of these fine creations.

Ceramics

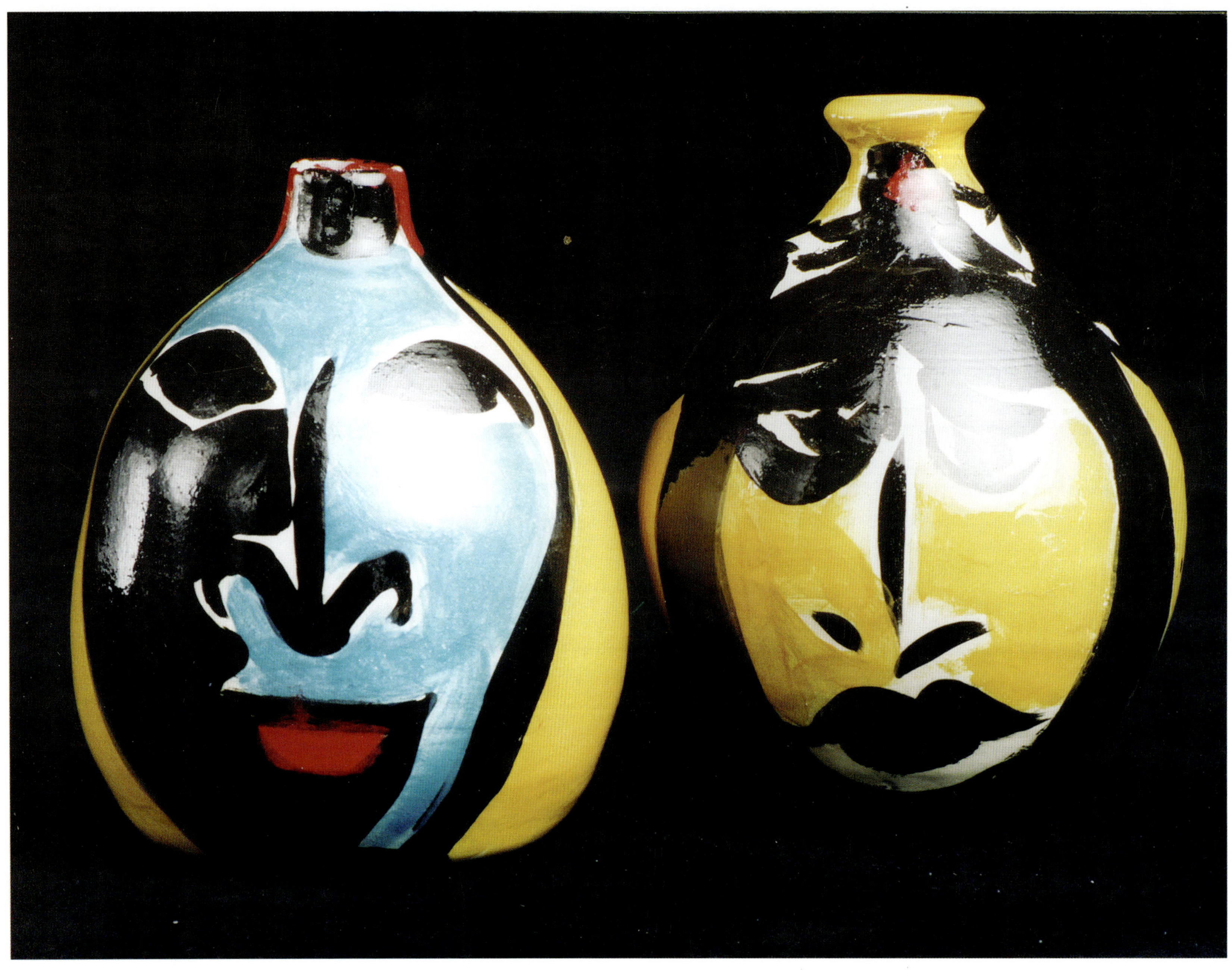

Untitled 8" x 18"   Untitled 7" x 16"

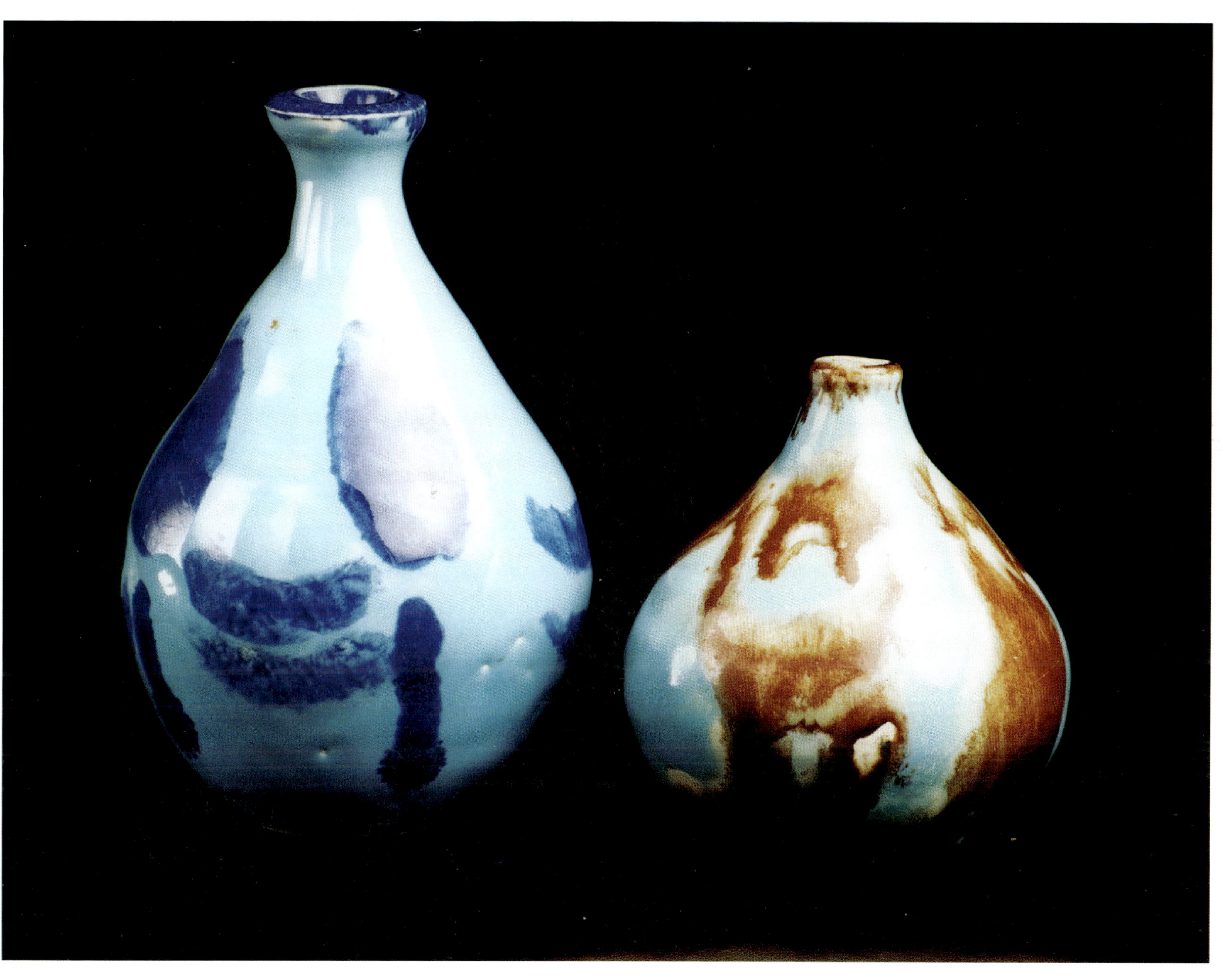

Untitled 8" x 16"   Untitled 4" x 10"

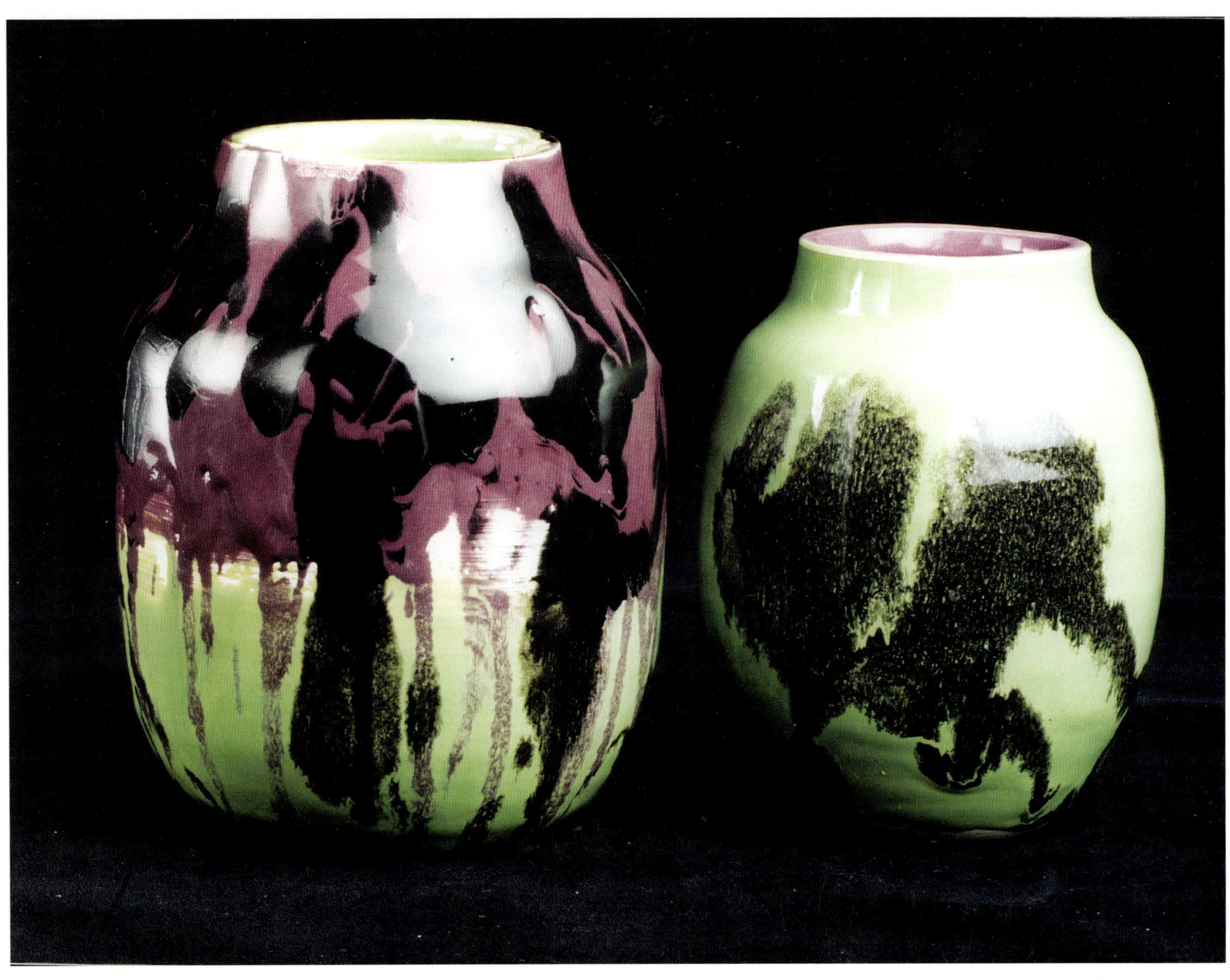

Untitled 8" x 19"   Untitled 7" x 16"v

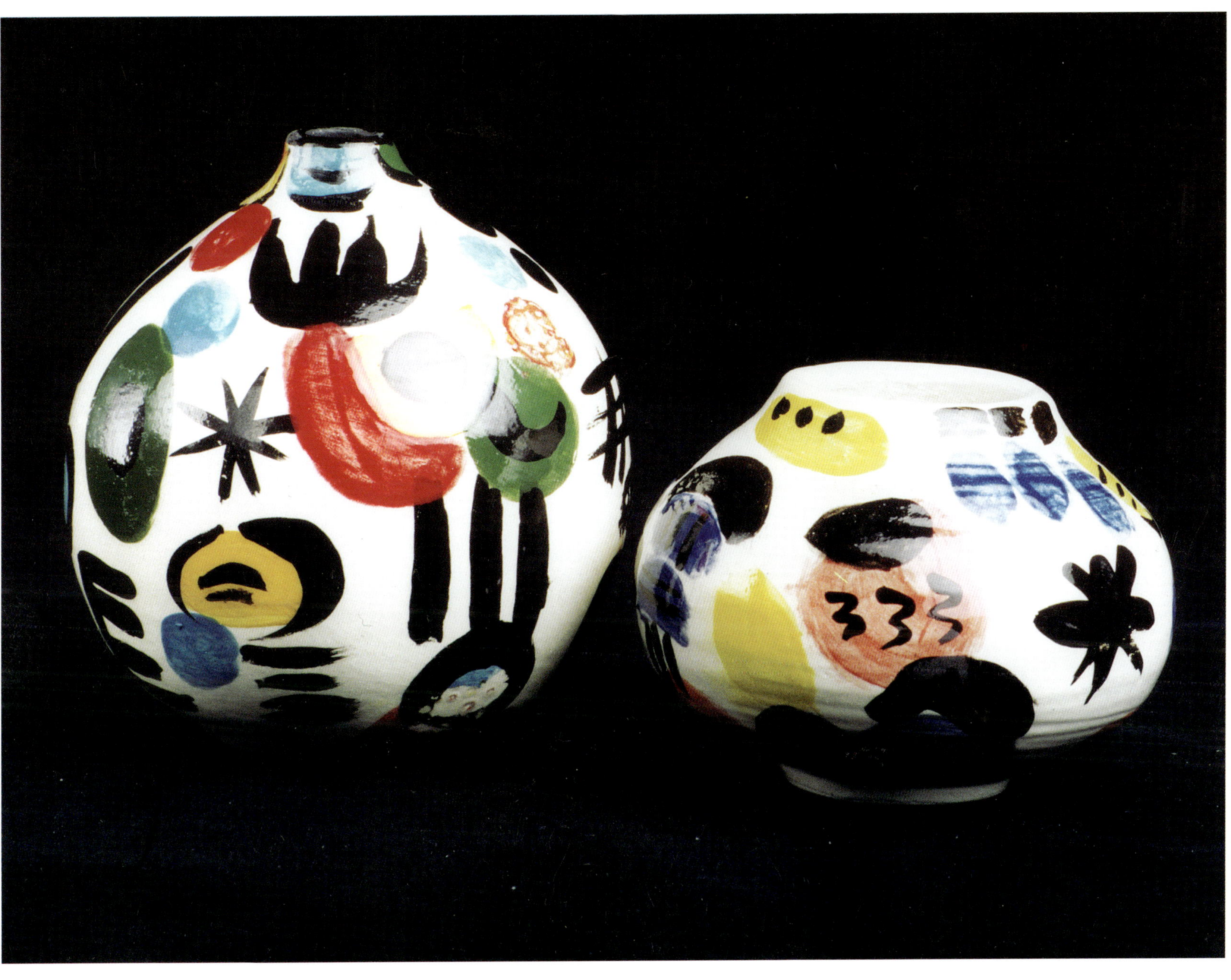

Untitled 7" x 16"   Untitled 4" x 12"

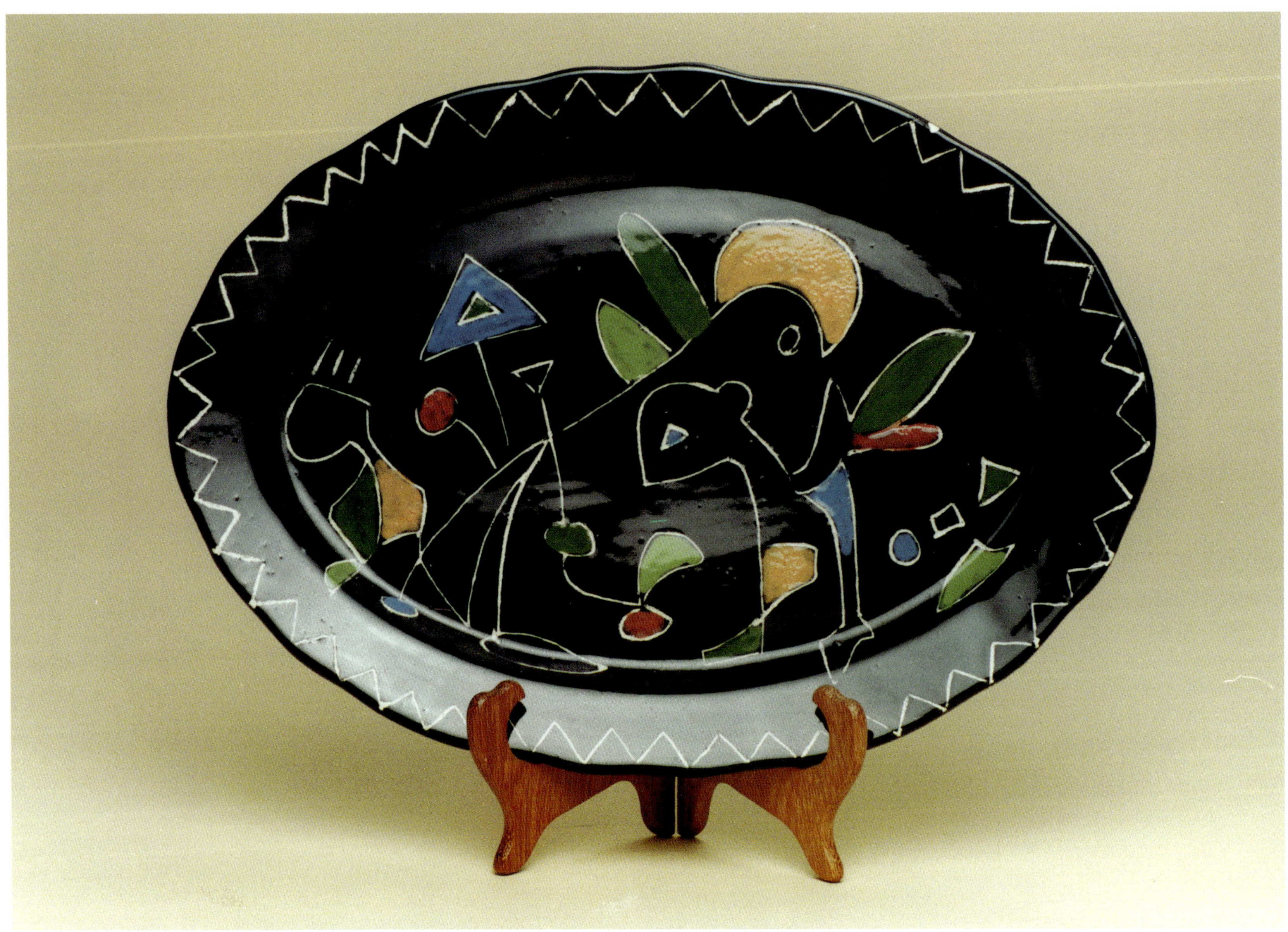

Low Fire Platter

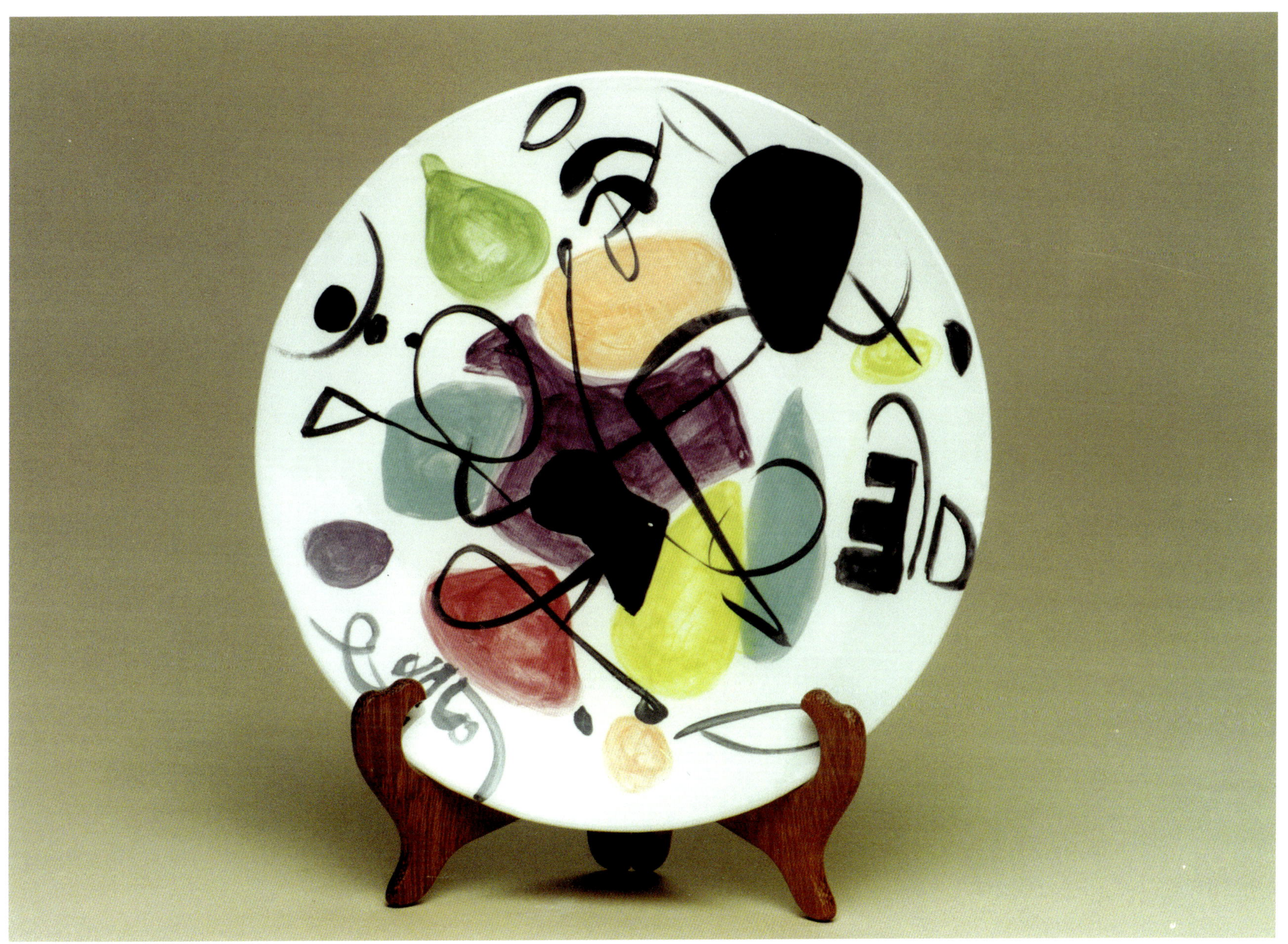

Hand Painted Low Fire Plate

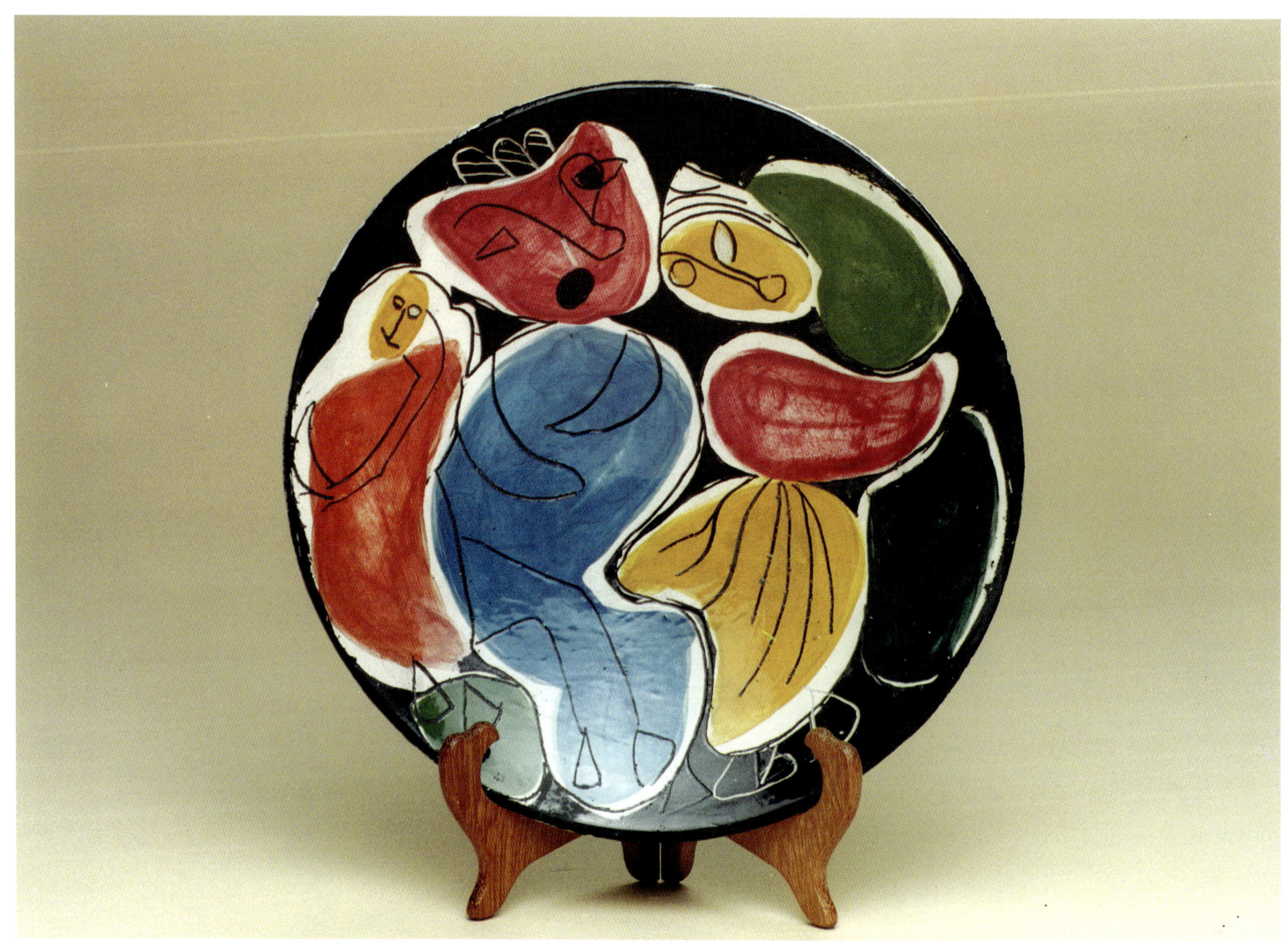

Low Fire Painted Plate

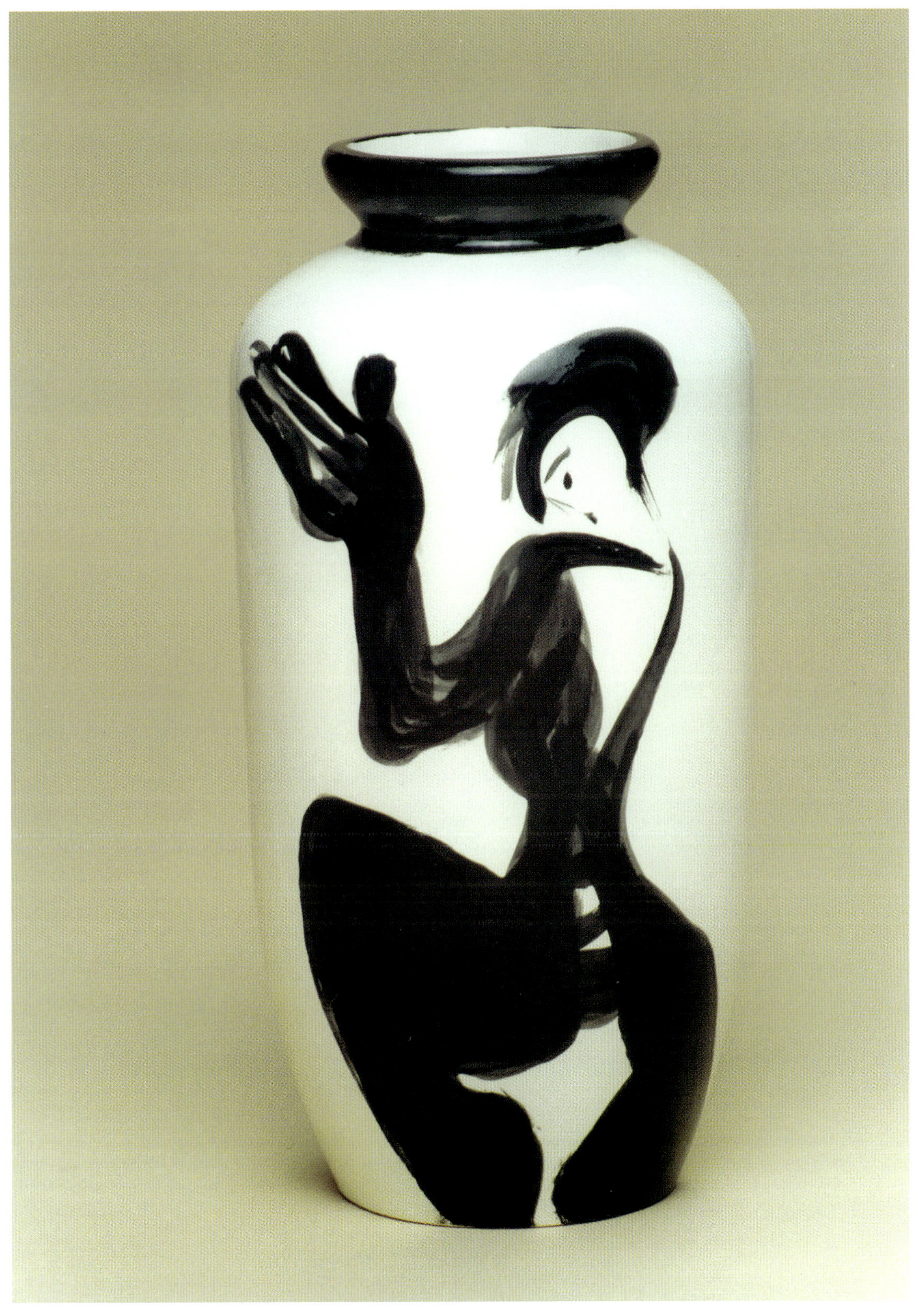

Painted Low Fire

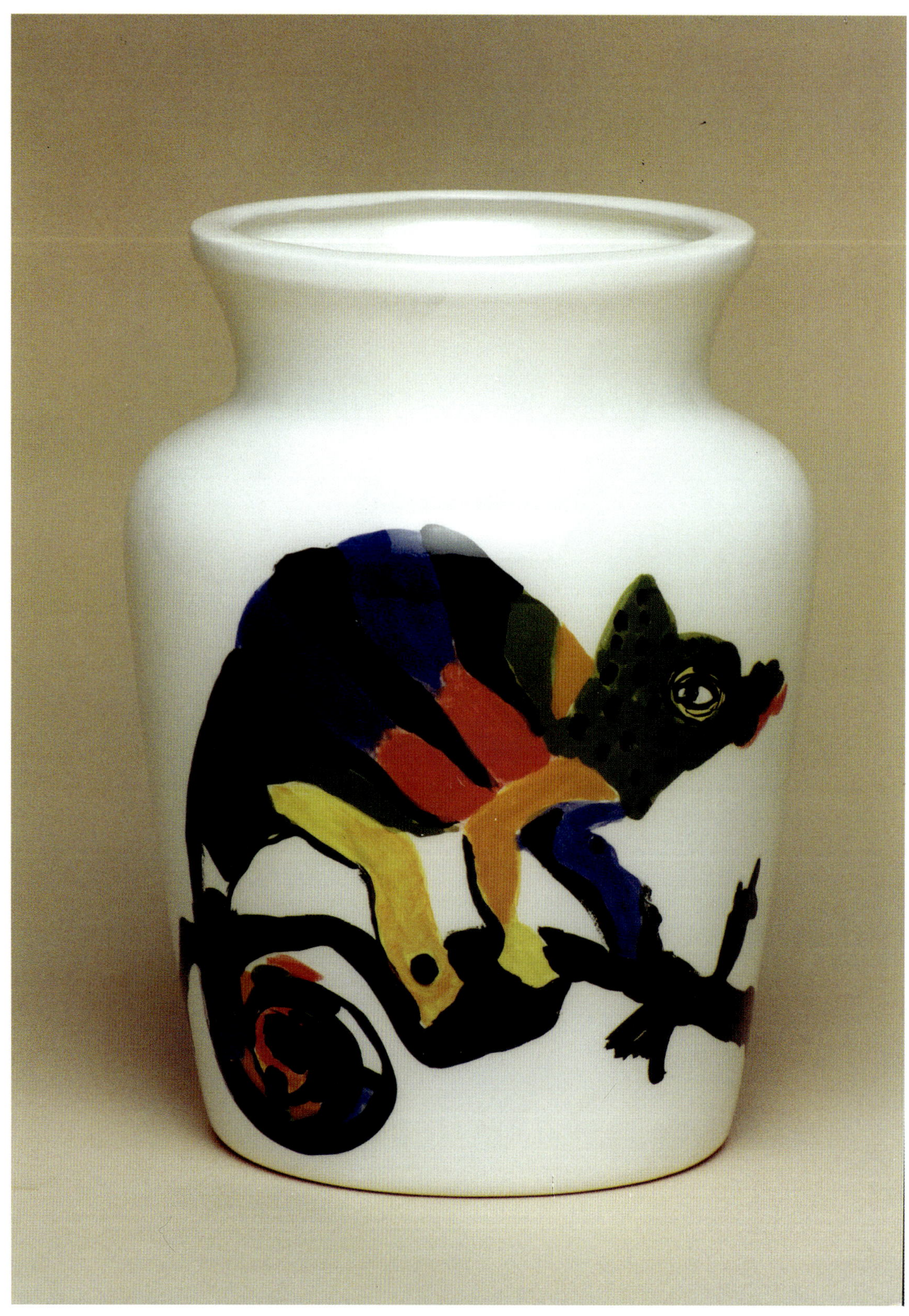

Low Fire Hand Painted

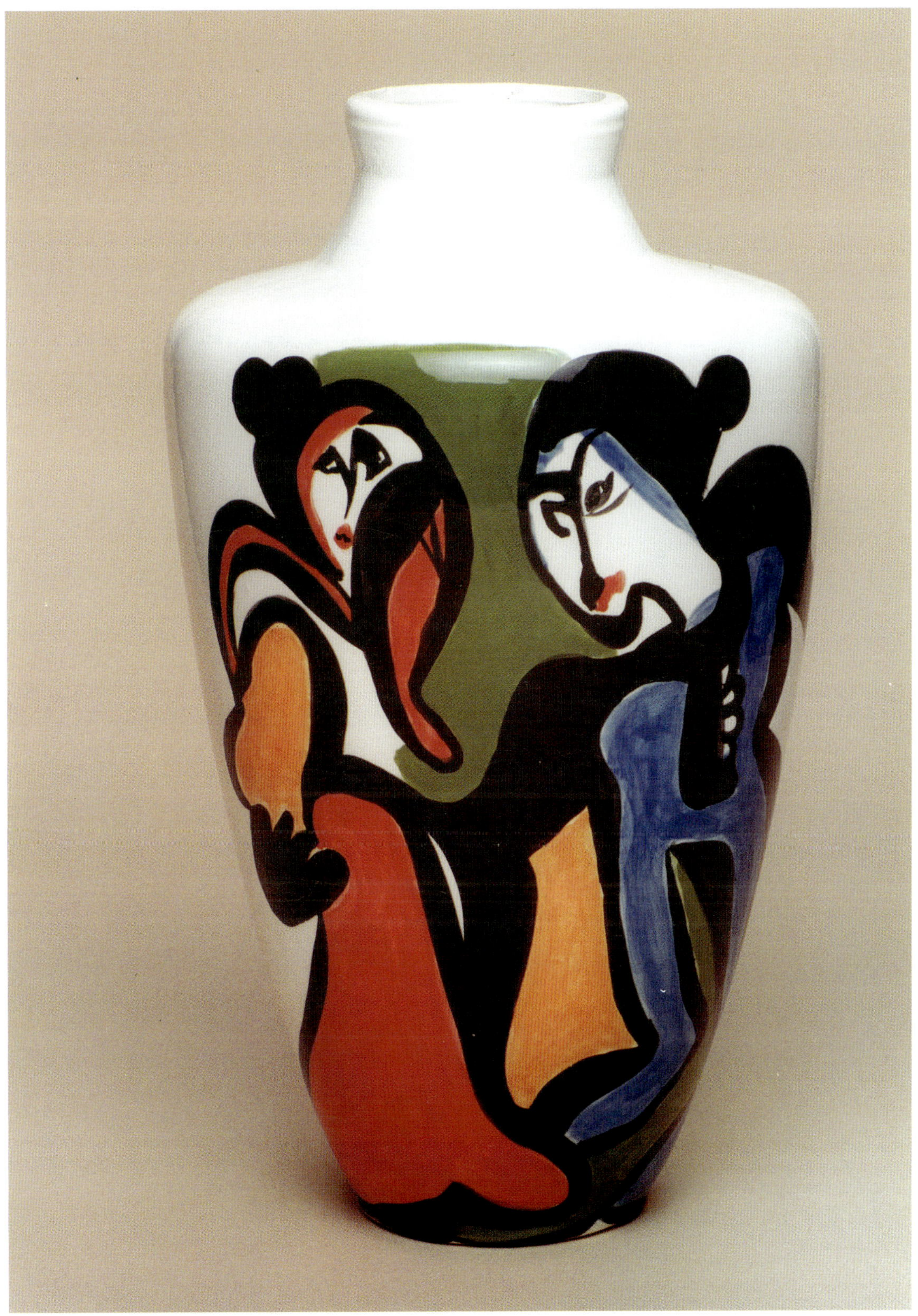

Low Fire Hand Painted Vase

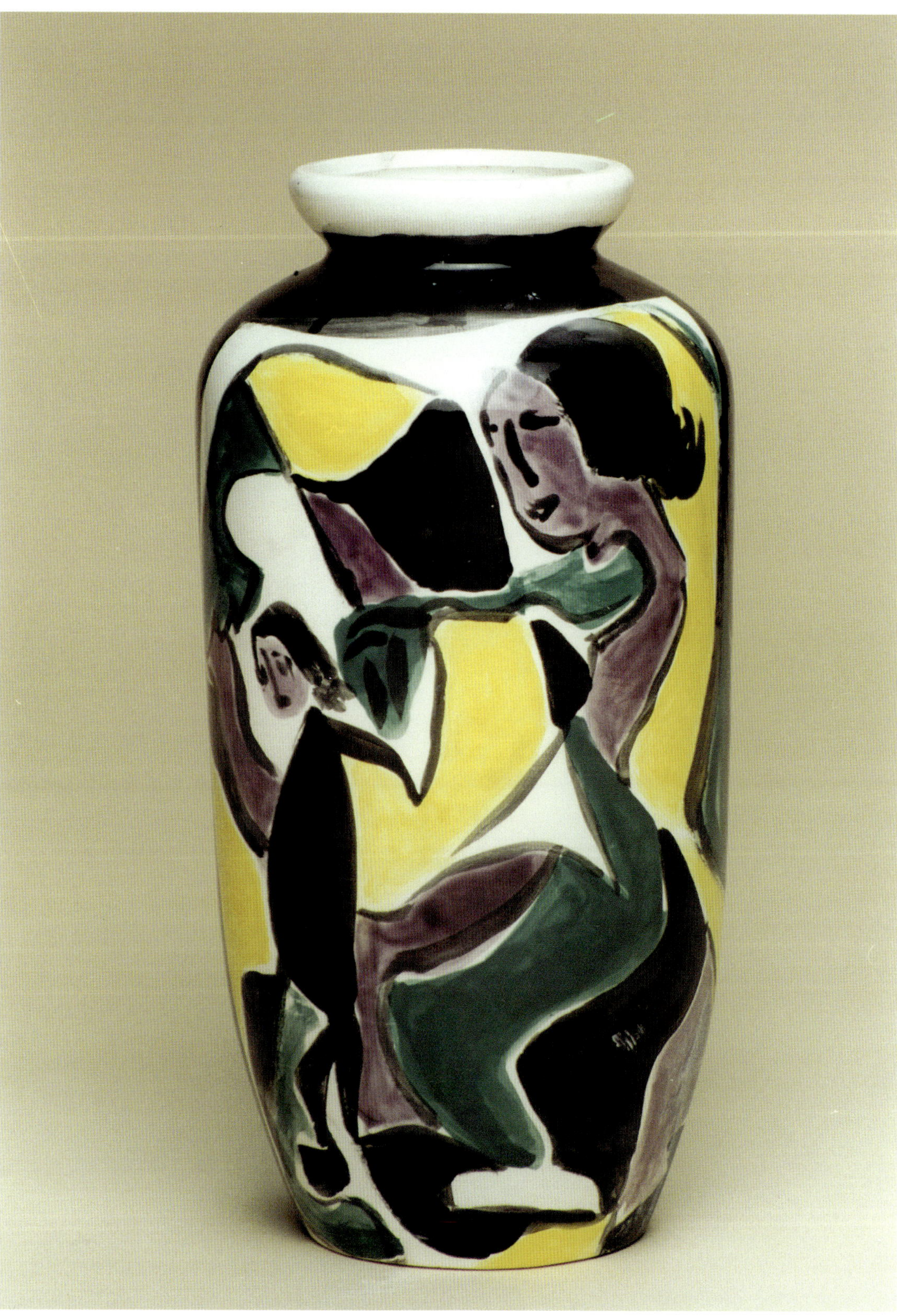

Low Fire Painter Vase

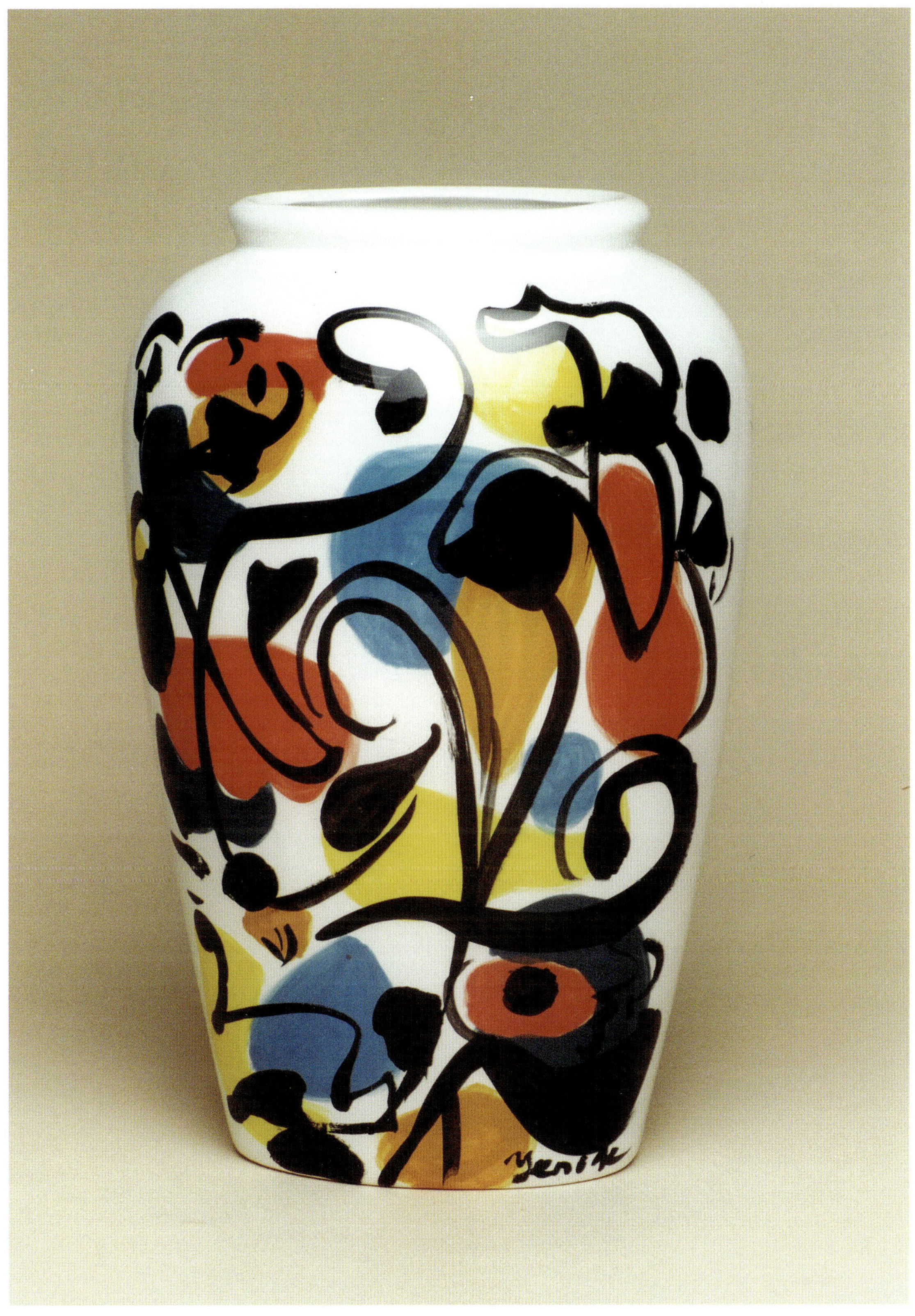

Low Fire Hand Painted Ceramic

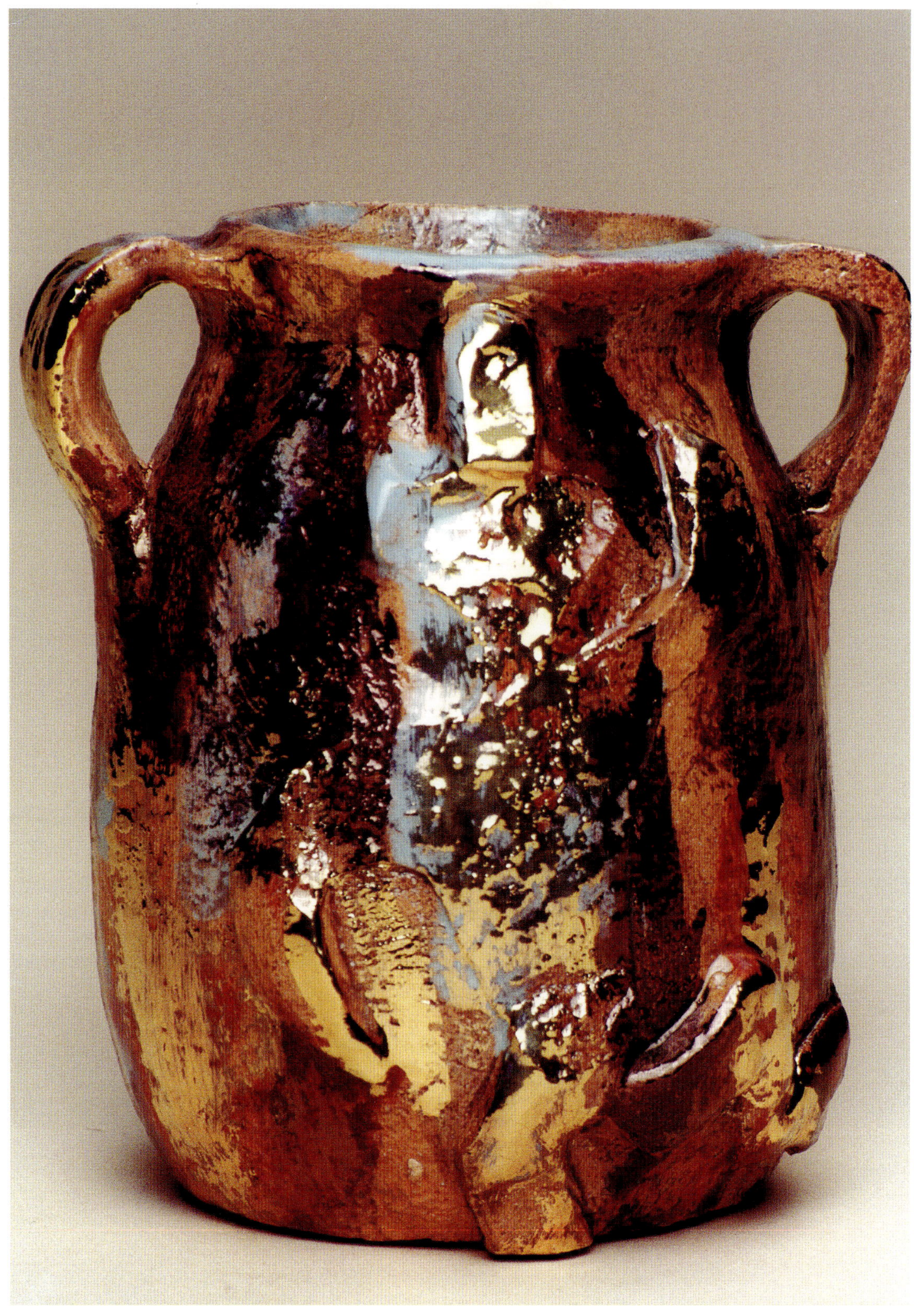

Hand Built   8" x 16"

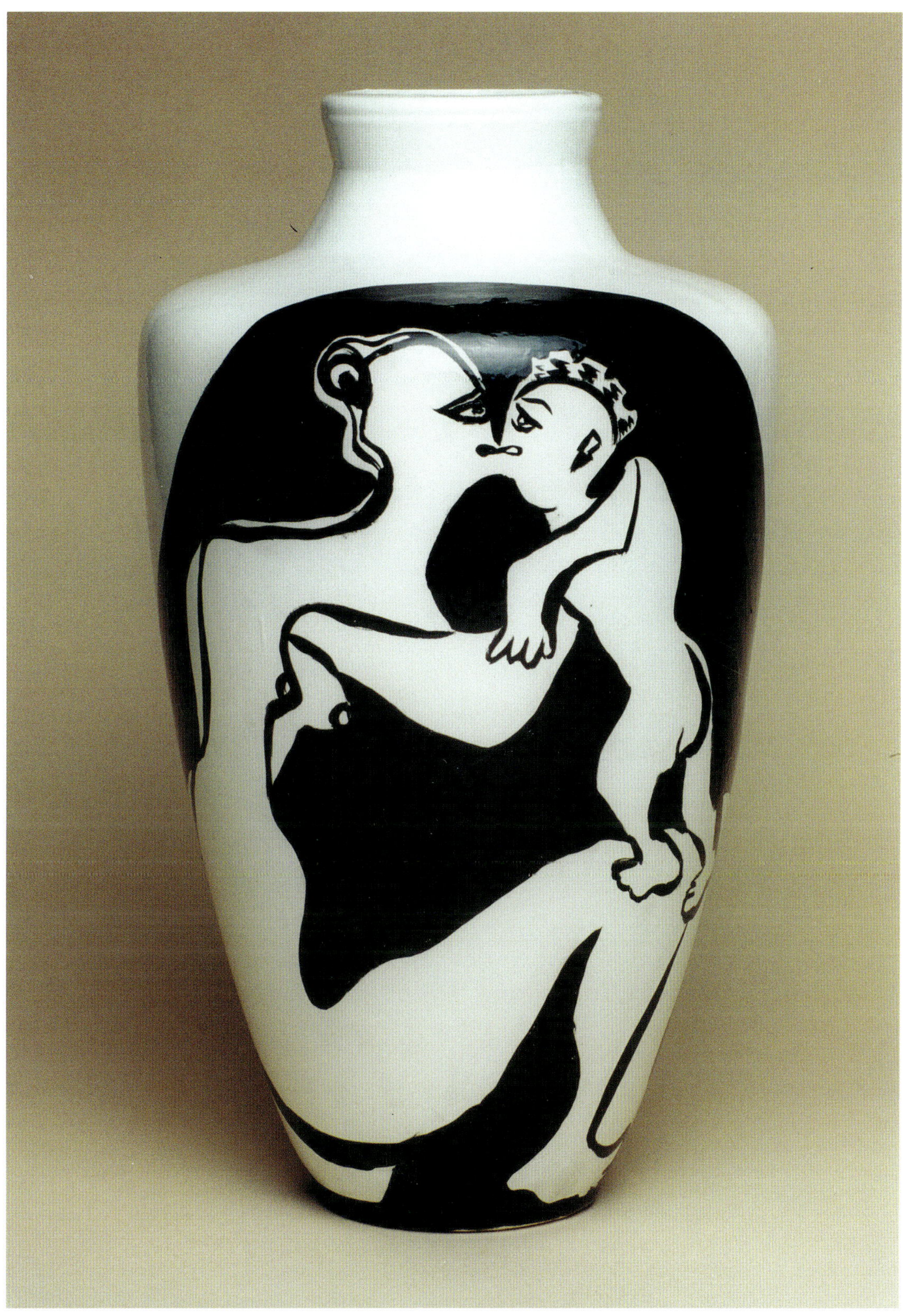

Low Fire Hand Painted

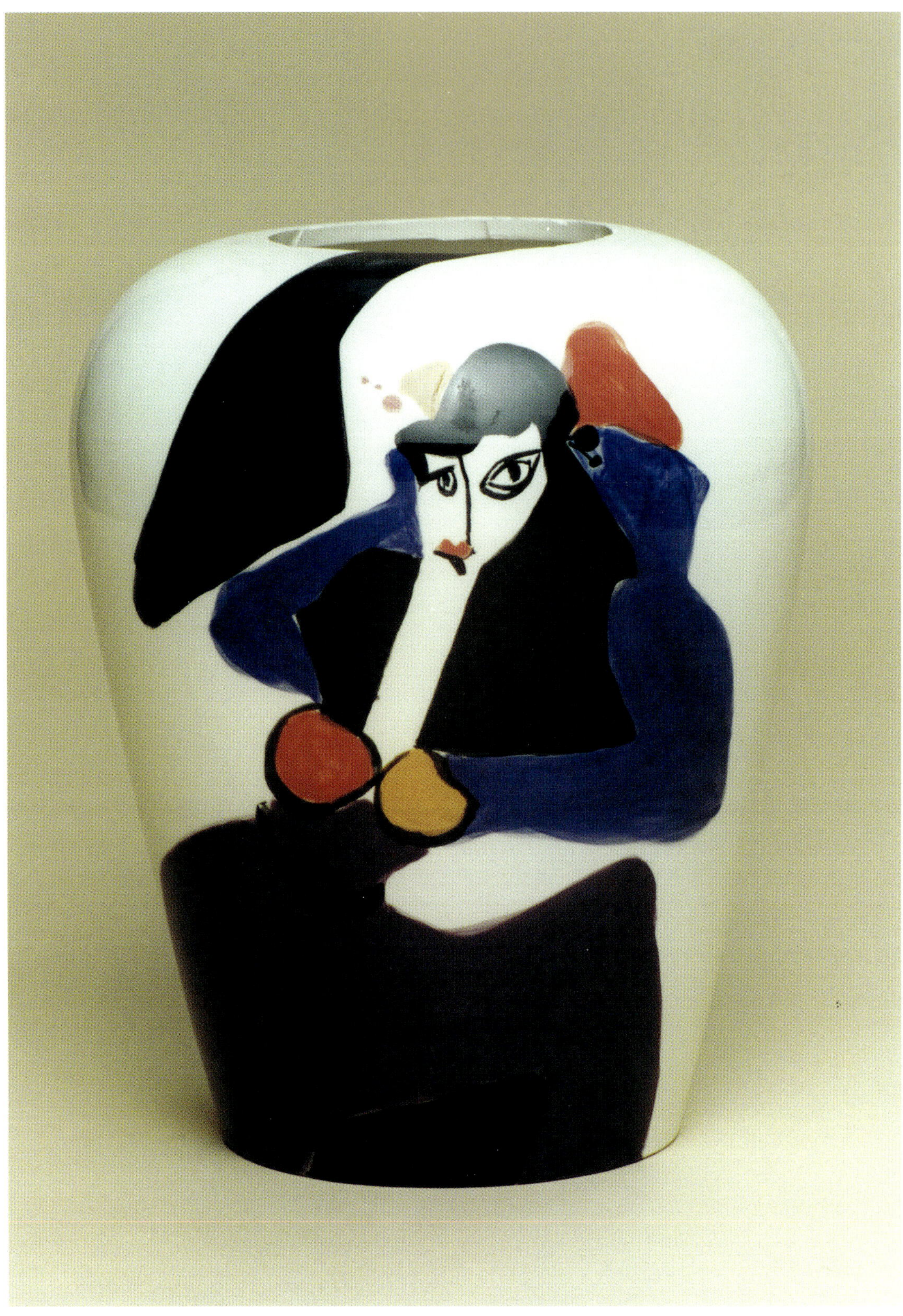

Low Fire Hand Painted Vase

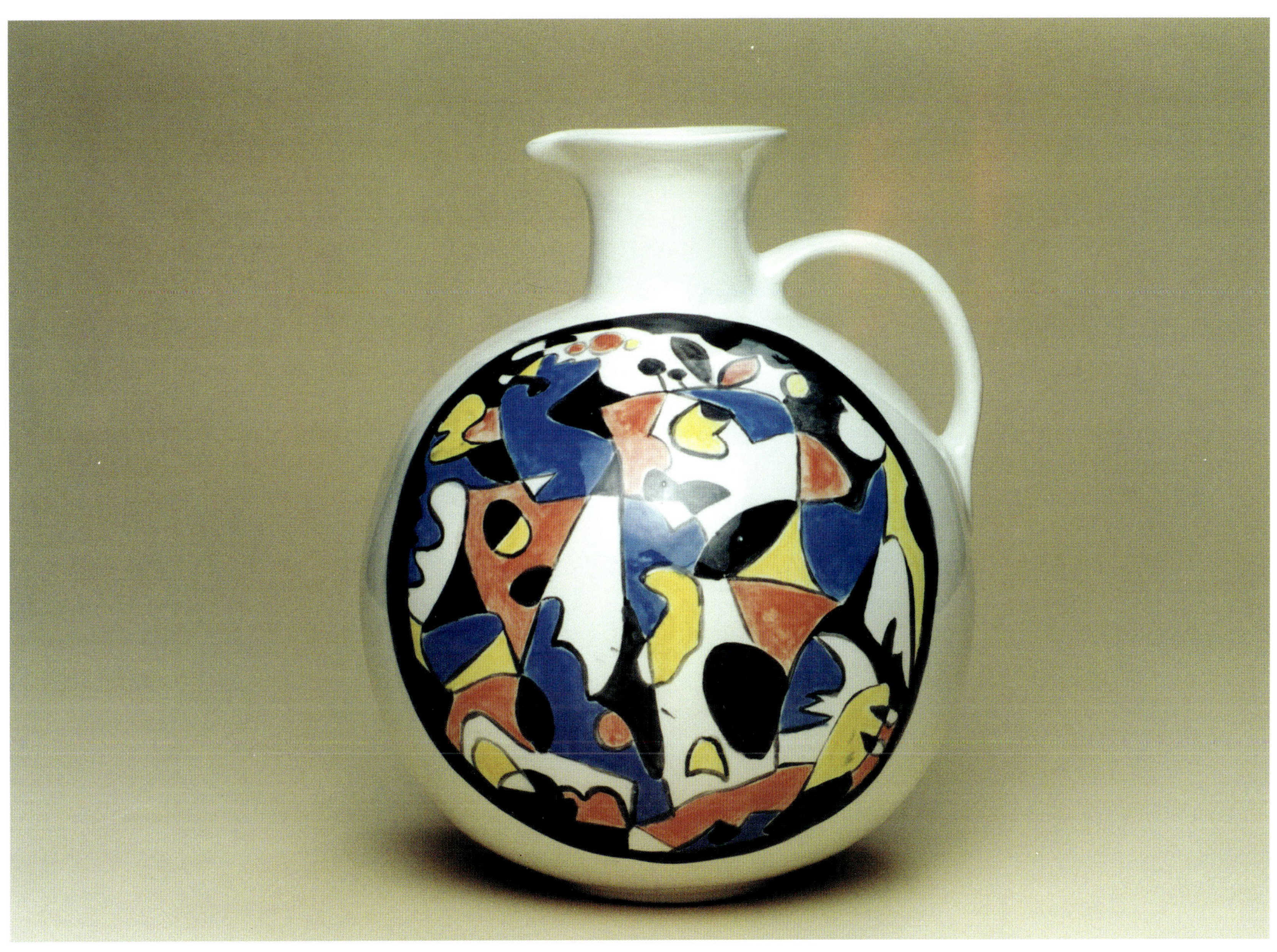

Low Fire Hand Painted Vase

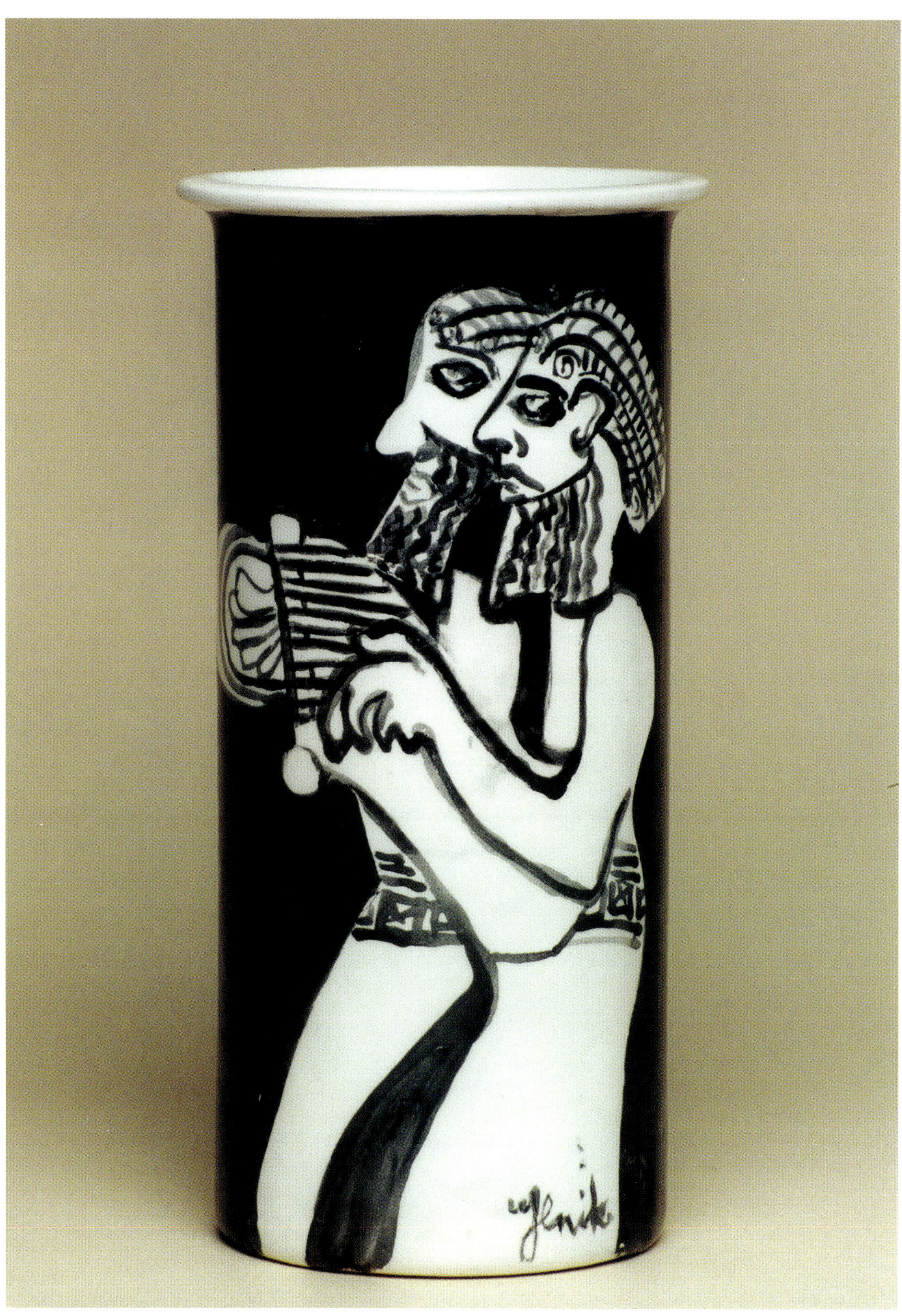

Low Fire Handpainted

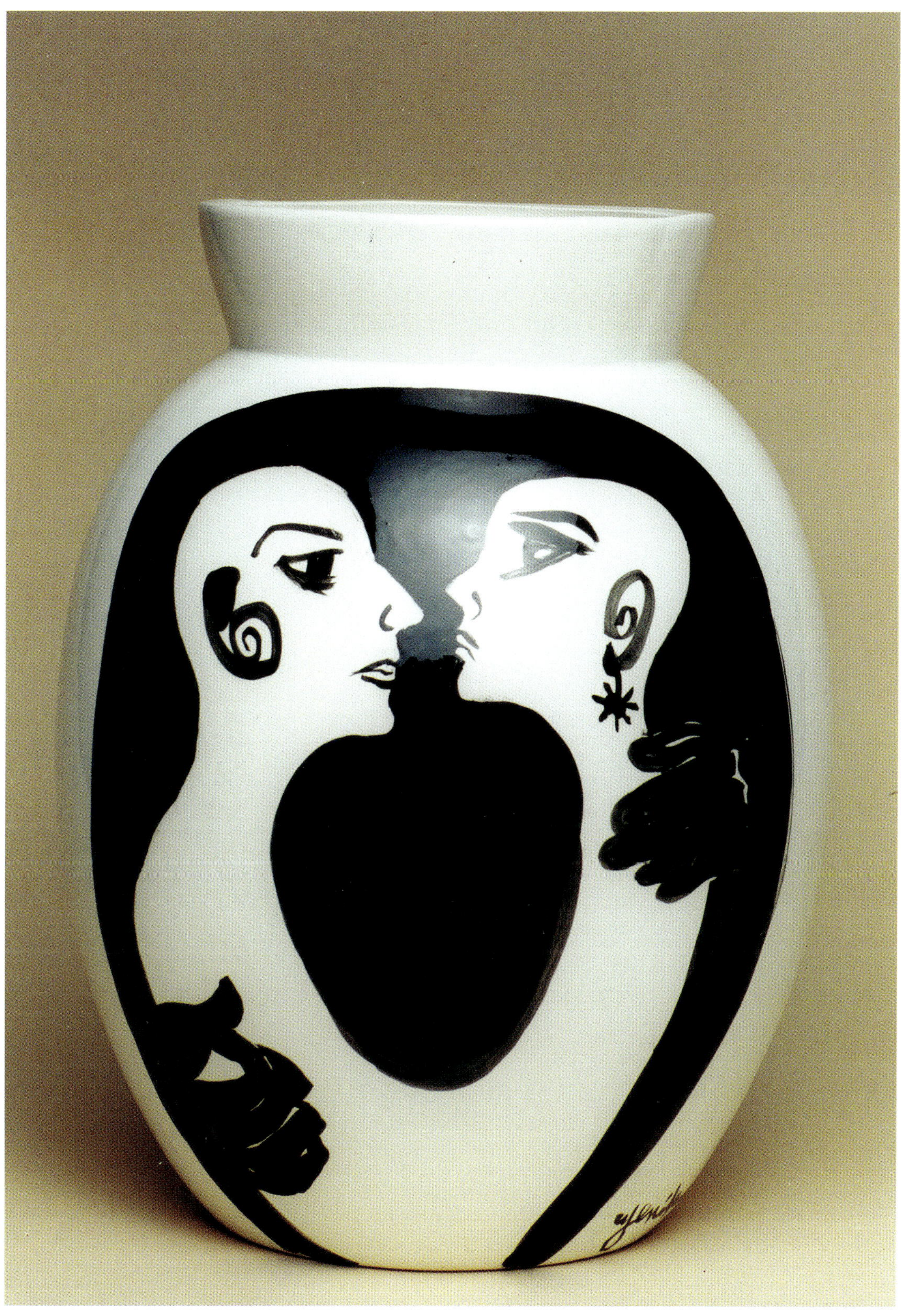

Low FireHand Painted

214

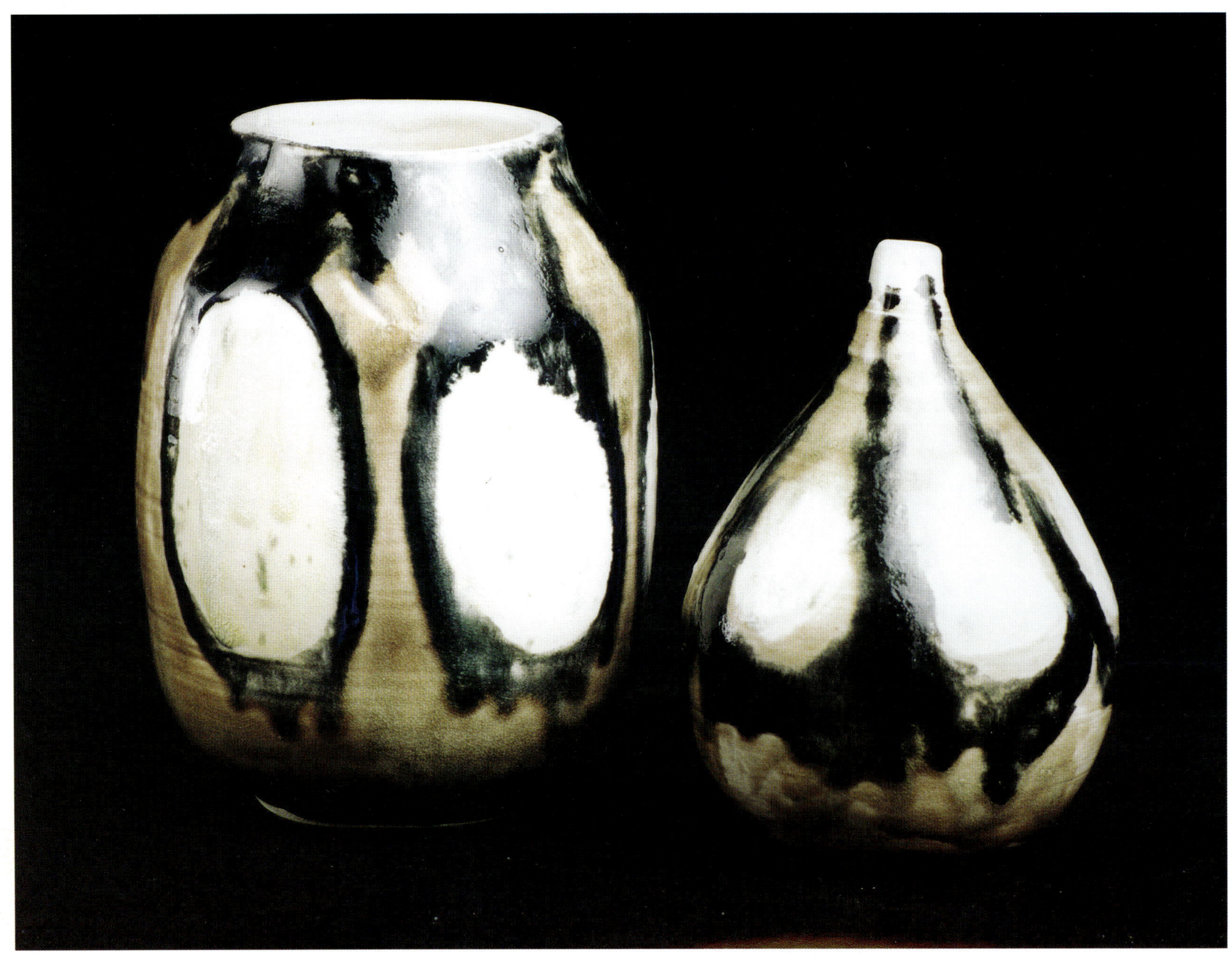

Untitled 12" x 18"   Untitled 5" x 12"v

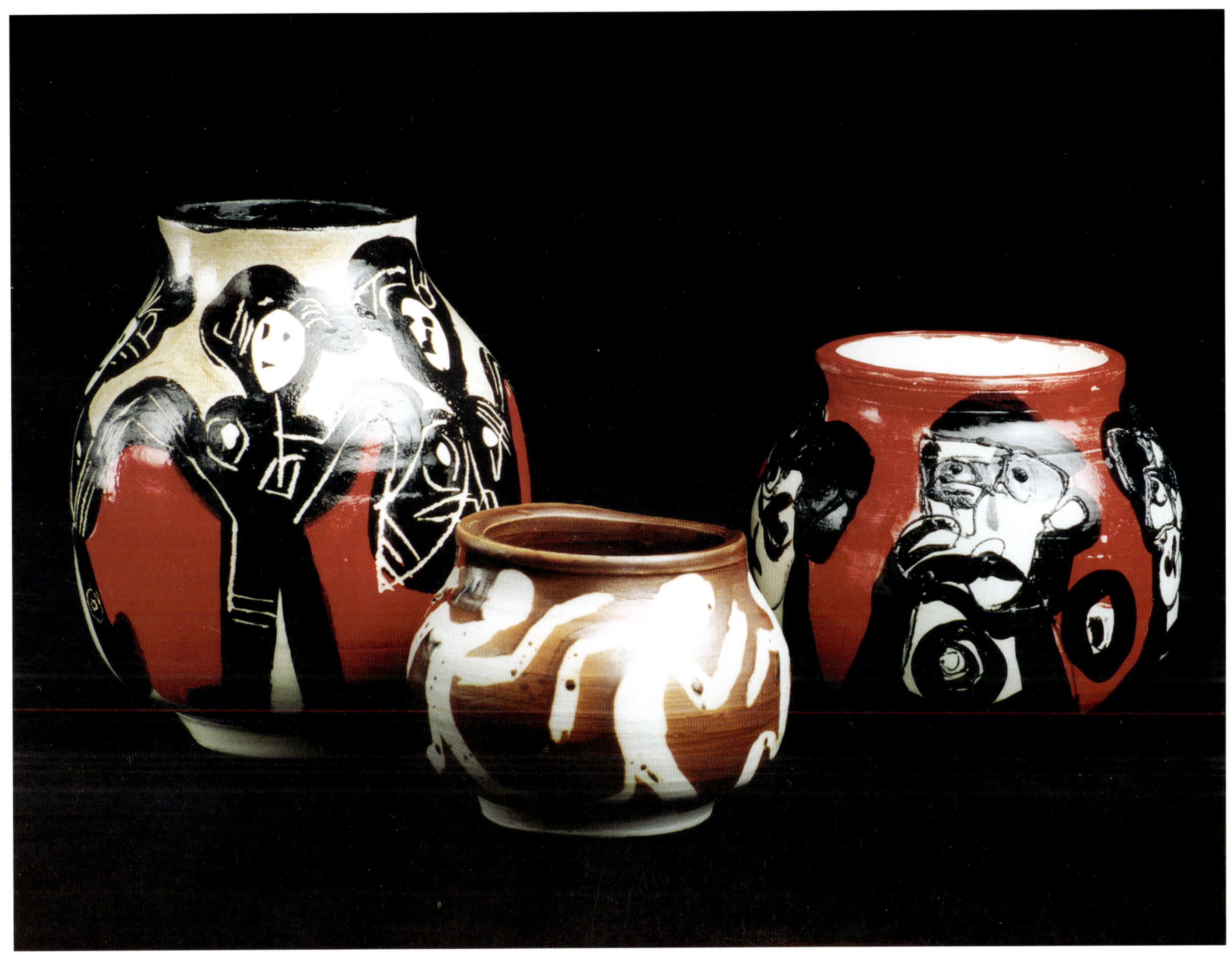

Untitled 6" x 14 "   Untitled 4" x 6"   Untitled 4" x 12"v

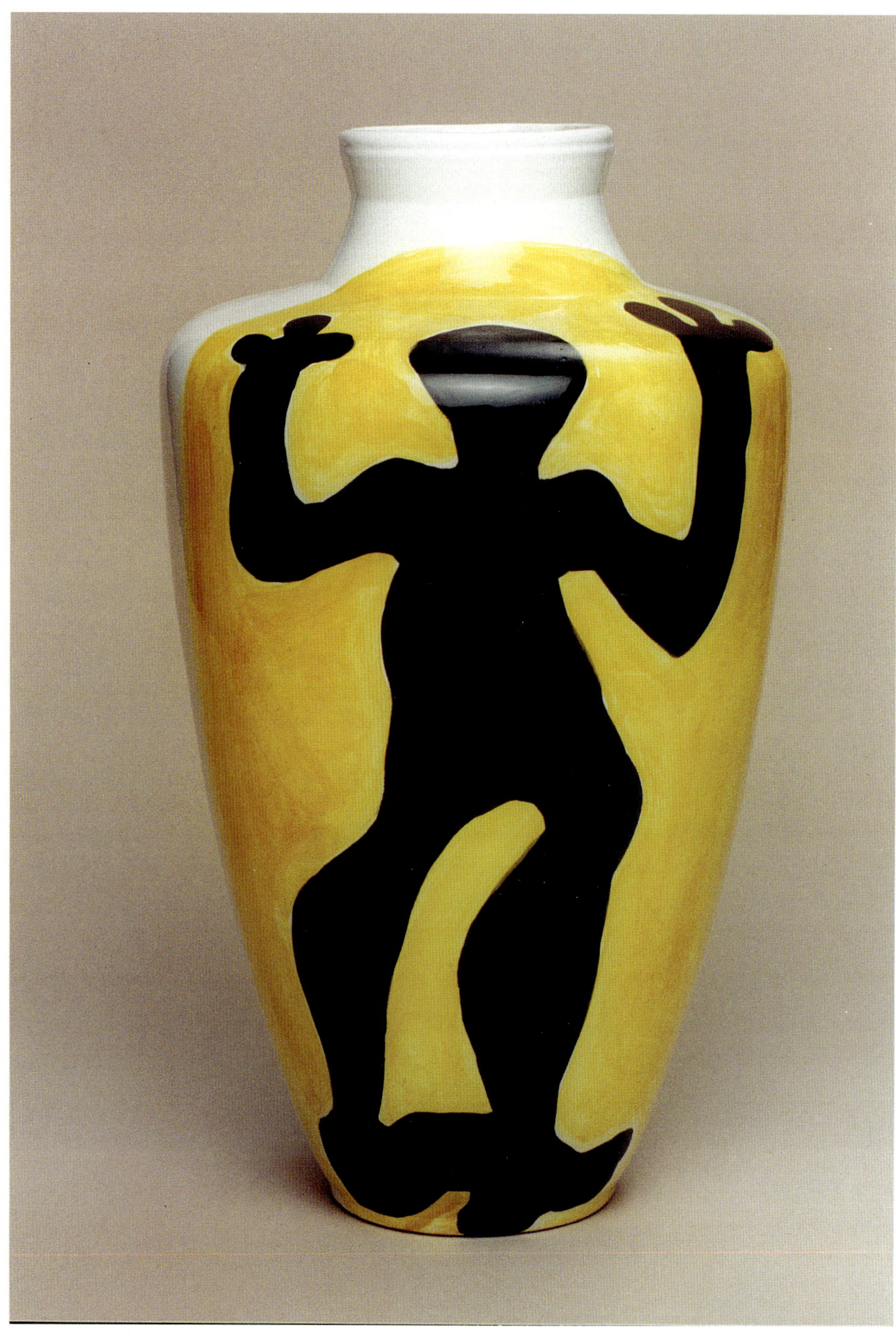

Untitled   18" x 32"

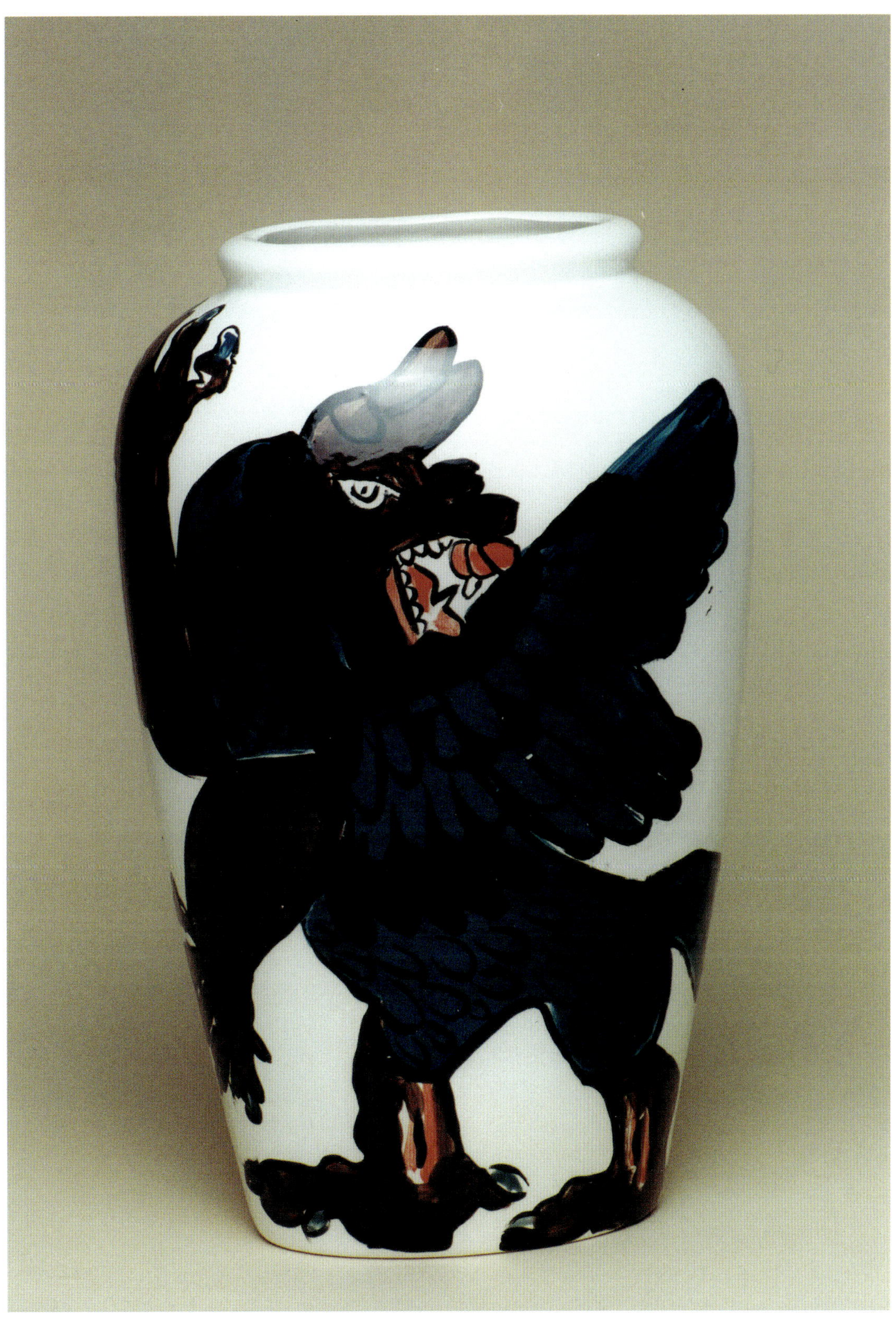

Untitled   11" x 22"

At the Roots of Vision

Notes from a Conversation with the Artist

It becomes clear in speaking with the artist Jenik Cook that the casual, nonchalant convergence of color and line upon canvas which conveys her images with such carefree intensity springs from a long process of discipline and depth.

"At the beginning, I had done the large drawings, the formal training," Jenik reflects, "looking to see and exploring color, style; studying about different artists and just trying to find a place in the whole scheme of things in the history of contemporary art.

"Whatever you're doing, (behind it) is always trying to accept your own uniqueness. Every individual human being is unique, obviously, not necessarily just in art but in everything else. That uniqueness is what I've been trying to find and befriend and come to terms with..."

The greatest hurdle facing the artist, in Jenik's viewpoint, is dispensing with conventions and preconceived ideas of one's relationship to art and learning to accept that uniqueness of self. This implies a confidence in one's own vision, founded upon knowledge.

"When you take that leap into your own realm, it's very scary but you make it," Jenik asserts. "You've always got to overcome the fear of what people and your colleagues are going to say. You're not conforming now; you're on your own. You're on a limb when you 'find your own stroke.' All the words in the world cannot express what you do in art. Painting is totally nonverbal expression but, even though it's nonverbal, it's very expressive. It all comes because of your intense working. It's a constant process and the process is eventually what brings you to yourself because you're most natural when you're allowed to be yourself...when you allow yourself to be who you are."

It would seem, from Jenik's example, that singing in someone else's voice induces an artificial strain which relaxes when you find your own key. She speaks mysteriously of "something that appears and reappears again in your silence of self" which will guide you. It is something, apparently, which you do not have to seek in the solitude of a mountainside cave but which can be accessible even in the suburbs of California. Something that is with you wherever you happen to be.

"I have been all over the world, so I've been exposed to many different environments," she notes. "California is a very pleasant place. The air here is very conducive to art. There's a lot of sunny days. The colors are beautiful. The flowers are beautiful. The fruit is beautiful. And there's a very active art scene to interact with."

The West Coast art scene she ventured into has included several mentors in whom Jenik found paths of self-discovery, validation and energy, varying from an accomplished Disney animator to an internationally recognized painter in an *avant garde* Los Angeles art group who was also a philosopher, architect and martial artist.

But influence, even from the greatest of instructors, does not guarantee inspiration and, when questioned about her sources of inspiration, Jenik bubbles with enthusiasm.

"To be honest, *everything* inspires me!" she laughs. "I love life and, of course, I love flowers- they are *great* inspiration, colorwise. I love people, colors, everything about life. Air is beautiful and just the whole activity of life is what goes into the art. Colors, in particular, make me 'run my juices' and start them flowing."

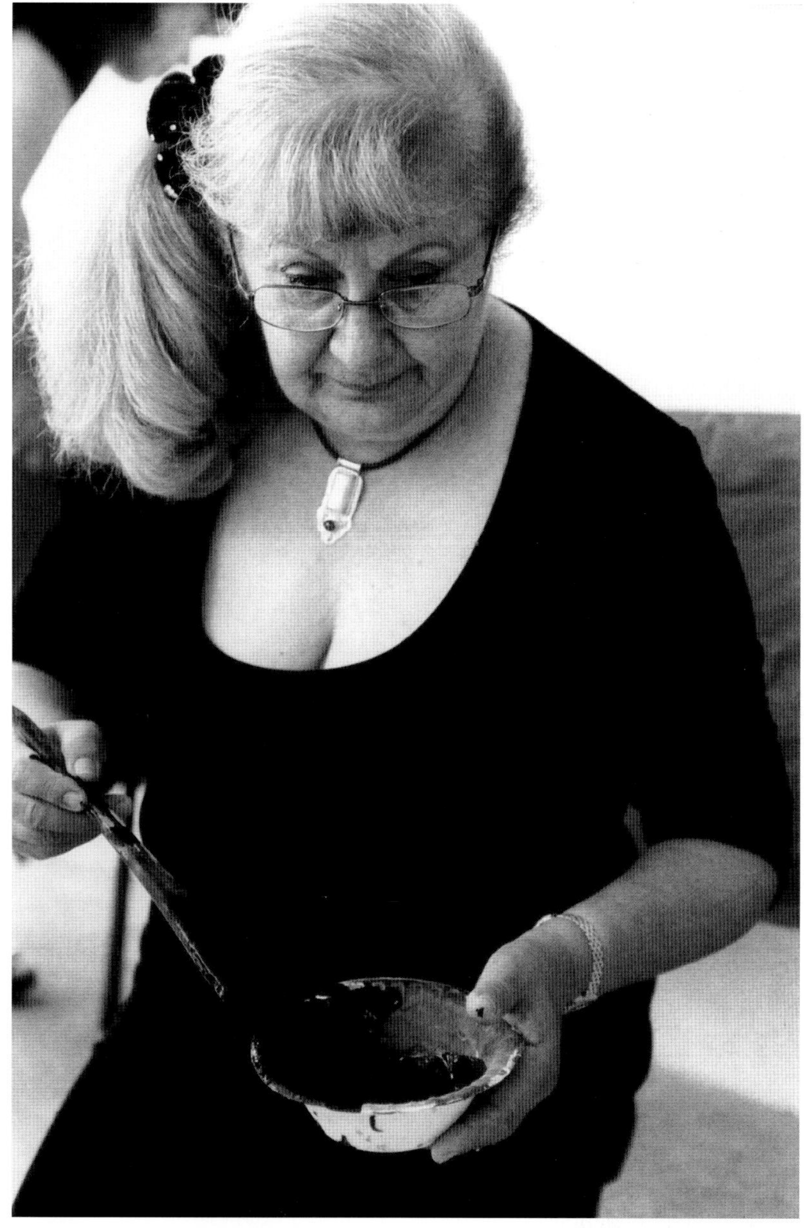

Photograph by Lei Elbag

The lure of discovery is another driving force in the work; one which she finds arrives serendipitously.

"Every day, I know that it's a new day and I'm a new student at this because it expands so much everyday and *everyday* I have something to learn," she observes. "You can't help but see the discoveries. They reveal themselves in the process."

There is, in this approach, a few key words which are worth emphasis because it may be said that there is more to be found in the *experience* of a Jenik Cook painting than in its analysis.

In terms of theme, the choice of subject matter can be almost inconsequential when measured against the *effect* of her compositions. Her most remarkable abilities center upon the *outlook* with which she addresses even the most mundane of visual topics and the *manner* with which she brings her ideas to visibility.

A knowing fluidity of *controlled abandon* propels her brush to capture an essential spirit of a subject- a spirit which is keyed to her very response to it. Making that response readily apparent within the work is a devotional act of *seeing* which transfers to the viewer a kind of *visible joy* which celebrates life.

It may seem an odd notion to reflect upon the work of a contemporary artist whose range of vision focuses upon prosaic subject matter to soar ebulliently into abstract realms as a "religious" artist but, when speaking with Jenik Cook about her artistic devotions, one is almost unavoidably struck by the correspondence between her perspectives and the ecstatic mind-sets of renowned mystics through the ages.

As a child, Jenik speaks of the same experiences of art- from playing with clay to childhood drawings and paintings- familiar to many if not most childhoods; experiences which she left behind as she progressed through her formal education. It wasn't until her early twenties that an inner hunger called her attention back to artistic endeavor.

"There was just a need for it," she recalls. "Because bare existence was very empty. There was nothing that was really catching my attention or keeping me satisfied for very long. Even though I was married, I had a beautiful child, a beautiful husband, everything... but, still, there was a hole there. It was very obvious I had to do something about it."

The intervening years from that moment of realization to the point of Jenik's breakthrough saw endless applications to study and creation; to reflection, focus and recognition which, in effect, mirrored the "prolonged techniques of meditation and concentration" which Walter T. Stage spoke of in *The Teachings of the Mystics*. In this work, Stage notes that "a genuine mystical experience, because it is formless, lends itself to transcription in many forms" not least of which, it may be argued, is artistic experience. In fact, it might be said that the very foundations of contemporary art are built, at least in part, upon the desire to express a somewhat mystical experience of the world.

In excerpting an account of Arthur Koestler's contemporary mystical experiences from his autobiographical book, *The Invisible Writing*, Stage compares that author's view of "the X-ray texture of the world" to descriptions drawn from the history and tradition of mysticism from "the founders of religions, prophets, saints and seers" who unsealed themselves to "a *bona fide* conversion to any creed, Christianity, Buddhism, or Fire-Worship..." by their realizations of self and world. At its roots, it is a vision, an opening, which precedes doctrine and denomination but does not necessarily freeze into rigid theological interpretation.

Thomas Merton, who was equally at home with Eastern and Western concepts of mysticism, explained his life's pursuit as "united by one central concern: to understand various ways in which men of different traditions have conceived the meaning and method of the 'way' which leads to the highest levels of religious or of metaphysical awareness." It is a kind of awareness almost impossible to clearly communicate in words and may even be said to be more lucidly discerned in some exceptional examples of contemporary visual effort than in the familiar concepts of creed-sponsored classical art referred to as "religious."

Certainly, Jenik, herself, speaks of "being in touch" through her readings of the older mystics of varying traditions. Her Middle Eastern background, of course, brings her to an acquaintance with such masters as Zarathushtra, the inspired poet, Rumi, and her study of elder Sanskrit disciplines but her attentions extend to the Zen masters, fire worshipers, Joseph Campbell and even James Joyce. The central element in these diverse interests would seem, obviously, to be an appreciation of mystical consciousness.

"Somewhere in the art process is being in touch with these people who had another eye open besides their earthly eyes," Jenik explains. "They give you wings to fly to another, less mundane, level if you're able to be, at some moments in your life, where they lived or spent longer periods of time. It's not in the mundane where we do our creative work. It's in another sphere that we do it. Maybe we transcend while we're at work and don't even know it now or when the time goes but that's where we do our best work- in that state of being...I can't imagine life without being creative because there would be no meaning in it for me.

"I think being an artist is just a way of life... The colors or the movement or the joy of the day- or the sadness- it doesn't matter what kind of emotion it is but it's a living thing. It happens on a daily basis and you experience it; you're never indifferent. The emotions are constantly activated by different (stimuli). They could be color. They could be movement of a tree. They could be a living painting, a piece of pottery. Whatever it is, it keeps constantly active, moving..."

At this stage of her relationship to visual arts, with her "new eyes," Jenik sees a "living painting" everywhere and feels that the influence of other artists upon her work has declined.

"It seems now that I'm not so much looking at other artists' work. That need has decreased and now I'm just basically doing my own work. However, that does not make me appreciate less the modern artist- because that's who I really *do* appreciate more. When I see their work, I still love it and all of that but I'm not seeking it like I used to do. A long time ago, I used to seek to know more about them, to know how they were doing things. But, now I'm less curious about how other people do things. I'm only standing back and seeking what I can discover in my own work.

"I consider myself very fortunate to have the time that I do to paint, experiment. Life is very demanding for all of us in many different ways. I think the main thing is focusing but, if your focus is disturbed, it's harder to bring yourself back into focus again... I think art is about expressing your accumulated life experiences with one, maybe, brush stroke...Expressing your innermost essence with the least effort. But, it can be more truthful about you because, in art, you can't really lie. You lay the stroke out and it is going to tell all. It's not like words. It holds nothing back and the person who's looking at that can feel the state of the artist who imparted it."

Although not all of us, alas, are in touch with this knowing eye within, it seems to have been obviously useful to Jenik during the twenty years she taught art to children and adults. Effective artistic instruction goes beyond the academic basics and an ability to find joy in the combination and interplay of tones or inject ecstatic values into mundane subjects is essential in the formation of an artist. When she speaks of the years devoted to conveying these ingredients of self to her students, Jenik seems to aptly sum up the balance of her artistic philosophy.

"When you teach art, you see how the person sees and acts when they do this art," Jenik notes. "I had students who would come in and I'd ask them to do something spontaneous before I gave instructions. In this, I could see exactly which one was where- in which stage of creativity they were. Were they very tight? Were they trying to open up or were they very scared. You can tell everything just by looking at the process when they're doing it. And, of course, I learned a lot just by observing my students...I think everybody learns from each other. The whole thing is that we're looking and learning...You really are old if you can't learn anymore. Otherwise, you're never old."

-G. Alexander Irving

Bibliography

Solo and Group Shows

2004
Shacknow Museum of Fine Arts – solo exhibition – retrospective – Florida

2003
Galleria Centro Storico – group exhibition – Florence, Italy
Art Expo – group exhibition – Lebanon, Beirut
Noho Gallery – group exhibition – Los Angeles
New York Art Expo – group exhibition – New York
The Schacknow Museum of Fine Arts – group exhibition – Florida

2002
Borders Books – solo exhibition – Sherman Oaks, California
New York Art Expo – solo exhibition – New York
CSUN Art Galleries – group exhibition – Los Angeles
Orlando Gallery – group exhibition – Los Angeles
FDG Gallery – group exhibition – Los Angeles
BGH Gallery – group exhibition – Los Angeles

2001
Iranian Art Association – group exhibition – Los Angeles
Orlando Gallery – group exhibition – Los Angeles
Artesanos – group exhibition –Coral Gables, Florida
Atlanta Décor Exposition – group exhibition – Atlanta
Z Mart Galleria – group exhibition – Los Andeles
Art Exhibition New York – group exhibition – New York
Agora Gallery – group exhibition SOHO, New York

2000
2000 Art Expo New York – solo exhibition – New York
Orlando Gallery – solo exhibition – Los Angeles
Latin American Museum – group exhibition – Coral Gables, Florida
International Art Expo – group exhibition – San Francisco, California
Post Logic Studio – group exhibition – Los Angeles
Long Beach Art Abstract Exhibition – group exhibition – Los Angeles
Art 21 – group exhibition – Las Vagas
Emery Fine Art – group exhibition – Douglas, MI

1999
Art 21 – solo exhibition – Las Vagas
Federal Building – solo exhibition – Los Angeles

1998
Orlando Gallery – solo exhibition – Los Angeles
Los Angeles Art Expo – group exhibition – Los Angeles

Rheinfelden Town Hall – group exhibition – Germany
Galery Markel – group exhibition – Germany
World Contemporary Art 1998 – group exhibition – Los Angeles
Orlando Gallery – group exhibiton – Los Angeles

1997
Orlando Gallery – solo exhibition – Los Angeles

1996
Pacific Design Center – solo exhibition – Los Angeles
Orlando Gallery – solo exhibition – Los Angeles

1995
Art Space Gallery – group exhibition – Sherman Oaks, California

1993
Federal Building – group exhibition – Westwood, California
California Color Traveling Exhibition – group exhibition – Bad Sackingen, Germany
Fine Arts Pavilion Gallery – group exhibition – Los Angeles

1992
LA Art Gallery – group exhibition – Encino, Califorina

1990
Valley Watercolor Society – group exhibition – Los Angeles

1989
Los Angeles Contemporary – group exhibition – Los Angeles
Galleries – group exhibition – Los Angeles
Art Works Gallery – group exhibition – Bakersfield, California

1986
Cunningham Art Gallery – group exhibition – Bakersfield, California

1981
Betty Hay Gallery – solo exhibiton – Bakersfield, California

1979
Petroleum Woman's Club – solo exhibition – Aberdeen, Scotland

Education

1968-1970 – Studied with Hossenin Delrish, Iran
1970-1978 – Studied with Barbara Lae, Scotland
1981-1987 – Studied with Chalita Robinson, U.S.A
1987-1990 – Studied with Jake Lee, U.S.A
1990-1994 – Studied with Dr. AAlexander Vilumsons, U.S.A